# The Marvels of Cosmos

Philosophico-Theological Appraisal
Based on Science, Linguistics & Anthropology

# The Marvels of Cosmos

## Philosophico-Theological Appraisal Based on Science, Linguistics & Anthropology

**Rev. Lameswar Kanhor**

CWI
**Christian World Imprints**™

First Published in 2014 by

**Christian World Imprints**™
*Christian Publishing & Books from India*
H-12 Bali Nagar, **New Delhi-110015**
info@christianworldimprints.com
www.ChristianWorldImprints.com
Phone: +91 11 25465925 Fax: +91 11 25173055

ISBN-13: 978-93-5148-010-5 ISBN-10: 93-5148-010-0

**Cataloging in Publication Data--DK**
Courtesy: D.K. Agencies (P) Ltd. <docinfo@dkagencies.com>

**Kanhor, Lameswar,** 1963-
The marvels of cosmos : philosophico-theological appraisal based on science, linguistics & anthropology / Lameswar Kanhor.
p. cm.
Includes bibliographical references (p. ) and index.
ISBN 9789351480105
ISBN 9351480100

1. Nothing (Philosophy) 2. Philosophical theology. 3. Religion and science. 4. Numerals--Religious aspects--Christianity. 5. Quantum cosmology. 6. Big bang theory. 7. Anthropological linguistics. I. Title. II. Title: Nothingness as constitutive of reality.

DDC 111.5 23



Printed at Chawla Offset Printers

# Dedication

Dedicated to the People of Kandhamal
In the Catholic Archdiocese of
Cuttack-Bhubaneswar of Odisha

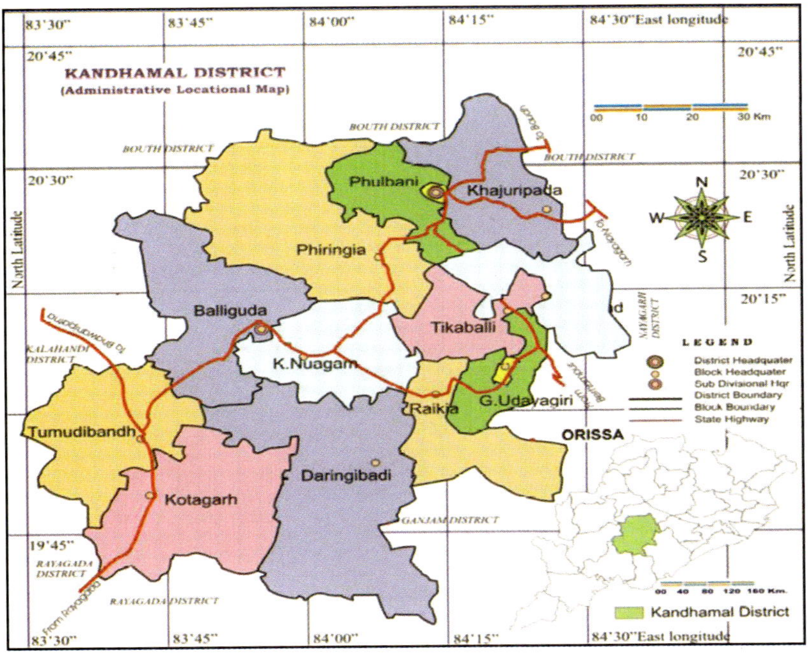

# The Book

We experience presence and absence, emptiness and fullness of things, events, facts and causes. It is we, human beings, who make statements about things, ourselves and others. Why is there Something instead of Nothing? The obvious answer is there might have been 'something', 'everything' or 'nothing.' Nothingness represents conceptual and numerical zero as empty placeholder in decimal system of mathematics. It also represents vacuum in science where the fluctuating energy in the vacuum is the same thing as the fluctuating amount of the mass as Albert Einstein put it E (energy) = m (mass) $c^2$ (speed of the light squared). Nothingness is a symbol, a concept, and a numeral (0) as a constitutive reality which represents and participates in the wholeness of reality. Reality is both presence and absence, paradoxical and relational as in our direct judgment we say two kinds of things about something: WHAT (essence) it is and THAT (existence) it is but when something is NOT, the concept 0 as a number represents what is 'not there.' The numerical zero fills the empty position in the decimal numeration whereas the vacuum points to fullness and wholeness in interdisciplinary disciplines of physical or social sciences.

The book is comprised of four chapters. The first chapter deals with the mathematical zero and its philosophical applications. The second chapter deals with the quantum reality and Big Bang cosmology. It deals with the quantum zero and the origin of the Universe. The third chapter deals with the philosophico-theological appraisal of the nothingness. Its linguistic, numerical, physical and inner nothingness is appreciated. The final chapter four provides a general critique and evaluation.

# The Author

Born in Uppar Khol, Kandhamal, on August 12, 1963, Fr. Lameswar Kanhor is a Catholic Priest in the Archdiocese of Cuttack-Bhubaneswar, and is currently the Staff of the St. Paul's Regional Institute of Spirituality at Padanpur, Odisha, where he was a staff member from 2001 to 2006. After that he went to Jnana-Deepa Vidyapeeth (JDV), Pune for Masters and Doctoral study in Philosophy of Science and Religion from 2006 to 2012.

He was in Raikia Parish for three years after his ordination on 29th May 1992. He was then given to look after Kattingia Parish for one year which he bifurcated into Salima Gochha Parish. He was given Pobingia and Betticola Parish for three years each before going to St. Paul's Regional Institute of Spirituality. He has been going to St. Albert's College, Ranchi, as a visiting professor for *Philosophical Hermeneutics* from 2012 onwards. St. Aquinas College, Gopalpur-on-Sea, has invited him to teach *Nastika* or Non-Vedic Philosophy from 2013 onwards.

# Foreword

I feel privileged to introduce Dr. Lameswar Kanhor's insightful book, "**The Marvels of Cosmos**." As the subtitle, "**Philosophico-Theological Appraisal Based on Science, Linguistics & Anthropology**," rightly indicates it is a book on dialogue between Science, Religion and related disciplines. It also relates our reality and existence to a larger cosmos, which is truly fascinating and marvellous.

Both as Master's student and Doctoral candidate, I came to know Rev. Dr. Kanhor very well. His studious nature, committed work and consistent life-style has impressed me tremendously. He has given his full life to long and dedicated research to bring out this work. He has been truly dedicated and committed to his research, with unimaginable intellectual rigour. Therefore, it has been my pleasure to guide him and accompany him in his doctoral work.

Drawing from contemporary mathematics, physics (quantum mechanics and theory of relativity) and cosmology, Kanhor has brought about an incredibly fascinating account of nothingness.

Though he has taken up a very difficult topic – on existence and non-existence of the marvellous cosmos, he has shown in simple and creative ways the importance of nothingness in our way of living and of thinking. His simple style and elegant writing enable us to approach a difficult subject with candour and transparency.

His has been an attempt to show that nothingness is very much part of our larger and complex cosmos. Emptiness is somehow constitute of existence. In this sense, the reality that we encounter is far more fascinating and complex. So the marvel of our cosmos in which we are privileged to dwell.

I believe that this book makes an invaluable contribution to our understanding of the cosmos – including ourselves. So I am very happy to recommend this book to anyone serious about the existence of the the world, the known universe and of human beings.

**Kuruvilla Pandikattu**
Jnana-Deepa Vidyapeeth
Pune 411014

May 4, 2014

# Acknowledgements

We are interconnected with being and non-being, fullness and emptiness, everything or something with nothing. We are precious in front of God, the creator who accompanied me throughout my journey of writing a Doctoral Dissertation on the *Nothingness as Constitutive of Reality*. Without God I am nothing, nobody, zero.

Archbishop Emeritus Raphael Cheenath, SVD allowed me in 2006 for Masters and later for Doctoral Studies in Philosophy of Science and Religion. *The Marvels of Cosmos: Philosophico-Theological Appraisal Based on Science, Linguistics & Anthropology* is a part of my doctoral dissertation,

I am grateful to Presidents, the Registrars of JDV (Jnana-Deepa Vidyapeeth) and the Chairpersons of Doctoral Committee of Philosophy Faculty from 2008 to 2012. I am indebted to the Deans, MPH (SP) and MPH (SR) Coordinators and M. Ph. Board members of the Faculty of Philosophy for their constant support and guidance. I am grateful to the Librarians of the JDV Library staff who went out of their way to help me with the library work. I am grateful to Missio Aachen, Germany, for providing me with the necessary scholarship to complete this project.

I am grateful to the Rectors, the Ministers and the staff members of Papal Seminary, Pune, for providing me accommodation during my study days. I am grateful to my doctoral guide Prof. Kuruvilla Pandikattu, SJ. and Prof. Job Kozhamthadam, SJ., and Prof. Noel Sheth, SJ. for their keen observations and valuable suggestions. Finally, I am indebted to my family members, friends and well-wishers. I am indebted to my new Archbishop John Barwa, SVD., who took the reign of Archdiocese after Kandhamal communal riots. I am truly indebted to the archbishops, professors, well-wishers and friends for their assured prayers.

May God, who *created* everything *out of nothing*, bless us with the *fullness* of abundant life!

**Rev. Lameswar Kanhor**

# Contents

# Table of Figures

# Introduction

On 4th July 2012, the CMS (Compact Muon Solenoid) and the ATLAS (A Toroidal LHC Apparatus) experimental teams at the Large Hadron Collider (LHC), at Geneva, independently announced that they each confirmed the formal discovery of a previously unknown boson of mass between 125–127 GeV/$c^2$, whose behaviour so far was 'consistent with' a Higgs boson.[1] A British theoretical Physicist and emeritus professor at the University of Edinburgh Peter Higgs (b. 1929), Belgian theoretical Physicists Robert Brout (1928-2011) and François Englert (b. 1932) suggested in 1970 "that all particles had no mass just after the Big Bang. As the Universe cooled and the temperature fell below a critical value, an invisible force field called the 'Higgs field' was formed together with the associated 'Higgs boson.'"[2] The Higgs field prevails throughout the cosmos: any particles that interact with it are given a mass via the Higgs boson.

In 1993, an American Physicist Leon Lederman (b. 1922) wrote a book called *'The Goddamn Particle'* describing the search for the (then) elusive Higgs, but his publisher made him change it.[3] Later the book, *The Goddamn Particle* written by Leon Lederman with Dick Teresi, is named as ***The God Particle: If the Universe Is the Answer, What is the Question?***[4] That is how a Higgs boson, crucial for the understanding of matter yet elusive, the origin of the particle mass, is known as God particle. In layperson's terms, the 'God particle' is the nickname of a subatomic particle called the Higgs boson which is responsible for giving matter different properties. One of the most mysterious and important properties of matter is mass. Mass can be defined as a quantitative measure of an object's stuff that is made of. The Higgs boson is believed to be the particle which gives mass to the material thing. In a layperson's understanding, it is God's particle rather than God particle.

Standard Model (SM) of Particle Physics tells us that everything in the Universe is made from twelve basic building blocks called fundamental particles (six quarks and six leptons), governed by four fundamental forces (the strong force, the weak force, the electromagnetic force, and the gravitational force). The SM particles are 12 spin-1/2 fermions (6 quarks and 6 leptons), 4 spin-1 'gauge' bosons and a spin-0 Higgs boson.[5] "The six quarks are paired in the three generations – the 'up quark' and the 'down quark' form the first generation, followed by the 'charm quark' and 'strange quark', then the 'top quark' and 'bottom quark.' The six leptons are similarly arranged in three generations – the 'electron' and the 'electron-neutrino', the 'muon' and the 'muon-neutrino', and the 'tau' and the 'tau-neutrino.'"[6] The 4 bosons (photons, W and Z bosons, and gluons) are particles that transmit forces and include the photon, which transmits the electromagnetic force.[7] The two forces, the weak force and the electromagnetic force, can be described within the same theory, which forms the basis of the Standard Model. All 12 fermions and all 4 gauge bosons have been observed. Seven of these 16 particles (charm, bottom, top, tau neutrino, W, Z, gluon) were predicted. One additional particle, Higgs boson, was not observed. Scientifically, the discovery of Higgs boson is a great insight for the understanding of the particle mass. This mass is very much connected with the material reality.

Any reality is being, the act of existence, the presence of something and meaning. The opposite or contrary of being is not-being or absence of being. It is nothingness.[8] *Nothingness* may be thought of as constitutive of reality. This is the marvel of nothingness, the paradoxical nature of existence. The reality we think about includes essences, events, facts and causes. It is the reality of being and essence. Reality appears to be the Universe, the Dynamic Now or the Existence, Consciousness, Intelligence or Will. Our view of reality is rooted in what we can observe, and our physical laws are based on replicable patterns in such observations.[9] In our observance space, time, energy/mass and gravity are the properties of this existing Universe. Reality is the state of things as they actually exist. The mystery of both life and death we live our lives is in relation to death.[10]

## Existence

Existence, the principle or source of being, can be attributed to anything which is not contradictory. To understand or grasp the wholeness of reality we search for symbols like Zero, *Śūnyatā,* Trinity, Brahman, etc. These symbols express the profound aspects of reality and manifest themysteries of human life for an integrative understanding of the Ultimate Reality. Concepts like zero, nothingness, eternity, void, emptiness, absence and singularity are pregnant symbols to express the reality.

There is a distinction between the three notions of *nothing, negation* and *non-being. Nothing* belongs together with entities like *every*thing, *some*thing, *many* things, *no* thing, *none* of them, *no*body, etc. It is a quantifier (*no*) combined with a variable (*thing*,…). There is an entity *no*. Mathematically it is an *empty set* or numerical zero (0). An entity is known as what it is and as what it is not according to its own features and the other objects from which it differs.[11] 0 is an entity, a number, a quantity. Thus, 0 being quantitative number is neither positive nor negative, nor both positive and negative, nor neither positive nor negative. It is neutral. So *nothingness* belongs together with *somethingness* and *everythingness*.[12] The word *nothing* must be distinguished from the *not*of negation and *non-being*. *No-being* is a *negated* being. It has two fundamental constituents: *being* and *negation, is* and *is not*. The two properties are not on equal footing. Negation belongs to *non entity*, opposite or absence. '*Not*' belongs to the world of *negation* as '*no*' belongs to the world of *quantity*. *Non-being* is *not a being*. Being and non-being are two abstractions. An object is abstract if it is the referent of an abstract idea. *Being* is fundamental and *no-being* is *negation* of being. An absolute negation is *nothing*, it is non-being. Non-circle is *not* a circle. In fact *non-being* may be said to exist yet there is *no separate entity* non-being, no property or feature of this sort. *Negation* is precisely one coordinated negative state of affairs to every positive state of affairs. It is a *relation* that constitutes a negative fact with anything else in the fact. In *non-being, no* entity or being is identical with the given thing even though we write, speak and think of it like a square circle. Quantum Mechanics and Big Bang can help us to challenge the two-valued logic and go to a multi-valued logic for understanding of being, non-being, not being (negated being), nothing (*no* entity/being), analogical, complementary and relational being etc. Zero, being the representation of the concept of *nothingness* as a quantity and number, is both metaphysical and relational being. Zero is metaphysical being because it is in human minds like any other concepts. It is relational being as a quantity and number because it is related any being as a basic quantity or quality like an empty set.

## Phenomenological Reality

Phenomenological reality is how the world appears or seems to each individual even though one is blind, deaf and dumb. The structural unity of the real is a substantive constitution. This substantivity has three constitutive characteristics: the physiochemical, the psychorganic solidarity and the moment or temporality of corporeality. Reality is the foundation of inanimate (material) and animates (living) with all its possible real moments and dimensions, static and dynamic.[13] It is the given gift. Phenomenology is the study of *human experience* and of the ways things present themselves to us in and through such experience.[14] It is a journey which has unfolded – as it must – within the horizon of personal self-consciousness.[15] Quantum theory states that prior to observation, nothing can be said about a physical system. The appearances of things are like parts without wholes, manifolds bereft of identities, and multiple absences without any enduring real presence.[16] Phenomenology insists that identity and intelligibility are available in things, and that we ourselves are defined as the ones to whom such identities and intelligibilities are given.[17] The Double Slit Experiment of Thomas Young (1773-1829) shows us that we create reality just by observing it. The subatomic particles take every possible path at the same time as a wave when not observed. When observed, the particle collapses down to one point as a particle. What can this mean about us? Do we all have powers that we are not aware of? What it does seem to prove that we create reality by observing it? At the high energy end of existence things are very different. A real entity or an event of fact has two faces, existence and nothingness; 1 & 0 or quantity and quality. The mathematical formulations of the Quantum Mechanics are abstractions of these quantities and qualities. "An amount of inadequacy is inbuilt into reality, an inadequacy that is both delimiting and enabling…Human beings themselves are products of such an ever expanding horizon, that is both elusive and enabling."[18] The biggest questions in Science, Philosophy, and Religion are about nothingness and eternity, the vacuum and the infinite, zeroand infinity. It is Nicholas of Cusa's (1401-1464) premise that there can be only one infinite and this infinite also precedes all plurality and differentiation. Therefore, at true infinity there is one only and all are one.[19] Whenever values or figures are raised to infinity in mathematics extraordinary things happen conceptually and logically. At infinity thorough going coincidence occurs. "The coincidence of opposites provides a method that resolves contradictions without violating the integrity of the contrary elements and without diminishing the reality or the force of their contradiction.... Coincidence as a method issues from coincidence as a fact or condition of opposition that is resolved in and by infinity."[20] Coincidence or necessary correlation as the method settles opposites into a harmony and as the principle views opposites as reconciled. Coincidence of opposites are like act and potency, rest and motion, a priori and a posteriori, past and future, subject and object, induction and deduction, diversity and identity, inequality and equality, divisibility and simplicity, universal and particular, etc.

## Nothingness

Nothingness is the philosophy and science of empty space or zero. Empty space speaks about the physical space or matter while zero (0) as a measurement quantity represents it. Is empty space an existence independent of the matter within it? The nature of an empty space and nothingness has left us with quantum mechanical vacuum filled with fluctuations. Is 'empty space' really empty, or is it an ocean seething with the creation and destruction of virtual matter? "A vacuum is a space entirely devoid of matter, but to Physicists the vacuum is the physical state having the lowest energy."[21] It is filled with a physical quantity called the Higgs field or boson which mediates a new force between particles. The electromagnetic waves (light, radio and UV waves) are consists of particles called photons; the newly discovered Higgs particles make up waves in the Higgs field: that is, waves in the properties of the vacuum itself.[22] The vacuum with its sub-atomic particles and waves is the metaphysical riddle of nothingness that science is experimenting to measure it properly day by day. The things are structured and differentiated as a whole as in process and change. So transcendence, transcendental identification in consciousness and transcendental agency are indispensable features of all humans.[23] Language, by its nature, delimits, encapsulates, and confines. Languages and words have the function of different marks. Different marks are used by humans. The notions like zero, nothing, *śūnya*, emptiness, *kenōsis,* etc., are found in various fields like mathematics, science, philosophy, religion and mysticism. Zero, *śūnya*, nothing, nihil, nonbeing, nonexistence, void and emptiness are not synonyms. Zero has different meanings in modern arithmetic. The integer zero is not the same as the fraction zero. Neither is rational zero same as the real zero. Zero as a number means 'nothing' or *0 quantities*. Zero as a natural number has countless meanings. We have a hierarchy of zeros: natural, integral, rational and real.[24] In science, we find two types of zeros: the zero of the scale which is relative, and the quantitative zero.[25] The origin of coordinate axes in geometry and the zero of the temperature scale are relative zeros. Zero grams, zero litres, zero metres etc. are quantitative zeros which imply 'nothing', 0 quantities. Metaphorically zero means worthless. Psychologically zero means meaninglessness, nihilism, denying all authority. Judicially zero means null and void, that section which is not valid. Zero has the most flexibility or elasticity and is the mark that has no 'original nature' at all. But zero as a placeholder represents a number, an empty set, Ø. Therefore, it has the possibility to develop all other numbers. The term 'nothing' is made of two words; *no* and *thing*, *no* entity, 0 quantities. Grammatically 'nothing' is an indefinite pronoun, refers to 'something,' nothing-as-an-absence-of-a-thing. 'Nothing' as a concept refers to a 'thing.' Equating nothing-as-an-absence-of-a-thing: 'no-thing' or 'not-some-thing', i.e., *no entity*, with nothing-as-a-thing is an invalid logic, the fallacy of terms. Fallacious conclusions follow when *nothing* is treated as a noun or pronoun because it does not have a formal object. It is necessary to respect reality as it manifests itself: the relative and correlative rapports between the existents, their internal and external structures, do not mortify the relations of respective priority and posteriority, of the container and the contained, of interiority and exteriority.[26] Reality is the ontology of internal structures, but also of dialectical movement.[27] There is undivided wholeness of dualities; Spiritual/Physical (theology), Form/Matter (metaphysics), Energy/Matter (physics). *Theology* has two realms; spiritual and physical. Spiritual realm has two basic categories; immortal and mortal spirit. Immortal spirit is rational and mortal spirit is irrational. *Metaphysics* is expressed in dual aspects of matterand form. Form is an abstract entity of a thing. There are many kinds of forms; individual and universal. We, humans, have two forms; human species and individual. Primordial state has three aspects (1) Essence, (2) Nature, and (3) Energy. So we have the three aspects of a reality: Primordial Form (Essence), Awareness (Nature), and Fullness (Energy) all together. *Physical things* are extended things in explicate order whereas spiritual things are unextended in implicate order. Movement or motion is an integral part of the material things. Earth rotates through $360^0$ in 24 hours, we have seen that each $15^0$ of rotation takes an hour and each degree of rotation takes 4 minutes.[28] Motion or change produces extension of matter or things. Motion presupposes the acquisition of something and the corruption of something else. There are *three things* necessary for change to take place. There must be something new that comes to be, something old that passes away, and something that stays the same throughout. These things receive the names *form*, *privation* and *matter*. Form is what comes to be, privation is what passes away and matter is what stays the same throughout the change. Zero corresponds to the dimensionless state of a thing. It represents the point of non-movement. A number or a point on a scale speaks of a movement either towards or away from a specific point on the scale. "By *zero* we mean only one number which has the implication of *nothing*; when added to another number the latter does not change, when multiplied by another number, we get back to zero, and when divided by any non-zero number our answer is zero."[29]

> In Indian theology, 0 is productive of All and None, the matrix of positive and negative values... the polarities of being and non-being, cause and effect, subject and object, time and eternity, finitude and infinity – the groundless ground, the unconditioned, 'origin' of all phenomena.[30]

## Mathematical and Quantum Zero

In the mathematical scale 0 has *no value*; it is nothing, absolutely nothing as quantity. In the temperature scale 0°C or –32°F is the freezing point of water. Numerically it is named 0 or nothing but truly it has a *basic value* in a scale. Zero is a basic value of quantity or quality in an integral part of the reality and of human life. Zero's path through time and thought has been full of intrigue, disguise and mistaken identity from the moment of its invention by the Babylonians, Mayans and Indians. While Babylonian and Mayan zeros disappeared, Indian 0 had already moved to Middle East then to Europe in the Middle Ages. With the invention of calculus in the West in the seventeenth century, zero became a linchpin of the scientific revolution. Modern mathematics and physics have shown that *zero can be basic source of everything*. Zero became the language of nature and the most important tool for mathematics. Zero is powerful because it is infinity's twin.[31] Zero has been symbolised as nothingness in the religious world. For Physicists adding infinities and dividing by zeros seemed utterly irrelevant to the workings of the Universe but, when they began to encounter zeros in the natural world, zero crossed over from mathematics to physics. In thermodynamics zero became unattainable state known as absolute zero. In the theory of relativity zero becomes a black hole, a monstrous star that swallows entire stars or suns.[32] In Quantum Mechanics zero becomes infinite source of energy even in the deepest vacuum. A zero in Quantum Mechanics means that the entire Universe – including the vacuum – is filled with infinite amount of energy: the zero point energy. The zero point energy concept describes the properties of a particle. This *point principle* applies to nature itself. This means that in a sufficiently small volume, even in a vacuum, we have some uncertainty about the amount of energy inside. "The vacuum, by definition, has nothing inside it – no particle, no light, nothing. Thus, the vacuum should have no energy at all."[33] According to Werner Heisenberg's (1901-1976) uncertainty principle, we cannot know how much energy there is in a given volume of the vacuum at any given time. The energy in a given time of vacuum must be fluctuating constantly. How could the vacuum have any energy at all? The answer comes from Albert Einstein's (1879-1955) formula E (energy) = m (mass) × $c^2$ (speed of the light squared).[34] *The fluctuating energy in the vacuum is the same thing as the fluctuating amount of the mass*. The vacuum is never truly empty. Quantum zero is the zero-point or infinite energy. Einstein's equations predicted the black hole; a star so dense even light cannot escape from its grasp. The gravitational attraction is so great that no force in the Universe can stop its collapse – not the repulsion of its electrons, not the pressure of neutron against neutron or quark against quark – nothing.[35] "The dying star gets smaller and smaller and smaller. Then … zero. The star crams itself into zero space."[36] The zero of black hole is a *singularity*, an open wound in the fabric of the Universe. The Universe was born in zero at the $0^{th}$ hour. Out of the void, out of nothing at all, came a cataclysmic explosion that created all energy and matter that the entire Universe is made of. As time runs forward the Universe expands continually. The Universe had a *beginning* about 13. 7 billion years in the past, and the space has been expanding ever since. At some point the Universe would shrivel and wither and then eventually disappear as *a point – the singularity* at the beginning of time and space. This is the primal zero, the birthplace of time and space, the Big Bang. Where did the Big Bang come from? Zero holds the secret. The zero of the vacuum must explain the lumpiness of the Universe. Zero also must explain the secret that created the cosmos. Perhaps the Universe is just a quantum fluctuation on a grand scale – an enormous *singular particle* that came into existence out of the ultimate vacuum. This cosmic egg would explode, inflate and create the space-time of our Universe. Thus, zero might hold the secret of our existence and the existence of other Universes. It may be responsible for the end of the Universe too. *Absolute Zero* is the utter *absence of temperature* of any kind. So it is the *motionless state* between the basest and unextended elements. Zero has a value in the distance scale. It starts here with 0 and ends there with other values, numbers or quantities. Mathematically it is *a point* which does not have a starting or an ending point and therefore it cannot be reached. Number is perceived as being, a basic mathematical entity conveying quantity. How many bunches of bananas do you have, if you have none? Well, none. And *none* is represented by *zero*. Numbers point to a background of reality in which psyche and matter are no longer distinguishable. Quality of number is the relation between the abstract thought of number and its physical dimension. A number is a quantitative essence of things which introduces unity and harmony. The numerals represent primarily as abstract quantities and qualities in the physical world.

## Philosophical Zero

*'Śūnya'* means 0 in Sanskrit. In Pali, *suñña* means empty, desolate, vacant, lonely, absent, void or devoid.[37] *'Śūnya'* is neither quantity nor quality of anything but stands for 'nothing.' *Śūnyatā* is translated as emptiness, void, nothingness, or even relativity, sometimes positively as openness. *Śūnyatā* is a combination of *'śūnya'* (stem) and *'ta'* (participle suffix), *'śūnya'* means empty and *'ta'* means nature, so *śūnyatā* means the nature of emptiness. The root of *'śūnya'* is *'svi'* which means to swell or swollen, so *'śūnya'* means things which are swollen with solid outside and empty inside. Religiously emptiness means to *remove wishes, desires even self to reach the Spirit*. Philosophically emptiness means no real substance, no self, and no original nature of things.

Original nature or self means an entity which is independent, self-sufficient, self-existent, decided, and cannot be separated. Mathematically 0 represents this emptiness and its practical function in business and science. 0 represents emptiness, void, blank, and impracticality, even the possibility of producing all things. Zero does not contain anything, but does instruct, represent, or include all things. Everything starts with zero, including knowledge, business, reputation, wealth, and … so on. So 0 symbolises the limitless latent force of vitality of being and non-being. We cannot think of emptiness (non-being), because all the 'think of' always belong to 'something', 'being' or *bhāva.* Nobody has an idea about non-being, nobody has an experience of non-being, and therefore we have no confidence in dealing with it. Emptiness is absolute transcendence which is beyond being or non-being, incomprehensible, indescribable by words, cannot be reached by words, languages, concepts, and thought. It is doubly hard to describe 'emptiness is form' or 'non-being is being.' Emptiness is that which stands right in the middle between affirmation and negation, existence and non-existence, eternity and annihilation.[38] It is form less but zero which represents nothingness has a form. Thus, nothingness as a quantitative or qualitative form is constitutive of reality. Every *reality* is a composite of *prime matter* and *form* while emptiness transcends all.

'Nothing' and 'void' are related to quantum reality and relativity. Relativity theory describes the phenomena without reference to absolute space and time. It is related to different events. The void or vacuum is not really empty it is always full of an electromagnetic radiation in any given region of space. So according to Einstein's theory of relativity mass can be converted into energy and vice versa under suitable conditions. In void, virtual particles appear and vanish in quantum phenomena. The subatomic existents behave either as waves or particles. A stream of electrons or a single electron can produce interference. So an electron can be at two places at the same time. The pairs of opposites are either *created from nothing* or annihilate each other. The riddles of modern science find some answers in Eastern mysticism which integrates science and spirituality.

## Anthropological Reality

Who are we? We are human persons. Our spirit is the immaterial soul, which our senses cannot feel. We have a spiritual soul which can exist apart from the body. Soul is immortal, being spiritual. The soul cannot be seen because it is formless. It has no parts, so it cannot come apart. The infusion of the soul with the body takes place at our conception and separates at death (CCC 366).[39] The soul, our genuine, true self, is the intellectual self-consciousness of the individual. It is the 'I' or the 'me' as some refer to it. The Greek word for soul is *psyche*, which is often translated as 'mind.' The mind, which receives immaterial forms or concepts (ideas), is therefore immaterial. There are not two immaterial principles within a human being but one. The soul of a human being is an intellectual one, capable of apprehending the natures of things. A person is an individual, complete, subsistent rational or intellectual substance embodied with free will. Rational nature of the person is expressed in consciousness. We are the only form of *living matter* endowed with *reason* and *will*. The *form* is the organizational or unifying principle of the building process. The form is not in the mind of some person. Rather, the form is in the organism itself. That is why it is called an organism. It is the form within the organism, the 'substantial form.' The soul is the 'substantial form' of a living thing, and so the soul is the organizing principle of the living substance. Can this be proved? Yes. The soul is clearly made known through its body that is either physical (human) or spiritual (angel). We have collective memory, better known as written language or history. Language, logic and science are due to the existence of reason. Reason is the property which allows living matter to produce language, logic and science. Our self or soul that holds an idea or concept is not material, but spiritual. Who or what is the self? What is that 'I', this 'I', which is always presupposed? I may find many answers: I am a man, a human being, an Indian, a teacher and so on. What does that mean? Why do I say, 'I am a teacher' and what does that mean? So this is a label, this is a word. This is a concept. We include this label as different concepts – me, self or I. The three most important people in the world are *me*, *myself* and *I*. It is the objective, reflexive and subjective form of the first person, speaker or writer. We cannot find one self, or what we call independent self. 'I' is a shifter: it is both a universal applying indifferently to any being who utters it; and a particular designating one and only one individual.[40] The paradoxical nature of the self is as follows: whatever it is that is said about the self, there is something other than that which is said which is tacitly presupposed.[41] We need to differentiate three concepts: the concept of ego, the embodied personality and the transcendentally real self.[42] 'I' in the sense of ego is any present here-and-now experience. It includes the memory, past experience, the abstract concept of self or ego. We become conscious of *me* or *ego* through the cognitive act of mind. It is through the formless mind that an individual is able to perceive. Even if mind and ego are inseparable yet *mind* is prior to *ego*. What we think or say, 'I have a mind' it means that mind belongs to the ego, the limited *embodied personality*, the subject possessor. Underneath embodied personalities is a transcendental real self which is the source of their causal agency and powers. The three unique activities of human beings which make them transcendental are conceptualization of language, creative art and religious faith.[43]

The doer, possessor, is the agent whom we call 'I. The self is the one who takes responsibility for the claims that it makes.[44] 'If you say 'I', it is equally true that you, and he, and she and indeed anyone can say 'I'; that is, 'I' is a universal.[45] In our being and acting as humans, we all presuppose the reality of subjectivity. It is the rational dignity of human person. According to Thomistic philosophy, the human person is not a composite of 'body and soul' as we may be led to think: it is prime matter informed by the human soul, which is its substantial form, that accounts for the human reality.[46] A human person is a substance consisting of twodistinct substantial co-principles, soul and matter as two principles of a being complementing each other. The soul is primarily an animating principle which is spiritual in essence for the activities of intellect and will.

*Intellectuality* or rationality of the person is thefirst foundation of human dignity. Possession of rational *consciousness* is the 2nd foundation of human dignity by which a person is aware of oneself and other beings. *Morality* is the 3rd foundation of human dignity. We can commit sins of pride, avarice, envy, anger, lust, gluttony and sloth. Physical evil is a lack, a defect, an imperfection or a privation of due being. Moral evil always exists in a subject that decides to do evil. Evil comes from our free will.[47]*Acceptance* of a person in the society is the 4th foundation of human dignity. A single cell zygote in the mother's womb is the 1st acceptance of human being. A genuinely learned ignorance recognizes the thoroughgoing transcendence of God-in-God's-self, always infinite, absolute, and hidden to human eyes.[48] Person is, as some of the Buddhists call, *empty of* substantial and autonomous existence. So that vacuum, that emptiness, is called emptiness of person or personality. That is called *śūnyatā*or no-self. There's only one self, one I, one so-called I. Me is the reflective concept of I or objective pronoun of I. If there is no me, why do we fool ourselves? Why do we call ourselves *me*, *I*, *we* or *us*? Why? The human person is not just a product of nature; it is our body, our genetics, which is a product of nature. The human person is not just a collection of atoms and molecules, however sophisticatedly organized, but is very much a product of his/her social, cultural, religious surroundings.[49] Either body-mind or body-soul is referred as ego or self. It is modern ego-problem. Human being is not an aggregate of separate parts but an integrated whole, human person, a mystery, in the Marcelian sense. Gabriel Marcel (1889-1973) was a French philosopher, drama critic, playwright and musician who converted to Catholicism in 1929. The human person is primarily a soul which has a body. The soul, an animating principle, is created by God at our conception, if we believe in the existence of the soul. Human beings are co-creators or partners in the on-going process of human creation. Belgian Jesuit of Fordham University, Joseph Donceel (1906-1994), writes, 'Human being is an embodied loving affirmation of God.'[50] "Whatever the self is, it is clearly very important in contemporary society, being the bearer of legal, social and religious rights and responsibilities. It is 'I' who comes of age and marries, possesses and owns, votes and talks, loves and fights, is punished and rewarded, becomes ill and dies – and event which 'I' either do or do not survive."[51] Our intelligence or brain is less powerful than the spiritual intelligence that our souls have. A spirit is a being that has understanding and free will, but no physical body, and will never die. The spirit is the soul of the body, the vital principle or the substantial form of the matter. There are thousand-and-one aspects to human being but they are many phases of one ultimate substantial reality, the human person. The person is both the subject and object of actions because the one who experiences is human and the one experienced by the subject of the experience is also a human. The human mind is capable of knowing reality through the use of both experience and reason. In every Direct Judgement we say *two kinds of things* about something: WHAT it is (its essence, its 'this-ness') and THAT it is (its existence).[52] In other words, the dynamic movement of the intellect *experiences* a limit, a check to its movement. This means that the intellect, in every affirmation, is always ultimately tending towards the Unlimited Being.[53]

## Ultimate Reality

Reality that is self-existent, necessary, uncaused, autonomous and absolute has been given many names – e.g. God, Self, Truth, Beauty, Goodness, Tao, Energy, World, Perfection, Consciousness, Conscience, Fullness, Void, etc. Once reason successfully intuits and formulates the first universal principles of being and correctly draws from them conclusions which are coherent both logically and ethically, then it may be called right reason.[54] The principles of non-contradiction, finality and causality, as well as the concept of the person as free and intelligent subject, with the capacity to know God, truth and goodness are self-evident principles.[55] Absolute Reality, Godhead or Absolute Consciousness or Enlightenment in metaphysics falls under the rubric of Theology. God is not Absolute Other, but the Ultimate in a radical relationship with all that exists.[56] Reality embraces all as cause of the finite world, includes all as real and transcends all as absolute and infinite. Words and language deal only with concepts, and cannot approach Reality fully. Concepts can only model, symbolize or represent something. They cannot, in fact, produce it. The basic form or structure that which is the universal ground of all conditions is simply Being-ness. The existence of structure requires form and form requires a boundary condition. A boundary condition separates something from something else. These two things (form and boundary condition) are relational to one another. This original and primordial structure is pure duality made manifest. The three: Being, the one and the other, are three conceptual aspects of the non-dual transcendental condition of Being Itself. These three; beingness or thatness or isness or suchness, the Absolute and the anthropomorphic Godhead are actually only One Thing arising together. Absolute Reality is described as unmanifest and manifest. The Godhead, the Essence of God, is unknown and unknowable in its Inscrutable Essence, is called by the mystics and theologians omnipotence, omniscience, omnipresence, Unity, Oneness, Absolute Existence, Pure Being, Non-dual Consciousness, Emptiness, Divine Nothingness, Darkness, Void, Abyss, Silence, Otherness, Beyondness and Mystery, and yet is beyond all of these. In the moment of arising, both the one and the other must arise simultaneously as a pair. Subject and object, limited and unlimited, positive and negative, presence and absence, quantity and quality, light and darkness or shadow exist together. Sides like left and right, rear and front, top and bottom, inside and outside exist together. Wave and particle also dance together. Modern physics has discovered that there is no actual, easily identifiable 'thing' at the basis of matter. How does the world of whirling atoms, electrons, neutrons and sub-atomic particles fit in with our own perception of reality? They are interconnected or interrelated to each other so that the living things can grow, mature and die? "Just as the material reality is ever approachable, but never attainable, so too beings could be understood in this paradoxical and ambiguous manner… our ideals, perfections, our relationship and even happiness, are approachable, but never realizable."[57]

## Endnotes

1. "Higgs Boson," in *Wikipedia: The Free Encyclopedia*, accessed July 10, 2012, http://en.wikipedia.org/wiki/Higgs_boson.
2. "Missing Higgs," in *CERN (European Organization for Nuclear Research),* accessed July 10, 2012, http://user.web. cern.ch/public/en/Science/Higgs-en.html.
3. Michael Hanlon, "The Goddamn Particle and the Prophets of CERN: Some Thoughts on the Higgs Boson," in *Mail Online*, accessed July 10, 2012, http://www.dailymail.co.uk/debate/article-2171448/The-God damn- particle-prophets-CERN-Some-thoughts-Higgs-Boson. html? ito= feeds-newsxml.
4. "The God Particle: If the Universe Is the Answer, What Is the Question?" in *Wikipedia:The Free Encyclopedia*, accessed July 15, 2012, http://en. wikipedia.org/ wiki/The_ God_Particle:_If_ the_ Universe_ Is_the_Answer,_What_Is_the_Question%3F.
5. Mike Woods, "Standard Model of Particle Physics," in *SLD*, accessed July 10, 2012, http://www-sldnt.slac. stanford.edu/alr/standard_ model.htm.
6. "Matter Particles," in *CERN (European Organization for Nuclear Research),* accessed July 10, 2012, http:// user.web. cern.ch/public/en/Science/StandardModel-en.html.
7. Woods, "Standard Model of Particle Physics," in *SLD*, accessed July 10, 2012, http://www-sldnt.slac.stanford.edu /alr/standard_ model. htm.
8. The concept of nothingness has been the best expression of the divine infinity or potentiality which is absolutely transcendent and indescribable. Words such as 'infinite', 'ineffable' and indescribable are obviously negative while potential and transcendental are positive.
9. Ernest Zebrowski, *A History of the Circle: Mathematical Reasoning and the Physical Universe* (London: Free Association Books, 1999), 185.
10. Mathew Jayanth, "Theology of Death: Experiencing the Fullness of Life through the Negation of Life in Death," in *The Depth of Death: Scientific Insights, Religious Openness*, ed. Kuruvilla Pandikattu (New Delhi: Serials Publications, 2010), 106.
11. John Peter Vallabados, "Abhāva," in *ACPI Encyclopedia of Philosophy*, 2 Vols., Vol. 1, ed. Johnson Puthenpurackal (Bangalore: Asian Trading Corporation, 2010), 3.

12. Reinhardt Grossmann, *The Existence of the World: An Introduction to Ontology,* The Problems of Philosophy: Their Past and Present Series, ed. Ted Honderich (London: Routledge, 1992), 122.
13. Joaquin Redondo, "Reality and Existence," in *Catholic Philosophy*, accessed February 20, 2011, http://catholicphilosophy.com/sys-tmpl/door/index.html.
14. Robert Sokolowski, *Introduction to Phenomenology* (Cambridge: Cambridge University Press, 2000), 2.
15. John Paul II, Encyclical Letter *Fides et Ratio (Faith and Reason)* (Mumbai: Pauline Publications, 1998), 3.
16. Sokolowski, *Introduction to Phenomenology*, 3-4.
17. *Ibid.,* 4.
18. Kuruvilla Pandikattu, "Ever Approachable, Never Attainable: Scientific and Philosophical Reflections on the Human Person," *Omega: Indian Journal of Science and Religion* 8, 1 (June 2009): 63.
19. H. Lawrence Bond, trans., *Nicholas of Cusa: Selected Spiritual Writings* (New York: Paulist Press, 1997), 22.
20. *Ibid.*, 22.
21. Cliff Burgess, "Higgs Boson Explains a Lot about Nothing," in *Thestar.com*, accessed July 8, 2011, http://www.thestar.com/opinion/editorialopinion/article/1223002--higgs-boson-explains-a-lot-about-nothing.
22. *Ibid.*
23. Roy Bhaskar, *Reflections on Meta-Reality: Transcendence, Emancipation and Everyday Life* (New Delhi: Sage Publications, 2002), 10.
24. Jayant Burde, *Śūnya and Nothingness in Science, Philosophy and Religion* (Delhi: Motilal Banarsidass Publishers, 2009), xviii.
25. *Ibid.,* xxi.
26. Luigi Bogliolo, *Metaphysics* (Bangalore: Theological Publications in India, 1987), 114.
27. *Ibid.,* 113.
28. Zebrowski, *A History of the Circle: Mathematical Reasoning and the Physical Universe,* 58.
29. Burde, *Śūnya and Nothingness in Science, Philosophy and Religion*, 112.
30. Bosco Correya, "Absence," in *ACPI Encyclopedia of Philosophy*, 2 Vols., Vol. 1, ed. Johnson Puthenpurackal (Bangalore: Asia Trading Corporation, 2010), 8.

31. Charles Seife, *Zero: The Biography of a Dangerous Idea* (New York: Penguin Putnam, 2000), 2.
32. *Ibid.,* 157-158.
33. *Ibid.*, 171.
34. *Ibid.,* 172.
35. *Ibid.*, 182.
36. *Ibid.*
37. Harsh Narain, *The Mādhyamika Mind* (Delhi: Motilal Banarsidass Publishers, 1997), 73.
38. Edward Conze, *Buddhism: Its Essence and Development* (New York: Harper Colophon Books, 1975), 131.
39. *Catechism of the Catholic Church (CCC)* {1994; 8th reprint, New Delhi: Theological Publications in India (TPI), 2006}, 73. Today, human beings may be playing God's role in IVF (in vitro fertilization), contraception and abortion.
40. Roy Bhaskar, *Reflections on Meta-Reality: Transcendence, Emancipation and Everyday Life* (New Delhi: Sage Publications, 2002), 69.
41. *Ibid.*, 70.
42. *Ibid.*, 76.
43. Cyril Desbruslais, *The Philosophy of the Human Person: An Introduction to Philosophical Anthropology*, ed. Kuruvilla Pandikattu (Pune: Jnana-Deepa Vidyapeeth, 1997), 15.
44. Sokolowski, *Introduction to Phenomenology,* 6.
45. Bhaskar, *Reflections on Meta-Reality: Transcendence, Emancipation and Everyday Life*, 75.
46. Desbruslais, *The Philosophy of the Human Person: An Introduction to Philosophical Anthropology*, 16.
47. We sin not only by freely choosing to do what God has forbidden but also by failing to do what God has commanded. There is no objective morality without God according to some thinkers. If there is no God, everything is permissible. Without God, morality would be just an opinion of few or might is right as Adolf Hitler (1889-1945) did to the six million Jews or communists did to the believers. Hitler, atheists or communists are right if there is no God.
48. Bond, trans., *Nicholas of Cusa: Selected Spiritual Writings,* 34.
49. S. George Valumkal, "Delaying or Defying Death through the Human Genome Project: Contribution of Science and Religion,"

in *The Depth of Death: Scientific Insights, Religious Openness*, ed. Kuruvilla Pandikattu (New Delhi: Serials Publications, 2010), 45.

50. Desbruslais, *The Philosophy of the Human Person: An Introduction to Philosophical Anthropology*, 30.
51. *Ibid.*, 70.
52. Cyril Desbruslais, *The Philosophy of the Human Person: An Introduction to Philosophical Anthropology*, ed. Kuruvilla Pandikattu (Pune: Jnana-Deepa Vidyapeeth, 1997), 26.
53. *Ibid.*, 27.
54. Paul II, Encyclical Letter *Fides et Ratio (Faith and Reason)*, 8.
55. *Ibid.*
56. Jacob Parappally, "The Significance of Jesus' Resurrection for Humans and the World," in The Depth of Death: Scientific Insights, Religious Openness, ed. Kuruvilla Pandikattu (New Delhi: Serials Publications, 2010), 132-133.
57. Pandikattu, "Ever Approachable, Never Attainable," 76.

*Chapter 1*

# Zero in Mathematics: A Study of Mathematical Nothingness

How is zero a part of our mathematical and conceptual world? What is the story of the evolution of zero? After taking up some of these questions, we dwell on its evolution and importance. So in this chapter, after studying zero from a mathematical and philosophical perspective, we briefly dwell on its philosophical significance.

## 1.0 Introduction

Mathematics is the science of numbers and their operations, interrelations, combinations, generalizations, and abstractions and of space configurations and their structure, measurement, transformations, and generalizations.[1] It is an expression of human mind that reflects the active will, contemplative reason and desire for aesthetic perfection. Its basic elements are logic and intuition, analysis and construction, generality and individuality.[2] Mathematics uses signs, symbols, and proofs and includes arithmetic, algebra, calculus, geometry and trigonometry. It is a precise and subtle language designed to express certain kinds of ideas more briefly, more accurately, and more usefully than ordinary language which uses the ordinary words and its behaviours. Mathematical language often serve as a starting point for the philosophy of language.

Arithmetic deals with the nonnegative real numbers including the transfinite cardinals and with the application of the operations of addition, subtraction, multiplication, and division to them. In arithmetic operations, dividing zero by zero cannot be done. Zero, depending on the context, either denotative or connotative means it includes 'total failure,' 'absence,' 'nil,' and 'absolutely nothing.' 'Nothing' is an even more abstract concept than 'zero' and their meanings sometimes intersect. 0 is NOT to 'nothing' as 1 is IS to a 'thing or being.' The concept of 'nothing' is a symbolic and numeral placeholder that really means 'the connection between some elements that we cannot see at the moment.' We have the word 'nothing' but it does not correspond to anything that we actually experience. The absence of something is still a thing that joins/divides/differentiates things in an entire thread of 'nothing.' Absolutely nothing is entirely dependent on something absolutely existing. 'Nothing' differs from zero in the way that zero is something, a finite amountwhich is defined. While 'nothing' overlaps the quantity zero, in the way that it also *is*, when finitely defined. 'Nothing' differs in the way that it has no specific basis like zero (0) in numbers. Mathematics and physics have shown that *zero* (numeral nothing) can be the source of everything especially bringing out natural numbers. Zero to the $0^{th}$ power ($0^0$) is undefined or nonexistent yet according to zero rules any nonzero number raised to the power of 0 is 1 ($1^0 = 1$ or $a^0 = 1$).

Zero derives from Indian *śūnya* – meaning 'void,' 'empty' – via Arabic *sifr*, Latin *cephirum,* and Italian *zevero*; *sifr* is also the origin of cipher.[3] *Śūnya* referred to empty, and was used to indicate the empty column on the abacus. There are ten designated numerals with a single digit: 0, 1, 2, 3, 4, 5, 6, 7, 8, and 9. Mathematical zero is a late comer in mathematics. It is symbolized by the numeric character 0. 0 is having no substantial numeral value of its own but plays the key role in the system of decimal notation, to express all numbers with nine digits. All Arabic numbers we use today are ideograms created by Abu Jafar Muhammad ibn Musa al-Khwarizmi (c.778-850) of Uzbekistan who later moved to Baghdad. Numbers 10 and greater are expressed by using a combination of the ten digits, with the place of the digit indicating the value of the digit. The value of each place from right to left is a successive power of 10, and the total values for all places are combined or added. In this positional number system, zero's place indicates 'nounits of this multiple.' For example, in decimal number 1908, there is 1 unit in the thousands position, 9 units in the hundreds position, 0 units in the tens position, and 8 units in the ones position or place. The number 13 is pronounced *trayo-daśa*, or three-ten, but is written ten-three. Notation for placeholders in positional numbers is found on stone tablets from ancient Sumeria around 3,000 BCE and later it was adapted by the Babylonians.[4] The Egyptians and the Mayans developed their positional numeral systems independently. The Greeks had no concept of a number like zero. After the destruction of the Babylonian and Mayan civilizations, the honour goes to the third inventor of zero, the Indus Valley civilization which was developed as early as 3,000 BCE.[5] Zero is traced to the Indian mathematician Āryabhaṭṭa (476-550) who, about 520 CE devised a positional decimal number system that contained a word, '*kha*,'[6] for the idea of a placeholder. By 876, the ***kha*** (empty space) had become the numerical symbol '0.' After Āryabhaṭṭa, another Indian, Brahmagupta (598-665), developed the concept of the zero as an actual independent number, not just a place-holder, and wrote rules for adding and subtracting 0 from other numbers. In mathematics, the sum of all real numbers is undefined, otherwise 0 would be a mathematical nothing and everything simultaneously.[7] In the 7th century, negative numbers were used in book keeping in India; positive quantities denoted assets, negative ones debts.[8] All the facts can be partitioned into two sets; positive and negative, neither of which, on its own comprises the totality of facts making up the world.[9]

Zero is an independent value midway between +1 and –1 of the number line. In the natural numbers, 1 is the only unit; in the integers, 1 and –1 are the only units (each of the things that exist). Galileo Galilei (1564-1642) of Italy and Isaac Newton (1643-1727) of Britain called numbers as the primary properties of things, the properties that can be measured.[10] Zero is synonymous with 'none,' 'empty' or 'nothing.' Zero is a number which quantifies a thing or an amount of null size. The value, or number, zero is not the same as the digitzero. For example, 02 and 20; the value of 20 is different than 02. In 002, there are two leading zeros which could be left blank for the sake of numeral value. Probably, zero was discovered almost as soon as numbers were discovered. What took thousands of years was to invent a special symbol for the number zero (0), and then to incorporate it into a decimal system of numeration or any other numeration. Two integers that have the same distance from zero in opposite directions of the number line are called opposites; + 2 and –2.

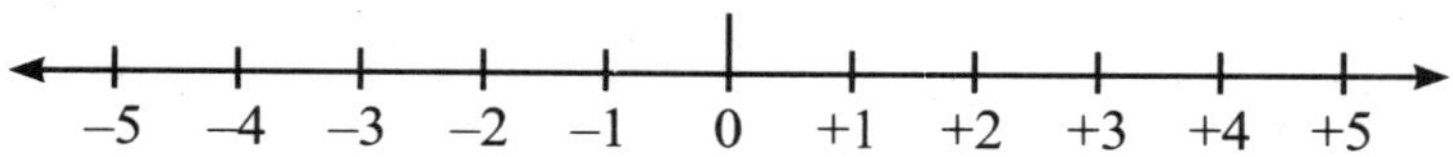


Philosophy of mathematics is the branch of philosophy that studies the philosophical or mathematical assumptions, foundations and implications of mathematics.[11] Here we want to deal with mathematical zero (0) and its philosophical implications. In mathematics, sets are convenient because all mathematical structures can be regarded as sets even natural numbers can be defined as sets. The sets and their theory are important foundational tools in mathematics, linguistics and philosophy. There are 10 mathematical fundamental assumptions on a set which is known as set theory. The proliferation of different numbers comes out from the cardinality of empty set which is represented as numeral 0.

## 1.1 Set Theory and Proliferation of Different Numbers

Set Theory is the mathematical science of the infinite, the uncountability of the real number line. Sets can be finite or infinite. The fundamental concept in the theory of infinite sets is the *cardinality* of a set. The sets are the fundamental objects to define all other concepts in mathematics. A set is an abstract object; its members do not have to be physically collected together for them to constitute a set. It can be any well-defined collection of objects or an unordered group of objects with no duplicates. The language of set theory is based on a single fundamental relation, called *membership* or elements. There are two special sets: the 'empty set' and the 'universal set.' The empty set (or null set) is the set which contains no objects and is denoted {}, or by the symbol ∅. The universal set is denoted by the capital letter U. Sets are used to define the concepts of relations and functions.

To tackle what a number is, mathematicians like Georg Cantor (1845-1918), Richard Dedekind (1831-1916), Gottlob Frege (1848-1925) of Germany, Giuseppe Peano (1858-1932) of Italy, Bertrand Russell (1872-1970), and Alfred North Whitehead (1861-1947) of Britain turned to a new branch of mathematics called Set Theory. Set theory features binary operations on sets. There are some set operations: union ( ∪ ), intersection (∩), set difference (\), symmetric difference (Δ), complementation (A'), Cartesian product (×) and power set P (A). The theory of sets was developed by German mathematician Georg Cantor in 1874 and promoted by John von Neumann (1903-1957) of Hungarian-American. A set is a collection, class, group or conglomerate of real or mathematical objects.[12] Cantor investigated ways of defining one-to-one correspondences between sets. This sets are considered to have the same cardinality (i.e. number of elements) called $\aleph_0$ (Aleph null). $\aleph_0$ is the cardinality of the set of all natural umbers. One set is a proper subset of another having the same number of elements. This is exactly the definition of infinite sets. The aleph numbers represent the cardinality of infinite sets. Cantor conjectured every infinite set of real numbers either is countable or has the power of the continuum.[13] The 'smallest level' of infinity has to do with countable things that can be put in some order like natural numbers. The set of all integers is countable while the set of all real numbers is uncountable. The cardinality of uncountable subsets of reals is equal to the cardinality of reals is continuum hypothesis.[14]

We may not be able to point out infinitely many objects in the real world; we can construct conceptual sets with an infinite number of elements. One of the basic principles of set theory is the existence of infinite sets which come in different sizes. The most basic set is the empty set denoted ∅ or { } which contains no elements; ∅ = 0 or ∅ = { }. $(\exists \varnothing)(\forall x)(x \notin \varnothing)$. Everything in set theory is based on the empty set. The Swiss mathematician Leonhard Euler (1707-1783) was largely responsible for the symbols $\varnothing, f, F$, as used in the theory of functions.[15] The empty set is a member of the universal set; it is also a subset of the universal set. In fact, the empty set is a subset of every other set ($\varnothing \in$ S, B, or any set), and any two empty sets are equal. When two sets are finite, then they have the same cardinality if and only if they have the same number of elements. So the fundamental concept in the theory of infinite sets is the *cardinality* of a set. In reality there exists no 'universal' set (the set of all sets), no set of all cardinal numbers, etc. It is like the barber who shaves all and only those that do not shave themselves. Set theory plays a central role in mathematics for providing the basic language and apparatus in which most of mathematics is expressed. If nothing is assumed, nothing will be deduced. A postulate is a statement that is assumed to be true without proof.

The Zermelo-Fraenkel (ZF) Axioms of set theory imply that there exists an empty set which has no elements. One constructs an empty set by starting with any set $A$ and then applying the axiom of separation to form the empty set $\varnothing = \{x \in A | \, x / x\}$. It is based on a certain picture of sets – the 'iterative hierarchy.' So the idea of the picture is that we have a series of levels of sets, each containing all members of the earlier ones, and they are constructed in a certain way: some by taking power sets of the previous member, others by taking the union of all the previous members. So every set shows up somewhere in the iterative hierarchy. There is *no set of all sets*, since that would not ever show up in the hierarchy. At each level, new sets are always added. They say there are two kinds of entities, classes and sets. There is a class that contains all the sets as members; it is just not a set. This is the approach of John von-Neumann (1903-1957) and Swiss mathematician Paul Isaac Bernays (1888-1977). The ZF approach just says there is nothing that contains all the sets. The natural numbers (N) are defined to be the intersection of all subsets of which are inductive sets and contain the empty set as an element. To define number 0 we choose sets having no elements. The cardinality of $\varnothing$ set is 0. There exists no more than one such set (empty set). We can proceed and define the set whose only member is $\varnothing$ it has one member $\{\varnothing\}$. Its cardinality is 1 which we can associate it with natural number 1. In the similar way a set having two elements {0, 1} shows its cardinality as natural number 2, {∅, {∅}}. They can be represented as { }, {∅}, {{∅}}, {{{∅}}}, etc. Numbers that denote the magnitudes of sets are called cardinal numbers (1, 2, 3, ...). Ordinal numbers (1st, 2nd, 3rd, ...) describe orderings while cardinal numbers measure the size in mathematics. Let us see few cardinal numbers which are finite ordinals[16] according to John von Neumann:

0 = ∅
1 = {0} = {∅}
2 = {0, 1} = {∅, {∅}}
3 = {0, 1, 2} = {∅, {∅}, {∅, {∅}}}
4 = {0, 1, 2, 3} = {∅, {∅}, {∅, {∅}}, {∅, {∅}, {∅, {∅}}}}
5 = {0, 1, 2, 3, 4} etc.

That is, in each case, we take the set of all the previous numbers. Each integer is a finite cardinal number. Different integers have different sizes. The set 0 has 0 elements, the set 1 has 1 element, the set 2 has two elements, set 3 has 3 elements, etc. Informally, the set *n* is the set consisting of the *n* elements 0, 1, 2, 3, …, *n* – 1, and *n* is both a subset of N and an element of N. An example of an infinite set is (∃A / ∅) ( ∀ x) >{∅, {∅}, {{∅}}, {{{∅}}} ...}. We get an infinite sequence of abstract Platonic mathematical entities – sets containing, respectively, 0, 1, 2, 3, ... elements, one set for each of the natural numbers, quite independently of the actual physical nature of the Universe.[17] 0 is before 1, 1 is before 2, etc. This notion of being 'before' is a relation. The relation of before is an entity, a finite set. Cantor classified infinite set according to power and proved that the cardinal of real numbers is larger than the cardinal of the integers (R > Z). "Now-a-days it is known to be possible logically speaking, to derive practically the whole of known mathematics from a single source, The Theory of Sets," expresses Bourbaki in '*Elements de mathematique*.'[18] The mathematical theory of the natural numbers or positive integers is known as arithmetic while

Algebra is the generalization of arithmetic. Arithmetic has some basic concepts: number, successor, addition, multiplication, etc. And it has some assumptions about how those work. In algebra, letters are used to stand for numbers like $ax^2 + bx + c = 0$ where the letters $a$, $b$, and $c$ stand for various known constant numbers called coefficients and the letter $x$ is an unknown variable number. Algebra studies relationships using symbols (numbers or letters), logic and formal proof.

Geometry is a mathematical study of points, lines, planes, closed flat shapes, curves, spheres and solids. Using any one of these alone, or in combination with others, it is possible to describe, design, and construct every visible object in the three dimensional space. In geometry we measure angles, perimeter, area and volumes in relation to their properties in the space. A point which shows position is 0-dimensional can lie on a line, in a plane, or in space. Euclidean or elementary geometry is of two and three dimensions (plane and solid geometry). Analytic geometry has been generalized to four or more dimensions and has been combined with other branches of geometry. It was introduced by French philosopher René Descartes (1596-1650) in 1637 and was of fundamental importance in the development of the calculus by Sir Isaac Newton (1642-1727) and German mathematician and philosopher G. W. Leibniz (1646-1716) in the late 17th century. It is concerned with geometric objects (loci) defined by algebraic relations among their coordinates. Descriptive geometry of Ptolemy (100-170) of Alexandria is concerned with the two-dimensional representation of three-dimensional objects which was introduced in 1795 by French mathematician Gaspard Monge (1746-1818). Differential geometry deals with the concepts of the calculus that are applied to curves, surfaces, and other coordinate geometric entities. The study of the relationships between the sides and angles in a triangle in terms of the trigonometric functions of angles is Trigonometry. Hipparchos of Nicea and Rhodes (190-125 BCE) is credited with inventing trigonometry and the term is invented by Bartholomaeus Pitiscus (1561-1613) of Germany in 1595.[19]

Calculus studies continuously changing quantities, slopes of curves at a given points, areas and volumes of curves and their problems. Isaac Newton and the German mathematician G. W. Leibniz, working independently, developed the calculus during the 17th century. Probability and Statistics deal with events whose results are uncertain. Probability is the ratio of the number of favourable outcomes to the total number of possible outcomes. It is based on the study of permutations and combinations and is the necessary foundation for statistics. Statistics deals with the collection, organization, and analysis of numerical data and with such problems as experiment, design and decision-making. Set theory establishes statements that are true of sets regardless of objects which make a set. Number theory deals with the properties of numbers primarily integers or whole numbers that are positive, negative or zero.

Counting, conceptualization of numbers and invention of four fundamental operations are the early activities of mathematics. The *four* fundamental operations of mathematics are addition (+), multiplication (×), subtraction (–) and division (÷ or /). Subtraction is the inverse operation to addition and division is the inverse operation to multiplication. For addition, 'the identity' is zero and the 'inverse' is additive inverse with the opposite sign. The most important arithmetic properties are *commutative*, *associative* and *distributive* laws of addition and multiplication.

For example,
1) $a + b = b + a$,
2) $ab = ba$,
3) $a + (b + c) = (a + b) + c$,
4) $a(bc) = a(bc)$,
5) $a(b + c) = ab + ac$.

The first two are known as the commutative laws of addition and multiplication interchanging (commuting) the order of the elements involved in addition and multiplication. The third is known as *associative law* of addition which gives the same result whether we add in any way either last two or first two elements at a time. The fourth is the associative law of multiplication tells us that we can group numbers in a product in any way we want and still get the same answer. The fifth is the distributive law which multiplies the terms in parenthesis and *distributes* its products. So with any two operations, first operation is distributive over the 2nd operation. The symbols + and – were first shown in 1489 by a German mathematician Johann Widman (1462-1498).[20] "The English mathematician William Oughtred (1574-1660) first used the symbol '×' for 'times.' The German mathematician Gottfried Wilhelm Leibniz (1646-1716) used a period (.) to indicate multiplication."[21] The Indians wrote the divisor under the dividend (÷). The most common way to write a ratio is as a fraction or division while comparing two things. Leibniz used the familiar form a: b. A proportion is a name we give to a statement that two ratios are equal. It can be written in two ways: $a/b = c/d$ or a: b = c: d. The quotients and ratios are equivalents but not equals. Eudoxus of Cnidus (408-355 BCE) is known for the theory of proportions as described in Euclid's *Elements*.[22] The symbol of equality, =, was originated by the English mathematician Robert Recorde (1510-1558) around 1557, and the symbols > and < for 'greater than' and 'less than' originated with Thomas Harriot (1560-1621), also an Englishman.[23] According to the definition of addition two integers may be defined in the relation of inequality, one may be greater or lesser. Dutch mathematician Simon Stevin (1548-1620) used a period (.) to set off the decimal part of a number as early as 1492 which Swiss mathematician Justus Byrgius (1552-1632) continued while a German mathematician, astronomer and astrologer Johannes Kepler (1571-1630) used comma (,). German mathematician and Physicist Karl Gauss (1777-1855) called number theory (the science of the natural numbers) the 'Queen of Mathematics.' In 1902, English philosopher Bertrand Russell (1872-1970) who showed that the assumption of existence of a set of all sets leads to a contradiction.

The set theory begins with an empty set symbolized as ∅ and represented by 0, a number, an empty placeholder in the decimal numeration. The rest of the numbers proliferate from this empty set which are abstract concepts that describe sizes of the sets or natural numbers. Let us see what a number is.

### 1.1.1 The Concept of the Number

A number is an idea that refers to amounts of things. It shows the oneness and unity of the things or concepts. It can express the quantity of things. It is a set, a fundamental concept in mathematics. It can also show the sequence of things like in the number line. This simple notion of *number line* leads us to the concept of *time*. It is the linear time which measures the magnitude of things. The notion of magnitude leads us to the concept of *space*. The number, time and space coincide together. India gave us the ingenious method of expressing all numbers by means of ten symbols: 0, 1, 2, 3, 4, 5, 6, 7, 8 and 9. Zero is a number as well as an empty placeholder in decimal numeration, and a concept for 'nothing' which is derived from the concept of *void* or *śūnya*.

> If we interpret Nagarjuna's *śūnya* as nothing or the null set, then the Sankarites would succeed, as the complement of the null set is the universal set; hence by negating that reality is nothing, they would obtain that reality is everything, which is Brahman.[24]

The concept of void existed in Indian philosophy and the Buddhist concept of *Nirvāṇa*, that is, attaining salvation by merging into the void of eternity. Zero is the only digit which cannot stand alone. *By itself it is nothing*! When we write 10, we mean 1 is in tens and 0 in ones position. 0 as marking a particular 'place' is empty and essential for other digits. The concept of *zero* represents '*something*' that is '*not there*,' while zero as a number represents the lowest of all non-negative numbers. Counting is as old as humans. We may say that any number is simply a 'unit' for counting. Humans invented *words* for numbers and later symbolic *numerals*. Real numbers involving zero, the following four categories: 'positive', 'negative', 'non-negative' and 'non-positive' are being used. The numeral system, we use today, originated in India with Indians. Numbers are invented to quantify the external world. The external world is *quantitative* and *qualitative* in its nature. The construction of all of mathematics assumes the empty set as the only primitive entity. Set theory builds on the empty set.

Empty set is the subset of any set. The integer 1 is defined as the set containing the empty set. Two is defined as the set that contains the empty set and 1 (0 and 1). 3 is the set that contains 0, 1 and 2. 4 is the set that contains 0, 1, 2 and 3. The other natural numbers are built as the previous ones are built.

The real numbers have no physical existence but describe magnitude or position.[25] They are a human creation. Number is the way we relate to the physical world. So far as we consider our minds as objective observers of that, number is in our heads, not in the material world. The maths is in our heads, but is reflected in the material view we produce. 1 and 1 make two, but 1 + 0 = 1. Who made them so? The answer is 'the human mind.' Our mind investigates things. The investigation of things is known as *science*. Science analyses or synthesises by induction or deduction to reach a certain *assumption*. These assumptions become fundamental *concepts*. They become *universals*. The notions of oneness and order, just as the notions of number and numbers, are universals. The 'one' is defined as undivided in itself and divided from everything else. We have the words 'single', 'common' and 'particular' which signify the same notion of 'one.' Being bound together and set apart in unity as one, unique, identical and distinct are attributed to the concept of *one*. Unity is a transcendental property of being and implies a certain interconnectedness within and separation from others.[26] Oneness or unity as *transcendental* is of the same nature as the transcendental being is. Being or existence has common traits as *one*, *true*, *good*, *beautiful*, *active* and *having duration* in space time continuum. So numbers are transcendental beings and exist in their own way. Unity of oneness is correlative of multiplicity of many things. In spite of things or numbers there is an order in the sense of a definite sequence. The concept of 'order' is fundamental to mathematics. This concept arises from the nature of 'time' and 'space.' The sequence of number line, numerals, letters of alphabets or milestones on the road refer to the continuous flow of time. They are units, one thing at a time: numbers, alphabets or milestones. Logically, they are universals in the sense of units or the order of sequences. In the science of mathematics the concept of number is a fundamental one. Mathematics involves the creation of truth which has an objective meaning. The essence of physical objects is immediate experience. Number is the mediator between the reality of here and now and our deeper existence as part of the unbounded creative process of evolving consciousness. The reality that contemporary physics paints is radically different than the conceptual framework we develop naturally. The objects in physical space in contemporary physics have a discrete structure, but time and space are still modelled as *continuous entities*.

Science must use the tools it has and these inevitably have limits and shortcomings. The continuous real line that we see is a creation of our brain and nervous system. Although objects in space-time are discrete, space-time itself remains continuous in special and general relativity. The structure of the Universe is simple, understandable, mathematical and finite. There is a relationship between the quality of experience and physical structure. This relationship is creative. Mathematics is the key to understanding the structure of this creative process and the conditions that make it possible. Natural sciences search for the laws of nature but mathematics depends on abstractions from the very nature of things.

We have invented integers to correspond to a definite position in a sequence of individuals of multiple realities. The oldest preserved samples of Indian, or Arabic, digits are inscriptions on a stone column found in India and believed to be from around the year 250 BCE.[27] So we count the things or numbers as 1, 2, 3.... There is a concept of quantity in each sequence of numbers. One milestone, two milestones, three milestones, etc., are applied quantitatively. Thomas Jefferson (1743-1826), the Space Secretary of State of the United States, suggested in 1790 that a decimal system of measurement would bring national uniformity of weights and measures. The metric system of the International System of Units (SI) was accepted by the U.S. in 1875. The SI unit symbols like millimetre (mm), microampere (μA), decibel (dB), kilobyte (KB, which is $2^{10} = 1024$ bytes), megabyte (MB, which is $2^{20} = 1\,048\,576$ bytes), gigabyte (GB, which is $2^{30}$ bytes), etc., are convenient for science and technology. When data is represented as binary (base-2) numbers, each binary digit is a single bit. In fact, the word 'bit' was coined by the American statistician and computer scientist John Tukey (b. 1915) in 1946 as an acronym for binary digit. The byte is equal to 8 bits (or 1 octet). This means that a byte (B) has $2^8 = 256$ possible states. The unit was named by IBM engineer Werner Buchholz (b. 1922) in 1956, and the 8-bit size was popularized starting in 1964 by IBM's System 360, a top-selling mainframe computer. Numbers are not in things; it is our mind that puts them into things.[28]

We have natural numbers (N*) or counting numbers, 1, 2, 3, 4…, where addition and multiplication apply. Natural numbers and zero are symbolized by 'N.' Zero (0) is the identity for addition and subtraction of numbers, since $1 + 0 = 0 + 1 = 1$ or $2–0 = 2$. In the 7th century India, negative numbers were used in book keeping; positive quantities denoted assets, negative ones debts. In the early 17th century, mathematicians of Europe began explicitly to use *negative numbers* but met with heavy opposition. Rene Descartes called negative roots false roots, and Blaisé Pascal (1623-1662) of France was convinced that numbers less than zero could not exist.[29] But, for subtraction we *need zero and negative* whole numbers besides positive whole numbers (N*), thus, we obtain the integers (Z), …,–3, –2, –1, 0, 1, 2, 3,…. Integers except 0 is symbolized as Z*. All whole numbers, including negative numbers (Z-), zero, and positive numbers (Z+), are called integers. We need ratio of integers or rational numbers (Q) for division like 0/1, 2/3, 6/5. Numbers like π (22/7) or equations like $x^2–2 = 0$, that is, $x = \sqrt{2}$, which are not represented by ratio of integers are known as *irrational numbers*.

Rational and irrational numbers are together named real numbers (R). Real numbers can not solve equations like $x^2+1 = 0$, that is $x = \pm\sqrt{-1}$. So there are complex numbers (C) like **a + bi,** where **a** and **b** are real numbers and i is the imaginary unit. $i^2 = –1$; $i = \sqrt{-1}$; $\sqrt{-4} = 2i$. These are pure imaginary numbers when **a** = 0. When **b** = 0 then we have real numbers. An integer larger than 1 that is divisible only by 1 and itself is called a *prime number*, or a prime.[30] They are 2, 3, 5, 7, 13, etc. The other numbers are known as composite numbers. Pierre de Fermat (1601-1665), a French lawyer and gentleman made a formula to find out primes. It is $F_n = 2^{2^n}+1$ (2 the power 2 to the power *n* plus 1) where n values from 0 to 4. French philosopher, mathematician, theologian, and scientist Marin Mersenne's (1558-1648) form for prime is $M_p = 2^p-1$ where p is a prime. It is known as Mersenne number or prime. "An integer number that is equal to the sum of all its possible divisors – except the number itself- is called *perfect number*. If the sum is less than the number itself, the number is said to be *defective* or deficient; if greater, the number is *abundant*."[31] "Two integer numbers are said to be *amicable*, or friendly, if each is the sum of all the possible divisors of the other; the smallest pair of friendly numbers is 220 and 284."[32] Irrational numbers can be *algebraic* or *transcendental*. Algebraic can be rational like $4a^2-9 = 0$; $a = \pm 3/2$ or irrational like $a^2-2 = 0$; $a = \pm \sqrt{2}$. Transcendental number is e (base of natural logarithm) = $(1+1/n)^n$. It is Swiss mathematician and Physicist Leonhard Euler's (1707-1783) $e = \lim_{n\to\infty}(1+\frac{1}{n})^n = 2.7\ 1828\ 1828\ 45\ 90\ 45\ ....$ $\pi = 22/7$ = ratio of the circumference of a circle to its diameter.

German mathematician, Georg Ferdinand Ludwig Philipp Cantor aka Georg Cantor (1845-1918), the inventor of the set theory, introduced *transfinite number* which measures the size of sets. It is symbolised as $\aleph_0$. It means infinite sets which are in one-to-one correspondence with the infinitude of natural numbers. The transfinite numbers which are not in one-to-one correspondence between two sets are denoted as $\aleph_1$, $\aleph_2$, $\aleph_3$, etc. In mathematics, however, infinity is not a number but a concept of increase beyond bounds.[33] Conceptuality is subjective while realization is objective. Most conceptuality is metaphysical; while reality is mostly physical though some part is transcendental or metaphysical.[34] The mathematical symbol of infinity ($\infty$) was introduced in 1655 by English mathematician John Wallis (1616-1703) in his *Arithmetica infinitorum*, but did not appear anew in print until the *Ars conjectandi* by Swiss mathematician Jakob Bernoulli (1654-1705), published posthumously in 1713 by his nephew Nikolaus Bernoulli aka Nikolaus I (1687-1759).[35]

Infinity has calculation rules of its own though it is not a number: $\infty + \infty = \infty$, $\infty \times \infty = \infty$.

In the integral system of numbers, zero is a late comer. A number is primarily an abstraction from things real. Zero as number could not associate with anything real. It is associated with nothing, void, vacuum, emptiness, which is not real. Zero came to fill the empty place with a value in positional system of numeration. As the natures of things have their properties, so also the numbers have their properties. Introduction of complex quantities (not complex numbers) in mathematical operations like roots, cubes, exponentials, etc., have given different meaning to the number systems. The notion of real numbers leads to the notion of a 'limit' for higher mathematics. The application of numbers leads to the investigation of physical laws and theories. Numbers are cultural phenomena; humans invented them to quantify the external world around them. The external world is quantitative in its nature. However, humans can only understand, compare and manipulate the numbers. "Numbers are not in things; it is our mind that puts them into things. Just as our minds abstracted them from things so in the same way and exactly by the reverse operation and with the same limitations, we can apply them to things."[36] Therefore, we use some measurable and numerical scales to quantify the world. If we cannot measure it, we cannot manage it. This is the essence of our understanding and decision-making process in *space* and *time* in an *orderly* manner.

The concept of number is real, abstract and expresses the quantitative quality of a thing. It is associated with the concept of a set, a collection of definite and separate objects of any kind of which we can decide whether or not a given object belongs. A thing is found in our dynamic Universe in space and *time* as we perceive. So there is an *order* in the Universe which we express in matter, time and *space*.

### 1.1.2 The Concept of Time, Order and Space

Most scientists prefer to avoid philosophical arguments about *what time is*; instead, they have reached consensus on *how time is to be measured.*[37] We have seen how Earth's natural celestial clock led early humans to count days, months, and years.[38] Time candles, oil lamps and water clock are used for physical time measurements.

All mechanical or electronic clocks need three functional elements:

> a source of energy, an oscillating system, and an escapement. The escapement is a device that feeds energy to the oscillator in small increments, just sufficient to keep the oscillating system in motion. The motion of the oscillator is coupled to an indicator that displays the time.[39]

Nature presents us two quite different cyclic systems, *astronomical* motion and our *earth-bound* clock, which can be brought into synchronicity and remain synchronized. The first practical pendulum clock was apparently built by the Dutch scientist Christiaan Huygens (1629-1695) around 1657 and the accuracy was available by the early 1800s.[40] We define 'here' as being where we are. Everything and everyone else is 'there.' Each of us thinks that we are the centre of the Universe. Let us take it a little further. Let us define 'now.' When is it? We cannot. The split second that we try to pinpoint 'now,' it becomes 'then.' We often find explaining the nature of 'now' after we ask people if they have ever stolen something. Their typical answer to the question is 'Yes, we have.' But that was in the past. We are even forced to define the reading of this sentence as something we did in the past. What is eternal is simply present without a before and an after. In other words, all of human history is present to God; there is no future, no past, only present. With us, we tell when an *event occurs*, place events *in sequence* one after the other, and we compare how long that *event lasted.* This is awareness of our physical time or psychological time. But real physical or earthly time is the time that measures the rotation of the Earth which is regulated by sunlight. In 1895, an English author Herbert George Wells (1866-1946) treated time as a fourth dimension in his science fiction novel *The Time Machine* while space is having three dimensions – length, breadth and depth.

There are four dimensions; the three dimensions of space, and the fourth, time. A figure that has all three dimensions of these exists, can be seen and felt. Then there is another dimension, the fourth dimension of time that we all seem to take lightly. The 'stage' on which the Universe goes is the three-dimensional space of geometry, as described by Euclid, the things change in a medium called time.[41] According to Aristotle, 'time is the number of precessions and successions in process.'[42] By time he meant measure of change or motion. Change is the actualisation of the potential, from potentiality to actuality. Any change is always in respect either of substance or of quantity or of quality or of place. A change, motion or movement is perceived by an observer. Motion in space is motion with respect to time. Physics is rooted in the notions of law – the existence of an ordered Universe that can be understood by the application of rational reasoning.[43] Why is there any *order* at all rather than none? Order is endowed or graced. A good life is an ordered life. In fact, peace is precisely an ordered life. The Latin word for peace is *pax*, which means order or harmony. The good life begins by bringing about harmony between the appetites and reason. There is order to the world around us. Those things are the way they are for a particular purpose, and that this presumes some intelligence behind the world. The things are designed. The activity of each thing or being reveals what it is. Beings act according to their natures. Agents act for determinate ends that are intelligible, meaningful and predictable. That is why a scientist studies the actions or reactions of things, to better understand their natures. The scientist begins to pursue knowledge of the world because s/he experiences it as ordered, meaningful, and knowable. There is a natural order of priority and subsequence in change. The scientist knows as a philosopher, not as a scientist, that when one event precedes another, it does not necessarily follow that the succeeding event was caused by the preceding event. The scientist has to distinguish between a *cause* and a *correlation*. All physical processes are part of a *one-directional*, essentially linear process. The prior and subsequent cannot be defined. It can be a flux or discontinuous change. *Flux* is a continuous change having two parts. Julius Wilhelm Richard

Dedekind (1831-1916), a German mathematician, says real numbers are continuous, continuity being an axiom of the flux. It can be measured provided we give meaning for a flux, segment or interval. So it is subject to quantity or magnitude.

Simultaneity of events is seen in the athletes' sports events. The instants are known as elements of time. These elements have the descriptive property of time. The single instant of the athlete is not a sufficient descriptive property of time, it needs aggregate of instants. We have three aspects of time; as a descriptive property, as an element and as an aggregate of instants. Time is continuous as an aggregate of instants. One will be prior and another subsequent. Time, being continuous or flux, is subject to quantity or magnitude. This is an axiom of time as an element. Between two instants at least there is one instant point. In the same way, point is part of a straight line or plane or space. In the time-flux we can measure any change. A stage of any change corresponds to a stage-instant or an event. Any change interval is known as occurrence. When two different occurrences are simultaneous they are contemporary. In the reality of time, the concept of 'instant' is one of a real entity, the physical instant. Every change occurs in time. It is the *change* that marks the *flow of time*. A change is a difference in the state or condition of a thing, yet something endures. What endures is a substratum, primary matter or simply matter. It is not the change we measure but the *time* involved in the change.

Can there be a universal measure of time? Change in local position is the most convenient to adopt as the standard. The most obvious is the change in the position of the Sun in the sky with respect to the vertical, or that of the Sun in the sky with respect to the stars. Each observer has a time, a notion of simultaneity, and a means of defining the equality of time-intervals and hence a measurable time. Our 21st century begins from 2001CE, not from 2000. According to the Holy Scriptures (Matthew 2, 1. 19), King Herod (73-4 BCE) was alive when Jesus was born, and Herod died in 4 BCE.[44] Does that mean the millennium actually started in 1996? No, the Greeks had no 0th year.[45] The monks Dionysius Exiguus (470-544) of Scythia Minor, Anicius Manlius Severinus Boethius (480-524/5) of Rome, and the Venerable Bede (672-735) of England had no zeros in their numerals.[46] Without the zero a millennium would make one year less. Millennium started actually in 1997. In the similar way, we begin 2000 years only in 2001 CE. Ordinal numbers, which the Gregorian (Pope Gregory XIII: 1502-1585) calendar uses, indicate sequence. Thus, '1CE' (the first year of CE) refers to the year that begins at the zero point and ends one year later. Cardinal numbers, which astronomers use in their calculations, indicate quantity. Zero is a cardinal number and indicates a value; it does not name an interval. Thus, 'zero' indicates the division between BCE and CE. There is a zero point; there is no '0$^{th}$'year before the beginning of CE or BCE. The 0 point is the starting point for both CE and BCE. The chronological year line is ← … , 4 BCE, 3 BCE, 2 BCE, 1 BCE, ←0→, 1 CE, 2 CE, 3 CE, 4 CE, …→. We refer to *years* with ordinal numbers (1st year, 2nd year, sequences – forward or backward) and to *ages* with cardinal numbers (12 years, 30 years, etc.). We look at a number as a point on time or a time interval. Years are intervals (on 2nd year, we become 1 year); numbers are points. 0 is a number. It is the starting point in the number line for the 0$^{th}$ year CE or BCE. Year 0 was rectified by Jacques Cassini (1677-1756) in 1740 CE, which other Italian astronomers from Paris observatory published in his *Tables Astronomiques*.[47] There are12 months each from 0 to 1CE or to 1 BCE, which are time intervals of one year. Therefore, treat years as interval points. When was the Big Bang or when was Jesus born depends on our calculations of historical realities in reference to time intervals. We are measuring the chronological time with seconds, minutes, hours, days, weeks, months and years. Why are there 24 hours in a day? No one really knows, yet it is we, who have observed, located, measured or named accordingly. The sidereal time of every planet is different according to its distance though earth remains the referential planet for time measurement. A mean sidereal day is about 23 hours, 56 minutes, 4.091 seconds (23.93447 hours or 0.99726957 mean solar days), the time it takes the Earth to make one rotation relative to the vernal equinox.[48] Time is the measure of the universal progression of uniformity between matter and space accomplished by counting equal, standardized divisions of a cyclical system of regular motion. The earth has been spinning and orbiting regularly for years.

Time is a restless continuous set of changes. Ahead is a moment we call future – it quickly changes into present – then quickly changes into past. There is an order of past, present and future. In eternity – there is no change, there is no succession of time. The earth has rotationary and revolutionary motions. For us, there are days and nights because the earth takes 24 hours to make a rotation on its invisible axis. There are months and seasons because the earth takes 365 days to orbit the sun. We have named them as days, nights, weeks, months and years. We have taken 0th meridian as our standard time at Greenwich Mean Time (GMT) at London. For the sake of calculating our human history, we have taken 0th year as point for 1 CE or BCE. Previously CE and BCE were known as AD (*Anno Domini,* i.e., Year of the Lord) and BC (Before Christ).[49]

Where does space begin and end? The boundaries of space are impossible to define clearly. Space is thought to be absolute emptiness or nothingness or place occupied with something. Space is not an absolute void. It is dependent on masses by which it is influenced. If it is sheer nothingness, it would not exist and nothing could be located. The concept of space signifies a *place*. Space allows *objects* to have lengths in the left/right, up/down, and forward/backward directions. A dot or a *point* has a zero dimension. A point – which may be regarded as the intersection of two *lines* – has the dimension zero.[50] By international agreement in 1864, the 0° meridian passes through the former London observatory at Greenwich, England, and is generally known as the Greenwich Meridian Time.[51] The time with respect to this meridian is known as Greenwich Mean Time (GMT) of the earth. The rest of the local times are related to it. The 0° meridian has coordinates (0, 0). Coordinates are ordered sets of numbers. The coordinates (3, 2) and (2, 3) are not the same. A coordinate system enables the user to establish a correspondence between sets of numbers and points in space. Longitude and latitude form a system of coordinates that enables the user to identify any position on Earth. The coordinates are ordered pairs of numbers or points on the surface of a sphere.

Traditionally the first coordinate is the longitude. The longitude identifies how many degrees east or west the location of intersect is from the prime meridian, 0°. The second coordinate, the latitude, identifies how many degrees north or south of the equator the point is located. The point is located where the line of longitude and the line of latitude cross. But North Pole and South Pole have only one set of coordinates each: 90°N (north) or 90°S (south) of equator. A plain place has two dimensions: length and width. A solid place has three dimensions: length, width and height. A three-dimensional region is called space or 3-space.[52] What are the simplest concepts which are involved in our complex concepts of spatial figures? They are elements, adjectives of space and properties from which properties of spatial figures be derived. The axioms are the a priori properties of spatial elements. They are the statements without which no knowledge can be derived. Statements that are accepted without discussion or proof, and are found basic to the respective system, are known as axioms or postulates.[53]

Empirical statements like 'it is cold or hot' depend on sense experience. The axioms are abstractions from intellectual concepts, abstractions from abstractions; starts with sensation, perception, abstraction, complex notion, analysis and then we reach the axiom. In the concept of time we abstracted from matter the concepts of unity and multiplicity, and of order. They are a priori concepts. Geometry is the science of space where we have three spatial elements or figures like plane, line, and point which are a priori. The point is descriptive of the straight line and the plane, the straight line is descriptive of the point and the plane, and the plane is descriptive of the straight line and the point. They are considered under three aspects: as an element, as the descriptive property and as an aggregate of spatial element. They are interdependent on each other. Interconnected identification of two points is taken as the straight line, the base. Two straight lines have a common property, the point and the vertex. Points have a common property; aggregate of spatial element, when two points are joined it becomes a straight line. They have unity and diversity, identification and differentiation.

In outer space, there is no night and no day. Is space hot or cold? There is no simple answer. Space is said to be homogeneous when we can identify the spatial elements either directly by a common property or by intermediate steps with a sequence of elements, any two successive ones having a common property. It is said to be heterogeneous when we can distinguish between the spatial elements. The basis of the identification as well as of the differentiation of the elements is the points, the straight line, and the plane taken as descriptive. The spatial elements are the pre-requisite for quantity. The concept of 'order' in geometry gives a particular place to each element. The place is not a chronological one but spatial. But time gives us a chronological order as in counting or natural numbers. Order is an a priori which enables us to make one-to-one correspondences in the spatial elements. The process of making this correspondence is called projection. "Projective geometry, the geometry that began with attempts by Renaissance artists to represent three-dimensional figures on two-dimensional canvases, is an example of a geometry that is defined by a different set of motions. The motions that define projective geometry are called projections."[54] Projections neither preserve the length of a line nor the measure of an angle. It enables us to recognise the relative position of points or straight lines or planes. We can have natural order from A to B along the straight line or curve. We can also have artificial order by mentally putting points into the line or curve. There is an axiom of continuity in the number system. There exists at least one number between two numbers. The order position does not refer to quantity.

The axiom of *order* acknowledges the order of spatial elements which are identifiable and distinguishable. We can have natural order of points or artificial order by mentally putting these points into correspondence with an already ordered set of elements. Or we can have continuous order in any planes, lines or curves. This order shows us the relationship with elements. The bases of relationship implied by order are the descriptive point, line and plane. As the order of elements is not resolved into finite number of elements, the axiom of continuity comes into geometry. When a complex descriptive property is not resolved into a finite number of points or lines we have a curve. A curve is classified by the maximum number of tangents that can be drawn to it from any point, or by the maximum number of points in which a straight line will meet it.

We abstracted spatial elements -- plane, line and point – from our sense-perceptions and obtained the idea of order and of one-to-one correspondence. They are all properties of the elements. *Quantity* is a property which is abstracted from material things. It is the property of having integral parts as the whole, i.e., parts of the same type as the whole and making up the whole, of which parts one is not another and each one is exclusive of every other.[55] Quantity itself is a pre-requisite for the consideration of the causal properties of things. It is not directly applicable to time but associated with mass, its causal and temporal effects are to be considered. There is no restriction of divisibility in geometry but physics has. There is indefinite subdivision in mathematics except in this case of ∞ and 0. Besides associative, commutative and distributive property of a number it could be either greater than some number or less than another number. The 'greater than' and 'less than' mean that an explicit quantitative meaning is given to numbers. 0 belongs to positive numbers, in whose properties it shares. But 0 as space element is a part but itself not having parts. Infinity (∞) belongs to the system of positive numbers as it is greater than every other number. It is only for a concept, and 'infinite quantity' is unmeasurable by any numerical scale. Therefore, one should never do any kind of arithmetic operations with it, such as $\infty + 100 = \infty$, which gives the silly result, $100 = \infty - = 0$. Infinity is not a mathematical number for mathematical operations. "We cannot understand infinity since we are unable to know an infinity of things simultaneously, unlike God, who can."[56]

Mathematical quantity associated with straight line is called linear magnitude or length. The straight line has threefold spatial elements: *point*, *plane* and *line*. Quantity is attributed to it. A *straight line* is an aggregate of points. If A and B are two points of the line L then these points can be indicated. The indefinite subdivision of segment $\overline{AB}$ can lead to a point with zero magnitude with no elemental point between the descriptive points A and B. With a definite number of subdivisions, we arrive at the concept of a point of more than zero magnitude in a straight line segment terminated by two descriptive points. The zero linear magnitude can be called the elemental segment or zero segments. We can identify elemental segments and distinguish them by means of their descriptive points. We can also identify descriptive points continuously. This continuous identification is called 'motion' and we speak of 'moving along a straight line' in this sense. We assume that each segment has an inherent metrical property called its length which is the integral sum of the quantitative parts making up the whole segment. When we equate two segments we are only identifying their intrinsic properties. This enables us to place our spatial linear magnitude into a closer relationship with the number system.

The limiting zero of area is that of a closed figure, and is not a point or a straight line; the figure is considered in the first instance as the descriptive property of a portion of the *plane*. So also the complete plane can be considered as having parts but itself not a part. We can associate quantity also with solid figures of space, which we call volumetric magnitude or *volume*. A solid figure is one of the descriptive elements of planes, lines and point or is reducible to planes, considered as elements, has only the common property of belonging to space. The volume of a closed solid figure is the integral sum of the parts making up the space bounded by the figure. "Einstein's creation of a new and spectacular theory of gravity allowed us to describe a space that is empty of mass and energy with complete mathematical precision. Empty Universe could exist."[57] "When mass and energy are absent, the space is flat. As masses are added, the space curves. If masses are large, the distortion of the flat surface of space is large near to the mass but decreases as one move far away."[58] There must be a simple law of nature which restores the vacuum and sets this vacuum energy equal to zero which would bring equilibrium in nature.

Albert Einstein's theory of gravity allowed us to describe a space that is empty of mass and energy with complete mathematical precision. So there could be an empty space or Universe. Space is the limitless, boundless, three-dimensional extent where objects and events take place. Physical space is conceived in 3 linear dimensions but today along with time it is four-dimensional continuum known as spacetime. In mathematics, 'spaces' are usually examined with different numbers of dimensions and with different underlying structures. So space is best described as the continuous extension in all directions in which all matter exists. Mathematically there is an empty set axiom which has become the foundational axiom in the set theory.

### 1.1.3 The Set Theory

German mathematician Ernst Zermelo (1871-1953) in 1908 and an Israeli mathematician born in Germany Abraham Fraenkel (1891-1965) in 1922 proposed the following axioms as a foundation for what is now called Zermelo-Fraenkel set theory, or ZF. If this set of axioms are accepted along with the Axiom of Choice, it is often denoted ZFC (Zermelo-Fraenkel with Choice).[59]

1) *Axiom of extensionality* or *Equality of sets*: The two sets are equal when they have the same elements. If $A$ and $B$ are sets, and $x \in A$ iff $x \in B$, then $A = B$. For any two sets A and B, if $A \subseteq B$ and $B \supseteq A$, then $A = B$. $\forall$ x (x $\in$ A $\equiv$ x $\in$ B $\Rightarrow$ A).
2) *Axiom of empty set*: There is a set having no elements. It is denoted Ø or { }. There exists a set A such that for all x, it is false that x $\in$ A. $\exists A \forall x (x \notin A)$.
3) *Axiom of unordered pairing* or *Pair set*: If $X$ and $Y$ are sets, then there is a set $Z$ containing only $X$ and $Y$ as elements. $\forall X \forall Y \exists Z (x \in Z \forall y \in Z)$. The posited set Z is denoted $\{x, y\}$ and called unordered pair of $x$ and $y$. $\{x, x\}$ can be denoted as {x}, singleton set of $x$.
4) *Axiom of union* or *sum set*: If $A$ is a set, then there exists a set that contains every element of each x $\in$ $A$.The posited set is $\cup$ B and called union of B. $A \cup B = \cup\{A, B\} = \{x \mid x \in A \text{ or } x \in B\}$.

5) *Axiom of power set*: If $A$ is a set, then there exists a set $P(A)$ with the property that $B \in P(A)$ iff any element $x \in B$ is also in $A$. $\forall A \exists B \forall x (x \in B \equiv x \subseteq A)$.
6) *Axiom of replacement*: Let $F(x, y)$ be some formula. If, for all $x$, there is exactly one $y$ such that $F(x, y)$ is true, then for any set $A$ there exists a set $B$ with the property that $b \in B$ iff there exists some $a \in A$ such that $F(a, b)$ is true. If $F$ is a function, then for any $X$ there exists a set $Y = F[X] = \{F(x): x \in X\}$.
7) *Axiom of regularity or foundation*: It can be stated as 'A set contains no infinitely descending (membership) sequence,' or 'A set contains a (membership) minimal element,' i.e., there is an element of the set that shares no member with the set.[60]

    $\vee S[S \neq \varnothing \Rightarrow (\exists x \in S)\ S \cap x = \varnothing]$.
8) *Axiom of infinity*: There exists a non-empty set $X$ with the property that, for any $a \in X$, there is some $b \in X$ such that $a \subseteq b$ but $a \neq b$. $\varnothing$ as a member whenever $a$ is a member, there is also $a \cup \{a, b\}$ as Zermelo states. It can be replaced by $\{a\}$ or $\{\varnothing, \{\varnothing\}, \{\{\varnothing\}\}, \ldots\}$.
9) *Axiom of separation* or comprehension or subsets: If $X$ is a set and $P$ is a condition on sets, there exists a set $Y$ whose members are precisely the members of $X$ satisfying $P$. $\exists x \forall y (y \in x \equiv x \in a \wedge P(y))$
10) *Axiom of choice:* Every family of non-empty sets has a choice function. $\forall x \in a \exists A(x, y) \Rightarrow \exists y \forall x \in a A(x, y(x))$. If A is a set the elements of which are non-empty sets, then there exists a function $f$ with domain A such that for member $x$ of $y$, $f(x) \in x$. Sometimes it is called Zermelo's axiom of choice, formulated in 1904 and states that, given any set of mutually disjoint nonempty sets, there exists at least one set that contains exactly one element in common with each of the nonempty sets.[61]

The above10 independent foundational axioms are the pillars on which the set theory rests. So we can have the language of set theory, and talk about logical consequences in that language. The standard form of axiomatic set theory, ZFC is the most common foundation of mathematics. Set theory begins with a fundamental binary relation between an object x and a set A ($x \in A$). Set begins with the membership. The empty set does not have any members like a barber who shaves everyone in the town except those who shave themselves. A derived binary relation between two sets is the subset relation ($A \subseteq B$). Empty set is subset of every set. The axiom of extensionality is uniquely defined by their members. Union of the sets A and B, denoted $A \cup B$, is the set of all objects that are a member of A, or B, or both.Intersection of the sets A and B, denoted $A \cup B$, is the set of all objects that are members of both A and B. Given a set A, the complement of A is the set of all element in the discussed universal set U, but not in A ($A^\circ = U-A$). Set difference of A and B, denoted A\B is the set of all members of A that are not members of B. Symmetric difference of sets A and B is the set of all objects that are a member of exactly one of A and B ($A \Delta B$). Cartesian product of A and B, denoted $A \times B$, is the set whose members are all possible ordered pairs $(a; b)$ where $a$ is a member of A and $b$ is a member of B. Power set of a set A is the set whose members are all possible subsets of A [P (A)]. The axiom of infinity implies the principle of induction on the integers. It says the set of all subsets of any set exists and is essential to define the set of all subsets of the integers. No consistent system of axioms is capable of proving all facts about the natural numbers. This implies that it is not possible to construct a "Theory of Everything." The best we could do is a "Theory of Almost Everything", which we could never prove was not self-contradictory! Even if that was only because we could not prove the mathematics we are using is not self-contradictory!

ZFC has a single assumption that all individual things of the Universe are sets. Mathematics usually deals with such sets known as structures. We define 0 as empty set Ø (0 or no elements), and 1 as {Ø} (one element, i.e., empty set) and proliferate successor operation on natural numbers.

### 1.1.4 The Proliferation of Different Numbers

Pythagoras (570-490 BCE) of Samos described number as "the first principle, a thing which is undefined, incomprehensible, and having in itself all numbers."[62] The number series as the series of successors to the number zero (0) is formulated by the Italian mathematician Giuseppe Peano (1858-1932) while Richard Dedekind (1831-1916) isolated it. Peano showed that the entire theory of the natural numbers could be derived from three primitive ideas and five primitive propositions in addition to those of pure logic.[63] The three primitive ideas are 0, *number* and *successor*. The five primitive propositions which Peano assumes are: 1) 0 is a number. 2) The successor of any number is a number. 3) No two numbers have the same successor. 4) 0 is not the successor of any number. 5) Any property which belongs to 0, and also to the successor of every number which has the property, belongs to all numbers.[64] The fifth postulate justifies mathematical *induction* that 0 and its successors are natural numbers. We can think of these axioms as saying what it takes for a given set of things ('numbers'), an operation ('successor'), and a given element ('zero'), to have the structure we demand of the natural numbers. Numbers are basic elements of mathematics used for counting, measuring, ranking, solving equations, and comparing quantities. Progressions of numbers are of great importance in the principle of mathematics. A number is anything which is the number of some class or set. Today's numbers, also called Indian-Arabic numbers, are a combination of just 10 symbols or digits: 0, 1, 2, 3, 4, 5, 6, 7, 8, and 9. We want our numbers to have meaningful properties for counting objects. Fibonacci, son of Bonaccio said the word 'zero' was coined by the Italian mathematician Leonardo Pisano (1170-1250). He transformed the Arabic word *sifr* (empty) into Italian equivalent *zefiro*, shortened to zero later. Many languages have adopted the word 'zero': English, Catalan, French (*zéro*), Portuguese, Romanian, Spanish (*cero*), Wallon (*zérô*) and so on. Europe is divided into two regions: the 'zero region' and the '*nullus* region' (*nullus*, 'zero' in Latin) like Germanic, the Skandinavian and some Slavonic countries. The Greek word for zero is μηδεν, read as '*meden*', which means, not even one (i.e. nothing). Indians used a dot (*bindu*, in Sanskrit) as the tenth number is not known. In working with abacus, they wanted to keep a written record of the answers on abacus. The used symbol '.' which is called *śūnya* to indicate a column on the counting board in which they had moved no beads. *Śunya*, the dot, was originally not zero, the number, but merely a mark to indicate empty space. But the natural numbers are the posterity of 0 with respect to the relation immediate predecessor. The number 0 is the number of terms in a class which has *no members*. 0 is the class whose only member is the null-class.[65]Only with a French-born mathematician Albert Girard (1595-1632) and Rene Descartes (1596-1650) did the symbol 0 gain full equality of rights as a number in the west.

The Babylonians used empty space as spaceholder for empty columns as far as 1700 BCE. They used the symbol like ", or yy for empty space around 1400 BCE. It was not a zero of base 10 but placeholder of base 60 only. The Mayans and Indians developed zero too. All we know is that as early as the third century BCE, two scripts were in use. One, called Kharoṣti, was derived from Aramaic. The other, known as Brāhmi, seems to have originated in India itself.

© G. Sarcone, www.archimedes-lab.org

Figure 1.1 Origin of the Indo-Arabic Numerals

The record of zero symbol in India is found in *Lokavibhaga* dated 458 CE where the names of the numbers are sometimes replaced by word-symbols and the word *śūnya* (void) and its synonyms are used as zeros.[66] From the $6^{th}$ century onwards the use of the place-value system and 0 begin to appear frequently in documents from India. Meanwhile decimal digits have reached through Brāhmi, Indian, Arabic and Medieval to Modern times.

R. C. Gupta quotes B. Datta and A. N. Singh that Indian numerals are found in several manuscripts of the Geometry of Boethius about the close of the 5th century.[67] These digits were introduced in Europe within the twelfth century by Leonardo Pisano (aka Fibonacci), an Italian mathematician who ended his travels around the year 1200 and at that time he returned to Pisa. L. Pisano (1170-1250) was educated in North Africa, where he learned and later carried to Italy the Indian-Arabic numerals. Zero is a number which indicates *no quantity*, size, or magnitude. It is denoted by the symbol, 0. Zero is neither negative nor positive. It is the additive identity; the number, when added to another number $n$, gives $n$. $n + 0 = n$. 0 as the additive identity is better known as the reflexive identity of addition. Zero's other fundamental properties are $n - 0 = n$, $n \times 0 = 0$ and $0/n = 0$ in which n is other than 0. There are two uses of zero; as a number and empty place holder in the place-value number system.

If mathematics is the language of science, the language of mathematics is numbers, its grammar being represented by the several kinds of numbers.[68] A number is a word or symbol or numeral which represents an amount or quantity. The numbers are used for counting objects, comparing quantities and expressing order. The whole numbers (W) are a set of numbers that includes zero and all of the natural numbers. W = {0, 1, 2, 3, …} = (x : x ∈ W). There are different type of numbers like natural numbers, prime numbers, integers, negative and irrational numbers, algebraic numbers, imaginary numbers and transcendental numbers. The counting numbers are natural numbers, or the numbers used for counting or ordering. The set of natural numbers, denoted N, can be defined in either of two ways: N = {0, 1, 2, 3, ...} = (x : x ∈ N) or N = (1, 2, 3, 4, ...} = (x : x ∈ N). The set N, whether or not it includes zero, is a denumerable set. Denumerability refers to the fact that, even though there might be an infinite number of elements in a set, those elements can be denoted by a list that implies the identity of every element in the set.

A multiple of a number is the product of that number and any other whole number. Zero is a multiple of every number. The product of zero and any number is zero ($1 \times 0 = 0$). This is known as the zero property of multiplication. The quantity n! is defined as the product of the n integers from 1 to n. 0! = 1.Why 0! = 1? Why is an empty product equal to one? Because $4! = 4 \times 3 \times 2 \times 1$ and $3! = 3 \times 2 \times 1$. Therefore $4! = 4\times3!$ In the same way $3! = 3\times2!$ and $2! = 2\times1!$ So it follows that $1! = 1 \times 0!$ So 0! must be equal to 1 or 1! Because it is a matter of 0 factors. 0! is an empty product, which always equals 1. For *any* real number base $x$, we define powers of $x$ as $x^0 = 1$, $x^1 = x$, $x^2 = x \cdot x$, $x^3 = x \cdot x \cdot x$, etc. The exception is $0^0$, which is termed indeterminate.

A negative number is a real number that is less than zero like –2. A positive number is a number that is greater than zero, such as +2. Zero is called the origin; it is neither positive nor negative. The non-negative numbers are the real numbers that are not negative which are positive or zero. Every number on the number line has an absolute value, which simply means how far that number is from zero. The opposites are the same distance from the origin 0; they have the same absolute value. The symbol for absolute value is two vertical lines; $|-2| = |+2| = 2$.

An odd number is a whole number that is not divisible by 2. An even number is a natural number that is divisible by 2. Cardinal numbers, or cardinals, are generalized numbers used to measure the cardinality or the size of sets. For finite sets, the cardinality is given by a natural number, which is simply the number of elements in the set. A cardinal number tells 'how many' showing the quantity. Ordinal numbers tell the *order* of things in a set showing the rank or the position. They tell the position of something in an ordered set. A nominal number names or identifies something like telephone or cell numbers, state or postal codes, etc.

All whole numbers (except 0 and 1) have minimum two factors: 1 and itself. Numbers, which are not divisible by any numbers except 1 and itself, are called *prime numbers or a prime.*[69] A prime number (P) is a natural number greater than 1 whose only factors are itself and 1. 2 is no longer a prime in Real numbers. Neither 0 nor 1 is prime number. Zero is not a prime or a composite number either. A number which can be factorized is composite which is not 0, not a unit, and not a prime. The composite has more than three factors while prime has only two. Prime is not a unit, and not the product of two non-units. Prime numbers are building blocks of all integers. The integers are the set of numbers containing zero, the natural numbers, and all the negatives of the natural numbers. They are abstract concepts that describe, not sizes of sets, but the *relative sizes* of two sets. The set of integers, denoted Z (*zahlen*, German, integer), is formally defined as follows: Z = {..., –3, –2, –1, 0, 1, 2, 3, ...} = (x : x ∈ I). We will let $Z_+$ denote the set of positive integers. $Z_-$ denotes the set of negative integers, $Z_{\geq 0}$ denote the set of nonnegative integers (which consists of the positive integers and 0). 0 is the only integer or the only real number that is neither negative nor positive. Fractions, decimals and percents are not integers.

A *number line* is a line on which every point represents a real number. The real numbers are abstract concepts that describe *measurements of continuous quantities*, such as length, weight, quantity of fluid, etc. The real numbers can be given by an infinite decimal representation like 13.548... Real numbers are the numbers which we use to measure real world quantities like length, width, depth, temperature or volume. A real number (R) may be either rational or irrational; either algebraic or transcendental; and either positive, negative, or zero. R = {x: $x^2$ is non-negative}. A real number set R, which is the union of the set of rational numbers and the set of irrational numbers (T). A rational or fractional number can be expressed as the ratio of two integers. The rational numbers are abstract concepts that describe *ratios of sizes of sets*. The set of rational numbers is denoted Q (quotient), and represents the set of all possible integer-to-natural-number ratios *p/q* where *q* is not 0, *p* is called numerator or dividend and *q* is called denominator or divisor. Q = {x: x = p/q; p, q ∈ Z, q ≠ 0}. The rational numbers can be written as terminating (ending) or repeating decimals (such as 0.5, 0.76, or 0.333333....). Fractions, mixed numbers, decimals and integers are rational numbers. Fractions were invented long before decimal numbers, as a way of showing portions less than 1. The set R gives rise to other sets such as the set of imaginary numbers and the set of complex numbers. The set R is sometimes called the continuum because it is intuitive to think of the elements of R as corresponding one-to-one with the points on a geometric line. The cardinalities (sizes) of the sets of rational and irrational numbers, is called the Continuum Hypothesis by Georg Cantor. In 1873 the German mathematician Georg Cantor proved that the continuum is uncountable – that is, the real numbers are a larger infinity than the counting numbers. The cardinality of the continuum is the smallest uncountable cardinal number.

An *imaginary number* (I) is a quantity of the form ***bi***, where ***b*** is a real number and ***i*** is the positive square root of –**1** which is a real number. The quantity ***i*** is called the unit imaginary number. In the electrical engineering, it is denoted ***j***,[70] and is known as the ***j*** operator. The set ***i*** of imaginary numbers consists of the set of all possible products ***bi***, where ***b*** is an element of the set R of real numbers. Therefore, the sets I and R are in one-to-one correspondence. A *complex number* is a quantity of the form ***a*** + ***bi***, where ***a*** and ***b*** are real numbers, and ***i*** represents the unit imaginary numbers equal to the positive square root of –**1**, a mystical quantity. It is then an ordered pair of real numbers (a, b). Swiss mathematician Leonhard Euler introduced the modern symbol ***i*** for √ –**1**. It is the answer to the question, 'What number squared is –1?' It was independently of one another, a Norwegian-Danish mathematician Caspar Wessel (1745-1818) in 1789, French-Swiss mathematician Jean Robert Argand (1768-1822) in 1806, John Warren in 1828 and a German mathematician, astronomer, and Physicist Carl Friedrich Gauss (1777-1855) around 1832 conceived the possibility of representing these complex numbers (***a*** + ***bi***) in a plane, the complex number plane.[71]

0 is considered to be a purely imaginary number: it is the only complex number which is both *real* and purely *imaginary*. Zero is a challenge for science and religion, for nothingness and eternity and for emptiness and infinite. The set C of all complex numbers corresponds one-to-one with the set R.

An *irrational number* is a real number that cannot be reduced to any ratio between an integer ***p*** and a natural number ***q***. It cannot be represented as fraction, terminating or repeating decimals. The union of the set of irrational numbers and the set of rational numbers forms the set of real numbers. The irrational numbers are $\sqrt[2]{2}$ (the square root of 2), $\sqrt[3]{3}$ (the cube root of 3), the circular ratio ***pi*** ($\pi$), and the natural logarithm base **e**. The decimal form of an irrational number does not terminate or repeat. $\pi$ = 3.1415926535897932384626433832795 (and more...). The popular approximation of 22/7 = 3.1428571428571... is close but not accurate. The number e (Euler's Number) is 2.71828182845 90452353602874713527 (and more ...). Hippasus (ca. 500 BCE) of Metapontum, a student of Pythagoras, was the discoverer of irrational numbers. *Transcendental* numbers are irrational numbers that are not algebraic. An *algebraic number* is any number that is a root of a non-zero polynomial with rational coefficients ($2x^2 - 4x + 2 = 0$, where x is algebraic). It is countable like whole numbers while transcendental is not.

Infinity, denoted by $\infty$, is a value greater than any computable value or a concept which indicates a quantity, size, or magnitude that is larger than any real number. In mathematics, $\infty$ is used as if it is a number like $\infty$ and $-\infty$ which are not numbers but conceptual entities. Neither $\infty$ nor $-\infty$ is a real number. In the first place, 'infinity' is not a number; it merely connotes the continuous increasing. The sets of numbers formulated by mathematicians are 'imaginary infinities' that have no corresponding parts in the Universe. English mathematician John Wallis (1616-1703) defined the negative exponent and first used the symbol ($\infty$) for infinity.[72] Infinity is an idea that philosophers, mathematicians, lay people even children have pondered for millennia. In mathematics questions about the infinite have often been expressed in terms of sets of numbers.[73] Cantor demonstrated different sizes of infinity. The infinity of decimal numbers that are bigger than 0 but smaller than 1 is greater than the infinity of counting numbers. There are infinitely many counting numbers, sets, fractions and infinities of points. Cantor denoted the number of natural numbers by the transfinite number $\aleph_0$ (aleph null) The set of all natural numbers are often called *denumerable* which can be written as an infinite sequence $\{a_1, a_2, a_{3, \ldots}\}$. There are infinite sets of different sizes or cardinalities. An infinite set whose elements can be put into a one-to-one correspondence with the set of integers is said to be countably infinite; otherwise, it is called uncountably infinite.[74]

Basic geometry is the study of points, lines, angles, surfaces, and solids of our Universe. In geometry there are only four imaginary items—simple ideas—upon which everything else is built: point, line, plane, and space. Plane Geometry is about flat shapes like lines, circles and triangles while Solid Geometry is about three dimensional objects like cubes, prisms and pyramids. Coordinate Geometry perceives geometric spaces as sets of numbers. The following pictures are points, lines and planes. A point shows a location but has no size or dimension. It is the only point where two lines or two rays of angle meet. It has no parts. A point shared by three or more sides of a solid figure is known as vertex. A straight line is the shortest distance between two points.

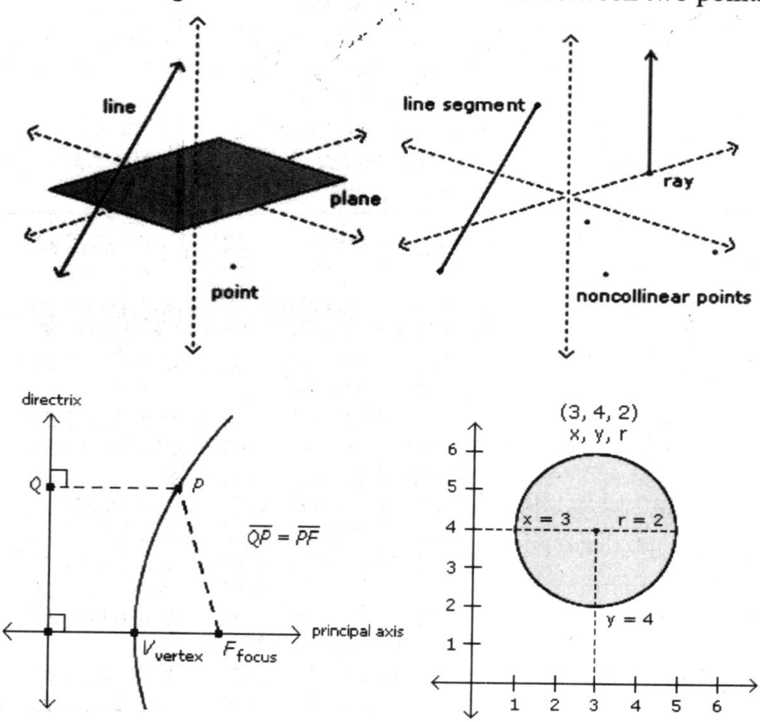


Figure 1.2 Lines, Plane and Points

A *line* is the path formed by a moving point. It is a set of points extends in two opposite directions without end. It is one-dimensional without width or depth. A length of a *straight line* is the shortest distance between two nonadjacent points and is made up of collinear points. A line segment has two end points. It has one dimension, length. Two lines can be related to each other in four different ways; intersecting, paralleling, perpendicularising and skewing. A ray is a part of line having one end point. An angle is the union of two rays having the same endpoint (vertex). There are four types of angles; straight, right, acute and obtuse. A straight angle is $180^0$.

A *plane* is a flat surface that stretches into infinity. It is a two-dimensional object, length and width without depth. The coordinate plane determined by a horizontal number line, called the x-axis, and a vertical number line, called the y-axis, intersecting at a point called the origin. The point (0, 0) on a coordinate plane, where the x-axis and the y-axis intersect is the origin. Each point in the coordinate plane can be specified by an ordered pair of numbers called Cartesian coordinates. The idea of graphing with coordinate axes dates all the way back to Apollonius (262-190 BCE) and Rene Descartes, who lived in the 1600s, gets the credit for coming up with the two-axis system as we use today.

A *point* is a location in a plane or in space, having no dimensions and noncolinear points. So space is the set of all points. It is everywhere having no boundaries and extends endlessly in all directions. A geometric point in ordinary spatial geometry is a just a particular spot in the space and has no extension but an event in spacetime is a particular point in a cosmological space at a particular moment of time. The space that we live in, has three dimensions: length, width, and height. This three-dimensional geometry or space geometry describes the buildings we live and work in, the tools we work with, and the objects we create. The straight lines and curves are one dimensional objects. The surface of a plane and curved surfaces of spheres, ellipsoids, cylinders and cones are two-dimensional objects. Solid spheres, ellipsoids, cylinders, cones, etc. are all three-dimensional objects. Although straight lines and circular geometries do exist in nature, ellipses seemed to arise only as illusions brought on by viewing a circle obliquely, and parabolas and hyperbolas seemed to have no natural counterparts at all.[75] We can see and feel one-, two- and three-dimensional objects. We cannot see and feel the fourth dimension. If we say higher dimension does not exist then we are limiting the word existence just to physical existence only but mathematics is par excellence the study of mental constructs too. Four coordinates, $x$, $y$, $z$ and t, are required to specify an event, and therefore the space of the relativity theory is a four-dimensional space.[76] To specify a moving point we requires six coordinates, viz., $x$, $y$, $z$, $u$, $v$, $w$, and since we require six coordinates we need a six-dimensional space which is for mechanics. For a mathematician, n-dimensional objects are as real as 1, 2, 3 ... dimensional objects. "We use Euclidean geometry as an abstract model – an ideal standard – against which to compare the real workings of nature. And frequently, Euclidean geometry informs us as much about what our Universe is not, as about what it is."[77]

Proliferations of different natural numbers are based on set theory and decimal numeration. The numbers 1, 2, 3, 4, etc., are the building blocks of our mathematical knowledge. These are numbers for counting or measuring things. These numbers being counted actually comprise the natural number set. With the universalization of decimal system we have units of measurements.

## 1.2 Decimal Numbers and the Units of Measurements

A number is primarily an abstraction from things real. Zero could not associate with anything real. It is associated with nothing, void, vacuum, emptiness, hole which is not real or physical. Zero came to fill the empty place in the decimal system and becomes a number. Numbers are not in things but our mind puts them into things. Our mind quantifies things. So numbers represent quantity of things. Our mind abstracts numbers from things and in the reverse way numbers quantify things.[78] Our mind measures things from 0 quantities to above. But the hierarchy of numbers begins from 0 either towards positive or negative integers. If we cannot measure the things we cannot manage them. We calculate or measure things with 10 numerical digits, known as decimal numeration. With the growth of mathematics and science we have 7 basic units and 22 derived units of measurements and weights.

The hierarchy of numbers begins from 0, 1, 2, 3, 4, 5, 6, 7, 8, 9, $10^1$, $10^2$, $10^3$, …. The higher powers of ten, in steps of a million, are given names compounded from a Greek number prefix plus million, thus, $(10^6)^2$ = bi-million = billion = $10^{12}$, $(10^6)^3$ = tri-million = trillion = $10^{18}$, $(10^6)^4$ = quadric-million = quadrillion $=10^{24}$, and $10^{600}$= centillion.[79] A large number googol was coined in 1930 by the 9 year old nephew of the American mathematician Edward Kasner (1876-1955) as $10^{100}$. 1 googolplex = $10^{googol}$, a 1 followed by a googol of zeros. *International System of Units* (SI) of Paris has named numbers with some prefixes and symbols from May 20, 1875 onwards; $10^1$ (number) = deka- (prefix) = da (symbol), $10^2$ = hecto- = h, $10^3$ = kilo- = k, $10^6$ = mega- = M, $10^9$ = giga- = G, $10^{12}$ = tera- = T, $10^{15}$ = peta- = P, $10^{18}$ = exa- = E, $10^{21}$ = zeta- = Z, $10^{24}$ = yotta- = Y, …The downward hierarchy of number can also begin negatively 0, –1, –2, –3, –4, –5, –6, –7, –8, –9, $10^{-1}$, $10^{-2}$, $10^{-3}$, $10^{-4}$, ….SI has named numbers with some prefixes and symbols; $10^{-1}$ (number) = deci- (prefix) = d (symbol), $10^{-2}$ = centi- = c, $10^{-3}$ = milli- = m, $10^{-6}$ = micro- = μ, $10^{-9}$ = nano- = n, $10^{-12}$ = pico- = p, $10^{-15}$ = femto- = f, $10^{-18}$ = atto- = a, $10^{-21}$ = zepto- = z, $10^{-24}$ = yocto- = y, …

In the International System of Units (SI), using the first two initials of its French name *Système International d'Unités*, signed the Treaty of the Meter in Paris on May 20, 1875, the basic unit of length (l) is the meter (m). The meter is the length of the path travelled by light in vacuum during a time interval of 1/299 792 458 of a second.[80] "The degree was a non-SI unit approved in 1969 by the *General Conference on Weights and Measures.* An established unit with a history of over 4,000 years, dating from the ancient Babylonian astronomers, the degree is 1/360th of the full circle. It is divided into 60 minutes, each minute into 60 seconds: $1^0$ =60′; 1'=60"."[81] The base units are consistent with the part of the metric system called the MKS system (metre, kilogram and second). A unit is a particular physical quantity which is defined and adopted by convention, with which other particular quantities of the same kind are compared to express their value. In all, there are seven SI base units:[82] 1) the metre (m) for length, 2) the kilogram (kg) for mass, 3) the second (s) for time, 4) the ampere (A) for electric current, 5) the kelvin (K) for temperature, 6) the mole (mol) for an amount of substance and 7) the candela (cd) for intensity of light. Let us see base units in detail.

1) The unit of length, metre (m), was intended to equal $10^{-7}$ or one ten-millionth of the length of the meridian through Paris from pole to the equator in 1889. This distance of metre marked on the platinum-iridium bar was replaced by the wavelength of krypton-86 radiation in 1960. In 1983, the CGPM (Conférence Générale des Poids et Mesures aka General Conference on Weights and Measures) replaced this latter definition by the following definition: The metre is the length of the path travelled by light in vacuum during a time interval of 1/299 792 458 of a second.[83]
2) The unit of mass, kilogramme (kg), was the mass of a cubic decimetre of water. In 1889, the 1st CGPM sanctioned the international prototype of the kilogram, made of platinum-iridium, kept by the Bureau International des Poids et Mesures (BIPM) aka International Bureau of Weights and Measures in Paris and declared: This prototype shall henceforth be considered to be the unit of mass.[84]
3) The unit of time, second (s), was defined originally as the fraction 1/86 400 of the mean solar day. The mean solar day is the time for Earth to make a complete rotation on its axis (24 hours) while mean sidereal time is 23 hours, 56 minutes and 4.091 seconds. The 13th CGPM (1967) decided to replace the definition of the second by referring to a caesium atom in its ground state at a temperature of 0 K: The second is the duration of 9 192 631 770 periods of the radiation corresponding to the transition between the two hyperfine levels of the ground state of the caesium 133 atom.[85]

4) The unit of electric current, ampere (A), is that constant current which, if maintained in two straight parallel conductors of infinite length, of negligible circular cross section, and placed 1 metre apart in vacuum, would produce between these conductors a force equal to $2 \times 10^{-7}$ newton per metre of length.[86] The unit is named in honour of the French Physicist André-Marie Ampère (1775-1836) who pioneered in studying electricity.
5) The unit of thermodynamic temperature, kelvin (K), is the fraction 1/273.16 of the thermodynamic temperature of the triple point of water.[87] The 10th CGPM (1954) selected the triple point of water as the fundamental fixed point and assigned to it the temperature 273.16 K, so defining the unit. The 13th CGPM (General Conference on Weights and Measures) adopted the name kelvin (symbol K) instead of 'degree Kelvin' (symbol °K) in 1967. The unit is named in honour of the British mathematician and Physicist William Thomson (1824-1907), later known as Lord Kelvin after he was named Baron Kelvin of Largs.
6) The unit of amount of substance, mole (mol), adopted by the 14th CGPM (1971):[88] a) The mole is the amount of substance of a system which contains as many elementary entities as there are atoms in 0.012 kilogram of carbon 12; its symbol is 'mol.' b) When the mole is used, the elementary entities must be specified and may be atoms, molecules, ions, electrons, other particles, or specified groups of such particles. The actual number of 'elementary entities' in a mole is called Avogadro's number after the Italian chemist and Physicist Amedeo Avogadro (1776-1856), and
7) The unit of luminous intensity, candela (cd), is the luminous intensity, in a given direction, of a source that emits monochromatic radiation of frequency $540 \times 1012$ hertz and that has a radiant intensity in that direction of 1/683 watt per steradian.[89] United States of America, France, and Great Britain decided to adopt

the *international candle* represented by carbon filament lamps in 1909. As early as 1933, the principle was adopted that new photometric units would be based on the luminous emission of a blackbody at the freezing temperature of platinum (2045 K). It was adopted on 16$^{th}$ CGPM (General Conference on Weights and Measures) in1979.

There are 22 *SI derived units*[90] which are defined algebraically in terms of 7 fundamental units. They include: 1) the radian (rad) for plane angles, 2) the steradian (sr) for solid angles, 3) the newton (N) for force, 4) the pascal (Pa) for pressure, 5) the joule (J) for energy, 6) the watt (W) for power, 7) the degree Celsius ($^0$C) for everyday measurement of temperature, 8) the coulomb (C) for electric charge, 9) the volt (V) for electric potential, 10) the farad (F) for electric capacitance, 11) the ohm (Ω) for electric resitance, 12) the siemens (S) for electric conductance, 13) the weber (Wb) for magnetic flux, 14) the tesla (T) for magnetic flux density, 15) the henry (H) for magnetical electric inductance, 16) the lumen (lm) for flux of light, 17) the lux (lx) for illuminance of a surface, 18) the hertz (Hz) for frequency for regular events, 19) the becquerel (Bq) for rates of radioactivity, 20) the gray (Gy) for radiation dose, 21) the sievert (Sv) for radiation dose received by a human or living organism, and 22) the katal (kat) for catalytic activity in a biochemistry. They are explained as follows:

1) The radian (rad), unit for plane angles, is used in mathematics and science. It was defined and named by James Thomson, the brother of the famous Physicist William Thomson or Lord Kelvin in 1873. One radian is the angle at the centre of a circle that cuts off an arc of length equal to the radius. Since the circumference equals 2π times the radius, one radian equals 1/2π of the circle, or approximately 57.295 779°. Thus, 2π rad = 360° means that 1 rad = 180/π degrees. It is the ratio between the length of an arc and its radius. The length of an arc is simply its radius multiplied by its angular

measure in radians, and the area of a sector of a circle is simply its angular measure in radians multiplied by half the square of the radius.

2) The steradian (sr), the unit for solid angles, originated in the 1870s by analogy with the radian. A steradian can be defined as the solid angle subtended at the centre of a unit sphere by a unit area on its surface. Just as there are $2\pi$ radians in a circle, there are $4\pi$ steradians in a sphere. Thus, 1 sr = 0.079 577 sphere. There are $129\,600/\pi = 41\,252.96$ square degrees in a sphere, so 1 steradian also equals about 3282.806 square degrees. It describes two-dimensional angular spans in three-dimensional space.

3) The newton (N), the unit for force, named after Isaac Newton (1642-1727), the British mathematician, Physicist, and natural philosopher, the first person to understand clearly the relationship between force (F), mass (m), and acceleration (a) expressed by the formula F = ma. The newton (N) is defined to be the force that accelerates a mass of one kilogramme at the rate of one metre per second per second. This means the newton is equal to one kilogramme metre per second squared, so the algebraic relationship is $N = kg{\cdot}m{\cdot}s^{-2}$. The newton is also equal to about 0.101 972 kilogrammes of force (kgf). On Earth's surface, a mass of 1 kg exerts a force of approximately 9.8 N (or 1kilogramme-force (1 kgf) = 9.80665 N by definition).

4) The pascal (Pa), the unit for pressure, is named after Blaise Pascal (1623-1662), French philosopher and mathematician, who was the first person to use a barometre to measure differences in altitude. It is a measure of force per unit area, defined as one newton per square metre ($1\ Pa = 1\ N/m^2$). One Pa equals to one newton per square metre or one 'kilogramme per metre per second per second' ($1\ Pa = 1\ kg/\ m.s^2$). In everyday life, the pascal is perhaps best known from meteorological barometric pressure reports.

5) The joule (J), the unit for energy or work, named after the British Physicist James Prescott Joule (1818-1889), who demonstrated the equivalence of mechanical and thermal energy in a famous experiment in 1843. J is defined to be the work done by a force of one newton acting to move an object through a distance of one metre (1 newton metre or N·m) in the direction in which the force is applied ($J = N.m = kg.m^2/s^2 = Pa.m^3 = W.s$) where W is the watt.[91]
6) The watt (W), the unit for power, 1 J per second, the name honours James Watt (1736-1819), the British engineer whose improvements to the steam engine are often credited with igniting the Industrial Revolution. One watt is the rate at which work is done when an object's velocity is held constant at one metre per second against constant opposing force of one newton ($W = J/s = N.m/s = kg.m^2/s^3$).[92] In terms of electromagnetism, one watt is the rate at which work is done when one ampere (A) of current flows through an electrical potential difference of one volt (V) ($W = V.A$).[93]
7) The degree Celsius (°C) is the unit for everyday measurement of temperature. The Celsius temperature scale is named in honour of Swedish astronomer and Physicist Anders Celsius (1701-1744). The Celsius scale is defined so that the temperature of the triple point of water (the temperature at which water can exist simultaneously in the gaseous, liquid, and solid states) is exactly 0.01 °C, and the size of the degree is 1/273.16 of the difference between this temperature and absolute zero (the temperature at which all molecular motion ceases).[94]
8) The coulomb (C), the unit (charge) of electrical quantity, is named in honour of Charles Augustin de Coulomb (1736-1806) who was the first to measure accurately the forces exerted between electric charges. One coulomb is the amount of electric charge accumulated in one second by a current of one ampere ($1C = 1A \times 1s$).

"Electricity is actually a flow of charged particles, such as electrons, protons, or ions. The charge on one of these particles is a whole-number multiple of the charge *e* on a single electron, and one coulomb represents a charge of approximately 6.241 506 × 1018 *e*."[95] The symbol *e* is often used as a unit of measure. 1 *e* is equal to approximately 1.602 176 487 × $10^{-19}$ coulomb, or 160.217 648 7 zeptocoulombs (zC).

9) The volt (V), the unit (potential) of electrical pressure, is named in honour of Italian Physicist Alessandro Volta (1745-1827), the inventor of the first chemical battery at the end of his life. In the 1880s, the International Electrical Congress, now the International Electrotechnical Commission (IEC), approved the volt as the unit for electromotive force. International System of Units (SI) derived the name from the proper name of a person; the first letter of its symbol is upper case (V). Electric potential is defined as the amount of potential energy present per unit of charge. Electric potential is measured in volts, with one volt representing a potential of one joule per coulomb of charge. A single volt is defined as the difference in electric potential across a wire when an electric current of one ampere dissipates one watt of power (V = A.Ω = W/A).[96]

10) The farad (F), the unit of electric capacitance, is named in honour of the British Physicist Michael Faraday (1791-1867). A pair of conductors separated by an insulator can store a much larger charge than an isolated conductor can store. Better the insulator, the larger the charge that the conductors can hold. The storage property of a circuit is called capacitance, and it is measured in farads. One farad is defined as the ability to store one coulomb of charge per volt of potential difference between the two conductors.[97] Or a farad is the charge in coulombs which a capacitor will accept for the potential across it to change 1 volt ($F = C^2/J = C^2/N.m$).[98]

11) The ohm (Ω) is the unit of electric resistance (R), reactance (X), and impedance (Z), named in honour of the German Physicist Georg Simon Ohm (1787-1854). If a conductor connects two locations having different electric potentials, then a current flows through the conductor. The amount of the current depends on the potential difference and also on the extent to which the conductor resists the flow of current. In direct current circuits, the property of opposition to current flow is called the *resistance*. In alternating current circuits, the opposing current flow is known as *reactance* and *impedance* measures the combined effect of resistance and reactance. Impedance is the total opposition to alternating current by an electric circuit, equal to the square root of the sum of the squares of the resistance and reactance of the circuit. All three quantities are measured in ohms. One ohm is the resistance, reactance, or impedance that requires a potential difference of one volt per ampere of current.[99] The ohm is defined as a resistance between two points of a conductor when a constant potential difference of 1 volt, applied to these points, produces in the conductor a current of 1 ampere ($\Omega = V/A = m^2.kg/s.C^2$).[100]
12) The siemens (S) is the unit of electric conductance, susceptance, and admittance, named in the honour of German electrical engineer Werner von Siemens (1816-1892). *Conductance*, *susceptance*, and *admittance* are the inverses of resistance, reactance, and impedance, respectively. To measure these properties, the siemens is the reciprocal of the ohm. In other words, the conductance, susceptance, or admittance, in siemens, is simply 1 divided by the resistance, reactance or impedance, respectively, in ohms ($S = \Omega^{-1} = A/V$).[101]
13) The weber (Wb) is the unit of magnetic flux (rate per unit of time). It is named in the honour of the German Physicist Wilhelm Eduard Weber (1804-1891), one of the early researchers of magnetism.

'Flux' is the rate (per unit of time) at which something crosses a surface perpendicular to the flow. If the something is a magnetic field, then the magnetic flux across a perpendicular surface is the product of the magnetic flux density, in teslas, and the surface area, in square meters. If a varying magnetic field passes perpendicularly through a circular loop of conducting material, the variation in the field induces an electric potential in the loop. If the flux is changing at a uniform rate of one weber per second, the induced potential is one volt. This means that numerically the flux in webers is equal to the potential, in volts, that would be created by collapsing the field uniformly to zero in one second. One weber is the flux induced in this way by a current varying at the uniform rate of one ampere per second. The weber is a large unit, equal to $10^8$ maxwells, and practical fluxes are usually fractions of one weber.[102]

14) Thetesla (T), the unit of flux density (or field intensity) for magnetic fields (also called the magnetic induction), is defined as the field intensity generating one newton of force per ampere of current per meter of conductor. The tesla, defined in 1958, honours the Serbian-American electrical engineer Nikola Tesla (1856-1943), whose work in electromagnetic induction led to the first practical generators and motors using alternating current.

The intensity of a magnetic field can be measured by placing a current-carrying conductor in the field. The magnetic field exerts a force on the conductor, a force which depends on the amount of the current and on the length of the conductor. One tesla is defined as the field intensity generating one newton of force per ampere of current per meter of conductor. Equivalently, one tesla represents a magnetic flux density of one weber per square meter of area. A field of one tesla is quite strong: the strongest fields available in laboratories are about

20 teslas, and the Earth's magnetic flux density, at its surface, is about 50 microteslas (μT).[103]

15) The henry (H), the unit of electric inductance, is named in honour of the American Physicist Joseph Henry (1797-1878), one of several scientists who discovered independently how magnetic fields can be used to generate alternating currents. The plural is sometimes spelled henrys, but in English it is correct to spell it henries.

    A changing magnetic field induces an electric current in a loop of wire (or in a coil of many loops) located in the field. Although the induced voltage depends only on the rate at which the magnetic flux changes, measured in webers per second, the amount of the current depends also on the physical properties of the coil. A coil with an inductance of one henry requires a flux of one weber for each ampere of induced current. If, on the other hand, it is the current which changes, then the induced field will generate a potential difference within the coil: if the inductance is one henry a current change of one ampere per second generates a potential difference of one volt.[104]

16) The lumen (lm) is the unit for measuring the flux of light being produced by a light source or received by a surface.

    The intensity of a light source is measured in candelas. One lumen represents the total flux of light emitted, equal to the intensity in candelas multiplied by the solid angle in steradians ($1/(4\cdot\pi)$ of a sphere) into which the light is emitted. Thus, the total flux of a one-candela light, if the light is emitted uniformly in all directions, is $4\cdot\pi$ lumens.[105]

17) Thelux (lx), the unit for measuring the illumination (illuminance) of a surface. One lux is defined as an illumination of one lumen per square metre. The intensity of the light source is measured in candelas; the

total light flux in transit is measured in lumens (1 lumen = 1 candela·steradian); and the amount of light received per unit of surface area is measured in lux (1 lux = 1 lumen/square meter).[106]

18) The hertz (Hz) is the unit of frequency, equal to one cycle per second for regular events. The hertz is used to measure the rates of events that happen periodically in a fixed and definite cycle; the becquerel, also equal to one 'event' per second, is used to measure the rates of things which happen randomly or unpredictably. The unit is named in the honour of the German Physicist Heinrich Rudolf Hertz (1857-1894), the discoverer of radioactivity, who proved in 1887 that energy is transmitted through a vacuum by electromagnetic waves. The frequencies of radio and television waves are measured in kilohertz (kHz), megahertz (MHz), or even gigahertz (GHz), and the frequencies of light waves in terahertz (THz).
19) The becquerel (Bq) is the unit for the rates of radioactivity and other random events. Radioactivity is caused when atoms disintegrate, ejecting energetic particles. One Bq is the radiation caused by one disintegration per second; this is equivalent to about 27.0270 picocuries (pCi). The unit is named for a French Physicist, Antoine-Henri Becquerel (1852-1908), the discoverer of radioactivity.
20) Thegray (Gy) is the unit for radiation dose. Radiation is a process in which energetic particles or waves travel through a medium from a source. "Radiation carries energy, and when it is absorbed by matter the matter receives this energy. The dose is the amount of energy deposited per unit of mass. One gray is defined to be the dose of one joule of energy absorbed per kilogram of matter, or 100 rad."[107] The unit is named in honour of the British physician L. Harold Gray (1905-1965), an authority on the use of radiation in the treatment of cancer

21 The sievert (Sv) is the unit for radiation dose used for measuring the effective or equivalent dose of radiation received by a human or some other living organism. The unit is named in honour of the Swedish Physicist Rolf Sievert (1898-1966), who worked over many years to measure and standardize the radiation doses used in cancer treatment. The sievert was recommended in 1977 by the International Commission on Radiation Units and Measurements (ICRU) as a substitute for the rem (roentgen equivalent man) named in honour of the German Physicist Wilhelm Conrad Röntgen (1845-1923).

22) The katal (kat) is a unit of catalytic activity used in biochemistry. A catalyst is a substance that starts or speeds a chemical reaction. Enzymes are proteins that act as catalysts within the bodies of living plants and animals. A catalyst has an activity of one katal if it enables a reaction to proceed at the rate of one mole per second (1 kat = 1 mol/s). The unit was added to the International System at the 21st General Conference of Weights and Measures in October 1999.

The SI permits the use of certain additional units though Myanmar, Liberia and United States have not officially adopted the International System of Units (SI),[108] specially: 1) The units for measuring angles (degree, arcminute, and arcsecond); 2) The units of civil time (minute, hour, day, and year); 3) Two metric units commonly used in ordinary life: the litre for volume and the tonne (metric ton) for large masses; 4) The logarithmic units bel (B) and neper (Np); a logarithmic measure of sound intensity, invented by engineers of the Bell Telephone Network in 1923 and named in honour of the inventor of the telephone, Alexander Graham Bell (1847-1922). One bel is equal to approximately 1.151 293 nepers. Neper is a unit expressing the ratio of two numbers as a natural logarithm. One neper is equal to about 8.685 890 decibels, and in general n nepers equal 20n/(ln 10) decibels. The unit recognizes the Scottish mathematician John Napier (1550-1617), the inventor of the logarithm. 5) Three non-metric scientific units whose values represent important physical constants: the astronomical unit (au), the atomic mass unit (amu) or dalton, and the electronvolt (eV). The SI does not encourage some of the other units.[109]

With the advent of decimal numeration we have been able to standardise the units of measurements and weights. Let us see some other numeral systems.

### 1.2.1 Different Numeral Systems

Counting is a basic life skill. Mesopotamia and India have made a major contribution for this. Numerals are signs or symbols for representation of numbers. There are three methods of arranging numeral characters to form numbers: additive, multiplicative, and positional notation.[110] The additive notation is done by juxtaposing single digits in a row in order of descending value and repeating each digit as required for composite number. Subtractive notation was done to deduce from the higher number. Multiplicative notation was obtained by writing the multiplied numerals in a row, and adding them up. Positional or place-value notation is done by its position, or place in the sequence of digits forming the composite number. Place value is the notion that where a digit sits in a number says something about its value.

Egyptians additive notation had many symbols for signifying numbers around 3400 BCE. Their number 1 was represented by a vertical line, 10 by a heel-bone, 100 by a coiled rope, 1000 by a blossoming lotus, 10, 000 by a bent finger, 100, 000 by a tadpole, 1, 000, 000 by a kneeling genie with raised arms.[111] They had strictly additive decimal (base 10) notation. Sumerians who lived around 3200 BCE had two additive notations; a sexagesimal (base 60) for astronomy and a decimal for everyday life. Mesopotamians around 3000 BCE had a special symbol for 10. Later numeral systems had symbols between 1 and 10. Babylonians numeral 1was used for numeral 60 and power of 60. They had special symbols for 10, 100, 1000 and 10,000. Greeks numerals were letters; *pi* ($\pi$) for 5, *delta* ($\delta$) for 10, *eta* ($\Pi$) for 100, *chi* ($\chi$) for 1000 and *mu* ($\mu$) for 10000. They added three more letters (digamma, koppa and san) from Phoenicians in 3rd century BCE. First 9 letters stood for units from 1 to 9, 2nd 9 letters for tens from 10 to 99 and last letters stood for hundreds from 100 to 900. Roman numerals had 7 symbols; I for 1, V for 5, X for 10, L for 50, C for 100, D for 500, and M for 1000 and read from left to right. LX = 60. They used additive principle for the requisite number in order of descending value. XII becomes 12. Subtractive principle was placed immediately in front of a higher value. IX becomes 9. The city of Florence, in 1299, issued an ordinance concerning the use of the 'new numerals', pointing out with what ease they could be falsified in the entries in the ledgers of the city and in tradesmen's books: a 0 might be made into a 6 or a 9, and a 1 into a 4, 7, or 9.[112]

Multiplicative notation is expressed by the multiplied numerals then added together. If A, B, C, and D represent 10, 100, 1000, and 10 000 then we can write 7D 5C 3B 1A 9 = 75319.

Positional notation values each symbol or digit depending on its position in the row of digits. Every integer greater than 1 can serve as a base in a positional notation requiring exact digit symbols indicated by the numerical value of the base. Two digits positional numeration system is known as binary, 3 digits base is ternary, 4 digits is quaternary, 5 digits is quinary, 6 digits is senary, 7 digits is septenary, 8 digits is octal, 9 digits is nonary, 10 digits is denary or decimal, 11 digits is undenary, 12 digits is duodenary, 16 digits is hexadecimal, 20 digits is vigesimal and 60 digit as base is known as sexagesimal numeration system.

Mathematicians had many numeration systems yet decimal or denary base (base 10) system has been accepted by all. It is the combined use of decimal numerals and place value first occurred on the Indian subcontinent as decimal place value system. The key contribution of the Indians, however, is not in the development of 9 numeral symbols to represent the numbers 1to 9, but the invention of the placeholder 0.

### 1.2.2 Decimal Numeration System

Indian-Arabic or Decimal Numeration System uses base 10 with ten digits which represent numbers on their own. We do not have a single-digit numeral after 9, for example 10. This is two digits; 1 stands for tens place and 0 stands for ones place. It gives meaning to strings of digits as a sum of powers of ten, the rightmost digit being the number of ones ($1 = 10^0$). The next digit to the left is the number of tens ($10^1$), next to the left is hundreds ($10^2$), next to the left is thousands ($10^3$) and so on. In the similar way decimal system also represents fractions too. As you move right from the decimal point, each place value is divided by 10. For instance, $1208.1963 = 1 \times 10^3 + 2 \times 10^2 + 0 \times 10^1 + 8 \times 10^0 + 1 \times 10^{-1} + 9 \times 10^{-2} + 6 \times 10^{-3} + 3 \times 10^{-4}$. From the decimal point it is read as 'and point one nine six three.' Each symbol is called a digit in the decimal numeration system, and each place value, is ten times that of the one to the immediate right. So, we have a *ones* place, a *tens* place, a *hundreds* place, a *thousands* place, and so on, working from right to left. In the decimal positional digits, we have a *tenth* place, a *hundredths* place and soon, working from left to right after the decimal point. When Gautama Buddha (560-483 BCE) sought the hand of the daughter of King Dandapani, he was tested for numerical knowledge by the mathematician Arjuna, who asked him to list all numbers above 100 *kotis* or $10^9$ (1 *koti* or 1 crore $= 10^7$), he gave till $10^{53}$ (*tallaksana*).[113] The Indians referred to 0 as '*śūnya*' meaning void, an empty column on their counting boards and clearly at some point this empty space was filled. A Mesopotamian origin for a placeholder, their 'zero' (two slanted bars) was not used in conjunction with a decimal base. The oldest preserved inscripted Arabic numerals on a stone column in India are found around 250 BCE.[114] The Indian numerals were fully developed in a book by the Persian mathematician al-Khowarizmi around 825 CE. The Arabic numerals reach Europe in 976 CE. The Englishman Robert of Chester translates *Liber algorismi de numero indorum* (The Book of al-Khowarizmi on Hindu Number) to Latin around 1120 CE.[115] Italian merchant Fibonacci wrote the *Liber abaci* (1202) and *Practicageometriae* (1220). The Samarkand mathematician Jamshid Al Kashi (1380-1428) described the decimal system in 1427. In Europe, the decimal was introduced by Simon Stevin (1548-1620) in 1584. "In 1585 CE, modern base 10 decimals literally erased 3,600 years of Egyptian

## Number Base Systems

| *Decimal Base 10* | *Binary Base 2* | *Ternary Base 3* | *Quinary Base 5* | *Octal Base 8* | *Hexadecimal Base 16* | *Vigesigesimal Base 20* | *Sexagesimal Base 60* |
|---|---|---|---|---|---|---|---|
| 0 | 0000 | 0 | 0 | 0 | 0 | 0 | 0 |
| 1 | 0001 | 1 | 1 | 1 | 1 | 1 | 1 |
| 2 | 0010 | 2 | 2 | 2 | 2 | 2 | 2 |
| 3 | 0011 | 10 | 3 | 3 | 3 | 3 | 3 |
| 4 | 0100 | 11 | 4 | 4 | 4 | 4 | 4 |
| 5 | 0101 | 12 | 10 | 5 | 5 | 5 | 5 |
| 6 | 0110 | 20 | 11 | 6 | 6 | 6 | 6 |
| 7 | 0111 | 21 | 12 | 7 | 7 | 7 | 7 |
| 8 | 1000 | 22 | 13 | 10 | 8 | 8 | 8 |
| 9 | 1001 | 100 | 14 | 11 | 9 | 9 | 9 |
| 10 | 1010 | 101 | 20 | 12 | A | A | 10 |
| 11 | 1011 | 102 | 21 | 13 | B | B | 11 |
| 12 | 1100 | 110 | 22 | 14 | C | C | 12 |
| 13 | 1101 | 111 | 23 | 15 | D | D | 13 |
| 14 | 1110 | 112 | 24 | 16 | E | E | 14 |
| 15 | 1111 | 120 | 30 | 17 | F | F | 15 |
| 16 | 10000 | 121 | 31 | 20 | 10 | G | 16 |
| 17 | 10001 | 122 | 32 | 21 | 11 | H | 17 |
| 18 | 10010 | 200 | 33 | 22 | 12 | J | 18 |
| 19 | 10011 | 201 | 34 | 23 | 13 | K | 19 |
| 20 | 10100 | 202 | 40 | 24 | 14 | 10 | 20… |
| Base 10 | Base 2 | Base 3 | Base 5 | Base 8 | Base 16 | Base 20 | Base 60 |

Figure 1.3 Number Base System

fraction arithmetic history. By 1900 CE, European and Arab scholars were unable to read medieval Egyptian fractions texts as well as the older Egyptian mathematical texts."[116] The Arabic system uses positional notation in which individual number symbols assume different values according to their position in the written numeral. It is possible due to symbol zero, 0. All numbers can be expressed in terms of ten symbols (0, 1, 2, 3, 4, 5, 6, 7, 8, and 9), the numerals from 1 to 9 plus 0. Each type of number has properties that are unique to it. Positional notation or decimal system is based on base10 and powers of 10. Therefore it is a base-10 system. The Babylonians had the sexagesimal system based on number 60, the Romans duodecimal based on number 12, the Mayans vigesimal based on number 20 and binary system is based on number 2 or 8 in computer systems. Here we have some of the number base systems.

Each digit can only count up to the value of one less than the base. In hexadecimal, the letters A to F are used to represent the digits 10 to 15, so they would only use one character.

Indian numeral system is a pure place-value system that is why we need a zero. Only the Indians, within the context of Indo-European civilisations, have consistently used a zero. The Arabs, however, played an essential part in the dissemination of this numeral system. In the decimal system we have ten digits; 0, 1, 2, 3, 4, 5, 6, 7, 8 and 9. In fact the meaning of 'digit' here is derived from the Latin word for a finger or toe: *digitus*.[117] The numerals 0, 1, 2, 3, 4, 5, 6, 7, 8 and 9 are more properly known as European digits. Where and when these 'finger numbers' were invented for the first time, it seems very likely that they arose from the needs of commerce; they are a language of trades-men. Besides the spoken number sequence, the number words, and the written number sequence, the number symbols, there once existed a third way of communicating the meaning of a number from person to person: the use of gestures. Number systems are nothing else but such auxiliary sets of a very special kind. Both the Egyptian and the Roman system are constructed by rule, in that all powers of ten (up to a certain limit) are assigned new symbols as collective units. The number ten therefore is called the base of the system.

With this positional notation we can represent any integer by using only the ten digit symbols in various combinations. It is expressed as $z = a.10^2 + b.10^1 + c.10^0 + d$ where a, b, c, and d are integers from 0 to 9 and integer abcd is represented by z. The number 1963 is abbreviation of $1 \times 10^3 + 9 \times 10^2 + 6 \times 10^1 + 3 \times 10^0$. In decimal system zero plays a double role; 0 represents null as a number and indicates the multiples of base 10. It can be represented as $z = a_n.10^n + b_{n-1}.10^{n-1} + \ldots + a_1.10 + a_0$. The integer z can be symbolically represented as $a_n a_{n-1} a_{n-2\ldots} a_1 a_0$. So in the number 1963, 3 is in the units place, 6 in the tens, 9 in the hundreds and 1 in the thousands place. For easier readability, commas are used to separate each group of three digits, which is called a period (1,963). When a number is written in this form, it is said to be in 'standard form.' Our decimal system lets us write numbers of all types and sizes, using a clever symbol called the decimal point. A percent can always be written as a decimal, and a decimal can be written as a percent, by moving the decimal point two places to the right like this: 0.63 = 63%. A number written in scientific notation is written as a product of a number between 1 and 10 and a power of 10. For example, to write 196,380,000 in scientific notation, we change the number to a number between 1 and 10 by moving the decimal point 8 places to the left. Then multiply by 10 raised to the power of the number of places we had to move the decimal point – that is, $10^8$: $196{,}380{,}000 = 1.9638 \times 10^8$.

With the coming of the decimal numeration, the units of measurements and weights also have been internationalised.

### 1.2.3 Units of Measurements

There are two clustering of metric units in science and engineering. One cluster, based on the centimetre, the gramme, and the second, is called the CGS system. The other, based on the metre, kilogramme, and second, is called the MKS system. The metre was defined to be one ten-millionth of the distance from the Equator to the North Pole. The litre was to be the volume of one cubic decimetre, and the kilogramme was to be the weight of a litre of pure water. The metric system was proposed in 1791, adopted by the French revolutionary assembly in 1795, and standards were adopted in

1799, was made compulsory in France in1837.[118] In 1875, the International Bureau of Weights and Measures, now called the International System of Units (SI) was signed. The metric system basing on metre and kilogram standards created and distributed in 1889 by the International Bureau of Weights and Measures (BIPM). In 1954, the Tenth General Conference on Weights and Measures (CGPM) adopted the metre, kilogram, second, ampere, degree Kelvin, and candela as the basic units for all international weights and measures, and in 1960 the 11th General Conference adopted the name International System of Units (SI) for this collection of units. The 'degree Kelvin' became the kelvin (K) in 1967. The 22nd General Conference met in October 2003. A committee of the International Committee for Weights and Measures (CIPM) has proposed revised formal definitions of the SI base units, which are being examined by the CIPM and which may be considered by the 25th CGPM, in 2014. The CGS system was introduced formally by the British Association for the Advancement of Science in 1874. There are CGS units compared with SI units.

| *CGS unit* | *Measuring* | *SI equivalent*[1]19 |
|---|---|---|
| barye (ba) | pressure | 0.1 pascal (Pa) |
| biot (Bi) | electric current | 10 amperes (A) |
| calorie (cal) | heat energy | 4.1868 joule (J) |
| darcy | permeability | 0.98692 x $10^{-12}$ square meter ($m^2$) |
| debye (D) | Electric dipole moment | 3.33564 x $10^{-30}$ coulomb meter (C·m) |
| dyne (dyn) | force | $10^{-5}$ newton (N) |
| emu | Magnetic dipole moment | 0.001 ampére square meter ($A \cdot m^2$) |
| erg | work, energy | $10^{-7}$ joule (J) |
| franklin (Fr) | electric charge | 3.3356 x $10^{-10}$ coulomb (C) |
| galileo (Gal) | acceleration | 0.01 meter per second squared ($m \cdot s^{-2}$) |

*contd...*

| *CGS unit* | *Measuring* | *SI equivalent*[1] 19 |
|---|---|---|
| gauss (G) | magnetic flux density | $10^{-4}$ tesla (T) |
| gilbert(Gi) | magnetomotive force | 0.795 775 ampere-turns (A) |
| kayser (K) | wave number | 100 per meter ($m^{-1}$) |
| lambert (Lb) | luminance | 3183.099 candelas/square meter ($cd \cdot m^{-2}$) |
| langley | heat transmission | 41.84 kilojoules/square meter ($kJ \cdot m^{-2}$) |
| line (li) | magnetic flux | $10^{-8}$ weber (Wb) |
| maxwell (Mx) | magnetic flux | $10^{-8}$ weber (Wb) |
| oersted (Oe) | magnetic field strength | 79.577 472 ampere-turns/ meter ($A \cdot m^{-1}$) |
| phot (ph) | illumination | $10^4$ lux (lx) |
| poise (P) | dynamic viscosity | 0.1 pascalsecond (Pa·s) |
| stilb (sb) | luminance | $10^4$ candelas per square meter ($cd \cdot m^{-2}$) |
| stokes (St) | kinematic viscosity | $10^{-4}$ square meters per second ($m^2 \cdot s^{-1}$) |
| unit pole | magnetic flux | $1.256\ 637 \times 10^{-7}$ weber (Wb) |

Figure 1.4 CGS Units Compared with SI Units

The units of measurements have become International System of Units (SI), abbreviated SI from French: *Système international d'unités*.Its headquarters are in Paris. Units are abbreviated or symbolised in parentheses. It is often used scientific (powers of ten) notation, like $10^6$. There are several Greek letters used as symbols. The 'micro' symbol is $\mu$ (lower case Greek letter mu). The French physician and mathematician Nicolas Chuquet (1445-1488) apparently coined the words *byllion* and *tryllion* and used them to represent $10^{12}$ and $10^{18}$ respectively. In 1600's they used *billion* and *trillion* for $10^9$ and $10^{12}$, respectively. A billion is $10^9 = 1\,000\,000\,000$ in the U.S. (American) system and $10^{12} = 1\,000\,000\,000\,000$ in the Non-U.S or European system.[120] The General Conference on Weights and Measures endorsed the European names in 1948. In 1974, the government of Prime Minister Harold Wilson announced that henceforth 'billion' would mean $10^9$ and not $10^{12}$ in official British reports and statistics. The 19th General Conference on Weights and Measures in 1991 extended the list of metric prefixes so that it reaches from yotta- at $10^{24}$ (one septillion) to yocto- at $10^{-24}$ (one septillionth). In English-speaking countries, the decimal marker (decimal point) is the period. In continental Europe and most other places, the decimal marker is the comma. The large numbers, like the billions above, is represented as groups of three digits separated by narrow spaces. In scientific notation, the exponent of the 10 should be a multiple of 3. The distance from the Earth to the Sun should be stated as approximately $149.6 \times 10^6$ km, not $1.496 \times 10^8$ km. No periods are used after abbreviations or symbols for units, and never uses an 's' on an abbreviation or symbol to indicate a plural. In science, the names of large numbers are usually avoided completely by using the appropriate SI prefixes. Moving from Latin-based systems to a Greek-based system in which, for $n > 3$, the Greek number $n$ is used to generate a name for $10^{3n}$. The names of thousand and million are retained for $n = 1$ and 2 and the special name *gillion*, suggested by the SI prefix giga-, is proposed for $n = 3$.

| $n$ = | $10^{3n}$ = | *American name* | *European name* | *SI prefix* | *Greek-based name (proposed)*[121] |
|---|---|---|---|---|---|
| 1 | $10^3$ | thousand | thousand | kilo-(k) | thousand |
| 2 | $10^6$ | million | million | mega-(M-) | million |
| 3 | $10^9$ | billion | milliard | giga-(G-) | gillion |
| 4 | $10^{12}$ | trillion | billion | tera-(T-) | tetrillion |
| 5 | $10^{15}$ | quadrillion | billiard | peta-(P-) | pentillion |
| 6 | $10^{18}$ | quintillion | trillion | exa-(E-) | hexillion |

*contd...*

| | | | | | |
|---|---|---|---|---|---|
| 7 | $10^{21}$ | sextillion | trilliard | zetta-(Z-) | heptillion |
| 8 | $10^{24}$ | septillion | quadrillion | yotta-(Y-) | oktillion |
| 9 | $10^{27}$ | octillion | quadrilliard | | ennillion |
| 10 | $10^{30}$ | nonillion | quintillion | | dekillion |
| 11 | $10^{33}$ | decillion | quintilliard | | hendekillion |
| 12 | $10^{36}$ | undecillion | sextillion | | dodekillion |
| 13 | $10^{39}$ | duodecillion | sextilliard | | trisdekillion |
| 14 | $10^{42}$ | tredecillion | septillion | | tetradekillion |
| 15 | $10^{45}$ | quattuordecillion | septilliard | | pentadekillion |
| 16 | $10^{48}$ | quindecillion | octillion | | hexadekillion |
| 17 | $10^{51}$ | sexdecillion | octilliard | | heptadekillion |
| 18 | $10^{54}$ | septendecillion | nonillion | | oktadekillion |
| 19 | $10^{57}$ | octodecillion | nonilliard | | enneadekillion |
| 20 | $10^{60}$ | novemdecillion | decillion | | icosillion |
| 21 | $10^{63}$ | vigintillion | decilliard | | icosihenillion |
| 22 | $10^{66}$ | unvigintillion | undecillion | | icosidillion |
| 23 | $10^{69}$ | duovigintillion | undecilliard | | icositrillion |
| 24 | $10^{72}$ | trevigintillion | duodecillion | | icositetrillion |
| 25 | $10^{75}$ | quattuorvigintillion | duodecilliard | | icosipentillion |
| 26 | $10^{78}$ | quinvigintillion | tredecillion | | icosihexillion |
| 27 | $10^{81}$ | sexvigintillion | tredecilliard | | icosiheptillion |
| 28 | $10^{84}$ | septenvigintillion | quattuordecillion | | icosioktillion |
| 29 | $10^{87}$ | octovigintillion | quattuordecilliard | | icosiennillion |
| 30 | $10^{90}$ | novemvigintillion | quindecillion | | triacontillion |
| 31 | $10^{93}$ | trigintillion | quindecilliard | | triacontahenillion |
| 32 | $10^{96}$ | untrigintillion | sexdecillion | | triacontadillion |
| 33 | $10^{99}$ | duotrigintillion | sexdecilliard | | triacontatrillion |

Figure 1.5 Names for Large Numbers

The name centillion ($n$ = 100) is $10^{100}$. A centillion is $10^{303}$ (1 followed by 303 zeroes) in the American system and a whopping

$10^{600}$ (1 followed by 600 zeroes) in the European system. The googol, the number is $10^{100}$ (1 followed by 100 zeroes). The name googol was coined and invented by the nine-year old nephew of the American mathematician Edward Kasner (1878-1955) in late 1930s (1938) and also defined the googolplex, equal to $10^{googol}$.[122] The googolplex (1 followed by a googol of zeroes) is far larger than any of the numbers. The prefixes hecto- (h-) for 100, deka- (da-) for 10, deci- (d-) for $10^{-1}$, and centi- (c-) for $10^{-2}$ is widely used in everyday life for smaller numbers. There are milli- (m-) for $10^{-3}$, micro- ($\mu$-) for $10^{-6}$, nano- (n-) for $10^{-9}$, pico- (p-) for $10^{-12}$, femto- (f-) for $10^{-15}$, atto- (a-) for $10^{-18}$, zepto- (z-) for $10^{-21}$, yocto- (y-) for $10^{-24}$. The rest of the small numbers are as follows:

| $n =$ | $10^{-3n} =$ | *American name* | *European name* | *SI prefix* | *Greek-based name (proposed)* |
|---|---|---|---|---|---|
| 1 | $10^{-3}$ | thousandth | thousandth | milli -(m-) | thousandth |
| 2 | $10^{-6}$ | millionth | millionth | micro -(µ-) | millionth |
| 3 | $10^{-9}$ | billionth | milliardth | nano -(n-) | gillionth |
| 4 | $10^{-12}$ | trillionth | billionth | pico -(p-) | tetrillionth |
| 5 | $10^{-15}$ | quadrillionth | billiardth | femto -(f-) | pentillionth |
| 6 | $10^{-18}$ | quintillionth | trillionth | atto -(a-) | hexillionth |
| 7 | $10^{-21}$ | sextillionth | trilliardth | zepto -(z-) | heptillionth |
| 8 | $10^{-24}$ | septillionth | quadrillionth | yocto -(y-) | oktillionth |
| 9 | $10^{-27}$ | octillionth | quadrilliardth | | ennillionth |
| 10 | $10^{-30}$ | nonillionth | quintillionth | | dekillionth |
| 11 | $10^{-33}$ | decillionth | quintilliardth | | hendekillionth |
| 12 | $10^{-36}$ | undecillionth | sextillionth | | dodekillionth |

*contd...*

| | | | | | |
|---|---|---|---|---|---|
| 13 | $10^{-39}$ | duodecillionth | sextilliardth | | trisdekillionth |
| 14 | $10^{-42}$ | tredecillionth | septillionth | | tetradekillionth |
| 15 | $10^{-45}$ | quattuordecillionth | septilliardth | | pentadekillionth |
| 16 | $10^{-48}$ | quindecillionth | octillionth | | hexadekillionth |
| 17 | $10^{-51}$ | sexdecillionth | octilliardth | | heptadekillionth |
| 18 | $10^{-54}$ | septendecillionth | nonillionth | | oktadekillionth |
| 19 | $10^{-57}$ | octodecillionth | nonilliardth | | enneadekillionth |
| 20 | $10^{-60}$ | novemdecillionth | decillionth | | icosillionth |
| 21 | $10^{-63}$ | vigintillionth | decilliardth | | icosihenillionth |
| 22 | $10^{-66}$ | unvigintillionth | undecillionth | | icosidillionth |
| 23 | $10^{-69}$ | duovigintillionth | undecilliardth | | icositrillionth |
| 24 | $10^{-72}$ | trevigintillionth | duodecillionth | | icositetrillionth |
| 25 | $10^{-75}$ | quattuorvigintillionth | duodecilliardth | | icosipentillionth |
| 26 | $10^{-78}$ | quinvigintillionth | tredecillionth | | icosihexillionth |
| 27 | $10^{-81}$ | sexvigintillionth | tredecilliardth | | icosiheptillionth |
| 28 | $10^{-84}$ | septenvigintillionth | quattuordecillionth | | icosioktillionth |
| 29 | $10^{-87}$ | octovigintillionth | quattuordecilliardth | | icosiennillionth |
| 30 | $10^{-90}$ | novemvigintillionth | quindecillionth | | triacontillionth |
| 31 | $10^{-93}$ | trigintillionth | quindecilliardth | | triacontahenillionth |
| 32 | $10^{-96}$ | untrigintillionth | sexdecillionth | | triacontadillionth |
| 33 | $10^{-99}$ | duotrigintillionth | sexdecilliardth | | triacontatrillionth |

Figure 1.6 Names for Small Numbers

For binary prefixes, a kilobit (kbit or KiB, pronounced *kilo bee*) is usually $2^{10}$ = 1024 bits instead of 1000 bits or 1 KB of decimal prefixes. In 1998 the International Electrotechnical Commission (IEC; Commission électrotechnique internationale (CEI), in French) approved new prefixes for the powers of 2. These prefixes are as follows:[123] Named kibi, symbolised as Ki is $2^{10}$ = 1 024 (KiB); named mebi, symbolised as Mi is $2^{20}$ = 1 048 576 (MiB); named gibi, symbolised as Gi is $2^{30}$ = 1 073 741 824 (GiB); named tebi, symbolised as Ti is $2^{40}$ = 1 099 511 627 776

(TiB); named pebi, symbolised as Pi is $2^{50}$ = 1 125 899 906 842 624 (PiB); named exbi, symbolised as Ei is $2^{50}$ = 1 152 921 504 606 846 976 (EiB). Thus, 5 gigabytes (GB) should mean exactly 5 000 000 000 bytes, and 5 gibibytes (GiB) should mean exactly 5 368 709 120 bytes.1GB is a metric prefix denoting $10^9$ or one billion while 1GiB (pronounced one *giga bee*) is 1 073 741 824 bytes.[124]

Numbers can be classified into sets, called number systems. Natural numbers or counting numbers symbolized as **N** started with 1. Natural number has a place value of one, and every other digit has a place value ten times that of the place value of the digit to its right. It is decimal numeration. Natural numbers can be represented by classes of equivalent sets in set theory. 6 can be represented as the class of all sets that have exactly six elements {0, 1, 2, 3, 4, 5}. Negative numbers are said to be less than zero and are usually written with a negative sign. Integer numbers or integers symbolized as **Z** are the set of the negatives of the natural numbers combined with the natural numbers. They are ..., –3, –2, –1, 0, 1, 2, 3, .... Rational numbers symbolized as **Q** are fractions written as two numbers, the numerator and the denominator, with a dividing bar between them. They are ½, –3/4, 5 etc. Real numbers symbolized as **R** are measuring numbers written using decimal numerals but not as fractions. The real numbers consist of irrational numbers and rational numbers, as well as the integers, whole numbers, and the natural numbers. If a real number cannot be written as a fraction of two integers, it is called *irrational* symbolized as **I**. Irrational numbers are those real numbers that cannot be represented as terminating or repeating decimals like π, e and √2 etc. The complex numbers symbolized as **C** consist of all numbers of the form $a + bi$ where $a$ and $b$ are real numbers. In the expression $a + bi$, the real number $a$ is called the *real part* and $bi$ is called the *imaginary part*. An imaginary number, when squared, gives a negative result. The 'unit' imaginary number is √(-1) and its symbol is i, or j. Imaginary numbers are not imaginary, they really exist, and we may need to use them one day.

The natural numbers and the units of measurements are quantitative concepts for knowing and measuring things. Decimal numeration has become a common system for measuring the things. The basic quantity of a thing begins with 0, a numeral quantity. Is 0 real or merely conceptual and relational number? How did 0 originate as a number and placeholder in decimal numeration? How do we know it? What are its philosophical implications?

## 1.3 Origin of Zero and its Philosophical Appraisal

Something coming from *nothing* arises out of realities which require at least three kinds of realities which require a cause for their existence: 1) Realities that have a beginning, in other words, prior to the beginning they were nothing – absolute nothing; they were zero, 0. 2) Realities which are conditioned in their existenceneed something beyond themselves to cause themselves to exist, transcendent cause, the Creator and 3) Realities that are conditioned by time need Eternal Necessary Being. "Though counting abilities were rare in the ancient world, numbers and the fundamentals of counting always developed before writing and reading."[125] The moment we experience or perceive we have an idea. We do *act before we know* the how and why of our operations. "We *walk before we know* anything of the nature of balance; we talk before we know grammar or idiom; we think and reason before we know aught of the science of logic or of psychology; and we 'do' mathematics before we understand its nature."[126] "In a sense the numbers were there all the time, waiting to be discovered."[127] It is India that gave us the decimal numeration, each symbol receiving a value of position as well as an absolute value. 0 (zero), alternatively called *śūnya*, is both a number and a numeral. It was the last numeral to be created. India transformed and reincarnated 0 into a *placeholder* as well as a *number*. There are two uses of zero. One use is as an empty place indicator in our *place-value* number system. The second use of zero is as a *number* itself in the form we use it as 0. 0 got its *own position* on the number line as the centre of all numbers.

Negatives do not quantify anything. They merely represent a quantity which belongs to another set. 0 is an *even* integer that precedes the positive 1. 0 was identified before the idea of 'negative integers' was accepted. Mathematical zero, a symbol to represent *nothing*, was invented three times in the history by the Babylonians, the Mayans, and the Indians. We say, 'there are no apples,' not 'there are zero apples.' 0 is another symbol for empty set. 0 also represents *nothingness,* which is better defined as 'the concept of absolute equilibrium.' It is the Babylonians who had positional system of numeration with base 60 and 10 around 1700 BCE and had two edged bars or yy symbols for empty space around 400 BCE. Let us see the origin of zero in Babylon.

### 1.3.1 Origin of Zero in Babylon

The earliest writers are the Mesopotamians (Iraqis) who used a pictographic script, on tablets of clay. The script was cuneiform with wedge-shaped marks. The Babylonians lived in Mesopotamia which was the centre of Sumerian civilization around 3500 BCE. Their culture became sophisticated as mathematics flourished and libraries appeared. Their counting was sexagesimal based on base 60. The Akkadians invaded Sumeria around 2300 BCE and had abacus for counting. The Babylonians establish themselves around 2000 BCE again. They had *positional system* with base 60 than 10 and around 700 BCE used three hooks to denote an empty place in the positional notation. It was around 400 BCE that the Babylonians put two wedge symbols ('') into the place where we would put zero to indicate which was meant, 21 6 or 21"6. They divided the day into 24 hours, each hour into 60 minutes (60'), and each minute into 60 seconds (60"). They had 59 symbols from basic two symbols; 1 and 10 ( 𒁹, 𒌋 ). 𒁹 is 60.

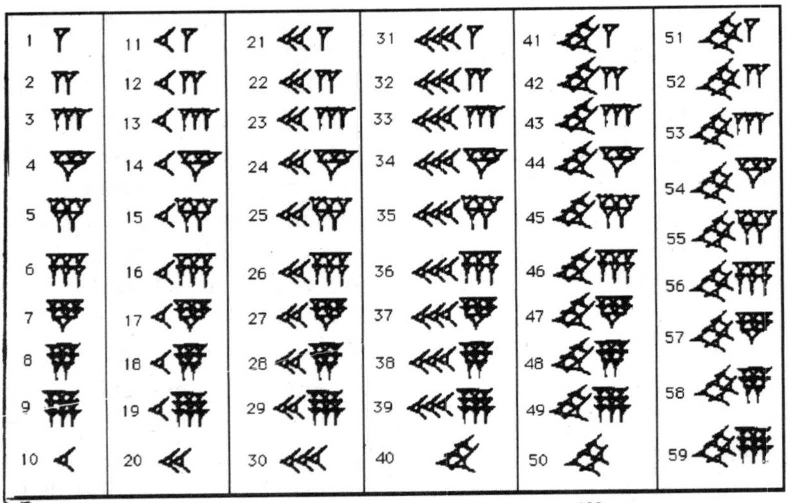

Figure 1.7 Babylonian Numerals[128]

Sexagesimal numeration is based on the number 60 and the powers of 60. One and 60 looked similar besides their size. The size of 60 looked greater than 1. Their *empty* position never occurred at the end of the digits but always between two digits. We find 21"6 but never find 216". The sexagesimal number system placed the rightmost units up to 59 and the position to the left is 60 $\times$ n where $1 < n < 59$. For example 1, 28, 19, 53 in sexagesimal is $1 \times 60^3 + 28 \times 60^2 + 19 \times 60^1 + 53 = 137993$. 1/2 is 0;30 in base 60. 1/50 is 0;1,12 in sexagesimal. Sexagesimal is used in measuring degrees in a circle, angles, geographic coordinates and time.

## 1.3.2 Origin of Zero in Mayan Culture

The Maya Indians of Central America used additive vigesimal (base 20) system of counting that had the remnants of an earlier base-10 system in it.[129] They are the first people to employ a special symbol for zero for their calendars in the 3rd century CE. They had three basic symbols; the dot's (.) value was 1, bar's (—) value was 5 and painted red seashell ( ) was 0. Their number unit was from 0 to 19. Seashell was 0. In base 20 system,[130] the first number would denote the units up to 19, the next would denote the number of 20's up to 19, the next the number of 400's up to 19, etc. It changes in the third place and denotes the number of 360's up to 19 instead of the number of 400's. The third term should be 400 but the Mayans took $18 \times 20$ because 360 was a closer approximation to the length of the solar calendar. After this, the system reverts to multiples of 20. So the fourth place was $n \times 20^2$, and the fifth, $n \times 20^3$ etc. For example, 9;13;5;1;11 would be $11 + 1 \times 20 + 5 \times 18 \times 20 + 13 \times 18 \times 20^2 + 9 \times 18 \times 20^3 = 1391431$. The numbers could be written or read from bottom to top or from right to left.

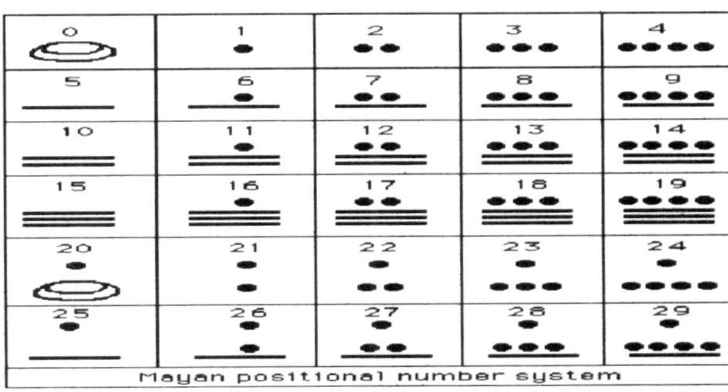


Figure 1.8 Mayan Positional Number System[131]

The Mayan system of numeration lacked the procedure of proper steps from level to level: "If a counting system of any base proceeds through levels which are each related to the previous one by a power of the base, whatever its value, then adding a zero to a symbol string will always have the effect of multiplying the number by the base value."[132] Indian place notation moved from left to right with ones place coming first. "The earliest example of the use of the Indian zero is in 458 CE, when it appeared in a surviving Jain work on cosmology (*Lokavibhaga),* but indirect evidence indicates that it must have been in use as early as 200 BCE. At first, it seems that it was denoted by a dot, rather than by a small circle."[133]

### 1.3.3 Origin of Zero in India

Our present number system is known as Indian-Arabic numeration. It is Indians who invented zero and the decimal numeration but the Arabs who spread it to the West. That is how it is known as Indian-Arabic numeration otherwise it is Indian decimal numeration. The earliest known mathematics in ancient India is from 3000 to 2600 BCE in the Indus Valley Civilization (Harappan civilization) of North India and Pakistan. Symbols for the first nine numbers of our number system have their origins in the Brahmi system of writing in India, which dates back to at least the mid-third century BCE.[134] With these nine figures and with the sign 0 which the Arabs call *zephir* any number whatsoever is written. In Indian number system, each number has an absolute value and its place values are units, tens, hundreds, thousands, etc., from right to left digits. The original Indian term for the *little circle* as placeholder was *śūnya* (empty). The Sanskrit word, *śūnya* means empty which was later translated as zero in mathematics. Its numeral sign is 0. 0 is an integer precedes 1 in number line. Zero as a number quantifies a count or an amount of null size. As the value, or number, zero is not the same as the digit zero (as in 03 where digit 0 is not always necessary). 0 is both an integer and placeholder in place value numeral systems. The concept of zero as 'nothing' is ancient we do not know exactly when it was incorporated into the system of numbers in India.

| Values | 0 | 1 | 2 | 3 | 4 | 5 | 6 | 7 | 8 | 9 |
|---|---|---|---|---|---|---|---|---|---|---|
| Bengali | ০ | ১ | ২ | ৩ | ৪ | ৫ | ৬ | ৭ | ৮ | ৯ |
| Devanagari | ० | १ | २ | ३ | ४ | ५ | ६ | ७ | ८ | ९ |
| Gujarati | ૦ | ૧ | ૨ | ૩ | ૪ | ૫ | ૬ | ૭ | ૮ | ૯ |
| Gurmukhi | ੦ | ੧ | ੨ | ੩ | ੪ | ੫ | ੬ | ੭ | ੮ | ੯ |
| Kannada | ೦ | ೧ | ೨ | ೩ | ೪ | ೫ | ೬ | ೭ | ೮ | ೯ |
| Malayalam | ൦ | ൧ | ൨ | ൩ | ൪ | ൫ | ൬ | ൭ | ൮ | ൯ |
| Oriya | ୦ | ୧ | ୨ | ୩ | ୪ | ୫ | ୬ | ୭ | ୮ | ୯ |
| Telugu | ౦ | ౧ | ౨ | ౩ | ౪ | ౫ | ౬ | ౭ | ౮ | ౯ |
| Tamil | ௦ | ௧ | ௨ | ௩ | ௪ | ௫ | ௬ | ௭ | ௮ | ௯ |

Figure 1.9 Indian Decimal Digits in Different Languages[135]

India has many languages; Tamil numerals were alphabets around 600 BCE.[136] Even Malayalam numerals are alphabets. Later numbers were written as the combination of symbols 1 and 0. Indian numerals, similar to Arabic numerals, were found near a Hindu temple around 250 BCE. "The symbol 0 was used as early as 200 BCE by Pingala (300-200 BCE) in his *Chanda Sutra*. The Bakshali manuscript employs a dot (.) for the zero."[137] Decimal writings are found in 5th century in Jain text *Lokabibhāga* (458).[138] One of the world's greatest mathematician and astronomer Āryabhaṭṭa (475-553), was born in Patliputra in Magadha, modern Patna in Bihar, made use of these numerals around 498 CE. Place to place in ten times in value is the origin of the modern decimal-based place value notation. "Varāhamihira (early 6th century CE) was familiar with the place-value. In his *Pañcasiddhāntikā* the number 1050 is expressed as *kha-indriya-diśaḥ*: *kha* for zero, *indriya* for five and *diśaḥ* for ten."[139]

In 628, the Indian astronomer Brahmagupta (598-670) of Bhinmal of Gujrat presently in North Western Rajastan, defined zero in this way and spelled out the algebraic rules for adding, subtracting and multiplying with it: "When *śūnya* is added to a number or subtracted from a number, the number remains unchanged; and a number multiplied by *śūnya* becomes *śūnya*."[140] Arab mathematician al-Khwārizmī (780-850) wrote a systematic introduction to algebra, *Kitab al-jabr w'al Muqabalah* (Book of Restoring and Balancing) around 825 CE. It was translated into Latin in 12th century. Mahavira (850) of Gulbarga from Andra Pradesh made rules for operation with zero around 9th century. Bhaskara II (1114-1185) of Bijāpur from Karnataka wrote *Lilavati* in 1150 CE in which he introduces the decimal system of numeration and rules for multiplication and division by zero.[141] It should be made clear straight away that the modern figures 1, 2, 3, 4, 5, 6, 7, 8, 9, 0 acquired their present form in the fifteenth century in the West, modelled on specific prototypes and adopted permanently when the printing press was invented in Europe.[142] The Indian mathematical writings were passed on to al-Khwarizmi (later the term algorithm) and thence to Leonardo Fibonacci (1170-1250) and to Europe around 13th century. There was a dispute between algorists and abacists (the supporters of the Roman numeral system) of Europe and finally abacus was abandoned in 18th century. Fibonacci writes *Liber Abaci* (Book of Calculation) in 1202. 'The Indian system is a pure place-value system. Only a pure place-value system needs a symbol for a missing amount, for a non-existent rank, the zero, 0. Only the Indians within the context of Indo-European civilisations have consistently used a zero.'[143] Zero is transliterated in Sanskrit as *śūnya* (void, nothing, empty), other words like sky, endless, *kha, gagan, ākāśa, nabha, ananta* are also used.

A number is a quantity, an abstraction of a collection of things; a numeral is a human-made symbol that represents the number. Numbers (quantities) are always the same value, no matter what symbol or word is used to represent them but zero (0) is a special case. The numeral zero (symbol 0) is invented but the number zero (abstract quantity of *nothing*) is discovered.

### 1.3.4 Philosophical Appraisal of Zero

In mathematics, we assign quantitative and qualitative properties to things so we may communicate about these things. A sentence is mathematically acceptable statement if it is either true or false but not both. If truth is symbolized by 1 or unity and 0 by nullity, then, by definition, our truth-seeking knowledge lies between two extremes. Our knowledge neither be absolute truth nor absolutely false. The assertion, by definition, lacks in cognitive claim. Knowledge may be virtuous or vicious, or permissible or impermissible, or obligatory or prohibitory, somewhere in between the extremes. The mean between the extremes is said to be ratio, fixed relation of number or degree, from which one derived words rational and reasonable.[144] An implication is a logical construction that tells us *if one condition is true*, then another condition must be true. It is written $\boldsymbol{a \rightarrow b}$ or $\boldsymbol{a \Rightarrow b}$ which would be read '***a*** implies ***b***', or '***a*** therefore ***b***', or 'if ***a***, then ***b***.' Implication is confused for 'if and only if', or the biconditional truth function (< >). They are not the same. The implication $\boldsymbol{a \rightarrow b}$ is true even if only ***b*** is true. For example 'dogs have wings, therefore it is raining today', is true if it is indeed raining, despite the fact that the first item is false. In fact, any implication $\boldsymbol{a \rightarrow b}$ is called *vacuously true* when ***a*** is false. By contrast, $\boldsymbol{a \Leftrightarrow b}$ would be false if either *a* or *b* was by itself false ($\boldsymbol{a \Leftrightarrow b} \equiv (a \wedge b) \wedge (\neg a \wedge \neg b)$, or in terms of implication as $(\boldsymbol{a \rightarrow b}) \wedge (b \rightarrow a)$.

It may be useful to remember that $\boldsymbol{a \rightarrow b}$ only tells that it *cannot* be the case that ***b*** is false while ***a*** is true; ***b*** must 'follow' from **a** (and 'false' does follow from 'false'). Alternatively, $\boldsymbol{a \rightarrow b}$ is in fact equivalent to $b \wedge \neg a$. The truth table for implication is therefore

| a | b | $a \rightarrow b$ |
|---|---|---|
| F | F | T (1) |
| F | T | T (2) |
| T | F | F (3) |
| T | T | T (4) |

Figure 1.10 The Truth Table for Implication

We assert a relation between the assertions *a* and *b*, which we can call formal implication. $a \supset b$. *If* one proposition *a* is true, *then* another *b* is true. When we translate the English 'if...then' or 'implies' with material implication we have four truth-tables: 1) When both are false, conclusion is true. 2) When *a* is false and *b* is true then conclusion is true. 3) When *a* is true and *b* is false, conditional is false. 4) When antecedent *a* and consequent *b* both are true, conclusion is true. Whenever the antecedent is false, the whole conditional is true. Whenever the consequent is true, the conditional is true. Mathematical propositions assert implications with variables. The mathematical use of 'if ... then ...' is importantly different from the everyday use. For example, if *n* is both even and odd, then *n* is certainly even. 1 +1= 2 could mean *x* is one and *y* is one, and *x* differs from *y*, then *x* and *y* are two (x + y = 2 units). This proposition may be expressed: 'Any unit and any another unit are two units.'[145] "A proposition is true if the reality it purports to describe is as that proposition depicts it – if the things referred to it (if any) have the properties they are said to have or stand in the relations in which they are said to stand."[146]

Mathematics studies class of relations possessing the formal properties of temporal priority – properties which are summed up in the notion of continuity. The properties identified with numbers are ones that exist necessarily, and that they necessarily stand in their arithmetical relations to be true. There are two types of implications; the material and the formal. Between two propositions whether we perceive or not but the mind perceives as sensible objects and infers, that is called material implication.[147] A formal implication is the affirmation of every material implication of a certain class.

Mathematics deals with an abstraction of reality: a 'model' of just *one aspect* of the reality. In addition, we perform an operation on numbers that is the abstract representation of things, in order to determine the number of things in the combined set. 'Equal' does not mean 'identical'; it means that they are two different ways to describe the same reality: I can view the apples as a set of two and a set of three, or as one set of five. The numbers have no reality in themselves, and that is in a sense true. What makes math 'work' is that numbers, which are not a part of the 'real' world, nevertheless describe it very accurately. They are simply a language that describes one aspect of the reality we perceive. Mathematics is just a set of logical truths. It assumes some things, defines some terms, and sees what follows logically from those assumptions. Descartes was skeptic in saying that nothing is certain. What he ended up with was his famous 'I think therefore I am' proof of his own existence. From there he argued that several other things followed logically. Many history books say 0 is the invention of a *symbol for nothing*. The concept of 0 is a new kind of number that represents the *concrete idea of nothing*. Carl Friedrich Gauss (1777-1855) said that what matters in mathematics is not notations but notions. Mathematical things have no existence in the real world; they are abstractions. A number is a process that has long ago been *thingified* so thoroughly that everybody thinks of it as a thing.[148]

Zero is absolute, in the sense that a number is either 0 or not. 0 has some properties which other numbers do not have: 1) For any number $0 \times n = 0$, 2) $0 + n = n$ and 3) $n/0$ = undefined. 15 divided by 3 is 5 because 3 times 5 is 15. 15 divided by 0 is $x$ would mean 0 times $x$ is 15. No value for $x$ works. It is indeterminate. 0/0 is also undefined. An even number is defined as one that is divisible by 2. *0 is an even number* because 0/2 = 0.

In fact, *0 is a whole number*. The set of numbers we use to answer quantitatively is the set of whole numbers. 0 by itself is *nothing,* no quantity. But as a whole quantity, it is not a fraction. In the place value, *0 is a placeholder*. In the whole numbers, 0 increases the whole number quantity. In the number line, *0 is the point of origin of positive and negative numbers*. Astronomically, a new Julian day number, starting with the day 0, began on the 1st of January, 4713 BCE at 12 o'clock noon, an arbitrary date was chosen in 1583 by the scholar Joseph Scaliger (1540-1609).[149] A new 0 hour was put at midnight on November 17, 1858[150] for civil purpose. Midnight is 0:00 in universal time. Midnight itself is neither a.m. nor p.m., but the minute between 12:00 midnight and 12:01 is a.m. Greenwich, England is defined as the 0° of longitude, and is the centre of the Greenwich time zone, relative to which other time zones are usually referenced. In geometry, *0 is a point*. In binary system, *0 is false* and 1 is true. 0 is not a directed or signed whole number but integers are directed whole numbers. *0 is a square number* ($0^2 = 0$) because it is an integer.

The concept of zero as number and placeholder in decimal system of numeration took many years for mathematicians to accept and apply in mathematics and other sciences. Today, the axiom of empty set from set theory also has helped us to understand the reality of zero.

### 1.3.4.1 Ontology of Zero

Both in the East and the West, we find the ontological views that numbers are bases of everything real.[151] Zero, 0, or *śūnya* is a number, an origin of any quantitative or qualitative amount things. Philosophical formulations concerning *śunyatā* - i.e. emptiness or the voidness may have facilitated in the introduction of the concept of zero. Whatever we think about in our daily life and surroundings is in one way or another dependent on our ability to count or measure. The aim of mathematical thinking process is to make our world measurable, calculable, predictable, and more manageable. An axiom is a basic principle that is assumed to be true without proof. We have assumed or axiomatised an empty set as 0 which has no elements as a basic set. The earlier demand that axioms be self-evident or basic truths gradually gave way to the idea that axioms were just assumptions, and later to the idea that the axioms are just designated sentences used to specify the theory.[152] 'No sentence can be true and false at the same time' (the principle of contradiction). Division by 0 is an operation by which you cannot find an answer. So it is not allowed. 8 divided by 4 is 2 because 4 times 2 is 8. 8 divided by 0 is $x$ *(any number)* means 0 times $x$ is 8. 0 times any number is 0. This operation does not work. The value of 0/0 is indeterminate. The familiar method of evaluating the indeterminate form 0/0 became incorrectly known, in later calculus texts, as l'Hospital's rule after Marquis de l'Hospital (1661-1704). 1/0 is undefined because division is defined in terms of multiplication. Division by 0 is not physically impossible but it is a violation of mathematical axioms or principles. Numbers have some properties and operations like adding, subtracting, multiplying and dividing give another number. Subtraction is the opposite of addition, as division is the opposite of multiplication. Any number multiplied by zero gives zero. Technically, division by 0 is not impossible; it is contradictory to our mathematical assumptions. We divide one number by another to get another number, but not in an abstract concept like infinity. Infinity is not a real number because it does not follow mathematical operations. The infinity we talk like 3/0 is a vague general infinity, whereas the infinity we get from the number of elements of the set {1, 2, 3, ...} is a very specific called 'countable' infinity ($\infty$) or aleph 0 ($\aleph_0$). Once one countable set is given, any other set which can be put into a one-to-one correspondence with it is also countable. This countably infinite sets have cardinal number aleph 0. Approach to infinity means whatever actual number we name, it eventually gets bigger than that. Real numbers do not include an object called infinity, though the sets of cardinal or ordinal numbers correspond to infinity in one of several senses. Jain mathematicians recognized *five* different types of *infinities*: infinite in one direction, in two directions, in area, infinite everywhere and perpetually infinite. There could be *three* types of infinites; *potential*, *actual* and *theological*.[153]

> Opposed to the finite are the potential infinite and the actual infinite. The potential infinite is an extension of the finite, constructible from the finite by some rule or process that is never in fact completed. The actual infinite, on the other hand, is conceived as an actually existing collection of an infinite number of parts. The actual infinite could be regarded as the completion of a process that builds the infinite from the finite. This is the actual infinite of set theory.[154]

Theological infinity is different from mathematical what Descartes and Leibniz call as absolute infinite. It is not a conception of an infinite collection but of the unlimited. The infinite has existence only as a process that can be repeated over and over again which is known as potential infinite. Aristotle's infinite has being only potentially and not actually which is denied by Cantor. Whereas for Aristotle the infinite has being only as this infinitely repeatable rule or process, Cantor's actual infinite could be seen as the completion of such a process.[155] The actual infinite is collection of an infinite number of parts, the completion of that process builds the infinite from the finite. The theological infinite is neither an infinite collection nor an extension of the finite but unlimited. Descartes calls potential and actual infinite as indefinite; only God is infinite without limits.

Zero is an integer, untouched or whole number which is the only integer that is neither positive nor negative. In order for a number to be positive, it has to be larger than 0. So, 0 is not positive. In order for a number to be negative, it has to be smaller than 0. So, 0 is not negative. Therefore, 0 is neither negative nor positive. Zero is less than any positive number, so $0 < 1$. Zero is greater than any negative number, so $0 > -1$. Zero is not the smallest number because any negative number is smaller than zero. Since zero is not bigger or smaller than itself, zero is neither positive nor negative. The only difference between the set of positive numbers and the set of non-negative numbers is that zero is not in the first set (empty set is the first), but it is in the second. In the same way the 'non-positive' numbers are the negative numbers together with zero. 0 is nonnegative or nonpositive. 0 being the centre, the number line extends to infinity in both the positive and negative directions.

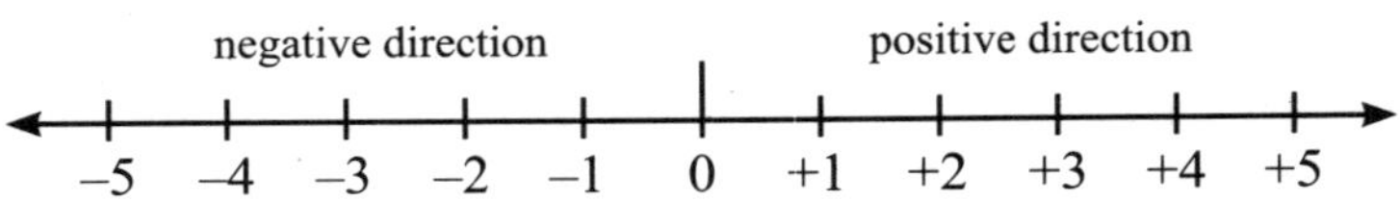

Figure 1.11 The Number Line

0 is even since 2 times 0 is 0. 0 can be divided by two, therefore it is even. Or it can be written $2 \times n$ where $n$ is an integer. An integer $n$ is called 'even' if there exists an integer $m$ such that $n = 2m$, and 'odd' if $n + 1$ is even. From this, it is clear that $0 = (2)(0)$ is even.

The reason for this definition is so that we have the property that every integer is either even or odd.

0 is neither prime nor composite. In geometry, 0 is a point to begin. In binary system, 0 and 1 are the only elements for computer language. 0 can be a natural number, squared number and an empty set. Empty set has no elements so its cardinality is 0. Sets are collection of things. Empty set is { } or Ø. 'Nothing' as a term describes the set itself, whereas 'zero' as a term does not describe a set, but an element. Empty set is nothing. Every set has an empty set as subset. Thus, all numbers can be built from empty set, the foundation of nothing.

All concrete things exist in space and time but space and time are not concrete things. Shadows and holes have locations but they are immaterial things. Reality reveals us as it is; solid, liquid, gaseous or immaterial. The Babylonians, Mayans and the Indians had discovered 0 to represent empty place but it is only Indians who could perceive 0 as *conceptual reality* and make use of it in decimal system as *empty place-holder* as well as a *number* bringing revolution in mathematics and science. It is 0 which represents absence, emptiness and nothing in the form of number 0. 0 by itself is nothing. It has no value in itself, but added any amount of value on being placed after a number.

The whole of mathematics or proliferation of natural numbers can be derived from the properties of empty or null set, Ø (the Danish and Norwegian alphabet[156]). Empty set has no members or elements. It can be identified as number 0 because the size or the cardinality of empty set is 0 or nothing. The empty set is not the same thing as *nothing* but it is a set with nothing *inside* it and a set is always full or empty of *something*.The natural number 1 can be defined as the set containing 0 elements {0} that contains the empty set as a member {Ø}. The cardinality of the set is 1 because it contains an element 0 or Ø. By the definition of subset, the empty set is a subset of any set. The number 2 be understood as the set, {0, 1}, with two elements of the empty set {Ø, { Ø}}. The number 3 can be defined as the set {0, 1, 2} which has three elements of empty set {Ø, {Ø}, {Ø, {Ø}}. Similarly, the number N can be defined as the set containing 0 and all the numbers smaller than N. So N = {0, 1, 2 ...N-1} is a set with N members. With the empty set {Ø}, each of the numbers in this set N can be replaced by its definition in terms of nested sets. In this way with empty set the natural numbers can be explained as sets.

Zero as the counting number does not have objects. It is only digit which cannot stand alone though 000000 stands for A in six-bit printer code.[157] 0 is a dependent number though its factorization is 1, 0! = 1, because the number of permutations of 0 elements is 1. As $4! = 4 \times 3 \times 2 \times 1 = 24$ or we can turn around (24 = 4!) the permutations and get the 0!

$$4! = 24 \text{ or } 4 \times 3! = 4!$$

$$3! = \frac{4!}{4} \text{ or } \frac{4x3x2x1}{4} = 6$$

$$3! = 6 \text{ or } 3 \times 2! = 3!$$

$$2! = \frac{3!}{3} \text{ or } \frac{3x2x1}{3} = 2$$

$$2! = 2 \text{ or } 2 \times 1! = 2!$$

$$1! = \frac{2!}{2} \text{ or } \frac{2x1}{2} = 1$$

$$1! = 1 \text{ or } 1 \times 0! = 1!$$

$$0! = \frac{1!}{1} \text{ or } \frac{1x1}{1} = 1$$

$$0! = 1$$

The most common mathematical fallacy is the proof that 1 = 2 as follows.

Let $a = b$, then $ab = a^2$ (1)
$ab - b^2 = a^2 - b^2$ (2) $b^2$ is subtracted
$b(a - b) = (a - b)(a + b)$ (3)
$b = a + b$ (4) $a - b$ is cancelled
$b = 2b$ (5) because $a = b$ So1 = 2 (6)

The incorrect step is (4), in which division by 0 ($a - b = 0$) is performed, which is not permissible in algebraic operations. Another common fallacy is that any number divided by 0 is ∞. Infinity (∞) is not a number because it does not follow the properties of numbers. It refers to something without any limit or boundary. It is opposite of finite, so whoever uses infinite must first give an indication for what is finite.An infinite number is a number greater than any real number.

Zero is known from its applications in mathematics. 0 as a concept and number has its own implications too such as no number can be divided by 0. Let us see its epistemological and hermeneutical implications.

### 1.3.4.2 Epistemological and Hermeneutical Approach to Zero

$0 + 0 = 0$ and $x \pm 0 = x$. Any number plus or minus 0 equals itself. So 0 is called the identity for addition. Zero is both a number and a numeral. The numeral or digit 0 is used in positional number systems, where the position of a digit signifies its value, with successive positions having higher values, and the digit 0 is used to skip a position. $3–3 = 0$, $0^1 = 0$, $0 \times 0 = 0$ or $0^2 = 0$, $1 \times 0 = 0$, $0! = 1$, $10^0 = 1$, $0/99 = 0$, $(a + b)^0 = 1$, $\log_a 1 = 0$, and $0/0$, $0^0$ or $10/0$ is undefined. Let us look at the nature of division...

$a/b = c$ means that $b \times c = a$

If we substitute with some numbers:

$12/3 = 4$ means that $3 \times 4 = 12$

Now we try the same thing involving zero...

$a/0 = c$ means that $0 \times c = a$

If we substitute with some numbers again:

$7/0 = c$ means that $0 \times c = 7$

What number multiplied with 0 gives 7? No number can give. So division by 0 is undefined.

$Ø = 0$, $0^0 = 180^0$ or $360^0$, $0 < 1$, $0 > -1$, $|0| = 0$, etc. Who made them so? It is our mind which investigates things. Our mind or intellect analyses and synthesizes by induction or deduction to reach a certain assumption. The assumptions become fundamental concepts or principles. They become universals. The greatest discovery of thought is *abstract objects*. Mathematical objects like sets, numbers, properties and relations are abstract ideas which are *universal*. Ideas are psychological entities while thoughts are contents of ideas which we express in sentences. A fundamental key for mathematical thinking is deductive reasoning. In deduction, a given statement has to be proven, often called conjecture or a theorem in mathematics. Valid deductive steps are followed; a proof may or may not be established. In contrast to deduction, in inductive reasoning, each case is worked on and a conjecture, theorem, hypothesis or formula is developed for generalization. They are formulated in terms of $n$, where $n$ is a positive integer. Each such statement is assumed as P (n) associated with positive integer n, for which the correctness for the case $n = 1$ is examined. Then assuming the truth of P (k) for some positive integer $k$, the truth of P (k+1) is established.

To prove such statements the well-suited and used-based principle is needed which is known as the principle of mathematical induction. Mathematical induction is a way of proving math statements for all integers. The concept of number is a fundamental one in mathematics. There are real, positive, negative, rational, irrational, transcendental and complex numbers besides 0. *The zero is defined as numerical function of nothingness that is used neither for an evasion but for an apprehension of reality.* 0 is a mathematical tool for dealing with reality. Mathematics depends on abstractions from the very nature of things. The '1' is defined as undivided in itself and divided from everything else. We have the words like single, common, particular and unique which signify *one*. *Unity* is a transcendental property of being and implies a certain inter-connectedness within and separation from others.[158] The reality of unity or *oneness* is of the same nature as the *transcendental being*. Being, reality or existence has common traits as *one, true, good, beautiful, active* and have *duration* in spacetime continuum. Thus, numbers are *transcendental beings* and exist in their own way. So we come to know the numbers from the things. Numbers are not in things, we put them into things. As our mind abstracts numbers from things so in the same way in reverse operation we apply numbers or quantity to them.[159] It is we, human beings, give meaning to the realities. We measure and quantify the world. We calculate, compare, manipulate and predict to manage the world.

There are *three* main schools of thought – *realism*, *nominalism* and *logicism* – arose to account for and resolve the crisis in the foundations of mathematics. I have put two schools together as one; realism as Platonism and realism, nominalism as structuralism and nominalism, and logicism as logicism and intuitionism. Let us see these schools as they have stood for realists, nominalists and logicists.

### 1.3.4.3 Platonism and Realism

Platonism and realism means the doctrine according to which the variables of true mathematical propositions denote objects with an autonomous identity, in the sense that their existence is independent of the cognitive subject. The notion of mathematical proof as the first firm foundation of mathematical understanding was laid by Greek philosophers, Thales (625-547 BCE) of Miletus and Pythagoras of Samos (570-490 BCE). The mathematical proof is an impeccable argument, using only the methods of pure logical reasoning, which enables one to infer the validity of a given mathematical assertion from the pre-established validity of other mathematical assertions, or from some particular primitive assertions – the axioms – whose validity is taken to be self-evident.[160] Plato (429-347 BCE) made it clear that mathematical propositions – the things that could be regarded as unassailably true – referred not to actual physical objects (like squares, angles, circles, spheres, and cubes that might be constructed from marks in the sand, or from wood or stone) but to certain idealized entities.[161] Mathematical Platonism believes mathematical entities exist as abstract entities though they lack causal power and spatio-temporal location. The abstract entities are non-spatio-temporal, eternal either as omnitemporal or atemporal, changeless and necessary existents.

Mathematical entities like numbers, sets, functions and limits, etc. exist objectively independent of our thoughts, concepts and language. Abstract simply means outside space and time, not concrete, not physical. In Mathematics, the term 'there exists' is used to negate a generalization using 'all.' 'There exists' corresponds to 'there is' in English. 'There exists *a* ...' means 'there exists at least one ....' The singular form in Mathematics does not exclude the plural, and the plural does not exclude the singular. In Mathematics that usage of 'some' is acceptable. The use of 'there exists' is slightly preferable. *There exists* an infinite number of prime numbers. The mathematical objects or structures would have the features that they in fact have even if there were no rational activities. Then how do we know them? Platonic mathematical world neither have spatial location nor extension of time yet Benoit Mandelbrot's (1924-2010) set as R. Brooks and J. P. Matelski in 1931 saw, had been in existence before its discovery.[162] We know the existence of things and the nature of concrete objects causally interact with each other indirectly like the butterfly effects. But mathematical numbers do not have causal effects. The external world, the past and future, other minds, mathematical objects, possibilities, universals, and moral or aesthetic properties are found in the world. They can be in three forms of existence – the physical, the mental and the Platonic mathematical – as entities belonging to three separate worlds. These are three mysteries affecting each other from mathematical principles to physical and mental world. Everything in the physical world is governed by mathematical principles.[163]

The Three Worlds and Three Mysteries are embellished with Platonic absolutes of Beauty, Morality and Truth which are to be found in mathematics. Beauty and Truth are intertwined, the beauty of a physical theory acting as a guide to its correctness in relation to the Physical World, whereas the whole issue of Morality is ultimately dependent upon the World of Mentality.[164] Indispensability argument states that mathematics is indispensable to all empirical sciences, and if we want to believe in the reality of the phenomena described by the sciences, we ought also believe in the reality of those entities required for this description. So Quine-Putnam indispensability refers to mathematical entities such as sets, numbers, functions and such is indispensable to our best scientific theories, and so we ought to be committed to the existence of these mathematical entities.[165] We ought to have ontological commitment to all and only the entities that are indispensable to our best scientific theories. Mathematical entities are indispensable to our best scientific theories. We ought to have ontological commitment to mathematical entities. Our thoughts, ideas, all the processes of logic which organize, interpret and abstract observations, are physical phenomena which take place in real time and physical space: namely, in the brains of human beings. Abstract objects, such as mathematical objects, are ideas, which in turn exist as electrical and chemical states of the billions of neurons in the human brain. In this way mathematical conceptions form representations which extrapolate from certain regions of our experience and intuition.[166] There is no such thing as a circle in the physical world. What is important is this: As the geometry of any physical object more closely approximates a true circle, the ratio of its circumference to its diameter more closely approximates is $\pi$.[167] The numerical constant number ($\pi$) is the most important and intriguing number in all of mathematics.

Everything about a mathematical proposition is independent of what appears to be the physical world. It all takes place in the mind. And the mind operates on *infallible principles* of deductive logic. It is not influenced by exterior inputs from the physical world, distorted by having to pass through the tentative, contingent Universe of the senses. "How the physical process brings about the belief is a very great mystery. It is just as great a mystery as how mathematical entities bring about mathematical beliefs."[168] Mind reconciles the contradiction between our belief in the certainty of abstract deductions and the empiricist principle that knowledge comes from observation of individual instances. Indeed, the very principles of logical deduction are true because we observe that using them leads to true conclusions. Aristotle's logic is replaced by symbolic logic of George Boole (1815-1864). The intuitionist school led by Dutch mathematician J. E. J. Brouwer (1881-1966) does not accept 'law of the excluded middle' in dealing with infinite sets. As a result indirect proofs including proofs by *reduction ad absurdum* of many well-known theorems in mathematics are rejected by the intuitionists who insist on 'constructive proofs.'[169] Mathematical representations are simply a language that describes one aspect of the reality we perceive. Platonism or realism takes mathematical entities to be real, independent objects of study about which discoveries can be made. It holds that mathematical notions are transcendent Ideals or Forms, independent of human consciousness. The slogan is 'to be is to be the value of a variable.'[170]

There are *three* non-platonistic accounts of mathematics like *logicism, formalism* and *intuitionism*. Logicists like Bertrand Russell and Whitehead reduce mathematics to logic. Basic principles of mathematical theories were articulated and logic was uncovered by Dedekind, Peano and Frege. If mathematics is a part of logic, then mathematical objects are reduced to logical objects. But what are the objects of logical concepts? The programme failed over the need to admit *sets as entities* subject to their own particular axioms, whose logical status was not at all obvious. For *formalists* like David Hilbert, mathematics manipulates the configurations of symbols according to prescribed rules independent of any physical interpretation of the symbols. The terms are mere symbols and the statements are formulas involving these symbols; the ultimate base of mathematics does not lie in logic but only in a collection of prelogical marks or symbols and in a set of operations with these marks. The material axiomatic of Euclid has extended to the formal axiomatic. In formalism (deductivism) if you assign meaning to the strings in such a way that the rules of the game become true (i.e., true statements are assigned to the axioms and the rules of inference are truth-preserving), then you have to accept the theorem, or, rather, the interpretation you have given it must be a true statement. The formalism was developed by David Hilbert to meet the crisis caused by the paradoxes of set theory and the challenge to classical mathematics caused by intuitionistic criticism. According to intuitionism, mathematics is something directly apprehended and capable of being constructed, an activity of construction as L.E.J. Brouwer proposes. Numbers, proofs and theorem are all mental *constructions*. Only a finite number of objects are constructed while actual infinities and the law of the excluded middleare rejected. In intuitionism, there are no proofs by contradiction, the terms like 'explicit construction' are not clearly defined, and that has led to criticisms. We ourselves construct what we talk about is known as *constructivism*. In this view, mathematics is an exercise of the human intuition, not a game played with meaningless symbols. Instead, it is about entities that we can create directly through mental activity. In addition, some adherents of these schools reject non-constructive proofs, such as a proof by contradiction. So realism and constructivism have emerged as the main contrasting ideologies.

Platonic realists see mathematical entities as real, abstract, structured and independent of all rational activities while constructivists or structuralists see them as human made constructed nominal things.

### 1.3.4.4 Structuralism and Nominalism

Mathematics is the science of structure. The study of mathematical structures (objects) and the ontology of these structures are known as structuralism. Geometry becomes the study of freestanding structures while arithmetic is the natural-number structure. Arithmetic is exemplified by the von Neumann finite ordinals, the Zermelo numerals, the Arabic numerals, etc. Natural numbers are the places of natural-number structure. Natural number-structure is our first infinite pattern. We get real numbers by considering sets of natural numbers. Peano axioms characterize the natural-number structure. Structures are prior to places. There are several ontological views on structures. Paul Benacerraf's dilemma is how we come to know mathematical objects if we do not stand in causal relation to them. Swiss linguist Ferdinand de Saussure (1857-1913) believed that there are subconscious structures in our language. French anthropologist Claude Levi-Strauss (1908-2009) took that notion and argued that there are also subconscious structures in our behaviour. Mathematics, like cultures and languages, can be viewed as systems of signs and analysed in terms of the structural relations among their elements. Central to structuralism is the notion that binary oppositions (e.g., male/female, public/private, cooked/raw, positive/negative, finite/infinite, left/right, night/

day, being/nothingness, hot/cold, magic/science, etc.) reveal the unconscious logic or 'grammar' of a system.

Philosophers postulate mathematical entities as either abstract objects or universals. *Nominalism* denies the existence of abstract objects or universals. It denies all objectivity, whether actual or potential. Abstract objects are that of non-spatiotemporal and causally inert objects. How much does the empty set or the real number 11 weigh? Asking this question is a category mistake because they do not constitute the spatio-temporal realm. Games and languages are supposedly abstract and yet they are temporal entities in our daily lives. Realists think that properties (e.g. whiteness), relations (e.g. between-ness), and kinds (e.g. gold) are universals. Nominalism is opposed to the philosophical idealism of Plato and to the moderate realism of Aristotle and Saint Thomas Aquinas (1225-1274). The defence of nominalism undertaken by the 14th century English Scholastic philosopher William of Ockham prepared the way for various modern nominalistic theories such as those of instrumentalism, pragmatism, semantics, and logical positivism.

Structures are prior to the names or things which we apprehend and name them. Natural structures are found in the physical objects which are based on the logical principles. Mental structures are found in human minds too. Let us see how logicists look at mathematics.

### 1.3.4.5 Logicism and Intuitionism

Mathematics is known by reason rather than sense experience is known as logicism. Where the mathematical exactness does exist? The intuitionist says: in the human intellect, the formalist says: on paper. Formalists view that mathematical statements are regarded as meaningless marks. Logicists sought to show that knowledge of mathematical truth is as certain as our knowledge of logical truth. The Logicists want to define mathematics in the language of logic. The intuitionists want to define logic in the language of mathematics.

The propositions of pure mathematics can be derived from the propositions of logic. Logic deals with the relationship between ideas and judgments as these are formed by our minds. The mathematical concepts are to be formulated in terms of logical concepts, and all theorems of mathematics are to be developed as theorems of logic. Logicism is the thesis that mathematics is reducible to logic. It is a part of logic to reason validly. It claims that the theorems of mathematics are logically necessary or analytic. The truths of mathematics are the same in all possible worlds. The proponents of the conception of a reduction of mathematics to logic are Gottlob Frege, Alfred North Whitehead (1861-1947) and Bertrand Russell (1872-1970) who trace back to Leibniz. Leibniz distinguishes truth from reason and truth from facts. Mathematical and logical truths are forms of truth from reason which are based on principle of non-contradiction. A truth from reason is a predicative proposition in the normal form: A is included in B or C in which A is the subject, B or C is the predicate and 'is included in' is the copula. The identical propositions are tautologies like the law of double negation or the principle of contradiction. Frege replaced Leibniz's identical proposition to his analytical proposition. So arithmetic depends on the fact that the laws of logic and the rules of inference are not given as evidence but have to be previously specified. $(\exists P)(x)(\sim P(x))$ means there is a P such that for all x, x does not have P or there is an empty property/set. In his last years, Frege came to the conclusion that such assertions of existence were not part of logic at all and repudiated logicism which he had himself founded.[171]

Intuitionism was founded by L. E. J. Brouwer (1881-1966) at the University of Amsterdam in 1907. It proposes that mathematical objects are constructed to carry out one's own constructions in one's own mind. This type of construction involves what Kant called 'intuition,' hence the name 'intuitionism.' We attach meaning to a mathematical term with a private mental object to which only we have access. Mathematical reality guarantees that it has one of these two truth-values either true or false. There might be no proof and no counter-example, in which case there is nothing to give the conjecture a truth-value. The principle of bivalence believes that every proposition is determinately true or false. It is based on the belief that truth can transcend evidence. The dispute between Platonists (realists about numbers), and intuitionists (anti-realists about numbers), the realist affirms the principle of bivalence and that truth may transcend evidence, and the anti-realist denies these two principles. The realist considers certain inferences to be valid which the intuitionist considers to be invalid. A implies B then not-A implies B according to the law of excluded middle but intuitionists have to prove either A or not-A too.

## Conclusion

Mathematical zero, nothingness or an absence of quantity, null quantity or cardinality is an empty set, {} or Ø represents numerically as 0. Probably, zero was discovered almost as soon as numbers were discovered. What took thousands of years was to invent a special symbol for the number zero (0), and then to incorporate it into a decimal system of numeration or any other numeration. Zero numeral indicates *no* quantity, size, or magnitude. It is a number and placeholder in decimal numeration. In decimal place value notation, the places are the exponents of the base 10. 0 as number is a word or symbol or numeral which represents an amount or quantity of 'nothing'or 'no' entity. 0 as a numeral is 'nothing' or 'no' entity yet represents the lowest value of non-negative numbers. Well, zero is not just another number but a different type of an operator. With the availability of zero, mathematicians were finally able to develop our present method of writing whole numbers. The path that leads to the discovery of '0' lies in the most advanced type of number system, which is called 'positional' because the value of a character depends on its position. The positional concept has emerged in only four places: in Babylon; in Egypt; among the Mayan astronomer-priests and Indians. 0 is a mathematical concept and numeral symbol indicating nothing, *no* magnitude, the *absence* of elements in a null set or *absence* of objects. The concept of zero represents 'something' that is '*not there*,' while zero as a number represents the lowest of all non-negative numbers.[172] Zero is a symbol for 'not there' which is different from 'nothing' or *no* entity. 'Not there' or 'absence' reflects that the number or item(s) exists but they are not just available. It is just an empty placeholder. 'Nothing' reflects nonexistence.[173] 0 is a number and numerical digit to represent a number in numerals. So 0 is not mere nothingness. Mathematical 0 is a placeholder of a digit as well as a number.It is called 'null,' 'nil,' 'naught,' 'zip,' and 'shit', '*śūnya*' or 'nothing.' It also becomes the power of 10 with digit 1 in the decimal system ($10^0$, $10^1$, $10^2$, ...) from right to left. The real discovery of *0* is that that the '*symbol for nothing*' that we are using is not just a placeholder, but an actual number: that '*empty*' and '*nothing*' are one. The null number is as real as '9.' When we calculate any value that is less than 1(it means 0 and lesser) and greater than nine (10 and greater) we need a symbol to represent the 'invisible', the *empty placeholder*. So, what better represents the 'invisible?' It is the *concept of nothing*, which is the *numerical zero*. As a number alone, 0 is the neutral ground, the starting point, or the centre of a point. 0 shows the paradox of empty place-holder and filler of the empty and invisible digits. $0^{th}$ year is the starting point interval for both 1CE and 1BCE for chronological time and 0° prime meridian is the starting point for measuring our space, the earth. The binary position has only two digits; 0 and 1. Zero is the hero for the number line, a mediator of numerical conflicts. It is the starting point. In a line graph, zero is the point in which the x-axis, y-axis and z-axis intersect with each other. It is the relative zero. It is the centre of the positive and negative points of different scales. 0 is the cardinality of the empty set. 0 stands for *nothing* but cannot stand without other numerals for its bigger values. Conceptuality is subjective while realization is objective. Most conceptuality is metaphysical; while reality is mostly physical though some part is transcendental or metaphysical. The great concepts of mathematics are number, length, area, volume, shape, dimension, rate of change, randomness, computation and computability, symmetry, motion, force, energy, curvature, space, continuity, infinity, axioms, sets and deduction. The nature of thought, language, and the cosmos are very much interconnected in mathematics.

How many types of zeros are found in mathematics? There are infinitely many zeros corresponding to infinitely many systems of the natural numbers.[174] Integer zero is not the same as fraction zero (0/1), rational zero is different from real zero. We have a hierarchy of zeros: natural, integral, rational and real.[175] They are the zero of the natural numbers, the zero of the integers, the zero of the rationals and the zero of the real numbers. Mathematical 0, a number which indicates nothing is known as commonsense or quantitative 0 or the natural number zero which is not the successor of any number. In the measurement of any plane line or temperature scale we choose an origin. This origin is called the zero of the scale which is known as relative 0. Fractional zero, any number divided by 0 or 0/0 is a nonsensical operation, therefore humans created a law to say that it is more-or-less 'not allowed' to divide by 0. Any number times 0 equals zero. So the answer to 0/0 could be any number. We call the answer 'undefined' because we cannot define an answer that would work. Strictly speaking, it is allowed, but we just do not get a useful answer when we do. Any number divided by itself equals 1. That would make 0/0 = 1, which is clearly impossible. There is *nothing* to begin with, so we can not end up with something. It is called *indeterminate*. One may ask when and how 0/0 became equal to 1. Since the right-side limit of x as x approaches positive-zero is one, but its left-side limit does not exists, therefore, one concludes that 0/0 is undefined.

Mathematics is an adventure into how things work and how humans describe reality with symbols, abstraction, generalisation, formalisation, proof, solution, etc. A *concept* and *symbol* that connotes *nullity* represents a qualitative advancement of the human capacity of *abstraction*. Being and non-being are two abstractions. An abstraction is a distinctive mental process in which new ideas or conceptions are formed by considering several objects or ideas and omitting the features that distinguish them. An object is abstract if it is the referent of an abstract idea. *Being* is fundamental and *no-being* is *negation* of being. An absolute negation is *nothing*, it is non-being. Zero is a numerical being which is abstracted and quantified as nothing. Today's zero, an empty set, an integer, a positional empty placeholder, a mathematical *nothing*, a symbol of physical vacuum, and an absolute 0 as a symbol of absolute equilibrium and religious self-emptying cannot be separated from science and religion. A meaningful symbol presupposes its existence. Zero as the symbol and number is the basic value of a quantity or quality in an integral part of the reality and of human life.

Zero has become the origin of all numerically. Natural numbers are counted to be infinite but they are imaginary. There could be *three* types of infinites; *potential*, *actual* and *theological.* The potential infinite is an extension of the finite, constructible from the finite by some rule or process that is never in fact completed. The actual infinite, on the other hand, is conceived as an actually existing collection of an infinite number of parts. Theological infinity is different from mathematical what Descartes and Leibniz call as absolute infinite. "God created human beings with an intellect that is innately equipped to grasp mathematical principles and to recognize them as true beyond all doubt."[176]

The invention of the mathematical zero became the turning point in the development of culture and civilization - without which the progress of modern science, industry and commerce was inconceivable. 0 has become an integral part of modern electronic computers, gadgets and machines. With the extension of the number system to negative as well as positive numbers, zero has become a starting position on the scale of integers between –1 and +1. It is used in this sense as 0°Celsius and –32° Fahrenheit temperature scales. 'Absolute zero' or 0 K is a term used by Physicists and chemists to indicate the theoretically lowest possible temperature. Scientifically, *absolute zero* is the lowest possible temperature at which matter can exist; a substance which has no thermal (heat) energy, no external force at constant pressure would shrink to *zero volume* (the amount of space occupied by a three-dimensional object). Absolute zero is equivalent to 0 K, –459.67°F, or –273.15°C. The zero is defined as numerical function of nothingness that is used neither for an evasion but for an apprehension of reality.

Something coming from nothing requires at least *three* kinds of realities which require a cause for their existence: 1) realities that have a beginning; 2) realities which are dependent for their existence on something else; and 3) realities that are conditioned by time. Realities which have a beginning, say, our Universe, has a beginning, then that beginning point represents the point at which the Universe came into existence with time. Prior to that point the physical Universe did not exist – in other words, it was nothing – absolute nothing. Mathematically it is 0. Cosmologically, here, something is coming from nothing. If the Universe was truly nothing, and if from nothing only nothing can come, then the Universe needs something beyond itself to cause (transcendent cause or Creator) it to exist – to bring it from nothing to something. There must be at least one being – and only one being (i.e. God) – that does not have a beginning, is not dependent on anything for its existence, and is not conditioned by time. All the realities which are nothing without the other realities, then they are nothing. Zero added to itself an infinite number of times is zero. If we do not have at least one 'reality which is NOT nothing prior to a beginning' (like God), then we have no reality at all. 'Why does the Universe have a cause?' or 'why do we have to explain how the Universe came from nothing to something?' is because there is an increasing amount of evidence from physics, the philosophy of mathematics, and metaphysics that imply and even require that the Universe has a Beginning. Zero is the sign of any reality which begins to have a beginning. As we express mutual relationship between zero as the symbol and nothingness as symbolised, we seek to express the fullness of 'symbol power' through this 'symbolic pregnance' which indicates the perceptive experience (the visible world) as sensual experience grasps at the same time a non-descriptive (the invisible world) significance of the symbolised, nothingness.[177]

When we move from mathematics to cosmology we are passing from nothingness to empty space, from conceptual nothingness to physical point reality. "We know that science as practised involves an organised process of observation, experiment, resource to prior theory, reliance on various metaphysical principles and so on, exploited via reason and argument to propose hypotheses, evaluate their promise for further progress, debate their adequacy, accept them as true or false."[178] Mathematical 0 helps us to understand nothingness (quantum 0) in Quantum Mechanics and Big Bang Theory (relativistic 0) which I would be dealing on the following chapter.

## Endnotes

1. Doctor Peterson, "Difference between Math and Arithmetic," in *The Math Forum @ Drexel. The MathForum. Ask Dr. Math,* accessed January 20, 2011, http://mathforum.org/library/drmath/view/52282.html.
2. Richard Courant and Herbert Robbins, *What is Mathematics?* 5th Printing (London: Oxford University Press, 1951), xv.
3. Jan Gullberg, *Mathematics: From the Birth of Numbers* (New York: W. W. Norton & Company, 1997), 26.
4. John D. Barrow, *The Book of Nothing* (London: Vintage, 2001), 20.
5. *Ibid.*, 35.
6. Robert Kaplan, *The Nothing that Is: The Natural History of Zero* (Oxford: Oxford University Press, 2000), 43.
7. Gevin Giorbran, "When Zero Equals Infinity (God's Math)," in *Everything Forever: Learning to See the Timelessness,* accessed January 1, 2011, http://everythingforever.com/st_math.html.
8. Gullberg, *Mathematics: From the Birth of Numbers*, 72.
9. Brendan S. Gillon, "Negative Facts and Knowledge of Negative Facts," in *Indian Philosophy: A Collection of Readings*, ed. Roy W. Perrett (New York: Garland Publishing, 2000), 83.
10. John Bigelow and Sam Butchart, "Number," in *Encyclopedia of Philosophy*, Vol. 6, 2nd ed., ed. Donald M. Borchert (Detroit: Thomas Gale, 2006), 670.
11. John Francis, *Philosophy of Mathematics* (New Delhi: Global Vision Publishing House, 2008), 1.
12. Thomas Foregger, "Set," in *PlanetMath.Org,* accessed January 2, 2011, http://planetmath.org/encyclopedia/ProperSubset2.html.
13. Akihiro Kanamori, "Set Theory," in *Encyclopedia of Philosophy*, Vol. 8, 2nd ed., ed. Donald M. Borchert (Detroit: Thomas Gale, 2006), 832.

14. R. H. Bingh, "Set Theory," in *McGraw-Hill Encyclopedia of Science and Technology*, 20 Vols., Vol. 16, 9th ed. (New York: McGraw Hill, 2002), 324.
15. Carl B. Boyer, "Mathematical Symbols," in *Microsoft Encarta Online Encyclopedia,* accessed January 3, 2011, http://encarta.msn.com/encyclopedia_761577100/Mathematical_Symbols.html.
16. Steward Shapiro, *Philosophy of Mathematics: Structure and Ontology* (Oxford: Oxford University Press, 1997), 5.
17. Roger Penrose, *The Road to Reality: A Complete guide to the Law of the Universe* (London: Jonathan Cape, 2004), 65.
18. Robert R. Stoll, "Set Theory," in *The New Encyclopedia Britannica*, 32 Vols., Vol. 27, 15th ed. (Chicago: Encyclopaedia Britannica, 1997), 226.
19. Gullberg. *Mathematics: From the Birth of Numbers*, 458.
20. Boyer, "Mathematical Symbols," in *Microsoft Encarta Online Encyclopedia,* accessed January 3, 2011, http://encarta. msn. com/ encyclopedia_761577100/Mathematical_Symbols.html.
21. *Ibid.*
22. Gullberg, *Mathematics: From the Birth of Numbers,* 365.
23. Boyer, "Mathematical Symbols." in *Microsoft Encarta Online Encyclopedia.*
24. Priyedarshi Jetli, "Zero," in *ACPI Encyclopedia of Philosophy*, 2 Vols., Vol. 2, ed. Johnson Puthenpurackal (Bangalore: Asian Trading Corporation, 2010), 1542-1543.
25. Gullberg, *Mathematics: From the Birth of Numbers,* 5.
26. Cyril Desbruslais, *The Philosophy of Be-ing: Introduction to a Metaphysics for Today*, ed., Kuruvilla Pandikattu (Pune: Jnana-Deepa Vidyapeeth, 1997), 48.
27. Gullberg, *Mathematics: From the Birth of Numbers*, 48.
28. J. B. Freeman, *The Number Concept* (Bangalore: St Joseph's College, n. d.), 5.
29. Gullberg, *Mathematics: From the Birth of Numbers,* 73.
30. *Ibid.,* 77.
31. *Ibid.,* 82.
32. *Ibid.,* 83.
33. *Ibid.,* 30.
34. Hossein Arsham, "Zero in Four Dimensions: Historical, Psychological, Cultural, and Logical Perspectives," accessed January 13, 2011, http://www.pantaneto.co.uk/issue5/arsham.htm.
35. Gullberg, *Mathematics: From the Birth of Numbers,* 30.

36. Freeman, *The Number Concept*, 5.
37. Ernest Zebrowski, *A History of the Circle: Mathematical Reasoning and the Physical Universe* (London: Free Association Books, 1999), 124.
38. *Ibid.*
39. *Ibid.*, 126.
40. *Ibid.*, 128 and 139.
41. Richard P. Feynman, *Six Easy Pieces: Essentials of Physics Explained by Its Most Brilliant Teacher*, originally prepared for publication by Robert B. Leighton and Matthew Sands (New York: Addison-Wesley Publishing Co., 1995), 27.
42. Aristotle, *Physics* IV c.11, tras. Richard Hope (London: University of Nebraska Press, 1961), 80.
43. Paul Davies, introduction to *Six Easy Pieces: Essentials of Physics Explained by Its Most Brilliant Teacher* by Richard P. Feynman; originally prepared for publication by Robert B. Leighton and Matthew Sands (New York: Addison-Wesley Publishing Co., 1995), xiv.
44. Charles Seife, *Zero: The Biography of a Dangerous Idea* (New York: Penguin Putnam, 2000), 54.
45. *Ibid.*, 55.
46. *Ibid.*, 55-56.
47. Kaplan, *The Nothing that Is: A Natural History of Zero*, 103.
48. "Sidereal Time," in *Wikipedia: The Free Encyclopedia*, accessed October 13, 2011, http://en.wikipedia.org/wiki/Sidereal_time.
49. From a Christian perspective, God's creation is ordered as king Solomon says: "You have *arranged all things* by measure and number and weight" (Wis 11, 20). See *Catechism of the Catholic Church (CCC)* {1994; 8th reprint, New Delhi: Theological Publications in India, 2006}, 62. "With creation, God does not abandon his creatures to themselves. He not only gives them being and existence, but also, and at every moment, upholds and sustains them in being, enables them to act and brings them to their final end" (CCC 301).
50. Gullberg, *Mathematics: From the Birth of Numbers,* 376.
51. *Ibid.*, 491.
52. *Ibid.*, 376.
53. *Ibid.*, 157.

54. John Tabak, *Geometry: The Language of Space and Form*, The History of Mathematics Series, 5 Vols., Vol. 2 (New Delhi: Viva Books Private Ltd., 2006), xv.
55. Freeman, *The Number Concept*, 11.
56. Adam Drozdek, "Number and Infinity: Thomas and Cantor," *International Philosophical Quarterly* 39, 153 (March 1999), 35.
57. Barrow, *The Book of Nothing,* 10.
58. *Ibid.,* 178.
59. Cameron McLeman, "Zermelo-Fraenkel Axioms," accessed January 4, 2011, http://planetmath.org/encyclopedia/ZermeloFraenkelAxioms.html.
60. Eric W. Weisstein, "Axiom of Foundation," in *Wolfram MathWorld*, accessed February 12, 2011, http://mathworld.wolfram.com/AxiomofFoundation.html.
61. Eric W. Weisstein, "Axiom of Choice," in *Wolfram MathWorld*, accessed February 12, 2011, http://mathworld.wolfram.com/AxiomofChoice.html.
62. Edward B. Burger, "Zero to Infinity," in *Teaching Company,* accessed January 6, 2011, /See http://www.teach12.com/ttcx/coursedesclong2.aspx?cid=1499&pc=Science%20and%20Mathematics.
63. Bertrand Russell, *Introduction to Mathematical Philosophy* (1919; reprint, London: George Allen and Unwin, 1930), 5.
64. *Ibid.,* 5-6.
65. *Ibid.,* 23.
66. Georges Ifrah, *The Universal History of Numbers II: The Modern Number System*, trans. David Bellos and others (New Delhi: Penguin Books, 2005), 130.
67. R. C. Gupta, "Spread and Triumph of Indian Numerals," *Indian Journal of History of Science* 18, 1 (1983): 23.
68. Gullberg, *Mathematics: From the Birth of Numbers,* 5.
69. Gullberg, *Mathematics: From the Birth of Numbers,* 77.
70. Gullberg, *Mathematics: From the Birth of Numbers,* 87.
71. Penrose, *The Road to Reality: A Complete guide to the Law of the Universe,* 81.
72. Boyer, "Mathematical Symbols," in *Microsoft Encarta Online Encyclopedia.*
73. John Tabak, *Numbers: Computers, Philosophers and the Search for Meaning*, 5 Vols., Vol. 4 (New Delhi: Viva Books Private Limited, 2006), xii.

74. R. Courant and H. Robbins, *What Is Mathematics? An Elementary Approach to Ideas and Methods*, 2nd ed. (Oxford: Oxford University Press, 1996), 77, accessed January 9, 2011, http://mathworld.wolfram.com/InfiniteSet.html.
75. Zebrowski, *A History of the Circle: Mathematical Reasoning and the Physical Universe*, 104.
76. J. N. Kapur, "Fourth and Higher Dimensions," *Science Today* 4, 10 (April 1970): 18.
77. Zebrowski, *A History of the Circle: Mathematical Reasoning and the Physical Universe*, 48.
78. Freeman, *The Number Concept*, 5.
79. Gullberg, *Mathematics: From the Birth of Numbers, 2*8.
80. Gullberg, *Mathematics: From the Birth of Numbers,* 409.
81. *Ibid.,* 410.
82. Russ Rowlett, "The International System of Units (SI)" in *How Many? A Dictionary of Units of Measurement*," accessed January 10, 2011, http://www.unc.edu/~rowlett/units/sipm.html.
83. Barry N. Taylor and Peter J. Mohr, "Unit of Length (Metre)," in *The NIST (National Institute of Standards and Technology) Reference on Constants, Units, and Uncertainty: International System of Units (SI)*, accessed November 11, 2011, http://physics.nist.gov/cuu/U nits/meter.html.
84. Barry N. Taylor and Peter J. Mohr, "Unit of Mass (Kilogram)," in *The NIST (National Institute of Standards and Technology) Reference on Constants, Units, and Uncertainty: International System of Units (SI)*, accessed November 11, 2011, http://physics.nist.gov/cuu /Units/kilogram.html.
85. Barry N. Taylor and Peter J. Mohr, "Unit of Time (Second)," in *The NIST (National Institute of Standards and Technology) Reference on Constants, Units, and Uncertainty: International System of Units (SI)*, accessed November 11, 2011,http://physics.nis t.gov/cuu/ Units/second.html.
86. Barry N. Taylor and Peter J. Mohr, "Unit of Electric Current (Ampere)," in *The NIST (National Institute of Standards and Technology) Reference on Constants, Units, and Uncertainty: International System of Units (SI)*, accessed November 11, 2011, http://physics.nist. gov/cuu/Units/ ampere.html.
87. Barry N. Taylor and Peter J. Mohr, "Unit of Thermodynamic Temperature (Kelvin)," in *The NIST (National Institute of Standards and Technology) Reference on Constants, Units, and Uncertainty:*

*International System of Units (SI)*, accessed November 11, 2011, http://physics.nist.gov/cuu/Units/kelvin.html.

88. Barry N. Taylor and Peter J. Mohr, "Unit of Amount of Substance (Mole)," in *The NIST (National Institute of Standards and Technology) Reference on Constants, Units, and Uncertainty: International System of Units (SI)*, accessed November 11, 2011, http://physics.nist gov/cuu/Units/mole.html.
89. Barry N. Taylor and Peter J. Mohr, "Unit of Luminous Intensity (Candela)," in *The NIST (National Institute of Standards and Technology) Reference on Constants, Units, and Uncertainty: International System of Units (SI)*, accessed November 11, 2011, http://physics.nist.gov/cuu/Units/candela.html.
90. Barry N. Taylor and Peter J. Mohr, "SI Derived Units," in *The NIST (National Institute of Standards and Technology) Reference on Constants, Units, and Uncertainty: International System of Units (SI)*, accessed November 11, 2011, http://physics. nist.gov / cuu/Units/units.html.
91. "Joule," in *Wikipedia: The Free Encyclopedia*, accessed November 10, 2011, http://en.wikipedia.org/wiki/Joule.
92. "Watt," in *Wikipedia: The Free Encyclopedia*, accessed November 12, 2011, http://en.wikipedia.org/wiki/Watt.
93. *Ibid.*
94. Russ Rowlett, "Degree Celsius," in *How Many? A Dictionary of Units of Measurements*, accessed November 12, 2011, http://www.unc.edu/~rowlett/units/dictD.html#celsius.
95. Russ Rowlett, "Coulomb (C)," in *How Many? A Dictionary of Units of Measurements*, accessed November 12, 2011, http://www.unc.edu/~rowlett/units/dictC.html#coulomb.
96. "Volt," in *Wikipdedia: The Free Encyclopedia*, accessed November 12, 2011, http://en.wikipedia.org/wiki/Volt.
97. Russ Rowlett, "Farad (F)," in *How Many? A Dictionary of Units of Measurements*, accessed November 12, 2011, http://www.unc.edu/~rowlett/units/dictF.html#farad.
98. "Farad," in *Wikipdedia: The Free Encyclopedia*, accessed November 12, 2011, http://en.wikipedia.org/wiki/Farad.
99. Russ Rowlett, "Ohm (Ω)," in *How Many? A Dictionary of Units of Measurements*, accessed November 12, 2011, http://www.unc.edu/~rowlett/units/dictO.html#ohm.
100. "Ohm," in *Wikipdedia: The Free Encyclopedia*, accessed November 12, 2011, http://en.wikipedia.org/wiki/Ohm.

101. "Siemens (Unit)," in *Wikipdedia: The Free Encyclopedia*, accessed November 12, 2011, http://en.wikipedia.org/wiki/Siemens_(unit).
102. Russ Rowlett, "Weber (Wb)," in *How Many? A Dictionary of Units of Measurements*, accessed November 12, 2011, http://www.unc .edu/~rowlett/units/dictW.html#weber.
103. Russ Rowlett, "Tesla (T)," in *How Many? A Dictionary of Units of Measurements*, accessed November 12, 2011, http://www.unc.edu/~ rowlett/units/dictT.html#tesla.
104. Russ Rowlett, "Henry (H)," in *How Many? A Dictionary of Units of Measurements*, accessed November 12, 2011, http://www.unc.edu/~ rowlett/units/dictH.html#henry.
105. Russ Rowlett, "Lumen (lm)," in *How Many? A Dictionary of Units of Measurements*, accessed November 12, 2011, http://www.unc.edu/~rowlett/units/dictL.html#lumen.
106. *Ibid.*
107. Russ Rowlett, "Gray (Gy)," in *How Many? A Dictionary of Units of Measurements*, accessed November 12, 2011, http://www.unc.edu/~rowlett/units/dictG.html#gray.
108. Russ Rowlett, "What Countries Besides the U.S. Have Not Adopted the Metric System?" in *How Many? A Dictionary of Units of Measurements*, accessed November 12, 2011, http://www.unc.edu/ ~rowlett/ units/index.html.
109. 1) The nautical mile and knot, units traditionally used at sea and in meteorology; 2) The are (a), a unit of area equal to 100 square metres and hectare (ha), metric unit of land area, equal to 100 ares; 3) The bar, a pressure unit, and its commonly-used multiples such as the millibar in meteorology and the kilobar in engineering; 4) The angstrom (A), and the barn (b), units used in physics and astronomy; angstrom, a metric unit of length, equal to 0.1 nanometre or 10-10 metre; One of the pioneers of spectroscopy was the Swedish Physicist Anders Jon Ångström (1814-1874), and in his honour the wave lengths of light waves are customarily stated in angstroms. One barn is equal to 10-28 square metres.
110. Gullberg, *Mathematics: From the Birth of Numbers,* 32.
111. *Ibid.*, 34.
112. Gullberg, *Mathematics: From the Birth of Numbers,* 43.
113. K. N. Malathi, "Number down the Ages," *Science Today* 26, 4 (May 1992): 51.
114. Gullberg, *Mathematics: From the Birth of Numbers,* 48.
115. *Ibid.,* 49.

116. Milo Gardner, "Egyptian Fraction," in *PlanetMath.org*, accessed February 14, 2011, http://planetmath.org/EgyptianFraction2.html.
117. Russ Rowlett, "Digit," in *How Many? A Dictionary of Units of Measurements*, accessed November 12, 2011, http://www.unc.edu/~rowlett/units/dictD.html.
118. Russ Rowlett, "The Metric System," in *How Many? A Dictionary of Units of Measurements*, accessed November 12, 2011, http://www.unc.edu/~rowlett/units/metric.html.
119. Russ Rowlett, "CGS and MKS Units," in *How Many? A Dictionary of Units of Measurement,* accessed October 12, 2011, http://www.unc.edu/~rowlett/units/cgsmks.html.
120. Gullberg, *Mathematics: From the Birth of Numbers,* 28.
121. Russ Rowlett, "Names for Large Numbers," in *How Many? A Dictionary of Units of Measurement,* accessed October 12, 2011, http://www.unc.edu/~rowlett/units/large.html.
122. Gullberg, *Mathematics: From the Birth of Numbers,* 29.
123. "Prefixes for Binary Multiples," in *The NIST Reference on Constants, Units, and Uncertainty: International System of Units (SI)*, accessed January 21, 2011, http://physics.nist.gov/cuu/Units/binary.html.
124. *Ibid.*
125. Seife, *Zero: The Biography of a Dangerous Idea*, 9.
126. Freeman, *The Number Concept*, 1.
127. Tabak, *Numbers: Computers, Philosophers and the Search for Meaning*, xii.
128. J. J. O'Connor and E. F. Robertson, "Babylonian Numerals," accessed January 11, 2011, http://www-history.mcs.st-andrews.ac.uk/Hist Topics/Babylonian_numerals.html.
129. Seife, *Zero: The Biography of a Dangerous Idea,* 16.
130. J. J. O'Connor and E. F. Robertson, "Mayan Mathematics," accessed January 11, 2011, http://www-groups.dcs.st-and.ac.uk/~history/HistTopics/Mayan_mathematics.html.
131. *Ibid.*
132. Barrow, *The Book of Nothing,* 33.
133. *Ibid.*, 37.
134. Fjordman, "A Brief History of Zero and Indian Numerals," in *The Brussels Journal: The Voice of Conservatism in Europe*, accessed January 12, 2011, http://www.brusselsjournal.com/node/4107.
135. "Indian Numerals," in *Easycalculation.com*, accessed January 11, 2011, http://www.easycalculation.com/funny/numerals/indian.php

136. Malathi, "Number Down the Ages," *Science Today* 26, 4 (May 1992): 54.
137. *Ibid.,* 53.
138. Priyedarshi Jetli, "Zero," in *ACPI Encyclopedia of Philosophy*, 2 Vols., Vol. 2, ed. Johnson Puthenpurackal (Bangalore: Asian Trading Corporation, 2010), 1541.
139. Jayant Burde, *Śūnya and Nothingness in Science, Philosophy and Religion* (Delhi: Motilal Banarsidass Publishers, 2009), 8-9.
140. Barrow, *The Book of Nothing,* 38.
141. Nagendra Kumar Singh, "Aryabhatta," in *Encyclopedia of the Indian Biography*, Vol. 1 (New Delhi: APH Publishing Corporation, 2000), 477.
142. Georges Ifrah, *The Universal History of Numbers II: The Modern Number System*, trans. David Bellos and others (New Delhi: Penguin Books, 2005), 25.
143. Berat Jusufi, Jon-Fredrik Stryker and Vegard Larsen, "The History of Indian Numerals," accessed January 12, 2011, http://home.c2i.net/greaker/comenius/9899/indiannumerals/india.html.
144. D. P. Chattopadhyaya, *Religion, Philosophy and Science: A Sketch of Global View* (Shimla: Indian Institute of Advanced Study, 2006), 210.
145. Bertrand Russell, *The Principles of Mathematics* (London: Bradford and Dickens, 1951), 6.
146. Paul Benacerraf and Hilary Putnam, eds., Introduction to *Philosophy of Mathematics: Selected Readings,* 2nd ed., (1964; Reprint. Cambridge: Cambridge University Press, 1998), 21.
147. Russell, *The Principles of Mathematics,* 33.
148. Ian Stewart, *Nature's Numbers: Discovering Order and Pattern in the Universe* (London: Phoenix, 2001), 43-44.
149. Seife, *Zero: The Biography of a Dangerous Idea,* 57-58.
150. *Ibid.,* 58.
151. Chattopadhyaya, *Religion, Philosophy and Science: A Sketch of a Global View*, 187.
152. Frederick Suppe, "Axiomatization," in *A Companion to the Philosophy of Science*, ed. W. H. Newton-Smith (Massachusetts: Blackwell Publishers, 2001), 9.
153. Jill Le Blanc, "Infinity in Theology and Mathematics," *Religious Studies* 29 (1993), 52.
154. *Ibid.*
155. *Ibid.,* 53.

156. "Empty Set: Notation," in *Wikipedia: The Free Encylopedia*, accessed February 11, 2011, http://en.wikipedia.org/wiki/Empty_set.
157. Roy Sorensen, "Blanks: Signs of Omission," *American Philosophical Quarterly* 36, 4 (1999), 318.
158. Cyril Desbrulais, *The Philosophy of Be-ing: Introduction to a Metaphysics for Today*, ed. Kuruvilla Pandikattu (Pune: Jnana-Deepa Vidyapeeth, 1997), 48.
159. Freeman, *The Number Concept*, 5.
160. Penrose, *The Road to Reality: A Complete Guide to the Law of the Universe,* 10.
161. *Ibid.,* 11.
162. *Ibid.,* 17.
163. *Ibid.,* 18-19.
164. *Ibid.,* 1029.
165. Mark Colyvan, "Indispensability Arguments in the Philosophy of Mathematics," in *Stanford Encyclopedia of Philosophy*, accessed January 12, 2011, http://plato.stanford.edu/entries/mathphil-indis/.
166. Paul Bernays, "On Platonism in Mathematics," in *Philosophy of Mathematics: Selected Readings*, 2nd ed., eds., Paul Benacerraf and Hilary Putnam (1964; reprint, Cambridge: Cambridge University Press, 1998), 259.
167. Zebrowski, *A History of the Circle: Mathematical Reasoning and the Physical Universe*, 11-12.
168. James Robert Brown, *Philosophy of Mathematics: A Contemporary Introduction to the World of Proofs and Pictures*, 2nd ed. (New York: Routledge, 2008), 16.
169. V. S. Huzurbazar, "Proof in Mathematics," *Science Today* 2, 9 (March 1968): 37.
170. Stewart Shapiro, *Philosophy of Mathematics: Structure and Ontology* (Oxford: Oxford University Press, 1997), 4.
171. Paul Benacerraf and Hilary Putnam, eds., introduction to *Philosophy of Mathematics: Selected Readings,* 2nd ed., (1964; reprint, Cambridge: Cambridge University Press, 1998), 13-14.
172. Hossein Arsham, "Zero in Four Dimensions: Cultural, Historical, Mathematical, and Psychological Perspectives," accessed January 13, 2011, http://home.ubalt.edu/ntsbarsh/zero/ZERO.HTM.
173. *Ibid.*

174. Burde, *Śūnya and Nothingness in Science, Philosophy and Religion,* 105.
175. *Ibid.*, xviii.
176. Mary Tiles, "Philosophy of Mathematics," in *The Blackwell Companion to Philosophy*, eds., Nicholas Bunnin and E. P. Tsui-James (Oxford: Blackwell Publishers, 1996), 330.
177. Kuruvilla Pandikattu, *Idols to Die, Symbols to Live: Dynamic Interaction between Language, Reality and the Divine* (New Delhi: Intercultural Publications, 2000), 237.
178. Victor Ferrao, "Hermeneutical Proximity between Science and Religion," in *Omega: Indian Journal of Science and Religion* 2, 1 (June 2003), 91.

*Chapter 2*

# Nothingness in Cosmology: A Study of Quantum Mechanics and Big Bang Theory

## 2.0 Introduction

"All things are made of atoms – little particles that move around in perpetual motion, attracting each other when they are a little distance apart, but repelling upon being squeezed into one another."[1] 'Atom' comes from a Greek word '*atomos*' meaning the smallest unit of matter. There are onlyfour stable charged particles – electron, proton, positron and antiproton – that are not a compound of other particles. Every matter has some quantity and energy. The study of the way heat and energy behave is known as thermodynamics. By statistical mechanics or statistical thermodynamics, the quantity of any matter would have to constantly radiate an infinite amount of energy; no matter what its temperature is (even ice cube) which is known as ultraviolet catastrophe (Rayleigh-Jeans catastrophe).[2] The ultraviolet catastrophe led to the quantum revolution. Quantum Mechanics got rid of the zero in the classical theory of light removing the infinite energy that supposedly comes from every bit of matter in the Universe. However, this was not much of a victory. "A zero in Quantum Mechanics means that the entire Universe – including the vacuum – is filled with an infinite amount of energy: *the zero point energy*."[3] Zero in Quantum Mechanics invests the vacuum with infinite energy. This, in turn, leads to the most bizarre zero in the Universe: the phantom force of nothing.[4] "In reality, it contains the *only mystery*. We cannot explain the mystery in the sense of explaining how it works."[5] It would be more intelligible in the context of a German theoretical Physicist Werner Heisenberg's (1901-1976) uncertainty principle.

The concept of uncertainty pertains to scientists' ability to describe the properties of a particle. The *position* and *momentum* of a particle cannot be simultaneously measured with arbitrarily high precision. There is a minimum for the product of the uncertainties of these two measurements. There is likewise a minimum for the product of the uncertainties of the energy and time. Even with perfect instruments and technique, the uncertainty is inherent in the nature of things. Uncertainty makes the Universe seethe with infinite energy. It holds everywhere in the Universe, in the centre of the earth and in the deepest vacuum of the space. This means that in a sufficiently small volume, even in a vacuum, we have some uncertainty about the amount of energy inside. The vacuum by definition has nothing inside it – no particle, no light, *nothing*. Thus, the *vacuum* should have *no energy* at all. According to Heisenberg's principle, we cannot know how much energy there is in a given volume of the vacuum at any given time. The energy in a given time of vacuum must be fluctuating constantly. How could the vacuum have any energy at all? The answer comes from German-born theoretical Physicist Albert Einstein's famous formula E (energy) = m (mass) × $c^2$ (speed of the light squared).[6] E is the total energy of a physical system, m is the relativistic mass and c is speed of the light in vacuum of that system. It is referred as 'the equivalence of mass and energy,' or simply 'mass-energy equivalence,' because one can choose units in which c = 1, and hence E = m. The mass of a body is a measure of its energy-content; only mass is a real property of physical systems and that we convert mass into energy. The fluctuation of the *energy* in the vacuum is the *same thing as the fluctuation* in the amount of mass. The vacuum is never truly empty. Instead it is seething with virtual particles; at every point in space an infinite number of particles are happily popping up and disappearing. This is the zero-point energy, infinity in the formula of Quantum Theory. Quantum zero is the zero point or infinite energy. This energy in a tiny volume of vacuum must be fluctuating constantly.

In classical mechanics, all physical quantities can be derived from an ultimate physical reality consisting of specification of the position and velocities of all the particles in the Universe. In Quantum Mechanics, the development of quantum theory strongly suggests that the physical Universe has no ultimate reality at the microscopic level in the way that the Newtonian physical Universe has.[7] The Big Bang Theory, a scientific hypothesis, proposes the development of the Universe from the *singularity*. Different religious cosmologies have their own explanations of the origin of the Universe.[8] Cosmology, astronomy and all sorts of dating techniques have been able to tell pretty reliably that the Universe has been around for a very long time.[9] The Big Bang Theory states that 13.7 billion years ago there was *nothing*. There were no material things in the Universe. Thus, there is a beginning of space, time and energy of our Universe. The beginning of the space, time and energy or the origin of the Universe is from the singularity, the primordial matter or the quantum reality as the Big Bang Theory proposes.

## 2.1 Quantum Reality and Origin of the Universe

Physics has two distinct concepts: *fields* and *states*. A field expresses local properties. Fields change in time according to the laws which are also *local*, in the sense that the way the value of a field at a given point of space changes is determined by the values of the field only at neighbouring points, and not by values at a distance.[10] The quantum *state* of a system is, by contrast, highly *non-local*. It is normally thought of as the state at a given time; but the notion of 'time' becomes questionable in relativity theory and this is probably not an accurate way of thinking about it.[11] Quantum physics (otherwise known as Quantum Mechanics or quantum theory) has two branches: Quantum *Mechanics* and quantum *field theory*. Quantum field theory is the theory of not only electromagnetic fields but other fields that were discovered subsequently. Max Born (1882-1970) of German-British Physicist and mathematician, Werner Heisenberg (1901-1976) of German theoretical Physicist, Pascual Jordan (1902-1980) of German theoretical and mathematical Physicist and Paul Adrien Maurice Dirac (1902-1984) of British theoretical Physicist had *theories of light* in 1926 but had pitfalls in calculating complexities and involved prediction of infinite quantities. The quantum theory of fields or quantum electrodynamics (QED), a quantum field theory of the electromagnetic forces, was developed by Richard Feynman (1918-1988), an American theoretical Physicist, Julian Schwinger (1918-1994), another American theoretical Physicist and Sin-Itiro Tomonaga (1906-1979), a Japanese Physicist in 1940.

The view of zero, empty space or vacuum in the theory of Quantum Mechanics is paradoxical. The empty space or 0 is not really empty. It is filled with fluctuating electromagnetic fields. The vacuum fluctuations explain the spontaneous emission. They produce small and measurable shifts in the energies of atoms and properties of particles like electrons. At low energies Quantum Mechanics is accurate but at high energies relativistic effects come into play. Quantum filed theory was for reconciling Quantum Mechanics with special relativity. Quantum field theory explains two fundamental classes of particles, namely, *fermions* and *bosons,* and their properties of intrinsic spin. It explains how particles like photons, electrons and positrons (anti-electrons) are created and annihilated. It explains the mysterious nature of identical particles that are created by the same underlying field. Quantum field theory also describes a class of particles called *leptons* that include the muon, tau lepton, meson, and their antiparticles. It also describes more complex particles called hadrons. Hadrons include protons, neutrons and mesons. Quarks are the constituents of hadrons. The force mediated between quarks is gluon. Quarks and gluons are confined within the hadron. They cannot be studied in isolation because forces like gravity, electricity, magnetism, strong and weak forces are interconnected. Physics so far has discovered *five layers* of matter:[12] 1) molecular level, 2) atomic level, 3) nuclear level, 4) hadronic level and 5) quark level, which is the innermost as of now. For hadrons a new theory had to be invented as generalization of QED, called quantum chromo dynamics or QCD. The synthesis of QED and QCD is known as Standard Model for particles.

To understand the ultimate nature of matter, Quantum Mechanics was created. Quantum Mechanics is a branch of physics that deals with the *motion of particles* by their wave properties at the atomic and subatomic level. The procedure for quantizing the gravity has failed. We cannot predict quantum behaviour in a black hole where gravity is very strong. We cannot also fully predict the properties of the basic elements of matter. We know that a particle has some volume, and even in vacuum some amount of energy resides. The energy inside the vacuum fluctuates constantly. How can a vacuum have any energy at all? It comes from Einstein's formula $E = mc^2$. It means the mass (m) of an object is equivalent to a certain amount of energy (E). The electron's rest mass is 0.511 MeV (million electron volts), an amount of energy.[13] Fluctuation of energy is fluctuation of mass. Vacuum is never empty but seethes with virtual particles at every point in space with infinite number of sparks. This is zero-point energy, virtually infinity. The zero-point energy is mathematically infinite, even though it is zero physically. Hendrik B. G. Casimir (1909-2000) and Dik Polder (1919-2001), two Dutch Physicists realised in 1948 that the zero-point energy cannot be ignored. Matter waves are similar to string waves. A given string in guitar cannot play every note, in the same manner some particle waves cannot appear in that particle. Casimir realized this forbidden particle waves would affect the zero-point energy of the vacuum. The force of the vacuum, a force produced by nothing at all, is known as *Casimir effect* or force. This force was measured by Steven Lamoreaux in 1995 by putting two gold-covered plates on a sensitive twist measuring device. Casimir force measured the weight of one slice of an ant that is chopped into 30,000 pieces.

Quantum Mechanics predicts the existence of what are usually called 'zero-point' energies for the *strong*, the *weak* and the *electromagnetic* interactions, where 'zero-point' refers to the energy of the system at temperature T = 0, or the lowest quantized energy level of a quantum mechanical system.

Although the term 'zero-point energy' applies to all three of these interactions in nature, customarily it is used in reference only to the electromagnetic case. The entire Universe – including the vacuum – is filled with an infinite amount of energy. Heisenberg's uncertainty principle makes the Universe seethe with infinite energy. This means that in a sufficiently small volume, even in a vacuum, we have some *uncertainty* about the amount of energy inside. The vacuum by definition has nothing inside it – a particle, any light, nothing. Thus, the vacuum should have no energy at all. According to Heisenberg's principle, we cannot know how much energy is in a given volume of the vacuum at any given time. The energy in a given time of vacuum must be fluctuating constantly. The fluctuation in the energy in the vacuum is the same thing as the fluctuation in the amount of mass. The vacuum is never truly empty. Instead it is seething with the virtual particles; at every point in space an infinite number of them are happily appearing and disappearing. This is the zero-point energy, infinity in the formula of quantum theory. Without Quantum Mechanics there would have been no global economy, because electronics revolutionized the computers. Photonics also revolutionized the information age. Matter is not a pure material in quantum physics. It is both particle and wave. It is wavicle. It is Complementary Principle of Niels Bohr (1885-1962), a Danish Physicist. Matter is neither a wave nor a particle; each picture is complementary not contradictory. It is the nature of the experiment which 'chooses' which aspect of matter is demonstrated. It is an abstract physical description. Then the observer chooses a set of 'consistent' measurement operators to analyse a specific situation. The choice of operators, called a framework, establishes the set of outcomes that can be talked about, i.e., it establishes a sample space. The space can be analysed using standard Boolean logic and probability theory. Events in differently defined sample spaces cannot generally be combined using standard logic. Science reveals the secrets of nature.[14] Nature has designed our eyes so that it can see only in certain wavelength regions, just as our ear can hear vibrations only of a certain range of frequencies. After all, we don't see the waves from a radio or a TV station; they are all in quantum level. Let us observe the unconcealment of quantum reality in the history.

### 2.1.1 History of Quantum Reality

The most profound scientific developments of the 20th century would include general relativity, Quantum Mechanics, Big Bang cosmology, the unravelling of the genetic code, and evolutionary biology – to name the most important of them. Quantum Mechanics brings revolution to the concepts of *position* and *speed*, cause and effect of the subatomic particles. It is a probability calculus which can be applied to a specific combination of measuring devices and quantum system. The waveform is not 'real'; it is a mathematical construction that represents the observer's knowledge of the system. The description of the world is inherently probabilistic. The 15th century physics had the final word for everything of nature with its principle of predictability. This classical omnipotent principle of determinism, realism and reductionism collided with new concepts of indeterminacy, randomness and unpredictability in the early 20th century.[15] The year 2000 marked the 100th anniversary of a German Physicist Max Planck's (1858-1947) creation of the quantum concept. But the beginnings of the quantum theory go back to 1859 when a German Physicist Gustav Kirchhoff (1824-1884) proved a theorem about *blackbody radiation.* A blackbody is an object that absorbs all the energy that falls upon it and, because it reflects no light, it would appear black to an observer. A blackbody is also a perfect emitter of energy. In 1879 Josef Stefan (1835-1893), an Austrian Physicist, proposed that the total energy emitted by a hot body was proportional to the fourth power of the temperature. Later Stefan stated this is false. The same conclusion was reached in 1884 by an Austrian Physicist Ludwig Boltzmann (1844-1906) for blackbody radiation, this time from the theoretical point of thermodynamics and a Scottish Physicist and mathematician James Clerk Maxwell's (1831-1879) electromagnetic theory. The result is known as the Stefan-Boltzmann law. Planck gave credit to Boltzmann for his statistical method but Planck's approach was fundamentally different.

In his thermal radiation experiments Planck saw the energy was transmitted and absorbed in certain *discrete packets*. The molecules vibrated only with certain acceptable energies, called *quanta*.[16] The energy is radiated and absorbed in discrete quanta, or energy elements, precisely matched the observed patterns of black body radiation. Planck hypothesised that the total energy of a vibrating system cannot be changed continuously. Instead, the energy must jump from one value to another in discrete steps, or quanta, of energy.[17] The radiant heat energy is emitted only in definite amounts called energy quanta. $E = \hbar n$, ($n$ = frequency of light, $\hbar = 6.626 \times 10^{-34}$ J/s). Later $\hbar$ is known as *Planck's constant*. He left the idea of energy quanta as fallow. It was Einstein who first named the microscopic 'bundles of energy' discovered by Max Planck as light quanta or photons, and that the amount of energy in each photon is $\hbar n$. This in contrast to the belief that light consists of electromagnetic waves. Albert Einstein recognised Planck's quantum in the implications of quantization for light in 1905. Quantum physics comprises two entities. The first is the theory of matter at the sub-atomic level which is known as Quantum Mechanics. The second is the *quantum theory of fields*. Thus, quantum physics is trying to understand reality in its discrete micro quantities. Measurements never return complex numbers. Only in recent years has science discovered that everything we see is composed of things that we cannot see – *invisible atoms*? What is seen was made from things that are not visible (Heb 11, 3). The Universe contains more than we can discover on our own.

The common observable things of the Universe follow the laws of cause and effect while Quantum Mechanics at the sub-atomic level faces quantum reality with randomness and multiplicity of force laws.

### 2.1.2 Basic Concepts of Quantum Mechanics

Mechanics is that branch of physics, which deals with the *movements of bodies*. Quantum Mechanics is that branch of physics which deals with the movement of quantum particles. Quantum physics was discovered in 1920 by an international

> group of Physicists, including Niels Bohr (1885-1962) from Denmark, Louis de Broglie (1892-1987) from France, Erwin Schrödinger (1887-1961) and Wolfgang Pauli (1900-1958) from Austria, Werner Heisenberg (1901-1976) from Germany, and Paul Dirac (1902-1984) from England.[18]

The quantum revolution emerged not from the studies of matter but from a problem in *radiation*. The problem was to understand the *spectrum of light* emitted by hot bodies, blackbody radiation. A blackbody is an *ideal body* that absorbs all the electromagnetic radiation that falls on it. If anyone stares at fire one can see the hot matter glows. The hotter the fire, the brighter it glows. The spectrum of light shifts from red to yellow and finally to blue as the temperature is raised. A high-energy light like blue bright light can kick an electron from one energy level to another. The ultraviolet beam of high frequency causes electrons to spark but if we lower the frequency close to red, it suddenly stops sparking. Heinrich Hertz (1857-1894), a German Physicist, discovered that a beam of ultraviolet light could cause a plate to spark; this photoelectric effect was discovered in 1887. Ultraviolet light takes some energy to kick an electron out of an atom. Max Planck assumed that the energies of vibrating electrons that radiate the light are quantised. But he felt the theory was physically absurd, 'an act of desperation' followed, as he described later. It could have ended, but Albert Einstein (1879-1955) in 1905 realised if a vibrator's energy is quantised, then the energy of the electromagnetic field must be quantised. Einstein imbued light with particle like behaviour. Experiments on the photoelectric effects revealed that when light absorbs its energy it arrives in discrete bundles. They appear sometimes as particles and sometimes as waves. Particle is confined to a very small volume while *wave is spread* over a region of space. The paradox of the dual nature of light, *particle or wave,* led to the discovery of the quantum theory. Quantum theory deals with the tiniest things we know, the particles that atoms are made of, which we call 'subatomic' particles. It began with the study of the interactions of matter and radiation in the beginning of the last century. German Physicist Max Karl Ernst

Ludwig Planck (1858-1947) is recognised as the originator of the quantum theory, while another German theoretical Physicist Werner Karl Heisenberg (1901-1976) formulated one of the most eminent laws of quantum theory, the Uncertainty Principle, which is occasionally also referred to as the principle of indeterminacy.

The first dilemma that led to the quantum theory was radiation. According to the Rayleigh-Jeans law,[19] even an ice cube would be radiating enough ultraviolet rays, x-rays and gamma rays to vaporize everything around which is known as *ultraviolet catastrophe*.[20] The ultraviolet catastrophe led to the quantum revolution.

The second problem was matter. Atoms contain positively and negatively charged particles. Oppositely charged particles attract them. The electromagnetic theory stated that particles should spiral into each other radiating light till they collapse. Niels Bohr proposed in 1913 that electrons exist in an atom only in certain stationary states. Electrons change their energy by jumping between the stationary states. Louis de Broglie proposed in 1923 that the particle behaviour of light should have its counterpart in the wave nature of particles. He brought wavelength to depend on the momentum of the particle: The higher the momentum, the shorter the wavelength. Satyendra N. Bose (1894-1974), an Indian mathematician and Physicist, proposed in 1924 a new way to explain Planck's radiation law. He treated light as a gas of massless particles. Now, photons do not obey the Boltzmann statistics but behave like particles. Einstein applied Bose's reasoning to a real gas of massive particles and found that energy is shared by the particles in a gas. It is known as Bose-Einstein distribution. Meanwhile Wolfgang Pauli (1900-1958), an Austrian theoretical Physicist, proposed the exclusion principle, proving it to be a basis for the periodic table. German Physicist Werner Heisenberg (1901-1976), with German-British Physicist Max Born (1882-1970) and a German theoretical and mathematical Physicist Pascual Jordan (1902-1980), discovered the matrix mechanics[21] or Quantum Mechanics. Erwin Schrödinger (1887-1961), an Austrian Physicist and theoretical biologist, invented wave mechanics which was opposed to Quantum Mechanics. Electrons obeyed the (Enrico Fermi: 1901-1954) Fermi-Dirac statistics or Bose-Einstein statistics. Heisenberg proposed the uncertainty principle which tells that we cannot measure a particle's position and its velocity with perfect accuracy at the same time. In fact, the better you know a particle's position, the less you know about its velocity, and vice versa. Paul A. M. Dirac developed a relativistic wave equation for the electron that explained electron spin and predicted antimatter. This explains the magnetic field. Bohr proposed the complementarily principle for wave-particle duality. Lord Rayleigh congratulated Bohr but never understood Bohr's theory.

Bohr and Heisenberg embraced the Quantum Mechanics but Einstein and Schrödinger were dissatisfied with the interpretation and validity of Quantum Mechanics. To appreciate the whole of Quantum Mechanics, Schrödinger's version of Quantum Mechanics (wave mechanics) is needed. Schrödinger's equations are known as *wave* functions. From the wave function one can calculate the possible values of every observable quantity. The probability of finding an electron in a given volume of space is proportional to the square of the magnitude of the wave function.[22] The location of the particle is 'spread out' over the volume of the wave function. The momentum of the particle depends on the slope of the wave function: the greater the slope, the higher the momentum. The *position* and *velocity* of the particle are thus, blurred in Quantum Mechanics. The Uncertainty Principle quantifies this: To locate a particle, the wave must be sharply peak. If a wave can follow several paths from source to receiver, then illumination will display interference fringes, two-slit interference. The double slit experiment of an English polymath Thomas Young (1773-1829) in 1803 shows us that we create reality just by observing it. The subatomic material will take every possible path at the same time as a wave when not observed. When observed, the particle collapses down to one point as a particle. Particles obeying a wave equation will do likewise, as in electron diffraction. A wave is a disturbance in a medium. There is no medium and wave in Quantum Mechanics when the wave function is itself our knowledge system.

The wave function of helium describes the position of each electron. There is no way to distinguish which is which electron. If two electrons are in the same quantum state, then the wave function of one of them has to be the negative opposite of the other. Consequently the wave function vanishes. The probability of finding two electrons in the same state is zero. No two electrons in an atom can be at the same time in the same state or configuration. This is called Pauli Exclusion Principle. All particles with half-integer spin follow the Pauli Exclusion Principle are known as *fermions*. Electrons get arranged themselves due to their fermion state. For particles with integer spin, including photons, the wave does not change sign. Such particles are known as *bosons*. Light is composed of bosons. The particles behave like fermions or like bosons only if they are totally identical.

What a wave function 'really is' and what is meant by 'making a measurement' were developed by Bohr and his colleagues, this being known as the Copenhagen interpretation (1930). The Copenhagen meeting of Physicists interpreted the probabilistic description of matter and events, and a sort of reconciliation was achieved of the wave and particle natures of things through Bohr's principle of complementarity.[23] Einstein never accepted quantum theory and the Copenhagen interpretation till his death in 1955. The main issue was whether the wave function contains all information about a system or was there a hidden variable to determine the particular measurement. John S. Bell (1928-1990), an Irish theoretical particle Physicist, showed that, if hidden variables existed, it would fall below certain limits, known as Bell's *inequalities*.[24] Experiments came against inequalities. This is described as quantum *weirdness*. The weird property of quantum systems is known as *entanglement*.

The quantum reality becomes uncertain and probable at the micro level due to its sub-atomic particles. Even though sub-atomic particles are describable by names yet they are probable in our approaches, not only in terms of common language, but also in the language of mathematics. Are the only sub-atomic particles the origin of our Universe? Where do the sub-atomic particles come from? How did our Universe originate? Did it come by itself or is there a creator of this Universe?

### 2.1.3 Origin of the Universe: The Big Bang Theory and the Creation

Origin of the Universe means the beginning of the Universe. It was not there in the beginning but came to be. Did the structure of it evolve by itself or created? Our Universe is dotted with over 100 billion galaxies, and each one contains roughly 100 billion stars.[25] Our Solar System belongs to the Milky Way Galaxy. Where and how did it all come from? What is the size and shape of it? How old is it? Is the Universe changing with time? What is the end of it? Study of the Universe in its totality – origin, structure, formation, history and future – is known as *cosmology* where science and theology meet. We are part of it. Astronomers study the stars and celestial bodies while cosmologists study the astrophysical properties of the Universe. We have passed through *three phases of cosmology;* religious, philosophical and scientific.[26] We describe the origin, evolution, shape, composition, structure, and an end of the Universe according to religion, philosophy and physics. There are *three revolutions in modern cosmology* which separate us from the shamans and story tellers of the age of mythology:[27] 1st was in 1500s with Nicolaus Copernicus (1473-1543), 2nd with Albert Einstein (1879-1955) in 1920s and the 3rd with Big Bang Theory in 1960s. Though "*this 'Big Bang' idea*" is coined by Fred Hoyle (1915-2001) during a BBC radio broadcast in 1950 yet it was first formulated by George Lemaitre (1894-1966), the father of the Big Bang Theory, a Belgian catholic priest who chanced to land on this insight while working with the equations of the General Theory of Relativity in 1927.[28] Lemaitre proposed that the Universe originated from the explosion of the concentration of matter and energy that he called a 'cosmic egg' or 'primeval atom.' Alexander Friedmann (1888-1925), a Russian mathematician and cosmologist who also found solution to Einstein's equations that showed that the Universe is expanding and he published it in the German journal *Zeitschrift für Physik* (*Journal of Physics*) in

1922.[29] The American astronomer Edwin Hubble (1889-1953) also discovered the expanding Universe continuously in every direction. He proposed in 1929 that a galaxy's velocity is proportional to its distance from the Milky Way. The galaxies moving away from each other are known through *redshifts*. The other galaxies have been moving away from us for last 13.7 billion ($1.37 \times 10^{10}$) years. If we move backward on the Big Bang clock we would appear to encounter a 'beginning' at which everything hits everything else, all the mass in the Universe is compressed into a state of infinite density, infinite pressure, and infinite temperature.[30] This point is described by cosmologists as *T (time) = 0* which is called as the *singularity*.[31] The Universe began with an 'initial singularity': all matter was packed into an infinitely dense space. The Singularity is a boundary or point of limit where all the laws of physics break down.[32] It is the beginning of the Big Bang which states that at some time in the distant past there was *nothing*. All of the matter, energy and space were compressed to an area of 0 volume and infinite density. It was extremely dense and hot. It was *vacuum fluctuation* what astrophysicists call a singularity. From that singularity, our Universe has expanded. It is an attempt to explain how the Universe developed from a very tiny, dense state into what it is today. It explains how matter took on its current form and shape. It does not attempt to explain what initiated the creation of the Universe, or what came before the Big Bang or even what lies outside the Universe. Is the Big Bang an explosion? It is neither an explosion nor a Big Bang. It is simultaneous appearance of space everywhere in the Universe from the tiny point, *singularity*. It is an expansion of space itself.

Whether the Universe and matter had always existed or evolved or had been created or designed? Are we alone in this Universe or are there other Universes too? Why were the laws of nature and the initial conditions of the Big Bang such as they were? Why would minimum differences in these conditions (such as expansion rate, masses of particles, and their charges) have led to a very different Universe than the one we have, one that excludes the phenomenon of life and of living beings? Natural science being limited cannot give satisfactory responses. So they fall within the domain of philosophers and theologians.

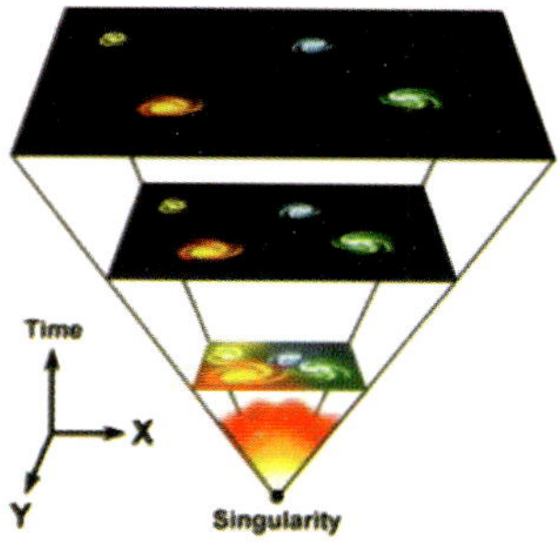


Figure 2.1 Singularity[33]

The tiny lights that meander through the sky are known as planets bearing the names of deities. "Each civilization invoked its own gods to explain the creation of the Universe, the existence of stars in the night sky, and occasionally the ultimate destruction of the cosmos."[34] Most of the religious or cultural cosmologies had grown all over the world around 6th century BCE. The philosopher-scientists abandoned the theologico-mythological explanations and started scientific explanations. They found nature is governed by laws. Cosmology emerged as a recognizably modern scientific discipline with the Greeks, first with Thales and Anaximander and then with the Pythagoreans who regarded numbers as the basis of all natural things.[35] Searching *scientific explanations* is the *first cosmological revolution* in science which began with Thales and culminated with Copernicus in 1543.[36] The geocentric golden age of Aristotelian-Ptolemaic cosmology was replaced by the heliocentric cosmology of Copernicus, a Polish clergyman and a doctor. Let us see some of the classical cosmologists.

Before Thales (620-546 BCE) of Miletus, most of the people explained the origin and nature of the cosmos with myths of anthropomorphic gods and heroes. Thales explained the world with reason without referring to supernatural entities or myths. The Earth floats on water. The earthquake takes place when the waves rock it. He regarded the earth as flat, thin, and circular, but there is no ancient testimony to support that opinion.[37] He saw earth is surrounded by water. Water evaporates and becomes air. It gets condensed and becomes ice too. He named water as the prime substance from which all things are made.[38] Thales, being one of the seven sages of Greece, is known as the father of science. He knew that the earth is a sphere and moon reflected light from the sun. Thales' predicted eclipse took place on 28th May 585 BCE which Herodotus (484-430 BCE) mentions in history.[39] Thales and Anaximander (610-540 BCE) brought structure to cosmology. Anaximander speculated that all matter results from the distillation of hot, cold, dry, and wet elements from an infinite, intelligent, living boundless whole. Anaximenes (?-528 BCE) is said to hold that condensation and evaporation of vapour or mist produces the physical world of earth, water, and fire. Thales, Anaximander and Anaximenes are known as cosmologists.

Pythagoras (580-497 BCE) of Samos, a disciple of Anaximander, is known as the father of the Number Theory of the Universe believed that planets and stars revolved on concentric spheres around a central fire producing a symphony. He taught that the earth is round and rotates on its axis.[40] The earth is a sphere but not like a disk floating in the air. The seven planets of that time – Moon, Venus, Mercury, Sun, Mars, Jupiter and Saturn – were fixed to a wheel and the air filled the heavens. It suggests that the earth is not stationary. The Pythagoreans held that the ultimate constituents of all material objects are numbers, perhaps understood as geometrical points. Nothing could exist without numbers. Numbers signify quantity of things. So celestial things obey some synchronized quantitative laws.

Plato (427-347 BCE) of Athens, the student of Socrates and the teacher of Aristotle, continued to spread the Pythagorean doctrine of a spherical earth and the circular motions of the planets.[41] The circular motions of the planets were advanced by Aristarchus (310-230 BCE) of Samos and revived still later and were given a scientific footing by Copernicus, Galileo, and Kepler. "Plato held that the circle, with no beginning or end, was a perfect form and therefore the celestial motions had to be in circles, because the Universe was created by a perfect being, God."[42] Eudoxus (408-355 BCE) of Cnidus, a contemporary to Plato held that the circular orbit of the each planet is fixed on a sphere. The Earth being the centre, Moon, Sun, Venus, Mercury, Mars, Jupiter, Saturn and sphere of stars went around the Earth.

Aristotle (384-322 BCE) of Stagira believed the earth was a round sphere rather than a flat plate.[43] Earth's shape must necessarily be spherical. The shadow of the earth on the moon is round during lunar eclipse.[44] The North Star appeared lower in the sky because it lies over the North Pole, but to someone looking from the equator, it appears to lie just at the horizon. These show that the earth is spherical. Aristotle required 55 spheres for its elaborate machinery to operate. The outermost sphere was fixed, being that of God, the Prime Mover, who caused the inner spheres to rotate. He devised a theory of the solar system with earth in the middle and the sun, moon, planets moved around the earth. The theory of Aristarchus of Samos who proposed that the planets including the earth revolved in circular orbits around the sun was abandoned.

Claudius Ptolemy (85-165CE) of Alexandria, a student of Theon of Smyrna, formulated a geocentric model of the solar system which remained the accepted model in the Western and Arab worlds until it was superseded by the heliocentric solar system of Copernicus. The adjective Ptolemaic is still used as synonymous with 'geocentric.' Ptolemy achieved this aim by imagining that the sun moved around the earth on a giant wheel.[45] Every planet was fixed to a smaller wheel which was perpendicular to the giant wheel. The planets danced in tiny little circles called epicycles as they spun around the earth. Ptolemy's *Almagest* (Greek title which means *The Greatest Compilation),* a treatise in thirteen books, is the first book which lays down mathematical and geometrical formulae for calculating the positions of the planets.[46]

Aristotelian-Ptolemaic geocentric system became well known in the West in the thirteenth century. Thomas Aquinas (1225-1274), an Italian Dominican priest of the Catholic Church, seized upon Aristotle's ideas and forged a synthesis of the Christian view of creation with the pagan cosmology of Aristotle which dominated till early 17th century.[47] Though the Copernican revolution replaced the geocentric Universe by the heliocentric yet it was small in size. Edwin Hubble (1889-1953) with the Big Bang brings the expanding enormous Universe which made the Milky Way galaxy miniscule and unstable.[48] Hubble's revolution and the discovery of the *cosmic microwave background radiation* showed that the cosmos had a beginning and an ending.[49] This is known as *second cosmological revolution.* According to this revolution we, as observers, do not inhabit in a special place in the Universe which is known as the Copernican principle, the forerunner of cosmological principle, namely, everything is the same everywhere. Let us recall some of the Renaissance cosmologists.

'The sun was stationary at the centre and that the earth and the planets moved in circular orbits around the sun' provided Polish canon Nicolaus Copernicus (1473-1543) a simple explanation for planetary motions around 1514.[50] He still clung to the classical idea that the planets should move in circular orbits at constant speeds as the ancient Greeks believed but later Kepler advocates that planets move in elliptical way. Relying on circular orbits forced Copernicus to retain some of Ptolemy's epicycles too. Copernicus' model of solar system we most readily associate with his name. Nicole Oresme (1325-1382), a French bishop had said if a man were in the sky then it would seem to him that the earth made a daily rotation. A direct observation of the Earth's motion came in 1838 when the German astronomer Friedrich Bessel (1784-1846) measured the tiny displacement, or parallax, of a nearby star relative to the more distant stars.[51] The heliocentric theory of Aristarchus of Samos and Nicolas (1401-1464) of Cusa became reality in Copernicus. Copernicus published his great work, *On the Revolutions of the Heavenly Spheres* in 1543 which was dedicated to Pope Paul III (1468-1549).[52] Galileo championed Copernicus' cause.

A Danish nobleman, Tycho Brahe (1546-1601) of Scania refused the Copernican system and advocated geocentric solar system. He drew a solar system in which the sun and the moon orbited the earth, while all the other planets revolved around the sun.[53] The 'geo-heliocentric' system of Tycho is known as Tychonic system where the sun, moon, and stars circle a central Earth, while the five (Mercury, Venus, Mars, Jupiter, and Saturn) planets orbit the Sun. Brahe's model of the Solar System was intermediate between the Ptolemaic and Copernican models. Heraklides (388-310 BCE) of Pontus had ascribed to the Earth a daily axial rotation in antiquity which Tycho did in 1583.[54] The first supernova in the West was recorded by Tycho in 1572 (but the Chinese had observed it in 1054) which destroyed the Aristotelian view that the heavens never change.[55] Tycho's accurate observations led to Kepler's discovery of the planets' elliptical motion. Kepler had removed the earth from the centre.

Galileo Galilei (1564-1642) of Pisa, often credited with being the first scientist,[56] who is also known as 'Father of Physics' and 'Father of Modern Science,' acquired a telescope in 1609 and discovered four large satellites of Jupiter. The four satellites of Jupiter were neither known nor observed by anyone before Galileio. He asked: If Jupiter appeared to have satellites orbiting around it why then could not the Earth and the other planets be orbiting the Sun?[57] It helped to demonstrate that Venus revolves around the sun and the discovery of sunspots helped to demolish Aristotelian immutability of the heavens. In 1611, Galileo visited the papal court in Rome and demonstrated his telescope, allowing priests, cardinals, and visitors to confirm what he had discovered.[58] Galileo believed that the earth revolved around the sun. He speculated that the Milky Way consists of stars like our sun. In 1616, Pope Urban VIII officially denounced the Copernican system as injurious to faith. In 1632, Galileo published his *Dialogue on the Two Chief World Systems*. For this he was arrested and tried by Inquisition. "The court spared his life, and he lived his remaining nine years under house arrest. A portrait painted two years before his death in 1642 carries the inscription *E pur si muove* (nevertheless, it does move), suggesting that to the end Galileo remained intellectually defiant. He was pardoned by Pope John Paul II in 1992."[59]

German mathematician and astronomer Johannes Kepler (1571-1630) of the Free Imperial City of Weil der Stadt (now part of the Stuttgart Region in the German state of Baden-Württemberg, placed the sun at the centre and the six known planets orbiting around it.[60] He was dealing with two problems: the *shape* of the paths of the planets and the cause of the motions of the planets. He inferred from Tycho's observations around 1605 that planets moved in ellipses. He published his first two laws in 1609 and the third law in 1619. Kepler's first law is the law of ellipses: The path of each planet is an ellipse, with the sun at one focus.[61] Second law is known as the law of equal areas: The line between the sun and a planet sweeps through equal areas in equal time intervals.[62] Kepler's third law is known as the law of harmonies: The ratio of the cube of the semi major axis to the square of the period of revolution is the same for each planet.[63] "Having discovered almost by accident that elliptical orbits fit the observations well, he could not reconcile them with his idea that the planets were made to orbit the sun by magnetic forces."[64] Much later, Sir Isaac Newton put forward a theory of how bodies move in space and time.

In 1668, Isaac Newton (1642-1727) invented a slightly different telescope that used a parabolic reflector and in 1672 he demonstrated his second prototype of this telescope to the Royal Society of London.[65] In 1687, Newton demonstrated that elliptical motions of the planets are explained by a universal law of gravitation which Kepler had initiated the process in 1619.[66] He showed that the gravitational force of attraction between two bodies varies inversely with the square of their distance of separation and is proportional to their masses.[67] Newton's theories were not proved until 1798 when Henry Cavendish (1731-1810) did a laboratory experiment that verified the law of gravitation.[68] If everything is attracted to everything else, then planets and stars and the earth should be constantly in erratic motion, constantly pulled one way or another yet he believed that the universal order could be explained only by the hand of a divine being.[69] God and science did not clash at all for Newton but worked in harmony.

In 1781, the astronomer William Herschel (1738-1822) discovered a new planet beyond the orbit of Saturn, which he named Uranus.[70] He and his son John's mapping the sky, Joseph Fraunhofer's running the starlight through prisms and lenses and Christian Johann Doppler's (1803-1853) discovery in 1842 that light, sound, or anything that moves in a wave changes frequency as it travels toward or away from the observer helped modern-day cosmology to start in 1905 with Albert Einstein.[71] Modern cosmology witnessed in 1917 at the Lowell Observatory, when Vesto Melvin Slipher (1875-1969) observed that distant galaxies are all receding from our own Milky Way. Alexander Friedmann in 1922 and Georges Lemaitre in 1927 independently discovered the solutions to Albert Einstein's equations of gravitation that describe the expanding Universe.[72] Both of them, Lemaitre and Friedmann, have fathered the Big Bang cosmology which is known as the *third cosmological revolution.* The supernovae are the harbingers of a third revolution. The third revolution has taken scientists by surprise, because they thought they already had a pretty good idea about how the Universe worked.[73] There is also twin developments in physical science, first, atomic theory and then quantum theory and second, the theory of relativity (both special relativity and general relativity of Albert Einstein).[74] Unfortunately, these two theories, the general theory of relativity and Quantum Mechanics, are known to be inconsistent with each other.[75] Many mathematicians, scientists, Physicists and astronomers have contributed for this moderncosmology.

Albert Einstein's (1879-1955) theory of special relativity shattered the illusion of absolute space and time. The theory of special relativity (1905) states that the laws of nature are the same for all observers in unaccelerated motion and the speed of light is independent of the motion of its source. In 1915, Einstein advanced the theory of general relativity, in which space is not only relative, it is also curved.[76] He created a Universe that had no centre, was finite, and was stable, a Universe where no energy would be lost. As he presented his theories of relativity, he still had a fudge factor, called a cosmological constant that would hold the Universe's expansion at bay. "The only reason for Einstein's positing the 'cosmological constant' was his confirmed belief in Newton's infinite static Universe, as he was resolute that any contrary view could not find justification."[77] He said later it was his biggest blunder. Edwin Hubble began to study the redshifts of distant stars which were moving away from us and the astronomical community became convinced in 1929.[78] It is Hubble's law now.

Alexander Friedmann (1888-1925), a Russian mathematician and cosmologist, solved Einstein's equations in 1922 and proposed that the Universe may be expanding. Einstein and Dutch mathematician Willem de Sitter (1872-1934) had published solutions earlier that assumed that the Universe did not grow or shrink. Friedmann's solutions revealed that it was possible for the Universe to expand over time, and that it was also possible for the Universe to undergo periodic expansions and contractions. Friedmann, Lemaitre, de Sitter and others constructed viable cosmological solutions to the Einsteinian equations which could be tested only by observations. Eventually, the experiment and theory resolved into two rival groups; the Steady State theory and the Big Bang theory.

Georges Lemaitre (1894-1966), a Belgian Catholic priest, mathematician, astronomer and professor of physics at the Catholic University of Louvain, developed the theory of the Big Bang in 1927. He was the first to explain British astronomer Arthur Eddington (1882-1944) the relation between the distance and the recession velocity of galaxies, the expansion of the Universe, misattributed to Edwin Hubble. The Universe could have originated from a single point like 'primeval atom.' He described the beginning of the Universe as a burst of fireworks. This burst of fireworks was the beginning of time, taking place on 'a day without yesterday.'[79] British theoretical Physicist and cosmologist Stephen Hawking (b. 1942) predicted that gravity would eventually slow down the expansion of the Universe and make the Universe fall back toward its centre but Lemaitre believed that the Universe would keep expanding. Einstein imagined an unknown force – a cosmological constant – which kept the world stable while Lemaitre believed that the Universe was expanding. In 1929, Edwin Hubble's systematic observations of other galaxies confirmed the redshift that galaxies are going away from us.

By the end of the 1920s, most astronomers were convinced that our Milky Way galaxy was but one of millions in the Universe. "In 1929, Edwin Powell Hubble (1889-1953) announced his discovery that galaxies in all directions appear to be moving away from us according to what is now called Hubble's law."[80] Hubble made the study of the spectra of 46 galaxies and concluded that the Universe expands uniformly. The expansion rate of the Universe is 500 kilometres per second per megaparsec (km/s/Mpc).[81] "A megaparsec, or a million parsecs, is a distance equal to about 3.26 million light-years; so a galaxy two megaparsecs away is receding from us twice as fast as a galaxy only one megaparsec away. This estimate is called the Hubble Constant, and scientists have been fine-tuning it ever since."[82] By calculating the distance and velocity of various galaxies and working backward, astronomers could determine when the expansion began – the age of the Universe.

Cambridge University became a centre of opposition to Lemaitre's theory of the Big Bang after Arthur Eddington's death in 1944. In fact, it was Fred Hoyle (1915-2001), an astronomer at Cambridge, who sarcastically coined the term 'Big Bang' in 1950. Hoyle, Herman Bondi (1919-2005) and Thomas Gold (1920-2004) made two contributions towards the development of the contemporary cosmology in 1948. First, they gave the Steady State Universe, an alternative to the Big Bang Universe. Secondly, Hoyle gave an explanation of the origin of different elements in the womb of the stars. He was the first to realise that all chemical elements are created inside the stars by nucleosynthesis. When the temperature in the core of a star reaches about 100 million degrees, three helium nuclei fuse to give one nucleus of carbon – this is known as helium burning. It is alpha-process when heavier nuclei are formed by successive fusion. Later Geoffrey Burbridge (1925-2010), Margaret Burbridge (b. 1919) and American astrophysicist William 'Willy' Fowler (1911-1995) continued to follow the quasi-steady state theory.

With Roger Penrose (b. 1931) Stephen Hawking (b. 1942) showed that Einstein's general theory of relativity (1915) implied space and time would have a beginning in the Big Bang and end either at the big crunch singularity or at a singularity inside a black hole.[83]According to Einstein the presence of matter causes the curvature of space in his view is gravity. Recently, attempts have been made to unify quantum physics and gravity and apply the results to cosmology. Proposals by Hawking and Hartle, Linde, Isham, Guth, Hawking and Turek, and others, are still in a speculative stage. Hawking says about his no boundary Universe:

> There would be no singularities at which the laws of science broke down and no edge of spacetime at which one would have to appeal to God or some new law to set the boundary conditions for spacetime. One could say: 'The boundary condition of the Universe is that it has no boundary.' The Universe would be completely self-contained and not affected by anything outside itself. It would be neither created nor destroyed. It would just BE.[84]

There are no singularities and boundaries of the Universe but space and time should be finite. Jim Hartle, a colleague of Hawking, worked out mathematical calculations for the no boundary Universe. The no boundary Universe is like a single point of North or South Pole. As one moves from the North to the South Pole its latitude increases up to the equator and decreases to a point at the South Pole. In a similar way the Universe also would increase and decrease in imaginary time. In imaginary time, the Universe has no beginning and no end. It exists in quantum state without boundary or edge.

But the curved Friedmann-Lemaitre Universe and the flat Einstein-de Sitter Universe form the core of the Big Bang theory.[85] George Gamow in 1940 surmised that if matter had been created during decoupling, then the primordial radiation should be present with an almost perfect uniformity everywhere in the Universe. By the discovery of the cosmic background radiation and light element abundances the Big Bang model has become the Standard Model of the Universe.

As we have observed that there is a growth of the different understandings of the Universe in the different periods of time from 6th century BCE to 20th century CE. We have understood the cosmos in *three cosmological revolutions*. The first has helped us to abandon the theologico-mythological understanding of the Universe to *scientific understanding* of the Universe. It began with Thales and culminated with Copernicus who replaced the geocentric Universe to the heliocentric one. The second cosmological revolution, with Einstein's general theory of relativity, made us aware that the homogeneous and isotropic *Universe has a beginning and the end* even though it is expanding. Finally, in the modern period, the third cosmological revolution challenges us to understand the spacetime (Hermann Minkowski, in 1908, was the first person to say that spacetime is fundamental and that space and time are just aspects of spacetime) reality of the hot Big Bang Universe which is fathered by Lemaitre and Friedman from Einstein's equations of gravitation.

Mathematics being the science of numbers is the queen of all other sciences. When 0 was understood as a number and placeholder its base extended from mathematics to physical sciences. The meaning of nothingness and void enter into the reality of vacuum. Evangelista Torricelli (1608-1647), Galileo Galilei (1564-1642), Blaise Pascal (1623-1662) and Robert Boyle (1627-1691) used pumps to remove air from glass containers and demonstrated the reality of the pressure and weight of the air above our heads. But there was always something left in the Universe: a vacuum energy that permeated every fibre of the Universe.[86] This vacuum has many states. Singularity is the point technically described by the cosmologist at a time equal to zero.[87] This is known as T (time) = 0. Absolute zero tries to find out the unity or the equilibrium of the cosmos in *triple temperatures*. The Kelvin (K) scale is an absolute, thermodynamic temperature scale uses its null point as absolute zero, the temperature at which all thermal motion ceases in the classical description of thermodynamics. Absolute zero is the point where no more heat can be removed from a system, where all motion within an atom ceases, according to the absolute or thermodynamic temperature scale. As kelvin is defined as the fraction 1⁄273.16 of the thermodynamic temperature of the triple point of water (273.16 K (0.01 °C; 32.02 °F)), water freezes at zero degrees Celsius, which is approximately 273.16 K. Absolute zero at 0 K is −273.15 °C (−459.67 °F). The micro world of Quantum Mechanics, the medium world of classical physics and the mega world of thermodynamics are fashioned in the roots of quantum zero, relativistic zero and absolute zero respectively.

Zero in the Quantum Mechanics brings infinite energy. As the Universe expanded with infinite energy it created black holes with relativistic zeros. These layers of dynamic zeros give us a clue for the beginning of the world, the Big Bang.

### 2.1.3.1 Cosmological Zero: The 0th Hour of Big Bang

The term Big Bang refers to the interval of time, roughly 13.7 billion years ago, when the photons in the microwave cosmic background radiation acquired their blackbody form. It refers to a hypothesized point in time when the observed expansion of the Universe began. At some time in the past there was nothing. Out of this *nothing* a process known as *vacuum fluctuation* created what astrophysicists call a *singularity*.[88] The singularity did not appear *in* space but space was inside the singularity. Prior to the singularity, *nothing* existed, not space, time, matter, or energy – nothing. Where and in what did the singularity appear if not in space? All we really know is that we are inside of it and at one time it didn't exist and neither did we. The singularity or *time (T) = (0) zero* of the Big Bang was a cosmic explosion which might have taken place around 13.7 billion ($13.7 \times 10^9$) years ago according to NASA's (The National Aeronautics and Space Administration) Wilkinson Microwave Anisotropy Probe (WMAP).[89] It was infinitely compact, dense and hot; since then it has expanded, becoming less dense and cooler clumping matter to form cluster of galaxies, galaxies, stars and planets. There are two observations:[90] First, our Universe began with an instant Big Bang, when space and time came into existence and all the matter started to expand uniformly. Second, the Earth is bathed in the cosmic background radiation (of George Gamow), fossil radiation (of Fred Hoyle) or a low, steady, mysterious noise (of Arno Penzias and Robert Wilson), an isotropic glow of radiation that has been the characteristics expected from the remnant of a hot primeval fireball. As the Universe rapidly grew, the temperature dropped, leading to the creation of the known forces of physics, elementary particles, and eventually hydrogen and helium atoms in a process called Big Bang Nucleosynthesis.

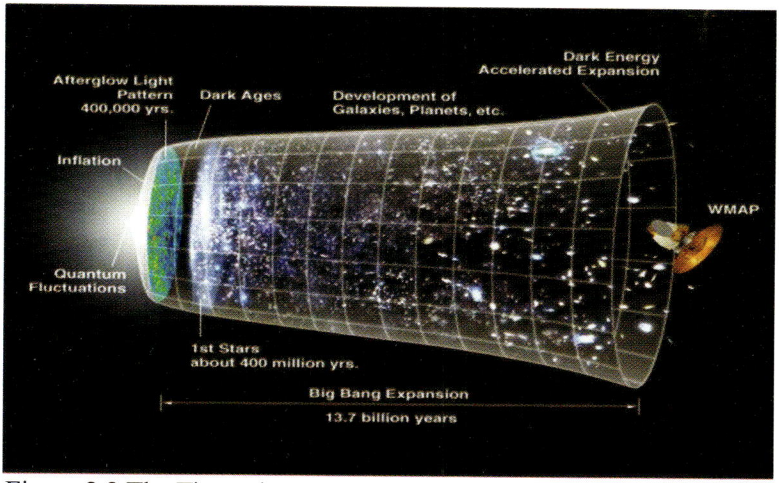


Figure 2.2 The Time Line of the Universe in Big Bang Expansion[91]

The revolution in the particle physics has helped us a lot to understand the Universe a microsecond after the Big Bang.[92] The time before $10^{-43}$ seconds is known as the Planck Era or *Quantum Gravity Era*. The temperature was $10^{32}$ K where all four fundamental forces or energies were unified into a single super force. All sub-atomic particle types (quarks, leptons, gauge bosons, Higgs bosons and undiscovered particles, e.g., sparticles, gravitons) and their anti-particles are in a thermal equilibrium (being created and annihilated at equal rate). The other three forces could not be distinguished from one another in their action on quarks and leptons. Here the gravity freezes out. This is the first instance of the breaking of symmetry amongst the forces. Perhaps the Universe existed in a perfect phase of '*nothingness,*' or empty higher-dimensional space.[93]

The Gravity split from the mysterious super-symmetry at $10^{43}$ seconds after the Big Bang when the temperature came down to $10^{32}$ K and a tiny bubble was formed, perhaps as the result of a random quantum fluctuation. This bubble was the size of the Planck length, which is $10^{-33}$ centimetres.[94] The Physicists have developed a theory called the Grand Unified Theory (GUT) which unifies the strong, weak, and electromagnetic forces. The grand unified era or GUT era lasted until about $10^{-38}$ second after the Big Bang. In 1981, the Inflation Theory developed by Alan Guth, Andrei Linde, Paul Steinhardt, and Andy Albrecht, proposed a period of extremely exponential expansion of the Universe prior to gradual Big Bang expansion.[95] Approximately $10^{-37}$ seconds into the expansion, a phase transition caused a cosmic inflation, during which the Universe grew exponentially. The huge inflation of space was driven by energy released from a separation of two forces that had previously been one: the strong force and the electroweak force.[96] At $10^{-35}$ seconds, this phase transition took place which is known as symmetry breaking.

An electroweak era lasted from $10^{-33}$ to $10^{-12}$ seconds which gave a seething soup of elementary particles at first photons, quarks, neutrinos, and electrons, and then protons and neutrons. At $10^{-32}$ seconds the temperature is too high for quarks to remain clumped to form neutrons or protons and so exist in the form of a quark gluon plasma. The LHC can study this by colliding together high energy nuclei. Here the strong force 'freezes' out and a slight excess of matter over anti-matter develops. "At $10^{-12}$ second, the weak and electromagnetic forces separated, leaving us with the four separate forces we know today. The weak nuclear force which governs radioactive decay acts only over very short distances. The more familiar electromagnetic force governs electricity, magnetism, and the propagation of electromagnetic radiation such as visible light."[97]

At $10^{-11}$ seconds the expanding Universe created pairs of particles and anti-particles which are known as *quarks* and *anti-quarks*. The particle era lasted from $10^{-10}$ to 1 second where quarks and anti-quarks annihilated each other, yet due to asymmetry of the number of particles surplus quarks began to form hadrons. The surplus matter over antimatter, one part in a billion, left behind the matter we see around us today. This is the energy range that we hope will be duplicated in the next few years by the particle accelerator the Large Hadron Collider.[98]

The *hadron era*, started approximately $10^{-6}$ seconds after the Big Bang, was then followed by the *lepton era,* started roughly 1 second after the Big Bang, where neutrons and protons were changing each other through the emission and absorption of neutrinos. The *photon era* started after most leptons and anti-leptons were annihilated at the end of the lepton era, about 10 seconds after the Big Bang. This is how the photons became quarks, quarks to *protons* and *neutrons*.

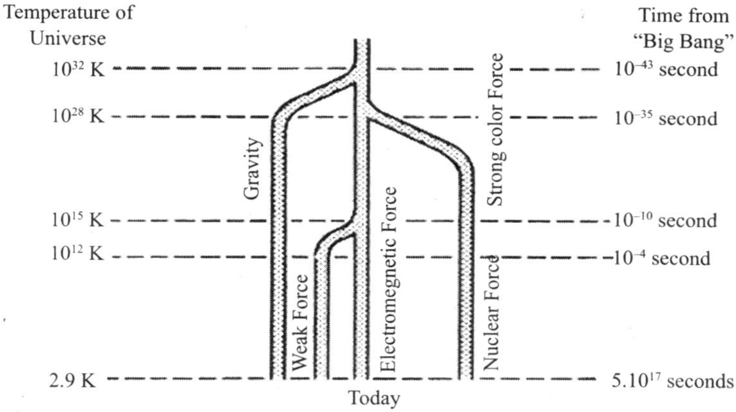


Figure 2.3 The Time Line of the Universe from the Big Bang to Today[99]

By the age of 1 second the Universe was cool. "Eventually huge numbers of hydrogen, helium and lithium nuclei are formed. The process of forming all these nuclei is called *Big Bang nucleosynthesis*."[100] Astrophysicists at Johns Hopkins University recently detected, in the intergalactic medium, the helium formed in the first two minutes after the Big Bang.[101] Nucleosynthesis lasted about three minutes. It sets the stage for the formation of atoms, galaxies and stars. After 10, 000 years, the era of radiation gives way to the *matter era*. The photons, massless particles, thermalize and start behaving as *thermal blackbody radiation* which we can measure as the cosmic background radiation today.[102] They are electromagnetic waves like radio waves, microwaves, x-ray waves. Their electric and magnetic fields move together. After 400, 000 years, the Universe became opaque and transparent which is known as the *dark ages* of the Universe, the years between the faded glow of creation and the lighting of stars. After 500, 000 years, electron and protons start to form atoms of hydrogen, helium and lithium. After one billion years, hydrogen gas is pulled together by gravity until the force causes the gas to collapse and ignite through hydrogen fusion to form the first stars.[103] The first stars were born at about the same time as the first galaxies.[104] As the star and galaxy formation begins, galaxy clusters emerge too. A vast disk of gas that swirls around this new star gave birth to planets, moons, and asteroids. The sun is formed within a spiral arm of the Milky Way galaxy. The heavier elements we see in the world today were all ejected from stars that had reached the end of their lifespan and exploded into supernovas before settling into old age as a white dwarf, a neutron star or a black hole.[105] With 3000° C, decoupling of matter and energy occurs that we detect today as the cosmic microwave background radiation. This radiation was stretched and cooled by the expansion of the Universe from 300° to –270.42° C. Today, the temperature of the Universe is 2.725 K (–270° C, –455° F), which is only a couple of degrees above absolute zero. The redshift of galaxies outside of our galaxy shows the Hubble expansion. When the expansion slows down, stops and contracts then it is known as *oscillatory Universe.* The contraction will continue till it reaches singularity which is known as the *big crunch.* The contraction occurs when the density of the Universe is greater than the critical density, then the strength of the gravitational force will stop the Universe from expanding and the Universe will collapse back on itself, the Big Bang singularity. We have events in an Inflationary Big Bang as follows:

| Events in an Inflationary Big Bang Cosmology[106] | | |
|---|---|---|
| Time since Big Bang | Temperature in Kelvin (K) | Reference Event |
| • < $10^{-43}$s | | *Quantum Era*<br>Universe consists of 'soup' of leptons & quarks |
| • ~$10^{-43}$s | $10^{32}$ K | *Grand Unification Era*<br>Gravity separates from other Grand Unified Forces |

| • ~ $10^{-35}$s | $10^{27}$ K | *End of Grand Unification*<br>Strong Force breaks symmetry with ElectroWeak Force. |
|---|---|---|
| • ~ $10^{-35}$s - $10^{-33}$s | | *Inflationary Epoch*<br>Universe inflates by a factor of $10^{30}$ or more (expands from size of an atomic nucleus to size of a cherry pit). |
| •~ $10^{-12}$s | $10^{15}$ K | *Particle Era*<br>Electromagnetic force and Weak Force break symmetry. |
| • ~ $10^{-6}$s | $10^{13}$ K | *Quark →Hadron transition*<br>Protons and neutrons (plus antiprotons and antineutrons) are formed from quarks - at this time the 'matter' particles have an excess of ~ one in a billion over 'antimatter' particles. |
| • 0.01s | $10^{11}$ K (100 billion K) | • The Universe is expanding rapidly, scale is doubling every 0.02s.<br>• As Universe expands it cools,<br>• Although the temperature is too low for protons and neutrons to be created from the thermal energy of the early Universe reactions yet they maintain an equal number of protons and neutrons.<br>• As the temperature decreases proton/neutron balance shifts in favor of less massive protons. |
| • 1s | $10^{10}$ K (10 billion K) | •Weakly interacting neutrinos 'decouple' from the rest of the Universe. |
| • 15s | 3 x $10^{9}$ K (3 billion K) | • Temperature is below the threshold for creation of electron/positron pairs.<br>• $e^+$/ $e^-$ annihilate: $e^+ + e^-$<br>• The Universe is 'reheated' about 35% by annihilation. |

*contd...*

| | | |
|---|---|---|
| • 3 min | $10^9$ K | *Era of Nuclear Reactions*<br>• Nuclei can begin to hold together<br>• At this time the baryons are divided into about 87% protons 13% neutrons. |
| • 3 1/2 m | $10^8$ K | *End of Nuclear Reactions*<br>Neutrons have been 'used-up' forming $^4$He<br>Universe is now 90% H nuclei( $p^+$) & 10% He nuclei |
| • $10^6$yr | 4000 K | *Era of Recombination*<br>Nuclei & electrons recombine to form atoms Universe becomes transparent |
| • $10^9$yr | | Era of Galaxy Formation |
| $4.7 \times 10^9$ yr | | Formation of the Solar System |
| $1.37 \times 10^{10}$ yr | 2.725 K | Today |

Figure 2.4 Events in an Inflationary Big Bang Cosmology

The Big Bang Model, known as *standard cosmology*, is based on two pillars of modern physics: 1) the cosmological principles and 2) on the field equations of the general theory of relativity of Albert Einstein which he discovered in 1916. Alexander Friedmann, a Russian Physicist, provided field solutions. Edwin Hubble, an American astronomer, provided redshift spectrum for distancing galaxies in 1929. George Gamow (1904-1968), Russian-American, in 1946, proposed that the primeval fireball, the 'Big Bang,' was an intense concentration of pure energy. It was the source of all the matter that now exists in the Universe. He supported Friedmann's equations in 1940 while Fred Hoyle opposed referring to it as a mere Big Bang in 1950, the name which stuck. The recent marriage between cosmology and high-energy particle physics has revolutionized the perspective, scope, and method of cosmology.[107]

The Big Bang is based on the cosmological principles: universality, homogeneity and isotropy. Universality principle says that the physical laws can be applied to anywhere in the Universe. The so-called cosmological principle states that the Universe is homogeneous and isotropic. That is to say the Universe appears much the same (homogenous) to observers wherever in the Universe they may be. The Universe is the same in every place (isotropic) as it is around us. There is no centre of the Universe.

#### 2.1.3.2 Foundational Cosmological Principles of the Big Bang

'The Universe is homogeneous and isotropic.' This statement is referred as cosmological principle. There is a uniform distribution of matter in the Universe on the larger scales. The Universe has neither a centre nor a special place. It looks the same everywhere and in all directions (up, down, or any). It looks the same whoever and wherever we are. Polish astronomer Konrad Rudnicki (b. 1926) summarizes *six cosmological principles* over different periods of human history: The Ancient Indian, the Ancient Greek, the Genuine Copernican, the Generalized Copernican, the Perfect and the Anthropic Principles.[108] A cosmological principle in general is a general law of nature. Cosmological principles are just the general assumptions serving for filling up blanks in the general 'map' of the spacetime. *The Ancient Indian Cosmological Principle* is described as the Universe is infinite in space and time and is infinitely heterogeneous.[109] It means there are many other 'earths' of equal significance in the Universe.[110] *The Ancient Greek Cosmological Principle* is reconstructed and formulated as the natural centre or quasi-centre of the Universe is the Earth, which is a unique feature in time and space. *The Genuine Copernican Cosmological Principle* says that the Universe observed from every planet looks roughly the same in every direction from every point in space. The Universe at every point is governed by the same physical laws. *The Generalized Copernican Cosmological Principle* is also called *The Ordinary, The Narrow* or *The Weak Cosmological Principle* which says that the Universe looks roughly the same not only when seen from every planet but from every point in every direction (the Universe is homogeneous and isotropic).*The Perfect Cosmological Principle* was introduced by Herman Bondi and Thomas Gold (1948) which says that the

Universe observed from every point in every direction and in every time looks roughly the same. *The Anthropic Principle* formulated by various authors in various manners can be expressed as follows: there exists in the Universe a physical intelligent human being striving for knowledge; out of this assumption all the physical laws and physical constants can be deduced in narrow intervals of their values. The observable Universe, as it is, must be compatible with our powers of observation. The Universe is for the sake of intelligent life. *The Weak Anthropic Principle,* which affirms simply that the existence of human life itself implies that nature must be consistent with having evolved carbon-based life, and *The Strong Anthropic Principle,* which is concerned with the possibility of alternative Universes, yet goes on to state metaphysically that our observable Universe must be the only kind of Universe capable of evolving human-like creatures as observers.[111] *Ancient Indian, Generalized Copernican* and *Perfect Principles* do not permit the existence of a centre of another privileged point in the Universe. The principles have come more or less consciously from the kind of scientific perceptions (observations, experiments) characteristic in a given epoch. The cosmological principles are not laws of nature but are products of human thinking, we can consciously evaluate the existing cosmological principles and strive to formulate more realistic ones combining elements of astronomy, physics and philosophy.[112]

Cosmological principle or models are used for understanding structures and processes not accessible to direct observation. The Big Bang is based on the general theory of relativity.

### 2.1.3.3 Foundational Principle: The General Theory of Relativity

Albert Einstein proposed in 1916 that the distribution of mass in the Universe determines the geometry of the space. John Wheeler (1911-2008) put it well: "Matter tells space how to curve, and space tells matter how to move."[113] It means matter and space are always in constant movement. Matter causes space to curve. It is the effect of gravitation on the shape of space and the flow of time.

This is the *relativity* of spacetime geometry or *curvature* of spacetime. "Energy determines the space and changes in the geometry of the Universe, and in turn, the geometry determines the movement of energy."[114] This description of geometry or equations describes the action of gravity. Newton's gravity is only valid for bodies at rest or moving very slowly compared to the speed of light but Einstein's for the Universe as a whole.[115] Spacetime is treated as curved rather than flat as in special relativity. The distribution of matter and energy in the Universe is homogeneous and isotropic.[116] It means that the Universe looks the same everywhere and in every direction. For Einstein, space is not simply emptiness; it's a real, stretchable, and a flexible thing. Einstein's theory of gravity describes a simple but universal relationship between space, time, and matter. Thus, Einstein's general relativity field equations are foundations for the Big Bang model of the Universe. The ten independent nonlinear partial differential equations imply that the Universe is expanding or contracting. In 1927 Georges Lemaitre of Belgium found solutions to the equations of general relativity that corresponded to an expanding Universe, and was the first to wind the clock backwards in time to infer the presence of an initial creation event.[117] De Sitter is the first to derive solutions of the equations of general relativity that describe an expanding cosmological model.[118] De Sitter's Universe had no matter, Lemaitre's had primeval atom and Friedmann's had a clump dense of matter. George Gamow, Ralph Alpher (1921-2007) and Robert Herman (1914-1997) state that the Universe expanded from a primordial state of matter called ylem consisting of protons, neutrons, and electrons in a sea of radiation.

The Universe has originated from a primeval atom with a Big Bang which has been substantiated by both theoretical and observational evidences. Georges Lemaitre in 1927 and Alexander Friedmann in 1922 had, independently from each other, theoretically posited the homogeneous and isotropic models of the Universe within the context of general relativity the necessity of an expanding Universe by mathematical formulas.

### 2.1.3.4 The Observational Evidence for the Big Bang

The standard hot Big Bang model has four key observational successes: 1) The Expansion of the Universe, 2) The Nucleosynthesis of the Light Elements, 3) Origin of the Cosmic Microwave Background (CMB) Radiation, and 4) Formation of Galaxies and Large-scale Structure.

1) The Expansion of the Universe

   Einstein's General Theory of Relativity showed that the Universe is expanding. In 1922, Alexander Friedmann, Russian meteorologist and mathematician, noticed that the Universe might be expanding. Einstein could not believe it and invented cosmological constant for a static Universe. Independently from Friedmann, Georges Lemaître, Belgian astrophysicist, developed the notion of a 'primeval atom' that had exploded marked the beginning of the expanding Universe. Later Edwin Hubble (1889-1953) discovered that the Universe is not static but expanding. The galaxies are moving away from us with a velocity which is proportional to their distance which is known as Hubble's Law named after Edwin Hubble who discovered it in 1929. When an object moves away from us, we get redshifts of spectrum, longer wavelengths. The wavelength increases as the source or the observer move apart from each other and decreases as they move closer to each other. The changing pitch of the siren of a passing motor vehicle is an example of the Doppler Effect (change in wavelength between a source of waves and the observer) on sound or light waves. Hubble also found that the ratio between a galaxy's distance ($d$) and velocity ($v$) was constant. $v = Hd$ where $H$ is Hubble's constant, $v$ is the recessional velocity and $d$ is distance of the galaxy from us. Hubble's constant ($H$) describes the rate of expansion of the Universe, and its value evolves as the Universe ages. The unit for measuring the distance to nearby galaxies is called the Megaparsec (Mpc) which is equal to 3.26 million light years.[119] The latest estimates place $H$ somewhere between 68 km/s/Mpc and 75 km/s/Mpc. The reciprocal of $H$ is called the Hubble time, the age of the Universe. One 's-Mpc/km' is 977 792 221 400 years. Now the Universe is 13.7 billion years. The Universe is still expanding.

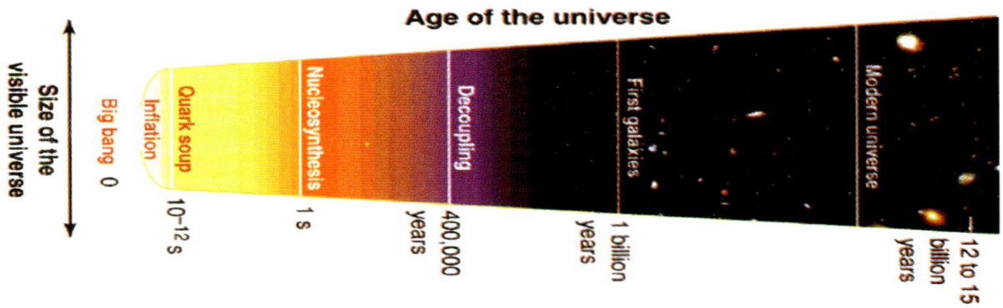


Figure 2.5 Age of the Universe[120]

2) The Nucleosynthesis of the Light Elements

The Big Bang has taught us that hydrogen and helium are the dominating elements in every spot of the Universe formed at the very beginning of the Universe. At its beginning, the Universe was a very hot mixture of protons, neutrons and electrons. The formation of heavier elements, atomic nuclei with many protons and neutrons, from the fusion of lighter elements is known as nucleosynthesis. A long time ago when the Universe was hot and dense its state of matter was a mix of nuclei and electrons, fully ionized *plasma,* full of protons, neutrons and electrons. As the Universe cooled, the neutrons either decayed into protons and electrons or combined with protons to make deuterium. During the first three minutes of the Big Bang, most of the deuterium combined to make helium and lithium. This process of light element formation in the early Universe is called Big Bang nucleosynthesis. As the Universe expanded, the density and temperature dropped, protons and neutrons collided to form light nuclei within a minute or two. After $3\frac{1}{2}$ minute's collisions between particles a lots of hydrogen, helium, deuterium and lithium appear. The result was three quarters of the mass of the Universe was hydrogen nuclei, and one quarter of the mass was helium nuclei. The nuclei were totally ionized. The electrons were scattering photons. There is an abundance of light elements like hydrogen and helium which supports the Big Bang model. We've roughly 75% hydrogen and 25% helium. Experiments are done in CERN (European Organization for Nuclear Research) of Geneva, Switzerland, Fermilab in Chicago, USA, and SLAC (Stanford Linear Accelerator Center) in San Francisco, USA to access the sub-atomic world where accelerator tunnels are constructed to simulate the hot mediums and to increase the velocity of sub-atomic particles.

3) Origin of the Cosmic Microwave Background (CMB) Radiation

As the early Universe was an extremely hot and dense, it expanded. As it expanded its gas cooled. Thus, its radiation, the remnant heat leftover, should be filled with the Universe. The leftover heat is known as the cosmic microwave background radiation (CMB). About 100,000 years after the Big Bang, the temperature dropped to about 3,000 K. Today, the CMB radiation is very cold, only 2.725K. This electromagnetic spectrum falls in the microwave range of 300 GHz. The CMB is a bath of photons coming from every direction, the afterglow of the Big Bang, an isotropic field of electromagnetic radiation – the redshifted relic of the Big Bang.[121] When we look at the Universe with radio telescopes in the microwave range, we see a spectrum which is exactly like that of a blackbody. It is like a fog, all the molecules of water scattered a photon into our eyes. The early Universe was extremely hot in the beginning and its remnant radiation, *echo* of the Big Bang, is discovered by Arno Penzias (b. 1933) and Robert Wilson (b. 1941) in 1965. The Cosmic Background Explorer satellite (COBE) was developed by John C. Mather (b. 1946), NASA Goddard Space Flight Centre, succeeded in sensitively measuring the temperature of the cosmic microwave background in 1992, which corresponded to a temperature of 2.725 Kelvin. It is 2.725K (–454.765°F, –270.425°C) Cosmic Microwave Background Radiation, which pervades the observable Universe. This reveals the tiny temperature fluctuations associated with the ripples which eventually led to the formation of galaxies, clusters of galaxies and planets. George Smoot (b. 1945),University of California, Berkeley, the principal investigator of the COBE project, described the picture of these ripples as the 'face of God' and one of the prime aims of cosmologists today is to study this 'face' in ever greater detail.[122] In 1994 the study of light coming from remote galaxies confirmed by the COBE that the cosmic microwave background radiation was higher in the past, as was expected. One of the significant characteristics of cosmic microwave background was its diffusion throughout space. The CMB radiation was emitted 13.7 billion years ago, only a few hundred thousand years after the Big Bang, long before stars or galaxies ever existed.

4) Formation of Galaxies and Large-scale Structure

From the perspective of a cosmologist, the basic building blocks of the Universe are the galaxies.[123] The Universe was homogeneous after the Big Bang. A large-scale structure of the cosmos was formed due to primordial fluctuations which later become galaxies. A galaxy is a system of stars, gas, dust and dark matter gravitationally bound together with a mass ranging from 10 million to 1000 billion times that of the sun.[124] The standard hot Big Bang model also provides a framework in which to understand the collapse of matter to form galaxies and other large-scale structures observed in the Universe today. "If density fluctuations with amplitudes between 1% and 0.01% were present before the decoupling era, the natural accretion resulting from this process of gravitational instability would have ensured eventual collapse – perhaps to form galaxies."[125] At about 10,000 years after the Big Bang, the temperature had fallen to such an extent that the energy density of the Universe began to be dominated by massive particles, rather than light and other radiations which had predominated earlier. This change in the form of matter density meant that the gravitational forces between the massive particles could begin to take effect, so that any small perturbations in their density would grow. Inflation ceased, the gentler Big Bang expansion resumed yet density fluctuations permeated, the seeds of future galaxies.[126] 13.7 billion years later we see the results of this collapse in the structure and distribution of the galaxies. As we gaze into the Universe it has revealed a vast hierarchy of structure and motion. Planets moving around stars; stars grouped together, moving around the centre of galaxies. Galaxies, some 100 billion of them, form galaxy clusters bound by gravity as they journey through the void. The largest structures are the superclusters, each containing thousands of galaxies and stretching many hundreds of millions of light years across space. These superclusters are arranged in filament or sheet-like structures, between which there are gigantic voids of seemingly empty space. Our scientific understanding of galaxy evolution is still evolving…

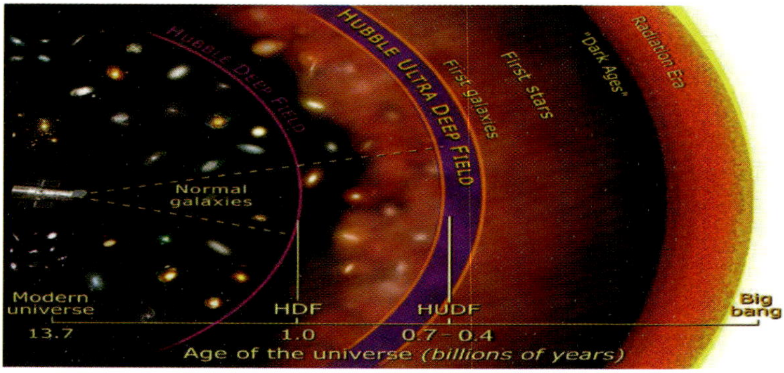

Figure 2.6 Hubble's Deep View of the Universe[127]

"The Hubble Deep Field (HDF), released on June of 2003, looked back to within 1.0 billion years after the Big Bang. The Hubble Ultra Deep Field (HUDF), released on March 2004, looks back even further to a time only 0.7 billion years after the Big Bang, close to the period when the first galaxies were formed."[128]

There are observational evidences of the Big Bang after 13.7 billion years. As the reality of the Universe is objective yet it depends on our perceptual observations. Let us see how the Big Bang and formation of the Universe came to be.

### 2.1.3.5 The Big Bang and the Formation of the Universe

We know what happens if too much energy is packed into too little a volume; it explodes. "The idea that space, time, matter and energy somehow 'exploded' or expanded from essentially nothing in the sudden 'Big Bang' that was the birth of our Universe, the first cosmic evolution," says Randal Niles.[129] An explosion occurred simultaneously everywhere, filling all space from the beginning, with every particle of matter rushing apart from every other particle.[130] It is hard to know the beginning of the Universe. The time before the Big Bang is known as Augustinian Era as George Gamow proposed in 1952. Time did not exist before creation. There was complete symmetry. The size of the Universe was the point of a needle $10^{-43}$ seconds after the singularity, which is known as Planck time.[131] The four fundamental forces were unified as one during this time. The grand unified forces were separated as the Universe expanded and cooled during the grand unified epoch. The Universe expanded $10^{50}$ times between $10^{-35}$ and $10^{-33}$ seconds after the singularity, which is known as inflationary epoch. It is flattened, homogeneous and isotropic. Inflation produced matter to fill the empty space so that the total energy of the Universe was conserved and remained 0.[132] The fundamental forces become distinct beginning with *gravity, strong* force, *weak* force and *electromagnetic* forces. The fundamental particles like quarks, electrons, pions, neutrinos, etc., smash together to form protons and neutrons by the first second. The early Universe formed the nuclei and neutral atoms. Some photons become quarks, quarks to neutrons and protons. An abundance of hydrogen, helium and lithium nuclei is formed. The process of forming the heavier elements from the light elements is known as nucleosynthesis. The photons, left over from the Big Bang, are known as cosmic microwave background. The energy of the Universe glows in the form of radiation with different wavelengths, x-rays, radio waves and ultraviolet rays from the radiation era. As the era of matter comes, the energy in matter and the energy in radiation become equal. The Universe becomes transparent in distributing the matter equally. Quasars, stars, galaxies, clusters and supercluster structures are formed from smaller size to bigger ones. Our star, the Sun, is within the spiral arm of the Milky Way Galaxy. The Sloan Digital Sky Survey (SDSS) is trying to map the position of over 100 million galaxies and determine their distances to each other.

Cosmologists now model the Universe back to $10^{-43}$ seconds after the Big Bang. They are searching the merger of gravity and Quantum Mechanics at that moment, which they have not found. Many think String Theory of Gabriele Veneziano (b. 1942), Leonard Susskind (b. 1940) and others in 1960s or membrane theory or M-Theory, first described by M-Theory pioneer Bert Ovrut in 2001, would help it. There is no way to detect the origin of the Universe. The Big Bang does not explain what was before it. A single force existed at the beginning. This force separated into four: gravity, electromagnetism, strong and weak nuclear force as we know. The GUT combines the three forces except gravitation. String Theory seeks to incorporate the force of gravity with the other three forces, providing a Theory of Everything (TOE).

Scientists are constantly adjusting the Big Bang to match the observed Universe. A 'standard model' of the Big Bang has been established by results from NASA's Wilkinson Microwave Anisotropy Probe (WMAP), launched in 2001. WMAP's observations suggest that the rate of expansion of the Universe, called Hubble's constant, is about 71 km/s/Mpc (kilometres per second per million parsecs, where a parsec is about 3.26 light-years). "The WMAP image also revealed the contents of the Universe: only 4% is made up of atoms or the physical Universe as we know it. The remainder is made up of poorly understood substances: dark energy (73%) and dark matter (23%)."[133] The dark energy provides antigravity or negative pressure for expansion. The matter is related to pressure, density and temperature. Temperature is a measure of the speed of the particles of the matter. Heat is produced of its collision with atoms or particles. When the pressure of the matter is 0 or very tiny, it is known as cold matter like stars, planets, asteroids, interstellar dust, and so on. Much of the cold matter does not glow which is called dark matter. Normal dark matter is also known as baryonic dark matter. The space is filled with energy even if there is no matter or radiation. This energy is known as dark energy, zero-point energy, zero-point fluctuations, vacuum energy, vacuum fluctuations, etc. This is constant and positive. The pressure, associated with dark energy is negative. If the negative pressure is larger than that of the positive energy density then the gravity will accelerate the expansion of the Universe. Dark energy also is connected with the cosmological constant of Einstein.

All matter is made up of protons, neutron and electrons, known as baryonic matter or visible matter which is named MACHOs (Massive Compact Halo Objects). The matter causes the gravitational forces. In 1970s and 1980s astronomers found mysterious material that also exerts a gravitational pull but neither emits nor absorbs light which is known as dark matter. There is also non-baryonic exotic matter which is called WIMPs (Weakly Interacting Massive Particles). There are new forms of non-baryonic matter supercolliders. The supermassive black holes are gravitationally collapsed masses where no light, matter or any kind of information can escape. There are VMOs (very massive objects) which are 100 times massive and heavier than our Sun likely to be found in the form of black holes.[134]

Albert Einstein's general relativity predicted either an expanding Universe or a contracting one. Einstein sighed and stuck in a mathematical constant to fix this problem by inventing an expansive quality of space itself, which today we call 'dark energy,' to balance the inward pull of gravitating matter.[135] "We live in a Universe that is not static as Einstein thought, and not just expanding as Hubble showed, but accelerating! We attribute this increase in expansion over time to a dark energy with a strange type of pressure. In its simplest form this might be Einstein's cosmological constant, which for 60 years was theoretical poison ivy."[136] Einstein discovered that the maximum velocity of any object is the speed of light. Therefore, if the escape velocity on the surface of an object is greater than the speed of light, then nothing, including light, can escape from it. We will then have a black hole. "A property of empty space, allowed by Einstein's general theory of relativity, that acts as a large negative pressure and pushes the Universe apart at a faster and faster rate... Unlike Einstein's famous fudge factor, the cosmological constant in its present incarnation does not balance gravity in order to maintain a static Universe; instead, it has negative pressure that causes expansion to accelerate.[137]

*General relativity* holds sway in the macroworld and Quantum Mechanics in the microworld. Black hole brings these worlds together at the centre. Zero transpires, becomes apparent, between these two theories. Black hole is a zero in the equations of general relativity; the energy of the vacuum is a zero in the mathematics of quantum theory.[138] The Big Bang is zero in both the theories. The Universe came from nothing and both theories break down when they try to explain the origin of the cosmos. The commonality of general relativity and Quantum Mechanics is zero. The zero space curving infinitely in black hole is infinite zero. In black hole, space and time are meaningless. In Quantum Mechanics, zero-point energy lies in the mathematical zero dimensionality of electron. Nobody knows the mass or charge of that electron. The true electron is hidden in the particles of zero-point electromagnetic fluctuations. The swarm of particles makes it very difficult to measure its mass and charge. It may be heavier because it moves faster. According to the rules of Quantum Mechanics, the zero-dimensional electron has infinite mass and infinite charge. When a scientist chooses a close distance, all calculations using the true mass and charge are made to agree with one another, which is known as renormalisation which Richard Feynman (1918-1988) called dippy process.

Certain Physicists (John Schwarz, André Neveu and others) treated particles as strings and produced string theory in the 1970s, using vibrating strings rather than dots as the elementary objects. They are treated as one-dimensional and as a result zero-dimensional point and infinity disappear. A string is in effect a one-dimensional loop instead of a point particle meeting at a point of singularity. Everything in the Universe is made up of these strings, which are about $10^{-33}$ centimetres. Zero has been banished from string theory to solve the infinity problem of Quantum Mechanics and general relativity. String theory needs 10 dimensions while we have only 4. What do these 6 extra dimensions mean? They are like imaginary numbers of maths. Scientists believe that there is a monster theory (M-theory), which lives in 11 dimensions. There is no instrument currently to observe strings directly.

Zero has not been banished but it seems to be at the realm of what created the cosmos. The Universe was born in zero at the $0^{th}$ hour. Out of the void, out of nothing at all, came a cataclysmic explosion that created all energy and matter that the entire Universe is made of. Aristotle rejected the creation of the Universe out of void. If it was not out of nothing then there must already have been a Universe. For him it was eternal. It had always existed in the past and would exist always. But the biblical cosmos toppled Aristotle. According to general relativity Einstein predicted that either the Universe will crunch or it will expand forever. If it expands it will become darker and darker becoming ever colder and dying by ice. To save from this death Einstein added a cosmological constant, an undetected force that counteracts the force of gravity. It balances the pull instead of the collapsing of the Universe. The stars and galaxies themselves destroyed Einstein's static and eternal cosmos: Edwin Hubble's discovery of Cepheid variable stars and the Doppler Effect show that says galaxies are speeding away from us in all directions. As time runs forward the Universe expands and expands. The Universe had a beginning about 13.7 billion years in the past, and space had been expanding ever since. At some point the Universe would shrivel and wither and then eventually disappear as a point – the singularity at the beginning of time and space. This is the primal zero, the birthplace of time and space, the Big Bang. Where did the singularity of the Big Bang come from? Zero holds the secret. The zero of the vacuum must explain the lumpiness of the Universe. Zero must also hold the secret of what created the cosmos. Just as the nothingness of the vacuum and the zero point energy spawn particles, they might spawn Universes.[139] The froth of quantum foam, the spontaneous death and birth of particles might explain the origin of the cosmos.

Perhaps the Universe is just a quantum fluctuation on a grand scale – an enormous singular particle that came into existence out of the ultimate vacuum. This cosmic egg would explode, inflate and create the spacetime of our Universe. It may be that our Universe may be simply one of many fluctuations. Thus, zero might hold the secret to our existence and the existence of other Universes. It will also be responsible for the end of our Universe.

Materially our Universe is composed of light, wave and time. Virtually all of our information about the Universe at large comes from studies of electromagnetic radiation – light, radio waves, x-rays and other variations on the theme – all of which travels at the speed of light, 30,000 million cm per second.[140] The existence of cosmic background radiation, the glow left over from the explosion itself confirms the Big Bang Theory. The radiation was discovered in 1964 by Arno Penzias and Robert Wilson, who later won the Nobel Prize for this discovery. The exponents of this Big Bang Theory are Alexander Friedman (1888-1925), a Russian meteorologist and mathematician, and Abbe Georges Lemaitre (1894-1966), a Belgian ordained priest and Physicist who had proposed it in 1927. Both of them showed the expanding world while contrasting Einstein's static Universe. Edwin Powell Hubble (1889-1953) also proved the expansion of the world in 1929. Astronomers estimate that the Big Bang took place around 13.7 billion years ago. All the mass in the Universe was compressed into a state of infinite density, infinite pressure and infinite temperature. With the instant of the Big Bang, explosion begins with time and space. This state is called as the singularity. The 1st microsecond explosion began with $10^{12}$ electron volts or $10^{16}$ K. At $10^{-10}$ seconds symmetrical four fundamental forces might have undergone a series of phase transitions. At $10^{-45}$ seconds super symmetry between the gravitational and other forces was lost. At $10^{-35}$ seconds the symmetry of strong and electro-weak forces was lost. Finally at $10^{-10}$ seconds the weak force split from the electromagnetic force. Before $10^{-4}$ seconds the Universe was a primordial soup of elementary particles; leptons (electron, muons, taus, and neutrinos) and hadrons (quarks and gluons). At a tenth of a millisecond ($10^{-4}$ sec) after the Bang there were no neutrons and protons but giant nuclei. The density of the Universe was very high. As it expanded, it cooled down. As the density decreased, neutrons and protons came to existence.

Years back, there was no space, matter, time, light, darkness, fullness, emptiness, etc. There was nothing. Nothing is presupposed 'before' the Big Bang. Suddenly Big Bang occurs, equilibrium is disturbed. Infinite density, infinite pressure, infinite temperature state or singularity explodes. Cosmological 0 is expanded. Equanimity or equilibrium is presupposed. With this motion, emerges the law of entropy – and the Universe, force, existence and matter appear. Where these no-things were getting from? From nothing, vacuum or 0 emerges matter, space and time. Is there any detectability? Detectability defines our limit of detection but not the limit of space and time. There can be no such thing as something outside of the Universe if it can be detected. It requires that the space be infinite. In the same logic time is also to be infinite. Time extends to the past and future. In any moment we define with the boundaries of space and time. The undetectability of the beginning and end shows that the Universe has and always existed. The theory of relativity has prediction that forces us to give up a static and everlasting Universe, which Einstein and most other people believed in at that time. He fudged the equations by adding a term called the cosmological constant, which warped space-time the other way so that bodies move apart. The repulsive effect of the cosmological constant would balance the attractive effect of matter and allow for a Universe that lasts for all time. But the Big Bang shows that the Universe has emerged. It is the dynamic Universe which has emerged from undetectable equilibrium or cosmological constant.

Where did the matter come from in the first place? What caused the Big Bang? How did life actually begin? How does one explain evolution's 'missing links?' How does one explain the tremendous odds against the evolution of species, many of which, for example, have a symbiotic need for other organisms in order to exist and survive?

Matter cannot create itself, because matter is finite. No finite thing could ever create itself. Therefore, simple logic demands that only something infinite which has no beginning and end is not subject to being created. This Universe did not always exist; it came into existence at the beginning of time. Christian faith explicitly states, that the world was created *in time,* which means that its past history is finite. There are three basic positions on the origins of the cosmos, life, and man: (1) special or instantaneous creation, (2) developmental creation or theistic evolution, (3) and atheistic evolution. The first holds that it was instantaneously and directly created by God. The second position holds that a given thing did develop from a previous state or form, but that this process was under God's guidance. The third position claims that a thing developed due to random forces alone. The Big Bang is in fact the first one, Big Bang-1, and refers to the transition from the vacuum to the Universe which now has about $10^{82}$ protons, neutrons and electrons.[141] These particles are an inert form of matter. The transition needed to go from inert matter to living matter is to be called Big Bang-2.[142] "Out of this enormous number of different forms of living matter there is one, and only one, endowed with a special property, called Reason. We are the only form of living matter having this incredible property, which generates Language, Logic and Science."[143] "Another Big Bang is needed to describe the transition from the innumerable number of examples of living matter to the unique one which is us. We call this transition Big Bang-3."[144] No one knows how to go from inert matter to living matter. No one can claim that Big Bang-2, Big Bang-3 and the evolutions following each of these basic transitions have been scientifically solved by Charles Darwin (1809-1882) and his successors. How did the Universe, life, and humans evolve is the question of *when* did they evolve.

Quantum reality seems uncertain and probabilistic at the micro level while macroworld seems boundless in measurement. There is an attempt to integrate the Quantum Mechanics (QM) and the general theory of relativity for better understanding of the middle Universe.

## 2.2 Integration of QM and General Theory of Relativity

Currently, Polish priest and Physicist Michal Heller (b. 1936) is researching the singularity problem in general relativity and the use of non-commutative geometry in seeking the unification of general relativity and Quantum Mechanics.[145] In his view, philosophy, history of science, science and theology, all of these different facets of science point to something truly important about the 'blueprint' of Creation and the teachings of the Church which help us to understand that blueprint. General relativity and quantum theory are the twin pillars of 20th century physics. The *Theory of Relativity* is Einstein's one-man show of the 20th century science. Contemporary cosmology rests on this theory. According to Newton gravitational action between two bodies takes place instantaneously, which is known as action at a distance. There was a difficulty how an action or force could be transmitted without a medium. So ether was brought in as medium for the discovery of the speed of light. Scientists were searching an absolute frame of reference for an absolute motion. Ether comes as the fixed absolute frame of reference. Thus, the epoch making Michelson-Morley experiment comes in. The theory of relativity was born in light, the speed of light. Albert Michelson (1852-1931) and Edward Morley (1838-1923), two American Physicists, tried to measure the speed of light in 1887. They found the speed of light was the same in every direction.

Albert Einstein (1879-1955) brings out the theory of relativity from Maxwell's equations for the motion of electromagnetic waves, which assumed the speed of light as constant, which was later fixed by the Michelson-Morley experiment.[146] Einstein's special theory of relativity is called special because it is concerned only with non-accelerated relative motion while general theory of relativity addresses the problem of gravity and accelerated motion. Einstein's general theory of relativity suspended Newton's 300 year old theory of gravity.[147] Newton's space and time were fixed quantities whereas Einstein's relative. "Relative is a theory which holds that concepts like mass, motion, length, time, simultaneity, etc., are not absolute but relative. They are relative to the frame of reference."[148] The gravitational forces affect electromagnetic radiation and bend rays of light, which has been validated in astronomical observations. The *special theory of relativity* is based on two postulates: 1) In any two systems that things move relative to one another with constant velocity, all physical laws and principles are expressed in the same mathematical form.[149] 2) The speed of light in vacuum has the same constant value, independent of the velocity of the source or the recipient.[150]

Albert Einstein presented this theory of relativity in 1905 breaking away from classical Newtonian physics where time is viewed independent of space. He abolished not only absolute space but time also. There is no absolute simultaneity at different locations. The present time, the right now, exists only at the location of observation; now is only here. Time is viewed as a coordinate like space coordinates. "Transformations of the coordinates of space and time takes place between two systems of reference moving at constant velocity relative to each other; length and time, and also mass, depend on the relative motion."[151] The effects of these spacetime transformations are known as Lorentz transformations after the Dutch Physicist Hendrik Antoon Lorentz (1853-1928). The observer is located in a system of reference S that moves at a constant velocity v relative to the system $S_1$ of the observed object; the speed of light in vacuum is c. A rod resting in system $S_1$ where its length is $l_0$, has when remeasured in system S shortened to $l = l_0.\sqrt{(1 - (v/c)^2)}$. The moving train looks shorter for the person who is on the ground. There is a contraction of length. If time measured in system S' is $T_0$, the observer in system S finds the longer period of time T, $T= T_0 /\sqrt{(1 - (v/c)^2)}$. If the object is moving closer to the speed of light, time is gained. Newton thought that light was made up of particles, but then it was discovered that it behaves like a wave. Now we say it is neither particle nor wave but *wavicle*. Light is both wave and particle. The uncertainty principle, presented in 1927 by the German Physicist Werner Heisenberg, states that position and velocity of a particle cannot, even in theory, be measured exactly at the same time: the more accurately one knows the position, the less accurately one can know the velocity, and vice versa.[152] An object that, at rest in system $S_1$, has the mass $m_0$ has in system S the mass m, where, $m = m_0 / \sqrt{(1 - (v/c)^2)}$. Einstein's energy mass relation is $E = mc^2$. It states that an object's total energy (E) is the product of its mass (m) and the speed (v) of light squared. The energy radiated every second by the Sun is $360 \times 10^{24}$J and the speed of light is $300 \times 10^6$ m/s; we can find the Sun's loss of mass per second.[153] The relation $E = mc^2$ means that every energy unit corresponds to the mass $m = E / c^2$, so the Sun's loss of mass per second is $m = 360 \times 10^{24} / (300 \times 10^6)^2 = 4.10^9$ kg = 4 teragrams.[154]

Einstein says if a number of people watch the same event – say, the flight of a raven towards a tree, the laws of physics are the same for each observer. But if you compare the notes of a person who is on the ground and a person on a train moving parallel to the raven, they will disagree about the speed of the raven and the tree. This is the principle of relativity; they are relative to each other's motions. Einstein's second assumption contradicts the principle of relativity; no matter at what speed they are travelling, the speed of the light remains constant, 300 million metres per second, denoted as c. If the raven were acting like a photon, then the observer on the train and the observer from the ground value for the raven's speed. Einstein realized that flow of the time changes according to the observer. The clock on the train is slower than the ground clock. Five seconds for the person on the train may be 10 seconds for the person on the ground. Not only time changes with the speed but length and mass also change. When the object speeds up they become shorter and heavier. A three feet stick may look one foot and a five kilos object may weigh 9 kilos. When Einstein applied the theory of relativity to gravity he did not suspect that his new equation would describe the ultimate zero, infinity or the black hole. When you accelerate an object, you subject it to force or gravity; you change its motion through time and space (spacetime). As space gets distorted (curved) close to a massive object, time too gets slower. Time gets slower and curvature becomes bigger and bigger. As you get into curved regions of space, masses of the body increase which is known as *mass inflation*. Light does not go in a straight line, but in a curved path around stars. Sir Arthur Stanley Eddington (1882-1944), a British astronomer, measured the position of a star during a solar eclipse and spotted the curvature that Einstein had predicted.

Integrating both the principles of general relativity and quantum theory is known as quantum gravity. It is the relationship between gravitation and quantized matter. It would measure the microstructure of spacetime, so-called Planck scale, at which all fundamental constants of the ingredient theories, c (the velocity of light in vacuum), *ħ* (Planck's constant), and G (Newton's constant), come together to form units of mass, length, and time.[155] Today this scale seems nearly impossible yet the quest for a quantum theory of gravity will continue. Let us see how the Quantum Mechanics measures the physical world.

### 2.2.1 Quantum Mechanics

Some basic ontological principles of space and time, of causality, of determination, of continuity, and the principle of the conservation of energy of the classical physics are violated or changed by Quantum Mechanics. Quantum Mechanics denied the exact simultaneous values of position and momentum that can be assigned to all physical quantities. Niels Bohr believed that an object and an objectively existing reality in the classical concepts of 'space,' 'time,' 'causation,' and 'continuity' were equivalent physical concepts of 'position,' 'time,' 'momentum,' and 'energy' respectively. The picture of space as a three-dimensional space, and of time as a separate thing, was *changed* by Einstein, first into a combination which we call space-time, and then still further into a curved space-time to represent gravitation.[156] There is a rule in Quantum Mechanics that says that one *cannot know both* where something is and how fast it is moving. The atomic world is nothing like our world, no matter how much we try to pretend it is. The uncertainty of the *momentum* and the uncertainty of the *position* are complementary, and the product of the two is constant ($\Delta x \ \Delta p \geq \hbar/2 \ \pi$).[157] Quantum Mechanics unifies the idea of the *field* and its *waves*, and the *particles*, all into one.[158] Quantum Mechanics started in 1900 when Max Planck (1858-1947) made the discovery that light, which was considered to be purely wave-like, was in fact composed of energy which came in discrete packets, called 'quanta.' The energy of the packets, $e$, is proportional to the light frequency, $f$, the constant of proportionality being Planck's constant, $h$. $E = hf$. From Einstein, $E = mc^2 = (mc).c = p.c$ (where $p$ = momentum, mass × velocity) $= p.f\lambda$ (treating the particle like wave $c = f\lambda$, $\lambda$ = wavelength). So from previous results, $E = hf = pf\lambda$ then $\lambda = h/p$.

There is an inevitable uncertainty about the position of the particle (due to the resolving power of the light used), the uncertainty in the particle's position being: $\Delta x \approx \lambda$. When the light particle (photon) hits the particle under observation it inevitably alters its *momentum* (speed) according to the result of Louis de Broglie: $\Delta p \approx h/p$. And on combining these two equations we get: $\Delta x \, \Delta p \approx h$ which is the Heisenberg's Uncertainty Principle. The electron does not have a precise position and a precise momentum at the same time. "The subatomic world is a world of puzzles, paradoxes and perplexities. Chaos, randomness and probabilities rule over the subatomic world."[159] So the mathematical description of the wave–particle duality of matter and energy is probable.

Microworld Quantum Mechanics seems probable and uncertain. Let us see the macroworld where space and time are fused into a single entity, spacetime, like a substance.

### 2.2.2 General Theory of Relativity

The zero in the modern theory of relativity creates the paradox of the infinite nothing of the black holes. Zero in Quantum Mechanics invests the vacuum with infinite energy. Einstein's equations predicted the black hole, a star so dense that nothing can escape from its grasp, not even light. When an extremely massive star collapses, it disappears. The gravitational attraction is so great that no force in the Universe can stop its collapse – not the repulsion of its electrons, not the pressure of neutron against neutron or quark against quark – nothing. The dying star gets smaller and smaller. Then zero (relativistic 0). The star crams itself into zero space. This is a *black hole*, an object so paradoxical that some scientists believe that black holes can be used to travel faster than light – and backward in time.

The key to black hole's strange properties is the way it curves space-time. A black hole takes up no space at all, but it still has a mass. Since the black hole has a mass, it causes the space-time to curve. Normally this would not cause a problem. As you approach a heavy star, the curvature gets greater and greater, but once you have passed the outer edge of the star itself, the curvature decreases again, bottoming out at the centre of the star. In contrast, a black hole is a *point*. It takes up zero space, so there is no outer edge, no place where space begins to flatten out again. The curvature of the space gets greater and greater as you approach a black hole, and it never bottoms out. The curvature goes off to infinity because the black hole takes up zero space; the star has torn a hole in space-time. The zero of black hole is a *singularity*, an *open wound* in the fabric of the Universe.

Even though the black hole is a star, none of the light it radiates ever escapes past the event horizon, and that's why it is black. The only way to look at the black hole's singularity is to go beyond the event horizon and see for us. Travelling beyond the edge of the event horizon is like stepping of the edge of the Universe. We will never return. This is the *comic censor*. Though scientists can detect black holes, they still have not spotted the relativistic zeros at their centres, since the singularities are shielded by the event horizon.

The Universe was born in zero at the $0^{th}$ hour. Out of the void, out of nothing at all, came a cataclysmic explosion that created all energy and matter that the entire Universe is made of. As time runs forward the Universe expands and expands. The Universe had a beginning about 13.7 billion years in the past, and space had been expanding ever since. At some point the Universe would shrivel and wither and then eventually disappear as a point – the singularity at the beginning of time and space. This is the *primal zero (quantum 0),* the birthplace of time and space, the Big Bang. Where did the singularity of the Big Bang come from? Zero holds the secret. The zero of the vacuum must explain the lumpiness of the Universe. Zero must also hold the secret of what created the cosmos. Just as the nothingness of the vacuum and the zero point energy spawn particles, they might spawn Universes too. The froth of quantum foam, the spontaneous death and birth of particles might explain the origin of the cosmos. Perhaps the Universe is just a quantum fluctuation on a grand scale – an enormous singular particle that came into existence out of the ultimate vacuum. This cosmic egg would explode, inflate and create the space-time of our Universe. It may be that our Universe may be simply one of many fluctuations. Thus, zero might hold the secret to our existence and the existence of other Universes. It will also be responsible for the end of our Universe. It may also hold a secret for future space travel.

Integrating quantum 0 with relativistic 0 seems paradoxical. Let us see some of the paradoxes of Planck time, temperature and big crunch.

## 2.3 Paradoxes of Planck Time, Absolute Temperature and Big Crunch

The moment at $10^{-43}$ second after the Big Bang is known as *Planck time*, named after the German Physicist Max Planck (1858-1947). The Planck length is the scale at which classical ideas about gravity and space-time cease to be valid, and quantum effects dominate. This is the 'quantum of length', the smallest measurement of length with any meaning. And roughly equal to $1.6 \times 10^{-35}$m or about $10^{-20}$ times the size of a proton. The Planck time is the time it would take a photon travelling at the speed of light to across a distance equal to the Planck length. This is the 'quantum of time', the smallest measurement of time that has any meaning, and is equal to $10^{-43}$ seconds. No smaller division of time has any meaning. Within the framework of the laws of physics as we understand them today, we can say only that the Universe came into existence when it already had an age of $10^{-43}$ seconds. Before a time classified as a Planck time, $10^{-43}$ seconds, all of the *four* fundamental forces are presumed to have been unified into *one force*. All matter, energy, space and time are presumed to have exploded outward from the original singularity. Nothing is known of this period. It is not that we know a great deal about later periods either, it is just that we have no real coherent models of what might happen under such conditions. The electroweak unification has been supported by the discovery of the W and Z particles, and can be used as a platform for discussion of the next step, the Grand Unification Theory (GUT). The final unification has been called a 'super grand unification theory', and becoming more popular is the designation 'theory of everything' (TOE). But 'theories of everything' are separated by two great leaps beyond the experiments we could ever hope to do on the Earth.

The visible light is the portion of the electromagnetic spectrum that is visible to the human eye. The spectrum has seven orderly colours: red, orange, yellow, green, blue, indigo, and violet. We are familiar with how heated metal first glows a dull red colour, then, as the temperature is increased, a brighter red, then moving to white and blue.[160] The quanta of blue light had more energy than the quanta of red light. "Infinity and zero are inseparable and are essential to mathematics. Mathematicians had no choice but to live with them."[161] For Physicists adding infinities and dividing by zeros seemed utterly irrelevant to the workings of the Universe but, when they began to encounter zeros in the natural world, zero crossed over from mathematics to physics. In thermodynamics zero became an uncrossable barrier: the coldest temperature possible. In the theory of relativity a zero becomes a black hole, a monstrous star that swallows entire suns. In Quantum Mechanics a zero is responsible for a bizarre source of energy – infinite and ubiquitous, present even in the deepest vacuum – and a phantom force exerted by nothing at all. In the realm of thermodynamics absolute zero is the state where a container of gas has been drained of all of its energy.[162] This is in actuality an unattainable goal. It is the lowest temperature possible. We can never cool an object to absolute zero. This barrier was the beginning of a new scientific revolution in thermodynamics. Thermodynamics is the study of the way heat, and energy in general, behave. It is impossible to create machines that eternally produce power without any source of energy or without wasting of energy. From thermodynamics came the discipline of statistical mechanics, the basic properties of matter, even the nature of light itself.

Our present complex cosmos manifests a huge range of temperature and density – from blazingly hot stars, to the dark night sky. What will be the fate of the Universe? Will it last forever or will it end? That question has been in our thoughts since humanity first began to think. In our current view of the Universe there are two possible futures. One possibility is that the Universe will come to an end in the opposite of a Big Bang called The Big Crunch. The Universe has an origin at a given point of time, 13.7 billion years ago, and it will die as a contingent being like all other living things. The other possibility is that we live in an Eternal Universe that will never come to end. Universe-time, the origin of the Universe has a beginning there is no infinite past.

The *Big Crunch* is one of the scenarios predicted by scientists in which the Universe may end. It is based on Einstein's Theory of General Relativity. That is, if the Big Bang describes how the Universe most possibly began, the Big Crunch describes how it will end as a consequence of that beginning. It tells us that the Universe's expansion, which is due to the Big Bang, will not continue forever. Instead, at a certain point in time, it will stop expanding and collapse into itself, pulling everything with it until it eventually turns into the biggest black hole ever. As gravity pulls on the matter, the Universe will begin to contract, falling inward until it has collapsed back into a super-hot, super-dense *singularity*. Well, we all know how everything is squeezed into that big black hole singularity. Hence, the name is Big Crunch. The Big Crunch is actually a consequence of the Big Bang.

All things were in one primordial matter, singularity, one spacetime, quantum zero, one unified energy or force before separating into four fundamental forces.

### 2.3.1 The Four Universal Forces

The four fundamental forces of nature appear distinct: gravity, electromagnetism and the strong and weak nuclear forces. The familiar force of gravity,discovered by Newton,pulls us down into our seat, toward the Earth's centre. Another force, electromagnetism which we learnt through the discoveries of Coulomb, Ampere, Faraday and Maxwell, holds the atoms of our seat together, preventing our atoms from intruding on those of our seat. "Electricity and magnetism were understood as two separate forces until the 1870s, when James Clerk Maxwell proved that they were one."[163] The remaining two forces work at the atomic level, which we never feel, despite being made of atoms. The strong force binds neutrons and protons inside the nucleus together. Lastly, the weak force is responsible for radioactive decay, specifically, beta decay where a neutron within the nucleus changes into a proton and an electron, which is ejected from the nucleus. The gravitational and electromagnetic interactions are long-ranged while the other two are short-ranged.

A force is defined as a push or pull that changes an object's state of motion or causes the object to deform. Newton defined a force as anything that caused an object to accelerate, $F = ma$, where $F$ is force, $m$ is mass and $a$ is acceleration. Isaac Newton envisioned gravity as a pull between any two objects that was directly related to their masses and inversely related to the square of the distance separating them. From 1687 until the early 20$^{th}$ century, Newton's idea of gravity as a 'tug-of-war' between any two objects dominated physics. In 1915, Albert Einstein realized that Newton's laws of motion and gravity did not, in fact, apply to objects in high gravity or at high speeds, like the speed of light. He envisioned gravity as a distortion of space caused by mass. Gravity appears to be the most powerful force but in atomic level, it has little effect because the masses of subatomic particles are so small. What is the agent that conveys the force of gravity through the vacuum of space? It is the subatomic particle graviton, quantum particle equivalent to photons, which carries light.

When we set the opposite poles of the magnets near one another, and the magnets will attract each other. These are familiar examples of electromagnetic force; opposite charges attract, while like charges repel. In 1785, French Physicist Charles Coulomb described the force of electrically charged objects as directly proportional to the magnitudes of the charges and inversely related to the square of the distances between them. In 1819, Danish Physicist Hans Christian Oersted discovered that electricity and magnetism were very much related, leading him to declare that an electric current generates a magnetic force. Michael Faraday weighed in on electromagnetism, showing that magnetism could be used to generate electricity in 1839. In the 1860s, James Clerk Maxwell, the Scottish math and physics whiz, derived equations that described how electricity and magnetism were related. Dutchman Hendrik Lorentz calculated the force acting on a charged particle in an electromagnetic field in 1892. Subatomic particles exerted electromagnetic forces on each other. They constantly exchange virtual photons during their electromagnetic interactions. But electromagnetism can't explain how the nucleus holds together.

The nucleus of any atom is made of positively charged protons and neutral neutrons. The force holding the nucleus together is called the strong force, alternately called the strong nuclear force or strong nuclear interaction. In 1935, Hideki Yukawa modelled this force and proposed that protons interacting with each other and with neutrons exchanged a particle called a *meson* – later called a *pion* – to transmit the strong force. In the 1950s, Physicists built particle accelerators to explore the structure of the nucleus. They found that protons and neutrons were made of smaller particles called *quarks*. So, the strong force held the quarks together, which in turn held the nucleus together.

In beta emission, a neutron decays into a proton, anti-neutrino and electron (beta particle). The electron and anti-neutrino are ejected from the nucleus. The force responsible for this decay and emission must be different and weaker than the strong force, thus, it's unfortunate name – the weak force or the weak nuclear force or weak nuclear interaction. W and Z bosons were discovered in 1983.

QED (Quantum Electro Dynamics) and QCD (Quantum Chromo Dynamics) describe the interactions between subatomic particles and nuclear forces. How does exchanging particles transmit a force? Physicists do not know how gravity transmits. Gravity is the weakest force at about $6 \times 10^{-29}$ times that of the strong nuclear force, however, it has an infinite range. In 1963, Physicists Sheldon Glashow, Abdul Salam and Steve Weinberg suggested that the weak nuclear force and electromagnetic force might combine at higher energies in what would be called the electroweak force. They predicted that this would occur at an energy of about 100 giga-electron volts (100GeV) or a temperature of $10^{15}$ K, which occurred shortly after the Big Bang. In 1983, Physicists reached these temperatures in a particle accelerator and showed that the electromagnetic force and weak nuclear force were related.[164]

Ernest Rutherford showed that an atom is mainly empty space, with electrons in orbit around a nucleus comprised of protons and neutrons.[165] Everything is made up of a few fundamental particles and that these interact through four forces: gravity, electromagnetism, the weak force and the strongforce.[166] All physical changes and motion are the result of the four fundamental forces. The objects or particles from which these forces operate bring about every physical change that occurs, either within themselves, or through interaction with other objects or particles. The motion of planets stars and galaxies are the result of gravitational forces. The chemical reactions are grounded in the electromagnetic forces. The strong nuclear force keeps sub-atomic particles within nuclei bonded together, and release tremendous energy when those bonds are broken. The weak nuclear force brings about radioactive decay about certain elements.

> "Electricity and magnetism were combined by Maxwell's theory of electromagnetism in the nineteenth century. The electromagnetic force was then combined with the weak force in the (now experimentally confirmed) 'electroweak' theory of the 1970s. Theorists have subsequently merged the electroweak force with the strong force as part of a Grand Unified Theory (GUT), although this has still not been verified experimentally. The final (and as yet incomplete) step is the unification with gravity, as attempted by superstring theory or M-theory."[168]

The key stages in the emergence of complexity: The first particles – protons and neutrons, the first stars and galaxies, the synthesis of the periodic table in stars, formation of planets around later-generation stars and the formation of biosphere. The strength of gravity, compared to other forces, is one of the key numbers of physics, not yet explained. The biosphere requires a balance between the nuclear force (the 'strong' interactions that binds together the protons in a nucleus) and the electric repulsive force that drives them apart. Otherwise there would be no periodic table. There must be some fluctuations for gravity to feed on. "Primitive Man was only aware of the mundane scales between, about $10^{-1}$ cm to $10^{7}$cm. The invention of the first microscopes and telescopes then expanded the range from about $10^{-5}$cm to $10^{17}$cm. Today the development of particle accelerators and space telescopes has expanded the range from $10^{-15}$cm to $10^{27}$cm."[169] New set of particles have been collected under the title 'supersymmetry.' We have supersymmetric boson particles for all the fermions and supersymmetric fermion particles for all the bosons. Supersymmetric quarks, leptons, photons, gravitons, gluons, W's and Z's are known as squarks, sleptons, photinos, gravitinos, gluinos, winos and zinos respectively.

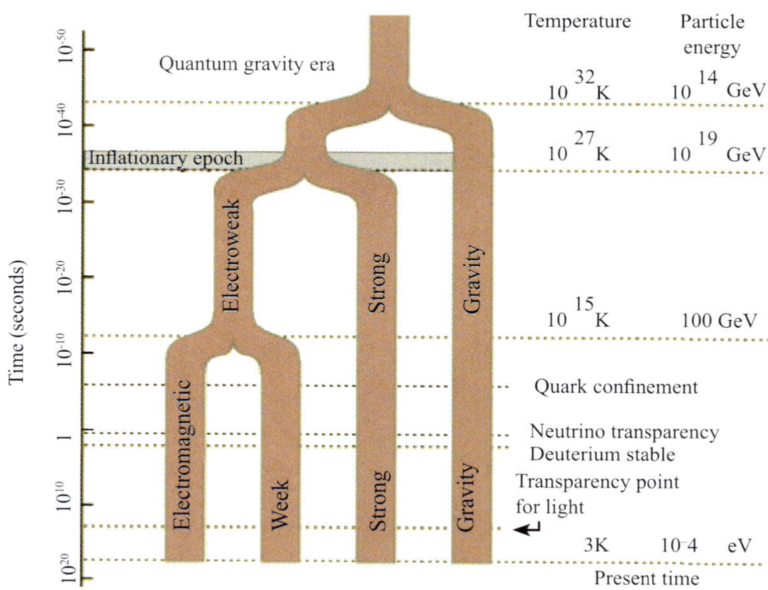


Figure 2.7 Unification of Gravity[167]

The matter has a certain quantity, which we call energy, which does not change in the manifold changes which nature undergoes. The law is called the conservation of energy. It is an abstract idea, a mathematical principle, a numerical quantity which does not change when something happens. We have no knowledge of what energy is. "The energy has a large number of different forms, and there is a formula for each one. These are: gravitational energy, kinetic energy, radiant energy, nuclear energy, mass energy."[170] Energy is associated with activity, with processes and this implies that the nature of subatomic particles is intrinsically dynamic – a continuous dance of energy. If nuclear energy centres come under some mad or fanatic people they can create a nuclear holocaust. According to Lemaitre, the primeval atom has become visible in the form of this Universe. The 7 continents have been discovered. The scientific community has discovered 118 elements out of which 90 occur naturally on earth. Our solar system is part of the Milky Way Galaxy. We have Andromeda galaxy as our neighbour. Other galaxies are far away. People have landed on the moon, gone into the deep oceans, have sent a rocket to the Mars. The 31st October is a symbolic date, which is based on interpolated data from the original 5-year period estimates prepared by the Population Division of United Nations, Department of Economic and Social Affairs. So on 31st October, 2011 we have become 7 billion people on this earth. The *anthropic principle* is the philosophical argument that observations of the physical Universe must be compatible with the conscious life that observes it. After all, all this things are for human life and love.

## 2.3.2 The Grand Unified Force of Life and Love

What sort of stuff constitutes the Universe? Some choose more unified and basic, such as numbers (Pythagoras) or the Void (Anaximander) or Water (Thales), or some combination of basic elements (Empedocles).[171] Democritus' basic stuff was atoms, Descartes had matter and mind and Plato had forms. There is interconnectedness between microworld and cosmos – between the inner space of atoms and the outer space of the Universe. There are links between small and large. Our everyday world is determined by atoms and chemistry. Stars are powered by fusion of nuclei within those atoms. Vera Rubin (b. 1928) discusses another link: galaxies are seemingly held together by swarms of subnuclear particles that make up the 'dark matter.' The way the Universe began is not within the realm of science. The General Theory of Relativity breaks down in the very strong gravitational fields in the early Universe. When the Universe is Planck size, a billion trillion trillionth of a centimetre, the two scales are the same, and quantum theory has to be taken into account. Unless gravity can be integrated with the three other fundamental forces, there can be no 'theory of everything', or 'grand unified theory', the holy grail of modern physics. We need to combine the General Theory of Relativity with Quantum Theory to understand the Origin of the Universe, the Big Bang Theory. The theory of relativity creates the paradox of the infinite nothingness of the black holes which are known as *relativistic zeros* while the primordial state of the Universe at the time of Big Bang is known as *quantum zero* in the quantum world.

The Big Bang theory postulates that the Universe had a beginning and it will come to an end. This fact repudiates materialistic philosophies. Once matter is considered eternal, the 'human being' or 'humankind' occupies the central place who is endowed with the consciousness that matter lacks. But the materialistic philosophy's ethics cannot be rationally grounded. When God is the creator, ethics is God-centred due to his superiority. Thomas Aquinas (1225-1274) gives us the five valid ways for God's existence. 1) The first argument reasons from *motion* to a prime or first mover, since everything that moves is moved by another, there must thereby exist an *Unmoved Mover*. 2) The second argument reasons from an order of *efficient causes* to a first efficient cause, the sequence of causes which make up this Universe must have a *First Efficient Cause*. 3) The third argument indicates the *necessity* of a being or one who brings material being, since all existent things depend upon other things for their existence, there must exist at least one thing that is a *Necessary Being*. 4) The fourth argument goes from the *degrees of* goodness, truth, nobility, or beauty, since all existent things can be compared as to such qualities as goodness, there must exist something that is an *Absolutely Good Being*. 5) The fifth argument arises from *design* or the *purposefulness* of things, also named as *'The Teleological Argument'* – The intricate design and order of existent things and natural processes imply that a *Great Intelligent Designer* exists. Processes that followed the Big Bang prove that there is a design in the Universe though the materialists deny the intervention of a conscious Creator. There is a design in the creation, a design that includes order and purpose, teleology and grace. This is the evidence of God's intervention, sovereignty and omniscience. The Universe operates within the framework of the laws of science and this is accessible to the human mind is one of the most interesting pieces of evidence of design in the Universe. To understand the Universe, human has to have the capacity of comprehension and memory. Science and causality do not explain whether the Universe was created or not, but the way it operates.

Common sense science reflects the Judeo-Christian Worldview that is based on *three* unprovable but reasonable assumptions:[172] 1) *Reality*: The world is real, and we can understand the nature of that reality. Objects are durable and continue to exist whether or not we think about them and whether or not we observe them. 2) *Causality*: Events in the Universe follow the law of cause and effect. Every event has a preceding cause. For example, an electron with negative charge is attracted by a proton with opposite charge and moves toward it. It doesn't move without a reason. 3) *Unity*: Nature is unified in two major ways. First, the forces between objects follow the same laws of physics whether the objects are large as galaxies or small as atomic nuclei. Second, the design and structure of atoms is the same everywhere in the Universe. Hot hydrogen gas emits the same colours of light whether the light comes from a distant galaxy or from a laboratory on earth. These assumptions of *reality*, *causality* and *unity* seem self-evident to many people. So Modern Science is built upon some opposite assumptions of *quantum* reality, *randomness*, and *multiplicity* of force laws.

The *reality* is ever approachable yet not fully attainable at the deeper level. It is an undivided wholeness. It consists of a steadily increasing number of parallel Universes. The world, made of ordinary objects, obeys its physical laws. It is twofold, consisting of potentials and actualities. Physics is not physical, but metaphysical at the deeper level. Lucretius (c.100-55BCE), not Charles Darwin, has been the principal spokesman for evolution during the last two millennia. Common Sense Science and the Judeo-Christian world view are rational approaches with reasons for events such as particle motion and emission of light. The Physicist James Jeans (1877-1946) declared that God was a mathematician. Paul Dirac (1902-1984), one of the inventors of Quantum Mechanics, went further, opining that He was a pure mathematician. Is mathematics invented or discovered? The word 'invention' means bringing into existence something that was not previously there. Thomas Edison invented electric light, Graham Bell invented the telephone. Mathematical objects lead a virtual existence, not a real one: they reside in minds, not embodied in any kind of hardware. What goes on is neither invention nor discovery, but a complex context-dependent mixture of both. Since the *abstraction* came out of reality, it is no surprise if it applies back to reality.

## Conclusion

All things are made of atoms or particles. There are four charged particles: electron, proton, positron and antiproton. Every particle or matter has some quantity and this quantity has to radiate constantly which is known as ultraviolet catastrophe. The position and momentum of a particle cannot be simultaneously measured with arbitrarily high precision which is known as Heisenberg's uncertainty principle. It means we cannot also fully predict the properties of the basic elements of matter. Science and Mathematics fail at some stage in describing the ultimate reality at micro level. The vacuum by definition has nothing inside it – no particle, no light, *nothing*. Thus, the *vacuum* should have *no energy* at all. The energy in a given time of vacuum must be fluctuating constantly as Einstein's formula says $E = mc^2$. The fluctuation of the *energy*in the vacuum is the *same thing as the fluctuation* in the amount of mass. This is the zero-point energy, infinity in the formula of Quantum Theory. The Big Bang Theory states that 13.7 billion years ago there was *nothing*. Thus, there is a beginning of space, time and energy of our Universe which is known as singularity, the origin of the Universe. We have understood the cosmos in three cosmological revolutions. The first is *scientific understanding* of the Universe, began with Thales and culminated with Copernicus who replaced the geocentric Universe to the heliocentric one. The second cosmological revolution is with Einstein's general theory of relativity, made us aware that the *Universe has a beginning and the end* even though it is expanding. The third cosmological revolution challenges us to understand the reality of the hot Big Bang Universe which has begun 13.7 billion years ago would one day come to an end in a big crunch or in a black hole in spite of its many years of existence. Or will it begin another Big Bang Universe with the black hole?

The hot Big Bang is the singularity. Singularity is the point technically described by the cosmologist at a time equal to zero. This is known as T (time) = 0. Absolute zero tries to find out the unity or the equilibrium of the cosmos in *triple temperatures*. The micro world of Quantum Mechanics, the medium world of classical physics and the mega world of thermodynamics are fashioned in the roots of quantum zero, relativistic zero and absolute zero respectively.

We have discovered different zeros like absolute zero, quantum zero, relativistic zero and cosmic zero which is just not nothing but has significant contribution to make and so they are 'something.' There are vacuums in space but they are not empty. They are representing vacuums and emptinesses like mathematical 0. In fact these physical vacuums or scientific zeros are *full of energies*, fields where the subatomic particles are constantly creating and annihilating particles in the micro level. As we see, matter exists in *three states: solid, liquid and gaseous*. Scientists are trying to find out an *absolute state* or absolute 0 where the solid, liquid and gaseous states can coexist. So it has become impossible to find out that temperature. Absolute zero is the temperature defined as the point at which all molecular motion ceases and it contributes significantly to our understanding of thermodynamics. No matter is in absolute rest. Even in 0 pressures matter is dynamic. They have got closer to absolute 0 (0 K). As we discover in Quantum Mechanics, matter is composed of *wavicles*. Though the mass of the particle or wave is negligible or 0, yet there is certain energy within them. *Quantum 0* is not just a vacuous matter, quantity or mass, it is a fluctuating of energy. It is a zero-point energy. It is an *infinite energy*. This is a Universe of infinite energy like an atom bomb.

A zero in the Relativity Theory creates other creative paradoxes like quantum 0, relativistic 0 and infinite energy. Relativistic zero is the infinite energy, 0 space of black hole. When the mass of the star becomes smaller and smaller and finally 0, the star crams itself into 0 space. This is a black hole. Some say black holes can be used to travel faster than light, which is another paradox, where we say speed of the light is not absolute. Cosmological zero is the origin of the Big Bang. In that singularity, time, space, speed, mass, matter, and energies of particles and waves have emerged. From that 0 has emerged the cosmos. At the macro level of the Universe it is expanding and we may say that it is expanding not into empty space, but into zero. Our Universe is dotted with over 100 billion galaxies, and each one contains roughly 100 billion stars. So our whole cosmos may symbolise zero, an empty space, a vacuum where particles and waves are constantly moving in dynamic ways to give life to humans and others.[173] A challenge for 21st century physics is to decide whether there have been many 'Big Bangs' rather than just one – and (if there are many) how much variety they might display.

Is not empty space pure nothingness? Is not a vacuum simply 'nothing?' *No.* "The Physicist regards space as more like an elastic medium than as emptiness....even the purest vacuum is a ferment of activity and is crowded with evanescent structures. To the Physicist 'nothing' means 'no space' as well as no matter."[174] The moment at $10^{-43}$ second after the Big Bang is known as *Planck time* after the name of Max Planck. And roughly equal to $1.6\times10^{-35}$m or about $10^{-20}$ times the size of a proton is the Planck length. Before a time classified as a Planck time, $10^{-43}$ seconds, all of the four fundamental forces are presumed to have been unified into one force. All matter, energy, space and time are presumed to have exploded outward from the original singularity. Nothing is known of this period. Some Physicists have proposed a Grand Unification Theory (GUT) or Theory of Everything (TOE) bringing all four fundamental forces of nature which are distinct: gravity, electromagnetism and the strong and weak nuclear forces.

Common sense worldview is based on *three* unprovable but reasonable assumptions: 1) *Reality*: The world is real, and we can understand the nature of that reality. Objects are durable and continue to exist whether or not we think about them and whether or not we observe them. 2) *Causality*: Events in the Universe follow the law of cause and effect. Every event has a preceding cause. 3) *Unity*: Nature is unified in two major ways. First, the forces between objects follow the same laws of physics whether the objects are large as galaxies or small as atomic nuclei. Second, the design and structure of atoms is the same everywhere in the Universe. Hot hydrogen gas emits the same colours of light whether the light comes from a distant galaxy or from a laboratory on earth. These assumptions of *reality*, *causality* and *unity* seem self-evident to many people. So, Modern Science is built upon some opposite assumptions of *quantum* reality, *randomness*, and *multiplicity* of force laws.

There was nothing before the primordial matter. "The evolutionary journey of spiritualised matter led it to become self-cognising in humans. The presence of humans in the Universe, far from being an unexplainable surd, in fact helps us to understand the Universe deeply."[175] Has the Universe come from primeval matter by chance or someone has created out of nothing and designed its being? Let us see nothingness as constitutive of reality in a philosophico-theological manner.

## Endnotes

1. Richard P. Feynman, *Six Easy Pieces: Essentials of Physics Explained by Its Most Brilliant Teacher*, originally prepared for publication by Robert B. Leighton and Matthew Sands (New York: Addison-Wesley Publishing Co., 1995), 4.
2. Charles Seife, *Zero: The Biography of a Dangerous Idea* (New York: Penguin Putnam, 2000), 164.
3. *Ibid.*, 165.
4. *Ibid.*
5. Feynman, *Six Easy Pieces: Essentials of Physics Explained,* 117.
6. Seife, *Zero: The Biography of a Dangerous Idea,* 172.
7. Chris Clarke, "Quantum Mechanics, Consciousness and the Self," in *Science, Consciousness and Ultimate Reality*, ed. David Lorimer (Charlottesville: Imprint Academic, 2004), 71.
8. It may be noted that the Catholic Church has no fear of science or scientific discovery. God creates freely 'out of nothing' (CCC 296) *Catechism of the Catholic Church (CCC)* {1994; 8th reprint, New Delhi: Theological Publications in India, 2006}, 61.
9. John F. Haught, "Evolutionary Naturalism and the Future of Theology," in *Faith. Science. Culture: A 40 Year Retrospective Converging or Diverging Realities,* Discussion Session 1, Proceedings of the ITEST 40th Anniversary Conference, September, 2008, eds. Marianne Postiglione and Thomas P. Sheahen {Missouri: ITEST (Institute for Theological Encounter with Science and Technology)}, 67.
10. Clarke, "Quantum Mechanics, Consciousness and the Self," in *Science, Consciousness and Ultimate Reality*, 72.
11. *Ibid.,* 73.
12. Augustine Pamplany, *Cosmos, Bios and Theos: Introduction to Philosophy of Science, Scientific Cosmology and Science-Religion Dialogue* (Aluva: Institute of Science and Religion – Little Flower Seminary, 2004), 37.
13. Seife, *Zero: The Biography of a Dangerous Idea,* 66.
14. See *Catechism of the Catholic Church* (CCC) 285: "Ancient religions and cultures produced many myths concerning origins. Some philosophers have said that everything is God, that the world is God, or that the development of the world is the development of God (Pantheism). Others have said that the world is a necessary emanation arising from God and returning to him. Still others

have affirmed the existence of two eternal principles, Good and Evil, Light and Darkness, locked in permanent conflict (Dualism, Manichaeism). According to some of these conceptions, the world (at least the physical world) is evil, the product of a fall, and is thus, to be rejected or left behind (Gnosticism). Some admit that the world was made by God, but as by a watch-maker who, once he had made a watch, abandons it to itself (Deism). Finally, others reject any transcendent origin for the world, but see it as merely the interplay of matter that has always existed (Materialism). All these attempts bear witness to the permanence and universality of the question of origins. This inquiry is distinctively human" (CCC 285).

15. Augustine Pamplany and Job Kozhamthadam, *East-West Interface of Reality: A Scientific and Intuitive Inquiry into the Nature of Reality* {Pune: ASSR (Association of Science, Society and Religion), 2003}, 34-35.
16. Seife, *Zero: The Biography of a Dangerous Idea,* 66.
17. Daniel Kleppner and Roman Jackiw, "One Hundred Years of Quantum Physics," in *Science, Pathways of Discovery*, ed., Ivan Amato (New York: John Wiley and Sons, 2002), 144.
18. Pamplany, *Cosmos, Bios, and Theos: Introduction to Philosophy of Science, Scientific Cosmology and Science-Religion Dialogue*, 33.
19. Lord Rayleigh aka John William Strutt (1842-1919) was British Physicist and mathematician; and Sir James Jeans (1877-1946) was an English Physicist, astronomer and mathematician.
20. Seife, *Zero: The Biography of a Dangerous Idea,* 164.
21. The mathematical property of matrices has an important physical significance connected with what quantities could simultaneously be measured in Quantum Mechanics. See John Polkinghorne, *Quantum Theory: A Very Short Introduction* (New Delhi: Oxford University Press, 2006), 17.
22. Kleppner and Roman Jackiw, "One Hundred Years of Quantum Physics," in *Science, Pathways of Discovery*, 151.
23. *Ibid.*, 153.
24. *Ibid.*
25. Simon Singh, *Big Bang: The Origin of the Universe* (New York: Harper Perennial, 2005), 3.
26. Augustine Perumalil, *Religious Cosmologies* {Delhi: ISPCK (Indian Society for Promoting Christian Knowledge), 2007}, viii.

27. Charles Seife, *Alpha and Omega: The Search for the Beginning and End of the Universe* (New York: Viking, 2003), 2.
28. Augustine Pamplany, *Theological Mysteries in Scientific Perspective* (Bangalore: Asian Trading Corporation, 2005), 64.
29. "Alexander Friedmann," in *Microsoft Encarta Online Encyclopedia,* accessed July 3, 2009, http://encarta.msn.com/encyclopedia_761586013/alexander_friedmann.html.
30. Edward W. Kolb, "The Big Bang Origin of the Universe," in *Cosmic Beginnings and Human Ends*, eds. Clifford N. Mattews and Roy Abraham Varghese (Chicago: Open Court, 1995), 72-73 cited by Augustine Pamplany, *Theological Mysteries in Scientific Perspective* (Bangalore: Asian Trading Corporation, 2005), 65.
31. Pamplany, *Theological Mysteries in Scientific Perspective*, 65.
32. *Ibid.*
33. Ellie Crystal, "Big Bang Theory," in *Crystalinks*, ed. Ellie Crystal, accessed July 3, 2009, http://www.crystalinks.com/bigbang.html.
34. Seife, *Alpha and Omega*, 3.
35. Peter Coles, ed. *The Routledge Companion to The New Cosmology* (London: Routledge, 2001), 5.
36. Seife, *Alpha and Omega,* 5.
37. Patricia O'Grady, "Thales of Miletus," in *The Internet Encyclopedia of Philosophy,* ed. James Fieser and Bradley Dowden, accessed January 3, 2011, http://www.iep.utm.edu/t/thales.htm.
38. Charles H. Patternson, *Western Philosophy*, Vol. 1 (Lincoln: Cliff's Notes, 1970), 2.
39. Seife, *Alpha and Omega*, 4.
40. Joseph Silk, *The Big Bang*, 3rd ed. (New York: W. H. Freeman & Co., 2001), 10.
41. *Ibid.,* 12.
42. *Ibid.,* 11.
43. Stephen Hawking, *A Brief History of Time* (London: Bantam Books, 1988), 2.
44. *Ibid.,* 2.
45. Silk, *The Big Bang*, 15.
46. Coles, ed. *The Routledge Companion to The New Cosmology,* 7.
47. *Ibid.*
48. Seife, *Alpha and Omega,* 26.
49. *Ibid.,* 50.
50. Hawking, *A Brief History of Time*, 4.

51. Educational Broadcasting Corporation, "Copernicus' Universe," in *Stephen Hawking's Universe*, accessed January 4, 2011, http://www.pbs.org/wnet/hawking/Universes/html/coper.html.
52. Seife, *Alpha and Omega,* 18.
53. Karen C. Fox, *The Big Bang Theory: What it is. Where it Came from, and Why it Works* (New York: John Wiley and Sons, 2002), 25.
54. American Institute of Physics, "The Start of Scientific Cosmology," in *Cosmic Journey: A History of Scientific Cosmology,* accessed January 4, 2011, http://www.aip.org/history/cosmology/ideas/start-of-scientific-cosmology.htm.
55. Bernard Carr, "Mind and the Cosmos," in *Science, Consciousness and Ultimate Reality*, ed. David Lorimer (Charlottesville: Imprint Academic, 2004), 35.
56. Fox, *The Big Bang Theory: What it is. Where it Came from, and Why it Works,* 28.
57. Coles, ed. *The Routledge Companion to The New Cosmology,* 8.
58. Ernest Zebrowski, *A History of the Circle: Mathematical Reasoning and the Physical Universe* (London: Free Association Books, 1999), 102.
59. *Ibid.,* 103.
60. Silk, *The Big Bang*, 20.
61. Zebrowski, *A History of the Circle: Mathematical Reasoning and the Physical Universe*, 96.
62. *Ibid.,* 98.
63. *Ibid.,* 100.
64. Hawking, *A Brief History of Time*, 5.
65. Zebrowski, *A History of the Circle: Mathematical Reasoning and the Physical Universe*, 113.
66. Coles, ed. *The Routledge Companion to The New Cosmology,* 8.
67. Silk, *The Big Bang*, 21.
68. Robert Crawford, *Is God a Scientist? A Dialogue between Science and Religion* (New York: Palgrave Macmillan, 2004), 9.
69. Fox, *The Big Bang Theory: What it is. Where it Came from, and Why it Works,* 34.
70. Zebrowski, *A History of the Circle: Mathematical Reasoning and the Physical Universe*, 121.
71. Fox, *The Big Bang Theory: What it is. Where it Came from, and Why it Works,* 38.
72. Silk, *The Big Bang*, 26.

73. Seife, *Alpha and Omega: The Search for the Beginning and End of the Universe,* 50.
74. Coles, ed. *The Routledge Companion to The New Cosmology*, 10.
75. Hawking, *A Brief History of Time*, 13.
76. Coles, ed. *The Routledge Companion to The New Cosmology*, 10.
77. Caner Taslaman, "Evidence of the Big Bang," accessed January 4, 2011, http://www.bigbang.ws/articles.asp?id=66.
78. Coles, ed. *The Routledge Companion to The New Cosmology*, 10.
79. Mark Midborn, "'A Day Without Yesterday': Georges Lemaitre & the Big Bang," in *Catholic Education Resource Centre*, accessed January 4, 2011, http://www.catholiceducation.org/articles/science/sc0022.html.
80. Coles, ed. *The Routledge Companion to The New Cosmology*, 217.
81. *Ibid.*
82. Lori Tyahla, "Edwin P. Hubble," in *National Aeronautics and Space Administration*, accessed January 4, 2011, http://hubble.nasa.gov/overview/hubble_bio.php.
83. Hawking, *A Brief History of Time*, 54.
84. *Ibid.,* 143-144.
85. Silk, *The Big Bang*, 28.
86. John D. Barrow, *The Book of Nothing* (London: Vintage, 2000), 11.
87. Binoy Pichalakkatt, "Dialogue with Symbols: Exploring Zero, Śūnyatā and Trinity for a Holistic Reality," *Omega* 5, 2 (December 2006), 27.
88. Kuruvilla Pandikattu, *Meaning through Science and Religion* (Pune: Jnana-Deepa Vidyapeeth, 1999), 3.
89. "Universe," in *National Aeronautics Space Administration (NASA)*, accessed January 5, 2011, http://map.gsfc.nasa. gov/ universe/uni_age.html.
90. Jay M. Pasachoff, "Big Bang Theory," in *McGraw-Hill Encyclopedia of Science and Technology,* 9th ed., 20 Vols., Vol. 2, eds., Elizabeth Geller and others (New York: McGraw-Hill, 2002), 719.
91. "Five Year Results on the Oldest Light in the Universe," in *NASA*, accessed January 5, 2011, http://map.gsfc.nasa.gov/news/index.html#timeline.

92. Pamplany, *Cosmos, Bios and Theos: Introduction to Philosophy of Science, Scientific Cosmology and Science-Religion Dialogue,* 58.
93. Michio Kaku, *Parallel Worlds: A Journey through Creation, Higher Dimensions, and the Future of the Cosmos* (New York: Anchor Books, 2005), 105.
94. *Ibid.*
95. "Our Universe," in *NASA*, accessed January 5, 2011, http://map.gsfc.nasa.gov/universe/bb_cosmo_infl.html.
96. David Darling, "Inflationary Model," in *Internet Encyclopedia of Science*, accessed January 5, 2011, http://www.daviddarling.info/encyclopedia/I/inflationary_model.html.
97. David Curtis and others, "Quark Soup - The Elementary Particle Era," in *Science for the Millennium* (Illinois: The Board of Trustees of the University of Illinois, 1995), accessed January 6, 2011, http://archive.ncsa.illinois.edu/Cyberia/Cosmos/QuarkSoup.html.
98. Kaku, *Parallel Worlds: A Journey through Creation, Higher Dimensions, and the Future of the Cosmos,* 106.
99. David Darling, "Big Bang," in *The Internet Encyclopedia of Science*, accessed January 6, 2011, http://www.daviddarling.info/encyclopedia/B/Big_Bang.html.
100. Pandikattu, *Meaning through Science and Religion,* 4.
101. David Curtis and others, "Big Freeze Out," in *Science for the Millennium* (Illinois: The Board of Trustees of the University of Illinois, 1995), accessed January 6, 2011, http://archive.ncsa.illinois.edu/ Cyberia/ Cosmos/ BigFreezeOut.html.
102. Patricia Schwarz, "Cosmology: The Big Bang," in *The Official String Theory Web Site*, accessed January 6, 2011, http://www.superstringtheory.com/cosmo/bang07.html.
103. *Ibid.*
104. Fred Adams and Greg Laughlin, *The Five Stages of the Universe: Inside the Physics of Eternity* (New York: Touchstone, 1999), 35.
105. Schwarz, "Cosmology: The Big Bang," in *The Official String Theory Web Site*.
106. Gene Smith, "The Big Bang: A Brief History of the Universe," in *Astronomy Education & Outreach*, accessed January 7, 2011, http://cass.ucsd.edu/public/tutorial/BB.html.
107. Job Kozhamthadam, "Creation Without a Creator: Reflections on Contemporary Scientific Cosmologies," *Philosophy in Science,*

Vol. 6, ed. Michael Heller, William R. Stoeger, and Jozef M. Zycinski (Tucson: Pachart Publishing House, 1995), 10.

108. Ofer Lahav and Yasushi Suto, "Measuring our Universe from Galaxy Redshift Surveys," in *Living Reviews,* accessed January 7, 2011, http://relativity.livingreviews.org/open?pubNo=lrr-2004-8&page=articlesu1.html.
109. Konrad Rudnicki, "The Importance of Cosmological Principles for Research in Cosmology," in *Apeiron*, no. 4 (February 1989), accessed January 7, 2011, http://redshift.vif.com/ JournalFiles/ Pre2001/ V0N0 4PDF/ V0N04RUD.pdf.
110. Frank Thomas Smith, review of *The Cosmological Principles* by Konrad Rudnicki (Cracow: Jagiellonian University, 1995), accessed January 7, 2011, http://southerncrossreview.org/22/rudnicki.htm.
111. Robert J. Russell, "Physics and Cosmology," in *Counterbalance*, accessed January 8, 2011, http://www.counterbalance.net/physics/creat-frame.html.
112. Smith, Review of *The Cosmological Principles* by Konrad Rudnicki.
113. "Big Bang Theory," in *NASA*, accessed January 8, 2011, http://map.gsfc.nasa.gov/universe/bb_theory.html.
114. Björn Fuerbacher and Ryan Scranton, "Evidence for the Big Bang," in *The Talk Origins Archive*, accessed January 9, 2011, http://www.talkorigins.org/faqs/astronomy/bigbang.html.
115. "Big Bang Cosmology," in *NASA*, accessed January 9, 2011, http://map.gsfc.nasa.gov/universe/bb_theory.html.
116. *Ibid.*
117. Coles, ed. *The Routledge Companion to The New Cosmology*, 248.
118. *Ibid.,* 161.
119. "Tests of Big Bang: Expansion," in *NASA*, accessed January 10, 2011, http://map.gsfc.nasa.gov/universe/bb_tests_exp.html.
120. David L. Alles, ed. "The Evolution of the Universe," accessed January 11, 2011, http://fire.biol.wwu.edu/trent/alles/Cosmic_Evolution.pdf.
121. Charles H. Lineweaver, "The Cosmic Microwave Background," in *The Routledge Companion to The New Cosmology,* ed. Peter Coles (London: Routledge, 2001), 77.
122. Carr, "Mind and the Cosmos," in *Science, Consciousness and Ultimate Reality*, 36.

123. Coles, ed. *The Routledge Companion to The New Cosmology*, 20.
124. José G. Funes, "Galaxy Evolution," in *Scientific Insight into the Evolution of the Universe and of Life: Plenary Session 31 October – 4 December 2008,* eds. Werner Arber, Nicola Cabibbo and Marcelo Sánchez Sorondo (Vatican: The Pontifical Academy of Sciences, 2008), 92, accessed January 23, 2011, http://www.vatican.va/roman_curia/pontifical_academies/acdscien/documents/newpdf/acta20.pdf.
125. Silk, *The Big Bang*, 170.
126. *Ibid.*, 172.
127. "Hubble's Deepest View Ever of the Universe Unveils Earliest Galaxies," accessed January 12, 2011, http://hubblesite.org/newscenter/archive/releases/2004/07/image/j/format/large_web/.
128. *Ibid.*
129. Randall Niles, "Theory of Evolution," in *All About the Journey*, accessed January 15, 2011, http://www.allaboutthejourney.org/theory-of-evolution.htm.
130. Steven Weinberg, *The First Three Minutes: A Modern View of the Origin of the Universe*, 2nd ed. (New York: Basic Books, 1993), 5.
131. Silk, *The Big Bang*, 3rd ed., 108.
132. Armand Delsemme, *Our Cosmic Origins: From the Big Bang to the Emergence of Life and Intelligence* (Cambridge: Cambridge University Press, 1998), 247.
133. "The Age and Composition of the Universe," in Science Section of *Fact Monster*, accessed January 18, 2011, http://www.factmonster.com/ipka/A0908644.html.
134. Pandikattu, *Meaning through Science and Religion,* 8.
135. Robert P. Kirshner, *The Extravagant Universe: Exploding Stars, Dark Energy and the Accelerating Cosmos* (Princeton: Princeton University Press, 2002), ix.
136. *Ibid.*, xi.
137. David Darling, "Dark Energy," in *The Internet Encyclopedia of Science*, accessed January 20, 2011, http://www.daviddarling.info/encyclopedia/D/dark_energy.html.
138. Seife, *Zero: The Biography of a Dangerous Idea*, 192.
139. Seife, *Zero: The Biography of a Dangerous Idea,* 208.
140. John Gribbin, *Companion to the Cosmos* (New Delhi: Universities Press, 1999), 1.

141. Antonino Zichichi, "Rigorous Logic in the Theory of Evolution," in *Scientific Insight into the Evolution of the Universe and of Life: Plenary Session 31 October – 4 December 2008,* eds. Werner Arber, Nicola Cabibbo and Marcelo Sánchez Sorondo (Vatican:The Pontifical Academy of Sciences, 2009), 102, accessed January 23, 2011, http://www.vatican.va/roman_curia/pontifical_academies/acdscien/documents/newpdf/acta20.pdf.
142. *Ibid.,* 103.
143. *Ibid.*
144. *Ibid.*
145. Matthew E. Bunson, "Fathers of Science," in *Catholic Answers Magazine*, accessed October 10, 2011, http://www.catholic.com/magazine/articles/fathers-of-science.
146. Gribbin, *Q Is for Quantum: Particle Physics from A to Z*, 236-237.
147. John D. Barrow, *The Book of Nothing* (London: Vintage, 2000), 176.
148. Pamplany, *Cosmos, Bios, Theos: Introduction to Philosophy of Science, Scientific Cosmology and Science-Religion Dialogue,* 25.
149. Jan Gulberg, *Mathematics: From the Birth of Numbers* (New York: W.W. Nortorn & Company, 1997), 904.
150. *Ibid.,* 904
151. *Ibid.*
152. *Ibid.,* 906.
153. *Ibid.*
154. *Ibid.*
155. Steven Weinstein and Dean Rickes, " Quantum Gravity," in *The Stanford Encyclopedia of Philosophy (Spring 2011 Edition)*, ed. Edward N. Zalta, accessed November 14, 2010, http://plato.stanford.edu/archives/spr2011/entries/quantum-gravity.
156. Feynman, *Six Easy Pieces: Essentials of Physics Explained by Its Most Brilliant Teacher*, 33.
157. *Ibid.,* 34.
158. *Ibid.,* 36.
159. Augustine Pamplany, "Quantum Mechanics," in *ACPI Encyclopedia of Philosophy*, ed. Johnson Puthenpurackal, 2 Vols., Vol. 2 (Bangalore: Asian Trading Corporation, 2010), 1116.
160. Clarke, "Quantum Mechanics, Consciousness and the Self," in *Science, Consciousness and Ultimate Reality*, 70.

161. Seife, *Zero: The Biography of a Dangerous Idea,* 157
162. *Ibid.,* 159.
163. Daniel C. Matt, *God and the Big Bang: Discovering Harmony between Science and Spirituality* (Vermont: Jewish Lights Publishers, 1996), 83.
164. Craig Freudenrich, "Uniting the Fundamental Forces," of What are the Fundamental Forces of Nature, in *howstuffworks?* accessed March 1, 2011, http://science.howstuffworks.com/environmental/earth/geophysics/fundamental-forces-of-nature5.htm.
165. Carr, "Mind and Cosmos," in *Science, Consciousness and Ultimate Reality*, 37.
166. *Ibid.*
167. Carl Rod Nave, "Unification of Gravity," in *HyperPhysics* (Georgia: Georgia State University, Department of Physics and Astronomy, 2005), accessed February 24, 2011, http://hyperphysics.phy-astr.gsu.edu/hbase/forces/unigrav.html#c1.
168. Carr, "Mind and Cosmos," in *Science, Consciousness and Ultimate Reality*, 38.
169. *Ibid.,* 44.
170. Feynman, *Six Easy Pieces: Essentials of Physics Explained by Its Most Brilliant Teacher*, 71.
171. Clarke, "Quantum Mechanics, Consciousness and the Self," in *Science, Consciousness and Ultimate Reality*, 66.
172. Thomas G. Barnes, David L. Bergman, Glen C. Collins and Charles W. (Bill) Lucas, "Our Consistent Approach to Life," in *Common Sense Science*, accessed February 15, 2011, http://www.commonsensescience.org/explaining_life.html.
173. The Bible is poetical and spiritual with regards to this scenario, when it proclaims: "Creation itself would decay and would share the glorious freedom of the children of God. We know that all creation has been groaning with the pains of childbirth up to the present time" (Rom 8, 21-22).
174. Paul Davies, *God and the New Physics* (Middlesex, New York: Penguin Books, 1983), 18.
175. Victor Ferrao, "An Involving God in an Evolving World: An Emerging Paradigm in Science-Religion Dialogue" (PhD diss., Jnana-Deepa Vidyapeeth of Pune, 2005), 156.

*Chapter 3*

# Nothingness as Constitutive of Reality: A Philosophico-Theological Appraisal

## 3.0 Introduction

Reality is the state of things as they actually exist. Existence is not the only part of reality but the concept of nothingness also encapsulates the reality. There is a distinction between the three notions of *nothing, negation* and *non-being. Nothing* belongs together with entities like *every* thing, *some* thing, *many* things, *no* thing, etc. It is a quantifier (*no*) combined with a variable (*thing*,...). There is an entity *no* in nothing. Mathematically it is an empty set, numerically 0 and generally a reality of absence or emptiness which *is*. So 0 is an entity, a neutral number, a quantity and an empty placeholder in decimal numeration which represents *nothingness*. The phenomenological reality of nothingness, emptiness and fullness is interconnected with nothing, something and everything respectively. Everything contributes to the oneness and wholeness of reality. A real entity or an event of fact has two facets, existence and nothingness, fullness and emptiness, 1 and 0, quantity and quality, etc. Nothingness is the philosophy and science of empty space. The nature of space and nothingness has left us with quantum mechanical vacuum filled with fluctuations.

So here we study some of the profound implications of nothingness, emptiness and fullness. First, we briefly study the linguistic nothingness which presupposes the presence of something. Then we describe mathematical nothingness that has brought different properties of 0, which in turn leads to physical nothingness that has given rise to vacuums in science. In the psychological or human level we study existential nothingness which gives rise to inner emptiness or nothingness of human beings. The people with inner emptiness have no hope in anybody including in themselves while self-emptying people have.

Can belief in *nothingness* be considered rational? Belief in nothingness or belief that God created the Universe *out of nothing*, is the test case for the rationality of religious belief.[1] "Why there is a correspondence between our intelligence and reality, this is the point where he [Pope Benedict XVI] asks: where does this rationability come from? Can it be the product of irrationality? Can it be the product of a mere random process without any rationality?"[2] A human being starts 'in' reality, not in the human imagination. Reality is the foundation of all its possible real moments and dimensions which is given to us. "Beyond being there is but nothingness. It is a perfection that transcends all the others, and it is never transcended."[3] This *perfection* is the paradoxical reality of nothingness. "Being is the act or perfection making the being present, making it *exist*, placing it outside of nothingness."[4] The common or particular being is made up of two inseparable components, *being* and *essence*. Our senses perceive the sensible properties of being while intellect perceives it as being. It is we, human beings, who are philosophising the world, ourselves and God. Metaphysics is the study of *what exists*, material and spiritual. Even a solipsist agrees there is at least one thing! Everything *has* nature. According to Scholastic philosophy, any change will involve *three elements*: matter (quantity), form (shape) and privation (absence) and the product of a change involves two things: *matter* and *form*.[5] What about the *nature of privations* and *negations* in which absence exists? The characterization of the subject matter prior to the change as *not having the form* is called privation. Change takes place in the categories of quality, quantity and place, and the terminology of matter, form and privation is used analogically. There must be a matter or subject but it cannot be matter in the sense of a substance which we can call the matter *prime matter*, first matter. But this prime matter is not a substance, and does not exist apart from any particular substance. It is always the *matter of some substance* that exists. The first matter or 'soul' will be defined as the substantial form of living bodies where human soul is immortal. Conservatives, coherentists and scientific gradualists all cast a suspicious eye on 'Why is there something rather than nothing?'[6] There is the probability of 'There is something' as opposed to 'There is nothing.' "Most philosophers would grant Peter van Inwagen's (b. 1942) premise that there is no more than one *empty world*. They have been trained to model the empty world on the *empty set*."[7] The principles of matter and anti-matter ensure that they cannot co-exist so the result would be an *empty world*. After all, an empty world would be free of objects trying to elbow each other out. Is there a limbo between being and non-being? 'Why is there something rather than nothing?' is not about the origin of the world. It is a *reflection* about the world of *presence* and *absence*. If the explanation cannot begin with some entity, then it is hard to see how any explanation is feasible. Every being or an entity is either a dependent being or a self-existent being. Not every being can be a dependent being or thing. So there exists a self-existent being or something whom we call God. If God exists, then something exists. After all, God is something or somebody. A concrete entity has a *position* in space and time. The spiritual entity transcends *space* and *time*. God, being spiritual, transcends time and space. *Points* in space have locations. "All material things are concrete but some concrete things might be immaterial. *Shadows* and *holes* have locations and durations but they are not made of anything material. There is extraneous light in shadows and extraneous matter in holes; but these are *contaminants* rather than *constituents*."[8] The holes are the empty spaces where the matter is *not*. So to admit the existence of holes is to admit the existence of immaterial objects! Our concepts, thoughts, ideas, memory, intellect, or will are immaterial! 'Nothing' as a grammatical subject in a sentence does not mean that the word designates *a thing*. The words 'all' and 'nothing' are not nouns but logical operators that say something about things that have certain properties.

Today's philosophers look back on at least five great revolutionary ideas that have radically changed our history: reason, person, experience, process and language:[9] 1) *Reason* as an instrument for divining truth by Presocratic philosophers in the 5th and 6th centuries BCE, 2) The emphasis of the *human subject* and the limits of the human thought by a German philosopher Immanuel Kant (1724-1804) in the 18th century, 3) The emphasis on the *sense experiences* by an English philosopher, statesman, scientist, jurist and author Francis Bacon (1561-1626), an English philosopher and physician John Locke (1632-1704) and by a Scottish philosopher, historian, economist, and essayist David Hume (1711-1776) in the 17th century in Britain, 4) The emphasis on dialectic *process* of becoming, progressing, willing and synthesising by a German philosopher Georg Hegel (1770-1831) and Friedric Nietzsche (1844-1900) in the 19th century, and 5) The boundaries of thought are delineated by the limits of the *language* as proposed by an Austrian-British philosopher Ludwig Wittgenstein (1889-1951) and other linguistic philosophers in the early 20th century. Our spoken language is immaterial until we can write or record it. Our emotions are also immaterial things! Although all concrete things are in *space* and *time* but neither space nor time are concrete things. Space and time are for contingent things. "But when read metaphysically, 'There might be nothing' seems true. So 'Why is there something rather than nothing?' is, so far, a live question."[10] 'There is nothing' would be a contingent, *negative fact*. But then it would have to be grounded on some positive reality. That positive reality would ensure that there is *something* rather than *nothing*. How can we perceive absences? We can perceive *absences* by abstracting the entities then we have negative truths. All abstract entities depend on concrete entities for their existence.

Mathematics makes *sets* central. Sets are defined in terms of their members. Therefore, any set that contains a contingent entity is itself a contingent entity. An empty set does not have any members. It symbolizes zero, quantitative nothingness. Physical nothingness gives rise to vacuums. The Church's anti-Aristotelian condemnation of 1277 by Etienne Stephen Tempier (?-1279), the

Bishop of Paris, prohibited the teaching of 219 philosophical and theological theses and required Christian scholars to allow for the possibility of a vacuum. Creation *out of nothing* presupposes the possibility of *total nothingness* of things but *fullness* of God. Following Galileo and Evangelista Torricelli (1608-1647), in 1646 Blaise Pascal (1623-1662) refuted Aristotle's followers who insisted that nature abhors a vacuum.[11] Rene Descartes (1596-1650) wrote Christian Huygens (1629-1695) that Pascal had too much vacuum in his head. Isaac Newton (1642-1727) resurrected Kepler's (1571-1630) hypothesis and suggested that the space between the moon and the Earth was filled with ether (a subtle substance).

Vacuum means empty. Physical vacuum is a *volume* of space that is essentially empty of matter, such that its gaseous pressure is much less than atmospheric pressure. A perfect vacuum would be one with no particles in it at all, which is impossible to achieve in practice. Zero is equated with nothing or *śūnya* but it is something involving something. Zero can be the absence of a quality or quantity. It can be a starting point like 0 degrees on a temperature scale or 0 in a number line. Zero being the centre of all numbers represents past, present and future. It is associated with time and creation, beginning and end of time. Scientifically it is Big Bang and religiously it is creation out of nothing and self-emptying. Science is engaged with the world of matter while religion is realising the inner world of the human mind and heart. How can the Universe come into existence from nothing as a result of physical processes? How did the counting or measuring of things, numbers, time and space originate naturally? It is the human beings who measure things. Physically or cosmologically matter, mass, space, energy, force, time and life began at $0^{th}$ hour or moment. It is to some extent mystical and so we do not know exactly when and how the Universe began and when it will end. We are related contingents with the earth and with its rhythmic motions. With the influence of Greek philosophy on Judaism, Christianity and Islam we see a succession of theological events – creation, fall, redemption, judgment, and resurrection – parallel to the concepts of order out of primeval chaos, origin of the earth, origin of life, origin of humans, destruction and decay in linear time. It is a dynamic and perfectible world, though some of the biblical scholars saw it as a perfect world. In short, mathematical zero, physical vacuum or philosophical nothingness has lots of implications for mathematics, science, philosophy and religion. Physics, mathematics and philosophy are based on logic, have their separate jurisdictions, aims and methods. Physics explains in terms of its concepts and theories of inanimate things. Mathematics as a logical science acts as a language of physics. Philosophy examines the nature of knowledge obtained through physics and other sciences. What relation does the physical world have with ultimate reality as scientific theories can change with time? Mathematical knowledge seems to be a case of pure rational knowledge, gained by thinking alone and independent of empirical verification.[12]

The physical zero and infinity are at the very nature of the Divine, which is the metaphysical source of the Universe. It is at this realm of integration of the zero and the infinity, which we encounter in physical and cosmological theory, that we may seek for traces of the possibility of the Divine; and it is at the realm of life of integration of the zero and the fullness of infinity that we may possibly seek for ways of integration of the zero and the infinity. I would opine that the religious concepts and practices of nothingness unto fullness are keys to construct a synthetic view of the theoretical zeros and infinities on the one side (e.g., the mathematical zero and infinity, absolute zero and infinity, quantum zero and infinity, relativistic zero and infinity and cosmological zero and infinity), and the practical zeros and infinities on the other (emptiness, nothingness, *śūnyatā,* divine fullness, *kenōsis*, etc.). The absence of anything may imply the absence of God, and harkens back to the void prior to the creation story in the Book of Genesis. The view, nature abhorred vacuum, was called *horror vacui*. Bishop Etienne Tempier of Paris condemned this view on 1277 which led to the conclusion that God could create a *vacuum* if he so wished.[13] Today vacuum, void or empty space has been accepted as physical reality. From a physical point of view, an empty cup is always full of something. Even in a vacuum a cup still contains space, light, radiation, as well as its own substance. Emptiness and fullness are always empty of or full of something.

In reality, there is an empty space, vacuum or void which could be expressed mathematically as 0 and religiously as nothingness, emptiness (or fullness?). Empty space is in process means activity. Activity implies change, becoming or fluctuating continually for perfection, from potentiality to actuality. Actuality of nothingness is constitutive of reality. In this chapter I would like to explain nothingness from the phenomenological, mystical and metaphysical point of view. Phenomenologically nothingness, emptiness and fullness are interconnected. The phenomenon of nothingness is expressed in languages, numbers, physical quantities and in our personal lives as inner nothingness, emptiness or fullness. Mystical nothingness is an *apophatic* approach of *netineti* (not this, not that), beyond our human description. Let us delve into the phenomenological reality of nothingness, emptiness and fullness.

## 3.1 Nothingness, Emptiness and Fullness: A Phenomenological Approach

'Nothingness' expresses some quantitative nature of a thing while 'emptiness' and 'fullness' express qualitative aspects of a thing. When we inquire into the nature of existence and of experiences we find some similarities and differences. Perception does not occur without both similarities and differences present. The positive and negative aspects of each thing occur together. Negation exists in as many ways as each thing is not every other thing, and is as dynamic and variable as are the relations between changing things. "Whenever we experience plurality, we experience difference, and when we experience difference, we experience negation."[14] "Nothing, in its various guises, has been a subject of enduring fascination for millennia. Philosophers struggled to grasp it, while mystics dreamed they could imagine it; scientists strove to create it; astronomers searched in vain to locate it; logicians were repelled by it, yet theologians yearned to conjure everything from it; and mathematicians succeeded."[15] Numerical nothingness or mathematical zero is a concept as well as a number has been a successful operator in mathematics. The evolution of zero has revolutionized the study of physical sciences. Phenomenological notion of nothing, something and everything are interrelated. In the same manner *nothingness*, *emptiness* and *fullness* are interrelated. "Western philosophers have understood nothingness to be directly related to being, insofar as nothingness simply stood for the negating of being, as in Heidegger's crossed-out being signifying nothingness as negation."[16] "The idea of creation *ex nihilo* added to the notion of non-being (change and otherness) the dimension of nothingness in the interpretation of world and man, giving rise to the need for justifying the very existence of things in their totality."[17] There are different things exist in the world. It means the world is full of many things[18] as Quantum Mechanics would say it is filled with infinite energy. The things are changing or becoming too. There is change within persons too as they grow daily. "The self discovers itself to be a bottomless contradictory identity and, as such, is both individual self and yet a manifestation of the whole of things as nothingness."[19] The encounter with the 'not' of essents enables us to shed our self-will, to see things in their true being and the 'not' itself as a manifestation of Being and integral to it.[20] 'Nothing' is 'not' a thing, 'not' a name of anything, and 'not' something else in the sense of negation. Affirmation is 'is' and negation is 'is not.' 'Nothing' is negation of the quantity one, many and all. There is a nonentity, opposite or absence. 'Not' is for negation and for quantity. "If God is simply identical with being – that is to say, if the terms 'being' and 'God' are in every sense convertible with one another, and if one means no more than the other – then God's entire substance would simply become one of two equally possible logical contraries."[21] The being of God and the being of created things are related analogically. God's 'essence' is 'wholly other' than being. If such a thing as nothingness is countenanced at all, it is understood to be contrary to, and entirely correlative to, being.[22] "Nothingness is God's face, your face, and my face *before* any of us were born – that is, before we or anything else was differentiated."[23] God has created and differentiated all realities according to their purposes.[24]

The word 'science' comes from the Latin verb *scire*, which means 'to know.' It is about possessing a certain kind of knowledge. In other words, one has science when one knows the cause of the fact. The word *question* comes from the Latin *querere*, which means to quest, to journey, or to search, search of something, namely the cause of a fact, or the reason for it. Thus, science is fundamentally knowledge of things through their proper causes. Causality, as 'causality' cannot be physically measured in the laboratory. Pursuit of knowledge in science often leads into philosophy. Philosophy is the pursuit of first or ultimate causes. Philosophical knowledge is the knowledge of things through their first causes. Experimental science is not a search for first causes, but rather proximate or secondary causes. The first cause is that which accounts for our being alive, the secondary cause accounts for our size and sight. Philosophy seeks an answer to the question: 'What does it mean to be a living thing as opposed to a non-living thing?' One must reason for the answer. Philosopher seeks to understand what it means to be a substance, or what makes a substance to be what it is, or what is the difference between substance and attribute, etc. Science investigates modes of being like living being, chemical being, energy, motion, psyche, human behaviour while philosophy studies simply being *insofar* as it is being. Philosophy inquires what it means *to be*, and its properties of being *as* being. Does non-being exist? Why is there anything rather than nothing? Is a thing good to the degree that it has being? What does it mean to know? Philosophy is the love of wisdom or truth begins on the level of ordinary experience and ascends upward by means of *human reason* in order to take in 'the whole picture' from a bird's eye point of view, a point of view that is beyond the realm of ordinary experience. This is phenomenological approach to the reality of anything. Thus, in philosophy, sensation serves reason and in the investigative sciences, reason serves sensation. Science presupposes the intelligibility of things but cannot explain why for its intelligibility. We cannot prove, through an experiment, that 'a thing cannot be both 'be' and 'not be' at the same time and in the same place' which is known as principle of non-contradiction (*absence* of contradiction) where the concept of *negation* is expressed. The truth and falsity are contradictory. There is no experimental proof for the principle of identity (a thing **is** what it **is**) and the principle of the excluded middle (a thing is either **be** or **not be**) too. That nothing remains in the middle of two contradictory terms. The three logical principles are our basic judgments or acts of our intellect or mind to say yes or no. As soon as a person experiences the concept 'being as such,' and the concept of 'non-being,' the two judgments that 'a being is what it is,' and that 'a being cannot both be and not be at the same time under the same aspect,' are immediately assented to by the mind.

To be able to understand that there is common or universal truth implies the ability to step *outside* of ourselves so to speak. We are able to know something other than ourselves. We have this common ability to 'exit ourselves' and know something other than ourselves. Denying this universal truth is entirely self-refuting. The first act of the intellect or mind is the act of simple *apprehension* of an idea; the second act is the act of intellectual judgment; and the third act is the act of reasoning which presupposes the priority of the first two acts. The intellect is an autonomous power of knowledge independent of sense experience. It reasons from first principles to conclusions. The first self-evident principle that is presupposed whenever we know anything at all, is the principle of identity, which runs: Each being **is** what **it is**. Each thing *is* what it *is*. And if nothing exists determinately, then nothing is known determinately. Knowledge is impossible if 'is' and 'is not' are the same and the identical at the same time with the same respect. Oneness or unity has been the state of things all along. Another first principle that is self-evident and presupposed whenever anything is known, is the principle of non-contradiction, which runs: Nothing can be both '**be**' and '**not be**' at the same time and in the same respect. The logical formulation of this principle runs: 'Nothing can be both *true* and *false* at the same time and in the same respect.' Nothing can be *true* and *not true* at the same time and in the same respect. The 3rd self-evident principle, the Principle of the Excluded Middle says, 'A thing is either *is* or it *is not*, there is no in between.' A thing either is or it isn't. No middle ground is possible.What could possibly exist between being and non-being? If it exists, then it is. If it does not exist, then it is not. 'Becoming' refers to change, that is, some existing thing that is changing. As the word 'becoming' indicates, to change is to 'come to be' in some way. If something is changing, then it '*is*.' So, becoming is clearly on the side of 'being.' There are only four possible forms of a categorical proposition, two are affirmative statements (universal and particular), and the other two are negative statements (universal and particular). We have three modes of knowing: science, philosophy and theology. Science studies the proximate causes of things via sensation. Philosophy studies the ultimate causes of things via reason. The truths of reason are the principles of identity, non-contradiction and excluded middle. For religious believers, God, who is outside of time, is the First Uncaused Cause of all that is.

The term 'nothing' is a concept which refers the absence of anything. It is an indefinite pronoun referring to something. The concept of 'nothing' itself is a thing which leads us to a fallacy of four terms (nothing, absence of anything, something and a thing).[25]

Mathematical zero can manifest as physical 0, the zero of empty space, the vacuum or the void. "Medieval science and theology grappled constantly with the idea of the vacuum, trying to decide questions about its physical reality, its logical possibility and its theological desirability."[26] Italian Physicist and mathematician Evangelista Torricelli (1608-1647) invented the barometer in 1643 and showed that an *empty space* appeared if the mercury tube was turned upside down. This phenomenon being known as the Torricelli vacuum and the unit of vacuum pressure, the torr, being named after him. Even Torricelli's teacher, the famous Galileo Galilei had previously been unable to adequately explain the sucking action of a pump. The dialectical method of German philosopher G. W. F. Hegel (1770-1831) consists of three steps. First, a thesis is given, which can be any postulate in logic. Second, the antithesis of the thesis is formed and finally a synthesis incorporates both thesis and antithesis. For example, Thesis: The Absolute is Pure Being, Antithesis: The Absolute is Nothing and Synthesis: The Absolute is Becoming. French existentialist Jean-

Paul Sartre (1905-1980) defines two kinds of 'being' *(être)*. One kind is *être-en-soi,* the brute existence of things such as a tree. The other kind is *être-pour-soi* which is consciousness. Sartre claims that this second kind of being is 'nothing' since consciousness cannot be an object of consciousness and can possess no essence. Can there be space independent of things? There is no such thing as absolutely empty space. All space contains fluctuating fields and particles. Even in the emptiest space that the Laws of Nature permit, there are energy levels about which the energies of the fields and particles fluctuate; and these energy levels are never sharply defined. Essentially, as space is created it is given some properties of 'non-emptiness.' Is it an ocean seething with the creation and destruction of virtual matter?

### 3.1.1 Linguistic Nothingness

What do words, whether uttered or written, refer to, what do they really point to? *They point to things 'out there' or* 'not out there.' A 'person' would point out three inalienable possessions: a soul, a body and a name. We will call this 'the out-there' as objective theory of reference. The second theory of reference, *not out there*, we will call the inner or subjective theory. It maintains that words point not to things out there but to our shared mental images, constructs or absences, to something inside our minds. These cogitations, or thoughts, are called concepts. The word 'concept' comes from Latin *con* = together, plus the verb *capio* = to catch, to hold, to grasp. So a concept is something that grasps and holds together many things, like a bundle or a bouquet, or many of our perceptions and memories. The concepts we use are not fixed, but change with time and place, they are historical. We use negative as well as affirmative words in our daily lives. There is nothing. There is something. Why is there something rather than nothing? Nobody is there. Somebody is there. There is no time. There is time. The vacuum has no gas. The vacuum is filled with energy field. Our human faculty can easily grasp things in the binary way: either ... or. It can also go beyond binary concepts: 'it may be' or 'may not be.' There is a possibility or probability.

It may be both: yes and no. 0 can be number as an integer but it is not a number as a counting number. So language becomes metaphorical and symbolic while expressing reality. We convert affirmative words into negative and vice-versa. When we use words like nothing, not, ineffable, incomprehensible, unknown, etc., we describe a thing negatively or *apophatically*. In the same manner when we describe things positively, it is a *cataphatic* way of emphasising positive properties of things. We use words that are divided into different kinds or classes, called parts of speech like nouns, adjectives, pronouns, verbs, adverbs, prepositions, conjunctions and interjections. We use phrases and clauses. We use antonyms. We use concepts to express thoughts. Concepts are words and thought is ordering of words into sentences. Concepts are non-physical yet they do not take us to immaterial realms. There is no non-linguistic realm. Thinking is talking to oneself. The thinking of Being becomes a thinking of language, or better, a 'speaking of language.'[27] Saying confers the 'is' on the things.[28] Even experience of pain and joy, happiness and sadness, health and sickness, good and evil can be talking to oneself, affirming the is-ness of the things. Heidegger speaks of historical presencing and absencing of being which is present. He expresses as "... unconcealedness, rising from the unconcealedness, the entry into unconcealedness, the coming and going away, the duration, the gathering, the radiance, the rest, the hidden suddenness of possible absenting."[29] Presencing and absencing of being is its limitedness in time and place. Even existentialists, in spite of their admitting existence, experience nothingness and emptiness. They are able to conceptualise nothingness in the presence of fullness of existence. Once experience is expressed or communicated, it becomes language. It can be vocal or body language.

When we say 'nothing' or 'there is nothing', semantically we mean 'no thing.' It is absence of the thing. It is empty. It is a presence of the empty location and absence of the thing. It is non perception. In the same manner we say 'nobody' or 'there is nobody.' What we mean is that no person is there. No body or object or thing is there. If we say 'no time' to somebody we are expressing the unavailability of our time or presence to that person.

When we say there is no space or place – it means somebody or something is occupying that space or place. These are the direct statements or judgements that we make. They directly or explicitly negate the objects: nothing, nobody, no time and no space. At the same time they implicitly affirm; there IS nothing, there IS nobody, there IS no time and there IS no space. Primarily there is IS. This IS is the existence. In every perception we are confronted with the 'nothing', 'nobody', 'something', 'somebody' which are fully dependent on the IS, the fullness of existence. Ontologically, the first is implicit affirmation or yes and the second is explicit negation or affirmation according to the statements. So we say no or yes accordingly. The third way, i.e., 'may be', 'probably', 'possibly', is our search for the new reality. In this way negative words become the participant words in affirming the reality. What is relevant for us is the affirmation that something exists: we may be mistaken in what concerns its essence (what it is), but that something does exist is undeniable.[30]

The linguistic analysis on nothingness leads us to appreciate deeper the mathematical nothingness.

### 3.1.2 Numerical Nothingness

Mathematics is one of the oldest of sciences. Numbers are cultural phenomena; humans invented them to quantify the external world around them. The external world is qualitative and quantitative in its nature. We can understand, compare and manipulate this world with numerical precision too. We use some measurable and numerical scales to quantify the world. The number 0 is the cardinality or size of an empty set which has no elements. Zero is a number which means nothing, null, void or an absence of value. Zero is the only digit which cannot stand alone. Its numeral is 0. When we write 10 we mean 1 in ten's place and 0 in one's place. It is filling the empty place of other digits. It is qualitative than quantitative. This is operational zero. It is a cardinal number as numeral zero or digital zero. Numeral zero is used in numeral position systems. Successive digits are higher than 0. In the number line it precedes +1 and follows –1. 0 is the lowest non-negative integer. Zero is even with integers but with natural numbers it is neither even nor odd. The cardinality of 0 is empty set. It is neither prime nor composite number. Adding or subtracting zero to a number leaves the number unchanged. It is an additive identity. The additive inverse of zero is itself. 0 has a multiplication property: multiplying any number with 0 gives 0. Zero has an exponential property: any number other than 0 raised to the power of 0 equals 1, $2^0 = 1$. A number cannot be divided by 0. It is indeterminate. It may be infinity but infinity is not a number. 0 is a must in decimal digit. The factorial zero is 1, 0! = 1. In geometry, the dimension of a point is 0. In trigonometry, sin 0 = 0, tan 0 = 0, arcsin 0 = 0 and arctan 0 = 0. In analytic geometry, 0 is the origin. Humans start numbers from 1, not from 0, but in computers they begin from 0. Programming languages start from 0. In telephones 0 comes first. Stopwatches and space shuttles begin with 0:00.00, the ground zero. Vehicle odometers begin with 00000. In counting it is cardinality and in order it is ordinality where 0 comes first then 1, 2, 3.... Baby was 0 years before completing 12 months. Once it completes 365 days it is 1 year old. So 0 is really something, a beginner.

The concept of zero represents 'something' that is 'not there', while zero as a number represents the lowest of all non-negative numbers. 0 is non-negative and non-positive number. 0 is neither even nor odd. Zero is a symbol for 'not there' which is different from 'nothing'. It is the presence of the location, the place, the space. It is the starting point of the number line, time, place, temperature, measurement of anything, etc. 'Not there' reflects that the number or item(s) exists but they are not just available. 'Nothing' reflects nonexistence. Henri Bergson (1859-1941) utilised the incompatibility theory of negation to mount an ontological argument for the existence of contingent positive realities: since a being can be absent only if its absence is entailed by some positive reality, the concept of a total absence, nothingness, is a contradiction in terms. The number 0 is the paradigm zero-member set: the empty set, Ø, { }. The set whose only member is 0 has one member. In absence of the concept of zero there could have been only positive numerals in computation.

The inclusion of zero in mathematics opened up a new dimension of negative numerals, the inverse of positives. Zero, when used as a counting number (such as zero defect), means that no such objects are present. A concept and symbol that connotes nullity represents a qualitative advancement of the human capacity of abstraction. As always, concepts are only real in their correct context.

Zero is the placeholder in the digits. It represents void, emptiness or absence of something. The first thing to say about zero is that there are two uses of it, which are both extremely important but are somewhat different. One use of it is as an empty placeholder in our place value number system. Hence, in a number like 2008, the zero is used so that the positions of the 2 (thousandths place) and 8 (units place) are clear. Clearly 2800, 2080, 0280, 0082, etc., mean something quite different. The second use of zero is as a number itself in the form that we use it as 0. There are also different aspects of zero within these two uses, namely the concept, the notation, and the name. One might think that once a place-value number system came into existence then the 0 as an empty placeholder is a necessary idea, yet the Babylonians had a place-value number system without this feature for over 1000 years. We can see from this that the early use of zero to denote an empty place is not really the use of zero as a number at all.

The ancient Greeks began their contributions to mathematics around the time that zero as an empty place indicator was coming into use in Babylonian mathematics. They, however, did not adopt a positional number system; ones place, tens place, hundreds place, thousands place, etc. It is worth thinking just how significant this fact is. How could the brilliant mathematical advances of the Greeks not see them adopt a number system with all the advantages that the Babylonian place-value system possessed? The real answer is that the Greek mathematical achievements were based on geometry. Although Euclid's Elements contain a book on number theory, it is essentially based on geometry. They didn't need to name their numbers since they worked with numbers as lengths of lines. Merchants, not mathematicians, used numbers, which required to be named for records. It is the practical people like scientists who sought for it.

Only three civilizations (Egyptian, Babylonian and the Mayan) used the zero, each of them far from cultures that would evolve into the so-called Western world, and each viewed its role and meaning in very different ways.[31] The third invention of the positional system (first and second being Egypt and Babylon) occurred in the remarkable Mayan culture that existed from about 500-925 CE.[32] The Egyptians had no zero. "Ten is denoted by an inverted u, a hundred by a coil, a thousand by a lotus flower, ten thousand by a bent finger, a hundred thousand by a frog or a tadpole with a tail, and a million by a man with his arms raised to the heavens."[33] "The destruction of the Babylonian and Mayan civilisations prevented their independent inventions of the zero symbol from determining the future of pattern of representation. That honour was to be given to the third inventor of the zero (India) whose way of writing all numbers is still used universally today."[34] But the Egyptian and Mayans were not able to make a conceptual jump from 0 being empty place-holder to the positional system. It is India which brought 0 and numeral position system to mathematics. In India a decimal system was already in place during the Harappan period, as indicated by an analysis of Harappan weights and measures. A bronze rod marked in units of 0.367 inches points to the degree of precision demanded in those times. In the Vedic period, records of mathematical activity are mostly to be found in Vedic texts associated with ritual activities. Philosophical formulations concerning *śūnya*, i.e., emptiness or the void may have facilitated the introduction of the concept of zero. While the zero (*bindu*) as an empty place-holder in the place-value numeral system appears much earlier, algebraic definitions of the zero and its relationship to mathematical functions appear in the mathematical treatises of Brahmagupta in the 7th century CE. Numerical nothingness passes to physical nothingness or vacuum. The conceptual jump is making a physical or material representation in physical sciences.

The Pythagoreans argued that number was the substance of things.[35] Everything is reducible to number, and number is ultimately the geometric point. The line is made up of points, and the surface is made up of lines, etc. Even numbers produce oblong figures, odd numbers produce square figures, etc. The elements are really arrangements of number. Fire is a composite of whole numbers (which form triangles), earth is a composite of square numbers, etc. So, at the basis of reality we have these discrete quantities, that are indivisible, unchanging, impenetrable, have shape and position in empty space. And so reality is made up of being and non-being. Non-being is the void, or empty space, and being is the 'indivisible', or in Greek '*atomai*', or atoms. The atom is the indivisible particle that is a pure quantity. What distinguishes one atom from another (i.e., air from fire) is quantity and shape (like Pythagoras, quantity is the basis of reality). The only properties an atom has are size, shape, impenetrability and position in space. The atoms of one element are alike in size and shape. The rest of the world is merely a conglomeration of atoms, which move through empty space and cluster and mechanically link up with one another by accident. So, the whole changes, but not the parts.

Reductionism is rooted in false premises (Pythagoras' number and Parmenides' notion of being and change, as well as Descartes identification of substance with extension). The parts are what they are by virtue of that form. The whole determines the parts. And so one can say that we are not humans because we have human DNA, rather, we have human DNA because you are humans. A human is not alive because human organs are alive, rather human organs are alive because the person is alive (the whole determines the parts). As we move towards the subatomic level, this becomes more and more the case. 'Being' is not the atom. It is the macroscopic level that is more real than the atomic or subatomic level. The reductionist tends to see the subatomic level as the primary level, the most real and the ultimate locus of causality. For example, we see this in Arthur Eddington's remarks about the table lacking in solidity, because atoms (thus, the table) are mostly in empty space. The electron is more open to determination (potential) than the atom, the atom more open to further determination than the molecule, the molecule more open or more potential than a flower, etc. A word has less 'interiority' than a sentence (a word does not literally have interiority. Rather, the interiority is in the mind of the writer), and a letter has much less 'interiority' than a word. By interiority I mean determination, meaning, intelligibility, and stability.

Similarly, the elementary particles, like a letter of the alphabet, are much more 'general', much more potential, and thus, far less 'self-centred', that is, less moved from within than the atom. And so the atom is more conservative, that is, it has more interiority, for it is more 'moved from within' (more determinate, in short, more formal). All the elementary particles are poor in property and inert. A proton, for instance, is so universal in its action not by virtue of what is has (it has very little), but rather by virtue of what it does not have. If the atom has less interiority than a rose, less determination and meaning, then it is less capable of maintaining itself through changes of quantity. It is more 'vulnerable' to being changed by being moved from without, as the word is more vulnerable to being altered by being moved externally than is the entire book (having sentences deleted).

But to conclude that the nature of a thing is determined by the quantity of parts would be a *non sequitur* (it does not follow). It is the *fallacy of reductionism* again. The meaning of the word 'truth' for example is not determined by the 't' and the 'r', etc. The meaning always precedes and determines matter (in this case the letters), just as the idea of the novel determines everything else, i.e., the sentences, chapters, parts, etc. The helium atom has a definite nature, one very different than sodium, for example. It behaves differently, it reacts differently, in short, and it is an essentially different substance. It has a different intelligible structure, that is, a different nature. Number alone (without looking at their activity) does not account for this difference, i.e, two electrons and eleven electrons. For we come to understand the nature of a thing by its activity, not its weight or its quantity. And yet because atoms are poorer in property than salt, or fructose, or a sunflower, or a worm, they are more vulnerable to being moved interiorly when there is a change of quantity. For they have less; they are less. They are more potential, and thus, have less 'actuality', less form.

Our understanding of the relationship between quantity and the essential nature of things begins at the pre-scientific level, and when we do science, we always do science within the framework of a large network of pre-scientific knowledge. At the pre-scientific level, 'what a thing is', that is, its nature, is always prior to quantity.

Linguistic and mathematical nothingness leads us to understand the physical nothingness.

### 3.1.3 Physical Nothingness

A physical vacuum is the state of minimum level of energy. The laws of vacuum are the laws of nature. The biggest questions in science, philosophy and religion are about nothingness and eternity, the void and the infinite, zero and infinity. Physical realities are the material things which we can feel and experience but mathematical realities are abstractions which we represent with signs and symbols. Though mathematics is an integral part of every science yet zero becomes a big puzzle in physics. A mathematical zero or conceptual nothingness works well with signs and symbols conceptually. But this mathematical 0 becomes a physical vacuum in physical realities, which has brought many Universes in the scientific world. A zero becomes an uncrossable barrier–the coldest temperature ever possible–in thermodynamics. Humanity is trying to represent physical vacuum of temperature, pressure, volume, mass, length, width and height of matter by use of conceptual 0. In Einstein's theory of general relativity, a zero became a black hole, a monstrous star that swallows entire suns and can lead us into new Universes. The infinite density of the black hole represents a division by zero. The Big Bang creation from the void is a division by zero. The infinite energy of the vacuum is a division by zero and is responsible for a bizarre source of energy in Quantum Mechanics. Yet dividing by zero destroys the fabric of mathematics and the framework of logic– and threatens to undermine the very basis of science. Vacuum is a valuable industrial tool in the 20$^{th}$ century with the introduction of incandescent light bulbs and vacuum tubes, and a wide array of vacuum technology has since become available. The recent development of human spaceflight has raised interest in the impact of vacuum on human health, and on life forms in general.

The Universe of general relativity is a continuous and very big extending to stars, solar system and galaxies. On the other hand, the Universe of Quantum Mechanics is jerky and discontinuous. It is related to atoms, electrons and subatomic particles. The two theories' common component is zero. The infinite zero of a black hole – mass crammed into zero space, curving space infinitely – is meaningless in relativity. The zero-point energy in the laws of Quantum Mechanics treats particles such as the electron as points which take up no space at all. The electron is a zero-dimensional object, and its very zero-like nature ensures that scientists do not even know the electron's mass or charge. The zero-dimensional electron has infinite mass and infinite charge. Scientists choose a close distance for calculations of mass and charge which is known as renormalization – "a dippy process" as Richard P. Feynman (1918-1988) called it. There is a unifying approach to quantum theory and general relativity called string theory where each elemental particle is composed of a single string and all strings are identical. The particles of matter and forces are the same. The particles have different vibrational notes. So there is no zero and infinity in string theory. The size of a typical string in string theory is the Planck length, i.e., about $10^{-33}$ centimetres. These theories may be precise and consistent mathematically yet can be utterly wrong. Zero and infinity can have no proof. Cosmos spawned from nothing and will it return to it?

The theory of nothingness investigates the fundamental forces in physics – gravity, electromagnetism, the strong and weak nuclear forces – which share a common factor, attraction to equilibrium.[36] Newton's Second Law of Motion asserts that moving force is the same as the mass of the body moved times its acceleration: $F = ma$. Jean Le Rond d'Alembert (1717-1783) rewrote Newton's equation in 1743 as $F – ma = 0$, to consider '–ma' as a force itself, the force of inertia. Inertia is now $I = –ma$. We have $F + I = 0$. The sum of forces, $F$ and $I$, produces equilibrium. The behaviour of the Universe and its constituent systems, including human thought, are driven by this inexorable pull to uniformity or equilibrium. Fahrenheit was a man before he was a scale. He chose 0 as the lowest temperature by freezing a mixture of ice and salt. Rene de Reaumur (1683-1757) made 0 the freezing point just of water. Anders Celsius (1701-1744) observed aurora in Lapland and devised Centigrade 0. William Thomson aka Lord Kelvin (1824-1907) set 0 degrees as the temperature at which motion ceases. So human is the measure of all things. Human, being searcher for measurements, is trying to find out equilibrium in the dynamic nature. 'M' or 'String' Theory[37] promises to unite all of the known models of physics – covering electromagnetism, nuclear forces, and gravity – into one all - encompassing supermodel. The fundamental unit of this supermodel is known as 'string' or one-dimensional vibrating chords, and from the various types of 'notes' that these fundamental strings play, one can derive every known particle and force in the cosmos. M-theory – the 'M' is for everything from Matrix to Membrane to Mystery to Mother, as the Mother of All Theories – is indeed an exciting and promising model.

Corey D. Kaup says, "Nothingness is a state of perfectly uniform static equilibrium constituting relative nonexistence."[38] Relative nonexistence is a state of uniform and static equilibrium undetectable by humans (like absolute 0 or black hole) due to the absence of spatial/temporal dynamics. Absolute nonexistence is the absence of existence like square circle or barren woman's child. Even though it cannot be properly referred-to, named, or defined yet it can be abstracted as non-existence and non-being in reference to existence and being. It is the non-state to which everything including nothingness is included.

Nothingness presupposes that it is not easy to peer into the void and ask what is there, but it is probably life's greatest adventure. The contemporary cosmological theories explore the notion of 'nothingness.' The Big Bang Theory is the present prevalent scientific view of creation. It maintains that the entire Universe originated in an enormous explosion. All matter, the stars and galaxies were concentrated into a very confined region in a primordial 'matter soup.' This matter soup cooled down, forming nuclei and then atoms and finally galaxies, stars and planets. This expansion is still going on today, except that the Universe is much older today. The creation of the Universe is the result of a series of events. Physicists believe that the whole physical, atomic and chemical mysteries behind the origin of the material Universe consist in the first three minutes after the Big Bang. Eventually the expansion may halt and reverse, culminating in a contraction back to zero size – the same state in which it apparently began. It is currently expanding and may eventually crunch too.

### 3.1.4 Inner Nothingness

Inner nothingness is the realisation of interior life of each one of us in our every day life. The interior life is the life of the soul with God, the necessary being. Though we are free yet we are dependent and relational human beings. As every contingent being is dependent on a necessary being so also every human soul is dependent on the Supreme Being. Inner nothingness is our humility, dependence, submission and obedience to Supreme Being for our life, freedom and experience. Our humility is our creatureliness, our authenticity, our limitedness and our openness to God and others. Without Supreme Being we would be nothing. "Nothingness is the absence of the world itself, a total absence of every positive contingent reality."[39] This is a very extreme view of reality. That could be symbolized as 0. Heidegger's "'nothingness' (das Nichts) is the 'other' than everything that is (entities) or 'that-which-is-not' (*das Nicht-Seinde*); but it is not an empty absence. It is the way in which Being 'presences' itself.... It belongs primordially to the unfolding of the Being of entities."[40] "Existential nihilists contend that human existence has no purpose, value, or justification. There is no reason to live, and yet we persist in living."[41] According to Parmenides, reality exists, always existed and cannot not be.[42] Aristotle agreed that Being could generate only being and there would be no logical ground for the deduction of Nothingness. Heraclitus says, 'all things are forever in a flux, nothing ever remains the same.'[43] "Nothing, logicians say, is not a thing, nor is it the name of anything, being merely a short way of saying of anything that it is not something else. Nothing means not-anything."[44] Nothing which is ready-at-hand or present-at-hand within the world functions as that in the face of which anxiety is anxious.[45] In this way, nothingness is physical emptiness, void and vacuum or numerical 0. Inner nothingness not only encounters fear, anxiety, dread, threat and death but inner divine presence, life, freedom, goodness and happiness. The Universe at large is fringed with nothingness, from which indeed it must have been created, if created it was; and its beginning and end, like that of all change within it, must similarly be viewed as a passage from one nothing to another, with an interlude of being in between.[46] Existential nothingness is the philosophy of negation, rejection, denial of some or all of thought or life. Existentialists hold that humans have no pre-given purpose or essence given by God, or by nature. So we have to decide what we want to be through our actions. Jean Paul-Sartre (1905-1980) says existence precedes essence. First we simply exist, are born into the world without our choice. Each one has to decide what to do. Thus, essence has to be chosen. Existentialists emphasise self as an existing individual who is free, responsible, self-creating and self-fashioning being. It is Hegel who deduced the conception of Nothingness from Being and kept it as the first antithesis in the first triad of the Doctrine of Being.[47] The most formidable mention of nothingness is Friedrich Nietzsche's (1844-1900) trumpeting of the 'death of God.' The 'death of God,' as Nietzsche intended it, is not a theological but a cultural malaise of the late nineteenth century – humans do not know what it means to be human. They may destroy moral, religious, social and metaphysical convictions.

Aristotle denied void can explain why things move. Movement requires a mover that moves the object. An object in a vacuum is not in contact with anything else. If the object did move, there would be nothing to impede its motion. Therefore, any motion in a vacuum would be at an infinite speed. It was refuted by experiments with barometers conducted by Evangelista Torricelli and Blaise Pascal. Their barometer consisted of a tube partially submerged, upside down in a bowl of mercury. What keeps the mercury suspended in the tube? Is there an unnatural vacuum that causes the surrounding glass to pull the liquid up? Or is there no vacuum at all but rather some rarefied and invisible matter in the 'empty space'? Pascal answered that there really was nothing holding up the mercury. The mercury rises and falls due to variations in the weight of the atmosphere. The mercury is being pushed up the tube, not pulled up by anything. Pascal's empty space or nothingness was popularized by existentialists in the twentieth century, leading to the interpretation of existential nothingness in terms of fear, anxiety, etc.

"Sŏren Kierkegaard (1813-1855), who pioneered studies in anxiety in *The Concept of Dread*, was first to make the keen distinction between fear and anxiety. While fear is confrontation with a situation that is comprehensible, anxiety is confrontation with a situation that is totally incomprehensible."[48] Emotions are intentional states; they are directed toward something. If angered, I am angry at something. If amused, there is something I find amusing. Free floating anxiety is often cited as a counterexample. But Kierkegaard says that in this case the emotion is directed at nothingness. According to Jean-Paul Sartre consciousness is in fact nothingness though it reflects Being. Being needs no proof. It is beyond thought. Consciousness is not even identifiable with the world of experience. Nothingness is really baffling to accord the status of reality to something which by definition is not. "If we can speak of it, it is only because it possesses an appearance of being, a borrowed being."[49]

"Nothingness does not nihilate itself; Nothingness is nihilated. It follows therefore that there must exist a Being of which the property is to nihilate Nothingness, to support it in its being, to sustain it perpetually in its very existence, a being by which nothingness come to things."[50] It must come out somehow from Being itself. If there were no existence, there would not be Nothingness. Nothingness is coeval and simultaneous with Being. Being-in-itself (*en-soi*) can stand alone but Being-for-itself (*pour-soi*) depends on Being-in-itself or consciousness, the substance. If a single atom is destroyed it would lead to the destruction of the world or entire solar system. This chaos is Being. By negating Being, nothingness or consciousness brings it into existence.

According to Heidegger, the mystery of Being cannot be resolved unless we understand the mystery of non-Being, that is, 'what is' can be known by the exclusion of 'what is not.' The

Being manifests itself by negating the negation. In the words of Heidegger, 'Nothing nothings itself.' 'Nothingness nothings' means it expresses, projects open and enowns Being, thus, bringing to effect the annihilation of Being. Negative judgment is based on nothingness. Nothingness is the source of negation and not vice versa. This negative approach of *neti neti* (not thus, not thus) of the ultimate reality is found in the Upaniṣads. The concept of nothing is included in the concept of being. Hegel asserted pure Being is pure Nothing. Dread proves that nothingness is experienced. Dread reveals Nothing. We shy away from our emotional encounters with nothingness. They are premonitions of the nothingness of death. They echo the groundlessness of human existence. Some have hoped that our recognition of our rootlessness would rescue meaningfulness from the chaos of nothing. Heidegger does think freedom is rooted in nothingness. He also says we derive our concept of logical negation from this experience of nothing. Science has no interest in 'nothing', it is concerned with 'what there is', while 'nothing' for science is 'what there is not.' It is against the rule of logic to think or speak of 'nothing.'[51] We cannot define 'nothing', still we speak of it. 'Nothing' is more original than 'not' and 'negation.'

Heidegger is sensitive to the hazards of saying that nothing exists and instead says 'The nothing nihilates.' To show illustratively that Being is not-a-being and no-thing, Heidegger writes Being with eraser. Thus, the question of Being leads us to the question of Nothing. Heidegger's main question is the traditional Greek metaphysical question, 'Why there is Something rather than Nothing?' Nothing has a positive connotation in Heidegger. It is the veil of Being. Werner Brook quotes Heidegger, 'Nothing belongs to the essential unfolding of entities as Such.[52] Rudolph Carnap (1891-1970) made this remark famous by exhibiting it as a paradigm of metaphysical nonsense. Heidegger gives no intelligible answer to 'Why is there something rather than nothing?' In many turgid passages of *Being and Time*, Heidegger appears to be sinking deeper with each step 'forward.' Logicians try to haul Heidegger out of the quicksand. They distinguish the quantifier 'no' from the logical operation of negation. The logicians prise apart senses of 'is' and clear up confusions about identity. They carefully compare and contrast 'exist' and ordinary predicates. Gradually, looking more like philosophers, they pass to more elusive characters such as non-being, negative facts, and so on. This falling away from real Being is one of the basic states of mind, the anxiety. Anxiety is a positive phenomenon which contrasts with fear which is an inauthentic state of mind. In fear, we have three elements: "That in the face of which we fear, the fearsome is in every case of something which we encounter within-the-world and which may have either readiness-to-hand, presence-at-hand or *Dasein*-with as its kind of Being."[53] The face or the fact of which we fear is a definite event or object which aggravates our fear. That which is feared about is the very entity of *Dasein*. Only *Dasein* can be afraid of oneself. In the act of fearing, the entity that is fearsome is freed to show itself as fearsome. Fearing shows the mode of *Dasein*'s being-in-the-world. In the same way, that in the face of which one has anxiety is Being-in-the-world as such.[54] What makes me anxious is the to-be-in-the-world, the thrownness in the world. That which anxiety is anxious about is Being in-the-world itself. Anxiety throws *Dasein* back upon that which it is anxious about. I am endowed or thrown in order to be myself. Finally the act of being anxious is the state of mind where I am not being at home with myself. What *Dasein* is anxious before is its 'facticity', the thrown Being-in-the-world; what *Dasein* is anxious about is its 'extentiality', the potentiality for-Being-in-the-world; and finally, the act of anxiety discloses *Dasein* in its fallenness, the uncanniness of *Dasein* in its complacent dependence on the world.[55] The characteristic questions of metaphysics–'what can I know' (epistemology), 'what must I do' (ethics), 'what I may hope for' (theology) – imply an intrinsic incompleteness–in the language of Being and Time, a nullity–and thus, reveal the basic finitude of the one who by these questions gives rise to metaphysics. In these ways *Dasein* has inner emptiness for-Being-in-the-world.

## 3.2 *Apophatic* and *Neti Neti*: A Mystical Approach

We can describe a reality in an *apophatic* or negative way, *neti neti* (not thus, not thus). Any claim can be expressed as a negative assertion. Negating of *anything*, on the contrary, is *confirming* it for a *world of possibilities*. The saying 'this thing does not exist', this-being is saying, at the same time, 'such a thing can exist, it already exists in our mind', and thus, is bringing into the world of being the very thing the existence of which is being denied in its judgment. Non-being or nothingness cannot be subject or predicate in an affirmative judgment. Even though there can be such logical constructions, nevertheless, they are empty in cognitive aspect because they cannot add anything to the notion of *nothing or non-being*. When non-being is still supposing a certain connection to the world of being, nothingness is supposing an absolute, total negation of being. Non-being is negation of being, however, not absolute but limited one. The contraposition of being and non-being, too, is highly relative, non-absolute one. The margin between being and non-being is not absolute one, and non-being still relates to the world of being, although as *negation* of being. For one thing, a real, actual law of logic is a negative, namely the law of non-contradiction. This law states that that a proposition *cannot* be both true and not true. Nothing is both true and false. Furthermore, we can prove this law. It can be formally derived from the *empty set* using provably valid rules of inference. Some say it is impossible to prove that Santa Claus, unicorns, the Loch Ness Monster, pink elephants, Weapons of Mass Destruction in Iraq, and Bigfoot do not exist. But we prove using the valid inference procedure of *modus tollens*: Latin for 'the way that denies by denying.'

1) If unicorns had existed, then there is evidence in the fossil record.
2) There is no evidence of unicorns in the fossil record.
3) Therefore, unicorns never existed.

Inductive arguments would not give us certainty about anything at all, positive or negative. We use inferences – induction – from past experiences in every aspect of our lives. Inductive arguments produce conclusions that are probable but not definite. Without induction we know basically nothing about the world apart from our own immediate perceptions. So we form negative beliefs as well as positive ones. The *apophatic* way is the way of negation to the infinite and nameless One who is beyond all finite comprehension. It is the favourite approach of those who favour a mystical experience of God in preference to a rational proof of his existence and understanding of his attributes. Meister Eckhart (1260-1327), a Dominican theologian and mystic of the medieval West, a writer in mystical theology, is best known for his writings on negative theology. He claimed that all creatures are an absolute nothing.

> In January, 1327, Archbishop Heinrich of Cologne undertook an independent inquiry, whereupon Eckhart and Father Nicholas appealed to Rome against his action and authority in the matter. But the next month, from the pulpit of the Dominican church in Cologne, Eckhart repudiated the unorthodox sense in which some of his utterances could be interpreted, retracted all possible errors, and submitted to the Holy See. His profession of faith, repudiation of error, and submission to the Holy See were declared by Pope John XXII (1249-1334) in the Bull "Dolentes Referimus" (27 March, 1329), by which the pontiff condemned seventeen of Eckhart's propositions as heretical, and eleven as ill-sounding, rash, and suspected of heresy.[56]

There is a legitimate use of negative theology to sharpen a believer's sense of God's incomprehensibility. The only way to describe God without limiting Him is to do it in 'negative terms.'

Dialectically we can move beyond both *cataphatic* and *apophatic* theology into the negation of the negation, which is the highest form of affirmation of transparent existence itself. The movement beyond affirmations and negations is part of a pervasive dialectical motion, which constitutes the very sinew of the Dominican's mysticism. Dialectic as existence, as praxis, as exercise, preserves both the stillness and the motion, celebrates both fusion and difference.

Mysticism has to do essentially with our experience of transcendence and our basic experience of God.[57] There is a desire of the human soul towards an intimate union with the Divinity. The union of the human soul with the Divinity could be through intuition, contemplation or love. What human cannot know by natural reason, s/he can know through revelation and faith; that what s/he cannot attain to by her/his natural power s/he can reach by the grace of God. God gives a very special grace to some souls by which they are enabled to feel His sensible presence which is true mystical contemplation. Negative experiences, sacrifices, pain and loss are explicit experiences of the mystery of God. Our daily life, loneliness, sickness, suffering, failure, rejection and dying are crosses. Every 'negative' experience, no matter how painful, has a 'positive' side to it.[58] "What lies behind all failures? Sometimes they are our own fault, the consequences of our sins. Sometimes failures are not our own fault but result from the sins others."[59] Sometimes failures involve no moral fault at all like games and sports or calamities.

### 3.2.1 Contingent and Necessary

The word 'contingent' comes from the Latin *'cum'* ('with') and *'tangere'*, ('to touch upon'). Contingent means 'that which need not be the case', or 'something which just happens to be the case.' A contingent being is a being that *need not be*. Contingent things are those which may or may not exist. A contingent being is a composite of essence and existence. It is 'what' it is, but it 'has' an act of existing. It is a unity of potency and act, or essence and existence. We can know *what* it is (essence), and we can know *that* it is (existence). The essence is related to the act of existing as potentiality is related to actuality. The act of existing (*esse*) *does not add* anything to the nature or essence of the thing.

What brings things into being? There are three possibilities: 1) A contingent being brings itself into being. If a being does not have an act of existing, then it is not a being. It is nothing. 2) Contingent beings bring contingent beings into being. Contingent beings cannot impart the act of existing. It is not possible to bring something into being from nothing. A simpler form of the principle of causality used by Gabriel Maréchal would be, "A limited being as such depends totally on the unlimited being."[60] We do not create our children. We reproduce. Contingent beings do not cause existence. A contingent being can cause, but it does not impart existence. So as a cause, a contingent being is a caused cause. 3) A non-contingent being brings things into being. We can rule out the first two possibilities. Only a non-contingent being causes being, that is, only an uncaused cause causes existence. Only a non-contingent being can account for the existence of contingent beings. A non-contingent being is not a possible being, but a being that *cannot* not be. Necessary things are those things which have to be present in order for us, the world and the Universe to exist. The reason why the world and the Universe are here must be found in that which has *necessary existence.* Its nature or essence is to be, whereas our nature is to be human. Its nature is not distinct from its existence. A non-contingent being is a being whose essence is *to be*. The uncaused cause is what we mean by *God* who is eternal, never came into existence, is the cause of the being of all other beings, and can only be one. God is that being whose essence is identical to His existence. God's essence is to be follows that God is His own to be, and therefore exists necessarily. There cannot be two beings whose essence is to be. What are they? Being Itself. Outside of Being Itself is non-being (nothing). Hence, nothing distinguishes them. They are not 'they' (plural), but one.

### 3.2.2 Limited and Unlimited or Finite and Infinite

Actual things are either finite or infinite. Finite things must be determinate, but infinite things can be determinate too. We quantify and count them. Infinite things are unlimited and indefinite, and hence not fully determinate in the required sense. Decimal numeration allows us to represent any finite quantity by using only 10 symbols 0, 1, 2, 3, 4, 5, 6, 7, 8, and 9. The mathematical meaning of the term 'actual' is practically synonymous with 'definite', while its meaning in the philosophy of nature includes 'physically existing' along with definiteness.

The question of whether whole numbers or reals form definite sets is therefore independent of the question whether infinite things exist actually in nature. Cosmologists were content with the notion that the Universe of space and time began at a singularity, where its temperature, its density and everything was infinite. They also realized later the notions like the beginning and end of the Universe, and the moments of the Big Bang and the big crunch. What does 'forever' or 'infinite' mean? Mathematics faced the reality of infinity in numbers. Georg Cantor (1845-1918) made some sense of the paradoxes of infinity. What is the nature of an infinite collection? Is there an ultimate infinity? Is God infinite? Is the Universe infinite? Is the past or future infinite? Does the Universe have an 'edge' or is it simply unbounded in size? What about an infinite temperature or an infinite brightness – can such physical things actually be infinite?[61] Counting numbers can go on and on, they are potential but not actual. The lazy eight, $\infty$, symbol for infinity came from the Oxford mathematician John Willis in 1655.[62] The Supreme Being, first among many is eternal, transcendent and infinite. Nicholas of Cusa (1401-1464) embraced the infinite as a place where opposites could be reconciled.[63] France drew a distinction between metaphysical infinity and mathematical infinity so as to be able to study geometry and arithmetical series.[64] Cantor defined a countable infinity (integers) to be one that can be put into one-to-one correspondence with the list of natural numbers 1, 2, 3, 4, 5, 6, ... which have the same size and symbolized as $\aleph_0$. The decimals which are never ending irrational numbers are uncountably infinite (real numbers) and symbolized as $\aleph_1$. Bernhard Bolzano (1781-1848) believed that all infinities are equal. Cantor used the name Absolute Infinity for the totality of everything, physical infinities for physical things and mathematical infinities for transfinite numbers.[65] Infinity comes in three flavours: Divine (Absolute), Human (mathematical) and Physical (physical Universe). Divine infinity is God.God to be almighty, eternal, immense, incomprehensible, infinite in intellect and will and every perfection, really and essentially distinct from the world, infinitely blessed in Himself and through Himself, and inexpressibly above all things that can exist and be thought of besides Him.[66] Mathematical infinite quantities are treated as actual infinities.Mathematical infinite may be taken as the potentially infinite that can be increased or diminished without end as a real quantity, or it can be taken as the actually infinite by which actual successive addition or division can never be reached. When we put things down in Einstein's space, then their mass and motion determine the shape of the space and the rate of flow of time at different places. When the mass is compressed into a small volume of space and objects move at speeds of light, space and time gets distorted where physical quantity becomes infinite, known as singularity. This is the physical infinity. "Can there be places in the Universe where measurable physical quantities like the density or the temperature of matter can become infinite? Could anything of finite extent be crushed to zero size and infinite density in a finite time from now?"[67] That is what Physicists are trying to measure the physical world with mathematical numbers while Anselm (1033-1109), Archbishop of Canterbury made an argument for the existence of God which is known as ontological argument.

> Anselm implicitly used the infinity of God to endow God with certain properties which he claimed made His existence logically necessary. He argued that if God is the greatest conceivable being, then He must have actual existence, not just potential existence, for otherwise a more perfect being could be conceived of: one that had the added attribute of actual existence.[68]

Mathematical infinity is human made while physical and divine infinities are divine made. Infinity is not a whole number. It is a concept which has no beginning, no end, no middle, no parts, no stopping point, no stopping off point, no past, no future, no time (only duration, in the widest sense of that word), no prior to, no next, nothing that we could conceivably think to be a positive property.

### 3.2.3 Negative and Affirmative or Absence and Presence

Negation is admitted as cognized by a separate and independent process of knowledge. 'There is no jug.' The non-existence of the jug is taken in the same act as the ground is perceived. It is the positive perception of the ground where the visible jug is absent that leads us to speak of having perceived the negation of the jug. But is this being without the jug identical with the ground or different? The ground without it, then call it 'ground, without the jugness' or 'the negation of jug,' it does not matter much, for a distinct category has anyhow been admitted. The relation between the negation and its negated is one of opposition, in the sense that where the one is the other is not.

The principle of sense-contact applies only to positive existents and not to negation or non-existence. Non-existence is not a positive substance for sense-contact. One could as well apprehend negation or non-existence of other places which are far away from him or her. Negation is not mere negativity or mere vacuous absence, but is what generates the cognition 'is not,' as position (*bhāva*) is what generates the cognition 'it is.' Whether negation be regarded as a positive being or becoming or of the nature of not becoming or non-being. In the first alternative it will be like any other positive existents, and in the second case it will be permanent and eternal, and it cannot be related to this or that particular negation.

In Vaiśeṣika School of Indian Philosophy, the four kinds of *abhāvas* [69] or non-existences are enumerated. Absence of an object and knowledge of its absence are different. Absolute negation is impossibility yet negation necessarily presupposes some affirmation or presence. Non-existence is of four kinds as:

1) Antecedent non-existence, *prāgabhāva* (the negation or absence preceding the production of an object– e.g. of the pot before it is made by the potter or creation before it was made by the creator);
2) Subsequent non-existence, *pradhvaṁsabhāva* (the negation or absence following the destruction of an

object– e.g. as of the pot after it is destroyed by the stroke of a stick);

3) Mutual non-existence, *anyonyābhāva* (mutual negation or absence– e.g. in the cow there is the negation of the horse and in the horse that of the cow) and
4) Absolute non-existence, *atyantābhāva* (a negation or absence which always exists– e.g., even when there is a pot here, its negation in other places is not destroyed. It is beginningless and endless, barren woman's child, sky-lotus etc.).

Negation and affirmation is what makes us human, imbuing us with the capacity to deny or accept, to contradict or affirm, to misrepresent or represent, to lie or tell the truth, etc. Negation and affirmation or absence and presence of an entity or proposition show its relational position in the world.

### 3.2.4 Nothing, Something and Everything

There is 'nothing' in the house. 'Nothing' is found in the house. They are not 'pure nothing.' They are identifiers, not properly nouns or pronouns. 'Nothing' as a grammatical subject does not mean that the word designates a thing. The words 'all', 'everything', 'something' and 'nothing' are typically not thought to be nouns, but logical operators that say something about things that have certain properties. 'Nothing is a round square' means that if a thing is round it is not also square. So 'nothing' is only a way of denying certain properties to the things that exist. It is not a thing in itself. It is a way of talking about the *absence* of all things. The contingency of a thing involves seeing it against the background of its *negation* or absence, it means seeing it against the background of 'nothing.' Nothing is the absence of anything, even of things we cannot talk about. *No-thing*, that is absence of *thing*, i.e., not only absence of being, *non-being*, but also absence of any *bearer* of that non-being. Quantitatively or qualitatively we perceive something. With this perception we can abstract into nothing (0). And when we want the wholeness of something (1 or a) or we want to quantify we say everything (all quantity or quality) of those things. There is an abstraction from something (1 or a) to nothing (0) and nothing or something to everything (all). So nothing, something and everything being quantifiers and logical operators are interrelated.

## Conclusion

A real entity or an event of fact has two facets, existence and nothingness, fullness and emptiness, 1 and 0, quantity and quality, presence and absence etc. The phenomenological reality of nothingness, emptiness and fullness is interconnected with nothing, something and everything respectively. When we say about a thing we say 'there is something' or 'there is nothing.' These 'something' and 'nothing' are participating in the unlimited existence of the direct statement 'there is...' even if they are absent or *no*thing. In the similar way fullness or isness of something is primary than emptiness or nothingness of any entity and they are necessary correlatives like left and right, top and down, east and west, north and south, day and night, light and darkness, life and death, etc. They constitute the paradoxical nature of reality of existence. At the very nothingness, fullness emerges. In every fullness, human beings experience some sort of 'lackness' that leads to further fullness. This is the reality of things as they actually exist. So the existence and the concept of nothingness encapsulates our reality. There is a distinction between the three notions of *nothing, negation* and *non-being. Nothing* belongs to a quantity. It is a quantifier (*no*) combined with a variable (*thing*,...). There is an entity *no*in nothing. A real entity or an event of fact has two facets, existence and nothingness, fullness and emptiness, 1 and 0, quantity and quality, and so on. 0 is an entity, a neutral number, a quantity and an empty placeholder in decimal numeration which represents nothingness. Mathematically it is an empty set, numerically 0 and generally a reality of absence or emptiness which is. Nothingness is the philosophy and science of empty space which is filled with fluctuations. Is empty space really empty or is it an ocean seething with creation and destruction of virtual matter? It is the riddle of nothing which science is never able to solve.

In reality, there is empty space, vacuum or void which is expressed mathematically as 0 and religiously as nothingness, emptiness or fullness. Its activity implies change, becoming or fluctuating continually for perfection, from potentiality to actuality. Any change will involve three elements: matter (quantity), form (shape) and privation (absence). The nature of privations and negations are absences. The characterization of the subject matter prior to the change as not having the form is called privation. We can perceive absences by abstracting the entities so that we have negative truths. All abstract entities depend on concrete entities for their existence. Being is the act or perfection making the being present, making it exist, placing it outside of nothingness. Creation *out of nothing* presupposes the possibility of *total nothingness* of things but *fullness* of God.

Phenomenological reality of nothingness, emptiness and fullness is expressed as nay or nothing in language, 0 in mathematics, vacuum in physical sciences, and emptiness or fullness in social sciences. In the psychological or human level existential nothingness which gives rise to inner emptiness or nothingness of human beings. Our sense of reality is always a derivative of language. When we abstract things linguistically, numerically, physically or anything from the Universe we are abstracting from something. When we are quantifying or talking of nothing, we are talking from something or everything quantitatively or qualitatively. Our mental acts or *direct judgements* are always directed at something beyond themselves: Seeing implies something seen, willing means something willed, judging points at something judged, knowing implies something known. Our *intentionality* links the subject and the object in a very powerful way. Nothing and everything, emptiness and fullness, absence and presence, negative and positive are interconnected and implied something beyond. Beyond being there is but nothingness. It is a perfection that transcends all the others, and it is never transcended. The term 'nothing' is a concept which refers the *absence* of anything. It is an indefinite pronoun referring to something.[70]

The concept, symbol and reality of nothing, something and everything are distinct yet inseparably interconnected to one another. In the similar way, the phenomena of conceptual and physical nothingness, emptiness and fullness are distinct yet they are interconnected in philosophy, science and religion. "It must be stressed that the individuation of symbol, its concretization, does not go against the totality within which symbol is made meaningful. It is here that the symbol radiates its symbolic pregnance."[71] The general critique and evaluation of nothingness is undertaken in the following final chapter, Nothingness and/as Fullness.

## Endnotes

1. Norman Brian Cubbage, "Nothingness and the Quarrel between Faith and Reason," in *American Catholic Philosophical Quarterly* 78, 1 (2004), 1.
2. Schönborn, "Pope Benedict XVI on 'Creation and Evolution' in *Scientific Insight into the Evolution of the Universe and of Life: Plenary Session 31 October – 4 December 2008.*
3. Luigi Bogliolo, *Metaphysics*, trans. Myroslaw A. Cizdyn (Bangalore: Theological Publications in India, 1987), 5.
4. *Ibid.,* 6.
5. Ralph McInerny and John O'Callaghan, "Saint Thomas Aquinas," in *The Stanford Encyclopedia of Philosophy (Winter 2010 Edition)*, ed. Edward N. Zalta, accessed February 24, 2011, http://plato.stanford.edu/entries/ aquinas/.
6. Roy Sorensen, "Nothingness," in *Stanford Encyclopedia of Philosophy*, accessed February 27, 2011, http://plato.stanford.edu/entries/ nothingness/
7. *Ibid.*
8. *Ibid.*
9. Nicholas Fearn, *The Latest Answers to the Oldest Questions: A Philosophical Adventure with the World's Greatest Thinkers* (New York: Grove Press, 2005), xii-xiv.
10. Sorensen, "Nothingness," in *Stanford Encyclopedia of Philosophy*, accessed February 27, 2011.
11. "Blaise Pascal," in *Wikipedia: The Free Encyclopedia* accessed November 12, 2011, http://en.wikipedia.org/wiki/Blaise_Pascal.

12. Saurabh Sanatani, "Physics, Mathematics and Philosophy – A Menage a Trois," in *The Journal of the Indian Academy of Philosophy* 31, 2 (1992), 27.
13. John D. Barrow, *The Book of Nothing* (London: Vintage, 2001), 81.
14. Archie J. Bahm, *Polarity, Dialectic, and Organicity* (Albuquerque: World Books, 1988), 257-258.
15. *Ibid.,* xi.
16. Robert E. Carter, "God and Nothingness," *Philosophy East & West* 59, 1 (January 2009), 1.
17. J. L. Mehta, "Being and Non-being," in *India and the West: The Problem of Understanding*, Studies in World Religions Series, No. 4, ed. M. David Eckel (California: Scholars Press, 1985), 106-107.
18. The Universe is not only filled with the material things but full of divine glory as Isaiah sees the vision of God in the Jerusalem temple where angels are praising God, "Holy, holy, holy is the Lord of hosts; the whole earth is full of his glory" (Isa 6, 3).
19. Carter, "God and Nothingness," 1.
20. Mehta, "Being and Non-being," 108-109.
21. Norman Brian Cubbage, "Nothingness and the Quarrel between Faith and Reason," in *American Catholic Philosophical Quarterly* 78, 1 (2004), 19.
22. *Ibid.,* 20.
23. Carter, "God and Nothingness," 13.
24. For Christians Jesus is the image of invisible God (Col 1, 15). In the person of Jesus Christ, in the hypostatic union of true God and true man, we see God's original intent and will for every human life – that we be "participants of the divine nature" (2 Pet 1, 4).
25. We see it in the following example.
    Nothing is beyond the Universe.
    Jack is beyond nothing.
    So Jack is beyond the Universe.
    The four terms are: Jack, the Universe, nothing-as-*a-thing* of which Jack is beyond and nothing-as-an-absence-of-thing which has *no entity* beyond the Universe. The term 'nothing' has been taken *equivocally* nothing-as-a-thing and nothing-as-an-absence-of-thing which is invalid. Many fallacious conclusions follow from treating 'nothing' as a noun or pronoun. Nothing as a noun is

contrasted with something and everything. The word 'nothing' does not function as a noun, as there is no object to which it refers.

26. Barrow, *The Book of Nothing,* 9.
27. Johnson J. Puthenpurackal, *Heidegger Through Authentic Totality to Total Authenticity: A Unitary Approach to His Thought in Its Two Phases* (Louvain: Leuven University Press, 1987), 213-214.
28. *Ibid.,* 217.
29. Martin Heidegger, *What is called Thinking?* Cited by Johnson J. Puthenpurackal, *Heidegger Through Authentic Totality to Total Authenticity: A Unitary Approach to His Thought in Its Two Phases* (Louvain: Leuven University Press, 1987), 141.
30. Cyril Desbruslais, *The Philosophy of Be-ing: Introduction to a Metaphysics for Today,* ed. Kuruvilla Pandikattu (Pune: Jnana-Deepa Vidyapeeth, 1997), 120.
31. John D. Barrow, *The Book of Nothing* (London: Vintage, 2001), 14.
32. *Ibid.,* 30.
33. *Ibid.,* 16-17.
34. *Ibid.,* 35.
35. Aristotle, *Metaphysics* I. 5, trans. W. D. Ross in *The Internet Classic Archive* by Daniel Stevenson, accessed February 27, 2011, http://classics.mit.edu/Aristotle/metaphysics.1.i.html.
36. Alice Thomas, "Scientific and Religious Implications of Nothingness," *Omega: Indian Journal of Science and Religion* 6, 1 (June 2007): 78.
37. String Theory attempts to provide a complete, unified, and consistent description of the fundamental structure of our Universe with one basic object, string. The fundamental objects in the Universe are not pointlike particles but small string like objects with ten dimensions even though we are aware of only three space dimensions and one dimension of time. This is a mathematical theory developed in the 1980s to explain the properties of elementary particles and the forces between them. String theory might be mathematically consistent, and even beautiful, it is not yet science.
38. Corey D. Kaup, "General Nothingness Theory," accessed January 15, 2011, http://www.nothingnesstheory.com/General%20Nothingness%20Theory10%20VII.htm.
39. Richard M. Gale, "Nothingness," in *A Companion to Metaphysics*, ed., Jaegwon Kim and Ernest Sosa (Oxford: Blackwell Publishers, 1995), 362.

40. Bosco Correya, "Absence," in *ACPI Encyclopedia of Philosophy*, 2 Vols., Vol. 1, ed. Johnson Puthenpurackal (Bangalore: Asian Trading Corporation, 2010), 10.
41 Donald A. Crosby, "Nihilism," in *Routledge Encyclopedia of Philosophy*, ed., Edward Craig (London: Routledge, 1998), 2.
42. Cyril Desbruslais, *Western Philosophy* (Pune: Jnana-Deepa Vidyapeeth, 1976), 5.
43. *Ibid.*
44. David Schmidtz, "Nothing," in *Encyclopedia of Philosophy*, 2nd Edition, 16 Vols., Vol. 6, ed., Donald M. Borchert (Detroit: Thomson Gale, 2006), 657.
45. Martin Heidgger, *Being and Time*, trans. John Macquerrie and Edward Robinson, 7th ed. (Tübingen: Harper San Francisco, 1962), 231.
46. Schmidtz, "Nothing," in *Encyclopedia of Philosophy*, 658.
47. Muhammad Kamal, "Consciousness and Nothingness," *Indian Philosophical Quarterly* 20, 4 (October1993): 373.
48. John Steffney, "Existentialism's Legacy of Nothingness," *Philosophy Today* 21 (Fall 1977): 217.
49. Jean-Paul Sartre, *Being and Nothingness: An Essay on Phenomenological Ontology*, trans. Hazel E. Barnes, First Indian Reprint (London: Routledge, 2004), 46.
50. *Ibid.*, 46.
51. Puthenpurackal, *Heidegger through Authentic Totality to Total Authenticity: A Unitary Approach to His Thought in Its Two Phases*, 100.
52. Bosco Correya, *Heidegger and Sankara: A Comparative Study of Thinking of Being and Advaita* (Kalamassery: Jyotir Dharma Publications, 2003), 136.
53. Puthenpurackal, *Heidegger through Authentic Totality to Total Authenticity: A unitary Approach to His Thought in Its Two Phases*, 26.
54. *Ibid.*, 27.
55. *Ibid.*
56. Arthur McMahon, "Meister Johann Eckhart," in *The Catholic Encyclopedia*, 15 Vols., Vol. 5 (New York: Robert Appleton Company, 1909), accessed December 3, 2011, http://www.newadvent.org/cathen/05274a.htm.
57. Felix M. Podimattam, *Kenosis Spirituality: Paschal Path to Holiness* (Bangalore: Claretian Publications, 2002), 73.

58. *Ibid.,* 79.
59. *Ibid.,* 81.
60. Cyril Desbruslais, *The Philosophy of Religion* (Pune: Jnana-Deepa Vidyapeeth, 2000), 23.
61. John D. Barrow, *The Infinite Book: A Short Guide to the Boundless, Timeless and Endless* (London: Vintage, 2005), 2.
62. Barrow, *The Infinite Book: A Short Guide to the Boundless, Timeless and Endless*, 4.
63. *Ibid.,* 33.
64. *Ibid.,* 38.
65. *Ibid.,* 93.
66. Otto Zimmerman, "Infinity," in *The Catholic Encyclopedia*, 15 Vols., Vol. 8, (New York: Robert Appleton Company, 1910), accessedMarch3,2011,http://www.newadvent.org/cathen/08004a.htm.
67. Barrow, *The Infinite Book: A Short Guide to the Boundless, Timeless and Endless*, 101-102.
68. *Ibid.,* 111.
69. Chandradhar Sharma, *A Critical Survey of Indian Philosophy* (2000, reprint; Delhi: Motilal Banarsidass Publishers, 1987), 182.
70. The concept of 'nothing' itself is a thing which leads us to a fallacy of four terms (nothing, absence of anything, something and a thing).
    Nothing is beyond the Universe.
    Jack is beyond nothing.
    So Jack is beyond the Universe.
    The four terms are: Jack, the Universe, nothing-as-*a-thing* of which Jack is beyond and nothing-as-an-absence-of-thing which has *no entity* beyond the Universe. The term 'nothing' has been taken *equivocally* which is invalid. Many fallacious conclusions follow from treating 'nothing' as a noun or pronoun. *Nothing* as a noun is contrasted with *something* and *everything*. The word 'nothing' does not function as a noun, as there is no object to which it refers. See Not 25.
71. Pandikattu, *Idols to Die, Symbols to Live,* 238.

# Chapter 4

# Nothingness and/as Fullness: General Critique and Evaluation

## 4.0 Introduction

In experiencing the coming-to-be of things, we experience the greatest of all wonders: that ***something is***! The idea of *something* or *being* is the first of all our ideas. In the first place, the predicate being is never univocally affirmed but analogically limited. Thus, we comprehend the *reality* which has two inherent principles; the spirit of change and fixation. What is absolutely real is Being. Being – which is all powerful, eternal, ultimate and unconditioned – is the principle of all finite beings.[1] Not-being is negation of being and non-being is unreal. "The way things appear is part of the being of things; things appear as they are, and they are as they appear. Things do not just exist; they also manifest themselves as what they are."[2] Things manifest us as *transcendent* and *analogous*.[3] In marvelling at the wonder of reality in its coming to be, human 'sees' the presencing of Being as the presencing of the Divine.[4]

We ask questions about reality, ourselves and our actions. The 'who' of a human person is the Acting Person – person with rational nature and subsistent subject of existence and actions.[5] "Feeling is now defined as the content of the *will*, which is the *act* of consciousness underlying all acts of consciousness, and therefore underlying all the contradictory aspects of the more abstract planes of consciousness."[6] "In the case of cognitive activity, the 'ego' or 'self' as the pure unity of mental acts can be conceived... in which the subject-object intentionality has emerged."[7] Through ones actions one becomes responsible for the action as good or evil. "In uttering (thinking) Being, thinkers, poets, artists, mystics gather the Divine traces to name them as holy. The Being-process is experienced by them as the Divine essencing in time and space."[8]

The essence of Universe is in time and space. The Universe is the sum total of *matter*, *space* and *time*. These three things depend on each other but self-moving things like animals and us are moved by desire or will and we human beings can transcend too. We regress our origin infinitely we come to our first human parents and finally to God, an Uncaused Being who does not have to receive existence like us. Our *linguistic terms* express our *mental concepts* which represent *real* essences or the *natures of things*.[9] Only God can create, that is, make something from *nothing*. "The Divine is not looked at as a static entity, but as a dynamic coming-to-be in the time – and space – bound event and things. To be open to reality is to be open to the Divine."[10]

Our cognitional acts (experience, understanding, judgment and decision) originate from the depths of our *conscious life* corresponding with *imperatives*:

1) Be attentive! → Experience
2) Be intelligent! → Understanding
3) Be critical! → Judgment
4) Be responsible! → Decision[11]

The imperatives (be attentive, be intelligent, be critical and be responsible) give rise to science which begins with *experience*. Philosophy studies the nature of *existence* as experienced as well as the *experience* of existence. When scientists attain an *insight* they express it in propositions known as *hypotheses* or theories. The third imperative is–be reflective and critical!–whether their hypotheses or theories are accurate. Then a tentative *judgment* whether their scientific propositions are approximately true. Both the scientist and philosopher claim to be lovers of truth. Thus, *philosophy* is a critical and systematic reflection leading to a wise worldview enabling us to have a wise and appropriate judgment. The fundamental criterion of truth is fidelity or *obedience* to the *imperatives* of the *mind.*[12]

Ultimately Reality or Existence is *Being Itself.* In India, great sages had reached the realization that Ultimate Reality was one, and that it was infinite; but they did not know that its name was "I."[13] All particular beings participate in Infinite Being-Itself. The first apprehension of the intellect is precisely *being*. Nothing can be known previous to the intuition of being; for there is nothing prior to being. Outside of being is only the darkness of non-being, or *nothing*. It is the *human person* who *encounters being*. The concept of 'person' is a *unitary one*, involving the notes of 'life', 'intellect' and 'will', with intellect involving both self-knowledge and knowledge of action.[14] In categorical thinking we move from the experience of simple objects to the presentation of intelligible objects.[15]*Being*, *substance* and *cause* are three most important ideas in understanding the reality.[16] The word 'Being', taken either as a participle or as a noun, has reference to the 'act' of existence (Be-ing) or the entity (being). "Our starting point, the direct judgment, is a critical reflection on an undeniable activity of ours: hence, it lands us already in the existential order (i.e. Be-ing)."[17] Being exists in mind or outside of mind, whether it is actual or potential, whether it inheres in subject or subsisting without it, it cannot be defined. It is conceptual and real. Real being is potential and actual. If anything distinct from being is added to being, what is added is 'nothing.' Being is that it is. The principle of reality is the identity of Being with Itself. Everything is *what it is*. Existence is limited and particularised in so many ways for the existence of many entities. Both existence and essence are realities, the one in the entitative order, the other in the quiddative order.[18] According to the scholastic tradition, every being is good, true, one, beautiful and in duration which are called transcendentals because they transcend, or exceed in extension. Real being is either finite or infinite. Finite being can be substance or accident. Accident is further divided into *quantity*, *quality*, *relation*, *action*, *passion*, *place*, *time*, *posture*, and habit (or *possession*). The truth is that substance brings out explicitly an existence which is neither explicitly affirmed nor explicitly denied but only implicitly contained in the concept of Being. So substance implicitly affirmstheunlimited Being. Everything that comes into being must have a cause. *Cause* as the correlative of effect which gives existence to, or contributes towards the existence of, anything; which produces a result; to which the *origin* of any thing is to be ascribed. Cause is that which in any way influences the production of an effect as an essence. The notion of cause is derived from observation of *changes*, whether local, quantitative, qualitative, or substantial. The explanation of any *change* leads to the doctrine of the four distinctions or classes, of causes as formulated by Aristotle (384-322 BCE). There are material, formal, efficient and final causes. The *material cause*, that out of which the effect is made or caused. The *formal causes* are the changeless essences of things in themselves amid the flux of accidental modifications, yet by actual union with the material cause they give shape to the objects. The *efficient cause* is the true cause by the operation or agency of which the effect is brought into being, an effect substantially distinct from the efficient cause. The action, or causality, of the efficient cause is conceived as one which reduces the actuality of the effect from its potentiality. The axioms of causality are: 1) Whatever exists in nature is either a cause or an effect. 2) No entity can be its own cause. 3) There is no effect without a cause. 4) Given the cause, the effect follows; the cause removed, the effect ceases. 5) An effect requires a proportionate cause. 6) The cause is by nature prior to its effect. 7) The perfection of the effect pre-exists in its cause. 8) Whatever is the cause of a cause is the cause also of its effect. 9) The first cause contributes more to the production of the effect than the secondary cause. Finally, the *final cause* is that principle on account of which the efficient cause moves towards the production of its effect. The final cause, like the efficient, is extrinsic to the effect. The end considered as the object desired, and the end considered as the desire of the object. All the four causes are really the cause of any given *physical effect*.

Being humans as efficient causes we ask *six questions* of philosophy due to the crisis of our inner being. We use *Why, How, When* and *Where* to delimit *What* and *Who*. External analyses in terms of Who (persons), What (objects), Where (places), When (events), How (instructions) and Why (reasons). Once grammatical categories are distinguished, enabling us to thereby distinguish the ontological category of objects by reference to the linguistic category of proper or common names.Aristotle identified 10 basic categories for knowledge. For example, 'A five-foot tall (quantity) man (substance) who was a thinker (quality) sat (position) on a bus (place) one morning (time), feeling hungry (state), but continuing to do a crossword puzzle (action) enthusiastically (passion).' The categories or modes of being exist in two ways: First way is primary, namely substance (what or who)and the secondary way is as accidents or predicables which are nine of them. A substance is a particular thing that retains its identity through time although its properties and attributes may change. The philosophical term 'substance' corresponds to the Greek *ousia*, which means 'being', transmitted via the Latin *substantia*, which means 'something that stands under or grounds things.'[19] Substance is beingness. "Aristotle analyses substance in terms of *form* and *matter*. The form is *what kind of thing* the object is, and the matter is *what it is made of*. The term 'matter' as used by Aristotle is not the name for a particular kind of stuff, nor for some ultimate constituents of bodies, such as atoms."[20] Substances could be corporeal and spiritual which exist independently. Related to the human body, matter is flesh and blood and form is prime matter which is known as soul. "Aristotle acknowledges that there are three candidates for being called *substance*, and that all three are substance in some sense or to some degree. First, there is *matter*, second, *form* and third, the *composite* of form and matter."[21]The secondary modes of being, accidents or predicables,'exist in' substances, dependently. Real being is analogously divided into finite and infinite. Finite being is divided into substance and accident. Accident is further divided into quantity, quality, relation, action, passion, place, time, posture, and possession. These nine accidents, together with the supreme genus, substance, are the ten Aristotelian categories.

"By the 18th century Immanuel Kant (1724-1804) found it necessary to reverse Aristotle, making 'substance and accidents' a sub-category of the broader category of 'relation'"[22] and distinguishes twelve pure concepts of the understanding and divided them into four classes of three: 1) *Quantity*: Unity, Plurality, and Totality. 2) *Quality*: Reality, Negation, and Limitation. 3) *Relation*: Inherence and Subsistence (substance and accident), Causality and Dependence (cause and effect), and Community (reciprocity). 4) *Modality*: Possibility, Existence, and Necessity. One may separately inquire after an object's quantity, quality, relation, and modality. It must be understood explicitly as categories *of objects of possible cognition*, not of the thing in itself. Aristotle used *language* as a clue to ontological categories, and Kant treated *concepts* as the route to categories of objects of possible cognition, Edmund Husserl (1859-1938) explicitly distinguished categories of *meanings* from categories of *objects,* and attempted to draw out the law-like correlations between categories of each sort. The highest existential categories on Roman Ingarden's list are the real (spatio-temporal beings), the ideal (abstract things), the absolute (completely independent, atemporal), and purely intentional (consciousness-dependent).[23] General terms as 'thing' 'entity' or 'object', on Michael Dummett's (b. 1925) view, are not genuine sortal terms, since they fail to provide any criteria of identity.[24] How does a substance change state? According to Quantum Mechanics, the world is not only made of ordinary objects rather peculiar quantum particle/wave objects. Quantum reality is fundamentally random; the movement of particles, creation of particles, destruction of particles, interaction between particles, the way atoms are tied to the nucleus, the nuclear forces, the properties of particles, the concept of the beginning of the Universe as a great leap, etc.

In modern times, however, quantum theory tells us that an electron is both in one position and at the same time in many other positions. This statement is *logically inconsistent,* and therefore nonsense. A square circle cannot exist, even in a dream, because if it were square, it would not be a circle! Without some innate knowledge, we would not be able to learn any language at all. The basic skills for communication or language, which philosophers have tried to identify are called *categories*. Categories are our basic assumptions we need in order to experience our world. Every being should be known by intellect. Not all words represent things in this Universe. The word represents a mental entity which contains the meaning of the word. Assumptions are part of our way of experiencing. Action at a distance has also been denied by scientists (because there is no mechanism whereby it can occur). Yet experiments in quantum physics have demonstrated action at a distance and instantaneous communication (violating relativity theory).

Reality is present as it **is**. We human beings experience, understand, judge and recognize this reality which manifests naturally, transcendentally and analogically. Being humans and as efficient causes we ask *six questions - Why, How, When* and *Where* to delimit *What* and *Who*.The linguistic terms of Who (persons), What (objects), Where (places), When (events), How (instructions) and Why (reasons) tell us the limited participation of the finite realities, like us too, in the Unlimited Reality of Infinite Existence. With our direct judgment, we affirm or negate entities directly while affirm existence indirectly but we cannot negate the being of existence. With the coming of the quantum physics, quantum reality or event is expressed in a paradoxical way.

Even if there is *no actual non-being* yet we represent empty set, empty placeholder, nothing, vacuum, empty space, non-being, non-existence, emptiness, nothingness or *kenōsis* as numerical 0. So nothingness as constitutive of reality of existence represents as mathematical zero, quantum zero, absolute zero, *śūnyatā*, *kenōsis*, emptiness or fullness. Here I make a synthesis, criticism and suggestions for complementarity on the paradoxical nature of the existence of nothingness. In fact if we analyse carefully, nothing points to fullness and fullness refers back to nothingness. In this sense, nothingness and fullness are not opposites, but they constitute reality, together with the limited something that we encounter.

## 4.1 Personal Synthesis

The objects, properties and events of the world are mere *facts of existence*. Only our perceptual *judgements* about those facts are termed either true or false. Truth cannot survive without its opposite non-truth (false) which is its epistemic precondition. In a way, *truth* and *knowledge* are inseparable. Truth comes in at least *two* different kinds: scientific *facts* and philosophical *wisdom*. We understand the whole, because it is nothing but the sum of its parts.Although the parts precede the whole in *the order of time,* it is the whole that is prior to the parts in *the order of perfection and completion.*There are no parts without a whole. Reductionism or mechanism in biology is simply a method and mode of thinking that is transferred over to the realm of *living substances*, as if substances are nothing other than the sum of their parts. The *form* of the machine exists in the mind of the engineer, but substances (whether living or non-living), have a *nature*, an intrinsic formal principle that renders them intelligible, determining matter to be 'what it is' (i.e., a substance with ordered parts). The whole determines the parts to be what they are. With regard to a living organism, *unity belongs to the whole*. The whole is one. It would not be a 'whole' if it were not one. If an organization loses its unifying principle, it becomes a non-unified multiplicity. Multiplicity is organized and made intelligible through unity, as it is in the realm of quantity (i.e., number organizes a raw multiplicity through a unit of measure, such as a foot, or an inch, or a litre). Number is multiplicity organized. Duration (quantity of time) is organized when it is numbered by a unit of time. To consider a part in isolation and treat that part as a whole unto itself is to forget that one would not be able to grasp this 'part' as a part, except in relation to the whole. Within the context of the whole living organism, parts exist for the sake of the whole, that is, they have a *function* in relation to the whole. They exist for the sake of the integrity (integration or oneness) of the whole organism. Because of that, parts do not determine the whole, but are themselves determined or defined by it. A living thing is characterized by *immanent activity*, that is, self-perfective activity.

Life is self-perfective self-movement: vegetative → animal → human → angelic → Divine (fullness of life). A vegetative life nourishes, reproduces, grows and repairs while an animal life adds locomotion and sensation to vegetative life. A non-living thing is not self-perfective and it moves as a result of being moved by some extrinsic principle. One existing substance that can move itself from 'within', grow, and is capable of nutrition and reproduction. A living thing is something that is self-perfecting, something whose activity is immanent, whose movement is from within (incretion, not accretion, as we see in crystals), which is why we look for self-motion (breathing or a pulse) to determine whether the body on the floor is alive or dead. The *form* that is the organizing or unifying principle must inhere not in the mind of the engineer as it does in the mechanical realm, but in the thing itself, in union with matter, determining it to be what it is, reducing it to an actually living entity. Organism is distinct from matter. That is another way of saying that *form* and *matter* are distinct. Matter that is organized into a kind of thing that is essentially different from inert matter is what we mean by a living organism. There is no self-organization without a 'self' and a thing cannot form or organize itself unless it has 'form' – otherwise, it would give to itself what it does not have, which is to get something from nothing. Potency does not reduce itself to actuality except by something already in act; multiplicity does not number itself, but is numbered by virtue of a principle, a unit, and disorder does not reduce itself to order except by a principle of order. To deny this is to equate something with nothing.

Organization is rooted in a principle, a unifying principle, and a unit is always distinct from the multiplicity, as order is distinct from disorder, or as determination is distinct from indeterminacy. The life principle is not matter, it is distinct (not separate) from matter. Hence, it is a non-material principle, a form, an intelligible configuration, and wherever there is form there is unity. Without unity, there is only multiplicity unorganized and unintelligible. The form of the living substance, distinct from matter but not separate, is what we mean by the *soul*. The difference between science and philosophy, between knowledge and wisdom, is not a difference in degree but in kind. Science is content with immediate proximate explanations and causes, while philosophy seeks ultimate explanations and causes. The difference is that *wisdom* always has a *value dimension*. Science is, or tries to be, values neutral. "Holistic science is a dynamic interplay of subjective research and objective research. Holistic science leads to *direct perception*, *verbal cognition* and *rational inference* (quantum logic) where all the three states are at different quantum energy potentials of the same mind spectrum."[25] *Freedom* cannot exist without *order*. They are inseparable. "Freedom of mind comes into being when there is no fear, when the mind has no desire to show off and is not intriguing for power, position and prestige... one who has a free mind is a true human being."[26] "Science looks at things that are measurable, physical, palpable, amenable to the senses. Spirituality looks at consciousness, thoughts, emotions, attitudes, values, character – all these are immeasurable, mental, not apparent to the senses."[27]

### 4.1.1 Metaphysics and Relational Zero

The object of metaphysic is being, the whole world of reality, whether subjective or objective, possible or actual, abstract or concrete, immaterial or material, infinite or finite. The nature of zero is the metaphysics of zero. Zero is construed as a number. In the standard set-theoretic definition of natural numbers zero can be identified with the number zero, 0. 0 is defined to be the empty set, this means that the number 1 is the set that contains the empty set as a member {Ø}. The existence of any number entails the existence of every other number but there are not any 'atomic' facts or properties in mathematical objects. The properties of any one thing (0 or 1) entail the properties of all the others. In the case of the notion of nothing at all ever having existed when construed as a real possibility, then our imagination breaks down because one always imagines some property or other. Zero as a number and empty placeholder has mathematical properties in decimal numeration. Platonists believe that zero is real or metaphysical. We are all entailed logically, physically and phenomenologically by the properties of zero otherwise our existence would have been logically incoherent. Quantum Mechanics (and Big Bang) helps us to go for a multi-valued logic from the two-valued logic for the better understanding of being, non-being, not being (negated being), nothing (*no* entity or being), analogical and relational being etc. 0 being quantitative number is neither positive nor negative, nor both positive and negative, nor neither positive nor negative but it is neutral yet it is connected, involved and associated or related with mathematics, science, religion and philosophy. Zero is both metaphysical and relational being. Let us see how the concept of immeasurable quantity or nothingness is used as mathematical 0.

### 4.1.2 Mathematical 0 as Quantitative and Relative 0

Mathematical 0 means *only one number* which has the implication of *nothing*. In the mathematical operation of addition, the later does not change (0 + 3 = 3). In multiplication, we get 0 (0 × 3 = 0). When divided by non-zero we get 0 (0/3 = 0). There are two types of zeros: relative and quantitative. The 0 of the scale, the origin of co-ordinate axes (0, 0), and 0 of the temperature scale are relative zeros. To specify relative positions we arbitrarily choose an origin as 0 of the thing. The origin of the three dimensions can be arbitrarily chosen by the triple (0, 0, 0) which is a relative zero. Relative 0 is not a number in the usual sense so it is a variable. To build a scale or a point on a line we need an 'order.' The 'order' is the minimum requirement for building a scale. In this way relative 0 is an ordinal 0. Relative zeros being abstractions have a hierarchy of zeros: natural 0, integral 0, rational 0 and real 0. Quantitative zeros imply 'nothing' of quantities like 0 litre, 0 gramme, 0 rupees, etc. Natural 0, the quantitative zero also is known as common sense zero. Bertrand Russell calls it logical 0. We call it right 0, rest higher level zeros are derived zeros (relative) or the ordered couple (0, 0) of the real zeros. 0 as a number is constant and not variable. So it may be called common sense 0, constant 0, absolute 0 or quantitative 0 of arithmetic. Mathematicians can be confident of their abstract truths; scientists can be at best be tentative about truth in the natural Universe.[28] In 1915, Einstein used mathematical logic to predict that light from a distant star would be deflected by a strong gravitational field.[29] Kurt Gödel's (1906-1978) incompleteness theorem says: Every formal logical system contains truths that cannot be proved within that system.[30] They have to be accepted as self-evident axioms.

### 4.1.3 Absolute 0 and Relativistic 0

The temperature of an object is a measure of how much energy that an object has. At absolute 0 K the object, atom or molecule, simply has no excess energy. Only that which it inherently possesses is called the 'ground zero state.' Each electron, proton and neutron is at its lowest permissible energy level. So atoms and molecules do continue to exist at 0 K and they are still uniquely different. As they lack extra energy they are very unlikely to actually interact with anything there. As yet no one has actually cooled anything to 0K but they have reached a few thousandths of a degree above 0 Kelvin. Absolute means unlimited, unconditioned, or free of any imperfect relation; it is perfect, complete, or total; permanent, inherent, or ultimate; independent, or valid without reference to a perceiving subject. Absolute is opposite of relative. Philosophically, it may be considered as the unknowable, the thing-in-itself; as that ultimate nonrelative that is the basis of all relation; as the ultimate, all-comprehensive principle in which all differences and distinctions are merged. Absolute 0 or truth still remains an unattainable ideal for scientists.

The relativistic 0 is the black hole. General relativity predicts that if a star of more than about 3 solar masses has completely burned its nuclear fuel, it should collapse to a configuration known as a black hole. Black holes are regions where the gravitational field of matter is too strong for anything, even light, to escape from its grasp.[31] Black hole begins as a hot gas like hydrogen. Left to itself it crushes to a tiny lump. As gas it gets hotter and denser. Hydrogen atoms hit each other with greater force. Due to increased heat and density, hydrogen gets fused and creates helium and releases more energy. A star life collapses due to uneasy equilibrium of energy. The bigger the star, the more hydrogen it has like in the Sun. Due to the Pauli Exclusion Principle, matter keeps itself intact without becoming a point. Wolfgang Pauli, a German Physicist, discovered in mid-1920s that no two things or rather two electrons can be in the same place at the same time. If pressure is increased on electrons they move faster. But there is a limit, electrons cannot move faster than light. They cannot move fast to collapse it. Subramanyan Chandrasekhar (1910-1995), an Indian-American Physicist, showed that a collapsing star that has 1.4 times the mass of our sun will have enough gravity to overcome the Pauli Exclusion Principle. It is the 'Chandrasekhar limit.' The electrons get smashed into protons and create neutrons and become a neutron star. When a dying star collapses it becomes smaller and smaller. Then zero space. This is black hole; a term coined by John Archibald Wheeler (b. 1911) in 1967. It is a closed surface through which gravity prevents light from propagating.[32] In the modern theory of relativity it creates the paradox of the infinite nothing of the black holes. Zero in Quantum Mechanics invests the vacuum with infinite energy. Einstein's equations predicted the black hole, a star so dense that nothing can escape its grasp, not even light. When an extremely massive star collapses, it disappears. The gravitational attraction is so great that no force in the Universe can stop its collapse – not the repulsion of its electrons, not the pressure of neutron against neutron, nor quark against quark – nothing. This is a black hole, an object so paradoxical that some scientists believe that black holes can be used to travel faster than light – and backward in time too.

The key to black hole's strange properties is the way it curves spacetime. A black hole takes up no space at all, but it still has a mass. Since the black hole has a mass, it causes the spacetime to curve. Normally this would not cause a problem. As we approach a heavy star, the curvature gets greater and greater, but once we have passed the outer edge of the star itself, the curvature decreases again, bottoming out at the centre of the star. In contrast, a black hole is a point. It takes up zero space, so there is no outer edge, no place where space begins to flatten out again. The curvature of the space gets greater and greater as you approach a black hole, and it never bottoms out. The curvature goes off to infinity because the black hole takes up zero space; the star has torn a hole in spacetime. The zero of black hole is a *singularity*, an open wound in the fabric of the Universe. The minimum speed needed to escape from a black hole is called escape velocity. If we get very close to a black hole, known as event horizon, escape velocity becomes faster than light. Einstein had denied black holes initially but he was wrong. "The supermassive black hole at the centre of the Milky Way galaxy is called Sagittarius A. It has a mass equal to about 4 million suns and would fit inside a very large ball that could hold a few million Earths."[33]

Black hole is the best example of nothingness and fullness which are not contradictory. As such blackhole constitutes reality.

### 4.1.4 Emptiness and Fullness: The Dynamic Relationship

The mystery of existence or emptiness-fullness embraces the absolute and the relative. The absolute is the ground of everything, the void, the deep silence and nothing – from all phenomena and all polarities. Fullness can be experienced – just by looking within what is left when anything related to the small self is taken away. The relative is the dependent evolving from the whole of absolute one. We speak of gratefulness, faithfulness or prayerfulness when we are full of gratitude, faith and prayer but for fullness in all its forms, emptiness is the necessary condition. The emptiness allows the fullness to be, the fullness gives richness to the emptiness. What we perceive as distinct phenomena are vortexes in the stream, temporary manifestations within the whole self. This self is part of the existence whole. It is an expression and manifestation of God/ Mind as all phenomena are, and the spacious awareness which functions through it is an aspect of God/ Mind – as all awareness is.

Emptiness and fullness seem as complete opposites but in the spiritual life, as well as in existential life, they are not. Emptiness is unmanifested or undifferentiated being while fullness is manifested and differentiated being. Emptiness is not mere emptiness but real emptiness is empty of phenomenal limitations.

It is the predicate absolute. "The term *śūnya* means both empty as well as full: the world is empty of intrinsic nature, it is non-existent; however the Supreme Body of Essence (*Dharma-kāya*) is empty of imperfections, but also full of perfections."[34] On the other hand fullness is full of predicates. Predicated properties or attributes, qualities, features, characteristics, and types are those predicated entities that can be predicated of things or persons attributed to them. The transcendental absolute reality is full of truth, consciousness and bliss (*Satcidānanda*).

## 4.2 Criticism

A 'thing' is primarily an activity - or series of activities (metabolism, breathing, growing, reproducing, etc.). But there is no entity as such, only activity. In other words, is there a predicate (growing, breathing, eating, etc.,) without a real subject? Self-perfective activity presupposes a subject of the activity that is distinct from its activity. There is no action without a subject to carry out the acting. "The mind is not only a receiver but also a transmitter of energy. When one is thinking, there is beta rhythm which implies that one is more attentive to the external world than to inner experience. When thinking is replaced by quiet contemplation, there is alpha rhythm which suggests a relaxed state."[35] Edmund Husserl (1859-1938) avoided the Cartesian, Lockean concept of consciousness as an enclosed sphere and restored the understanding of mind as public and as present to things.[36] Once consciousness is present to the things then it is aware of the quality or quantity.

### 4.2.1 Quality and Quantity

What is a 'thing?' Is it a quantity or a quality? Can a 'thing' exist without quantity and quality? Pythagoras (569-475 BCE) and his school showed the link between quantity and quality in the study of music: the length of a vibrating string on the harp (quantity) affects the pitch (quality) of a musical note. Hence the suggestion that number (quantity) is the basis of everything (quality). 'What' is a matter of quality, not quantity. When we ask 'what' a thing is, we are inquiring of its *nature*. It means 'essence' or 'being.'

Essences are not particular, they are universal, they are not subject to change, they are unchanging; they are not subject to quantity, they have no quantity; they are not subject to place, so they are nowhere. The intellect apprehends essences (which are universal), while the imagination internally perceives particulars. Intelligence is the ability to apprehend the essences of things (universals) by reducing universals, for instance, to linguistic constructs or concepts. A thing with a nature is a determinate, limited thing that is intelligible and definable. Non-quantitative aspects of existence, such as purpose, freedom, design, honesty, cannot be handled by science because they are not quantitative propositions.

Quality depends upon quantity in order to be. There is no such thing as pure quantity. There are only quantified things or substances. Quantity depends upon substance. The substance is first or primary. It is through the accident of quantity that substance is actually extended. If the substance was not quantified, that is, spread out in three dimensions, it could not be coloured. If it does not have sensible qualities like taste, smell, hardness or sound, it cannot be perceived. The only thing that can be perceived and imagined is a quantified/qualified substance. The senses cannot explore the substance of gold itself. This is the limit of our sense investigation, limit of investigative science. Intelligence alone can investigate the substance. The substance refers to the *kind or form* of a thing. The form determines the thing to be the kind of thing it is. *Form* gives the substance its 'whatness.' What is it? Its substantial form (goldness) is just a word, but it is a word that expresses the intelligible content of gold. What is it that has the substantial form? It is always matter that has form. Matter receives form. Matter = Potentiality, Form = Actuality. The source or principle that renders a new form possible is matter. The source or principle that makes the thing actually what it is, is the form. The substance gold is nothing other than prime matter. Prime matter is the ultimate matter, the ultimate potentiality. The prime matter has the form, is the subject of the form. It can acquire a new form. If it does, it becomes a new kind of substance. Prime matter is the ultimate principle of potentiality of a substance. Substantial form is the ultimate principle of actuality of a substance. These two principles are composite. Form actualizes prime matter, potentiality. Actuality actualizes potentiality. A substance is a composite of potency and act. The substantial form is not located anywhere in a substance? The form is found in every part, just as the substantial form of man is found in every part of man. 'What' is more fundamental than 'How much?' 'What' is a qualitative term while 'how much' is quantitative of a being.

### 4.2.2 Being and Non-being

'Being and non-being' or 'to be and not to be' are the most basic questions of philosophy. The word, being, functions as both a noun (pointing to a thing that exists) as well as a verb (denoting the activity of existing). The word *being*, in the primary sense, is the present participle of the verb *to be*. *To be* is the act of existence and *not to be* is non-existence. When Supreme Being is totally beyond human understanding, He is said 'not to be.' Being means which exists. It means a thing, an entity or reality. "Each thing is first of all *being* (if it is actual and real), then being is the first act, the root of every other act and perfection. It could be said that being is the *act of every act* or *perfection of every perfection*."[37] The term being is the expression of a concept; it has both a comprehension (connotation) and an extension (denotation). The comprehension or connotation of a concept is the sum total of all the attributes which constitute the concept, expressed in the definition of the content of the concept. The extension or denotation of a concept, on the other hand, is the sum total of all the individuals and groups to which a concept can be applied. Being is anything and everything that does or can exist. Existents are specific ways of existing while being is unspecified way of existing. Being (existence) makes entities but refuses to be an entity. A being can be actual or possible, substantial or accidental, necessary or contingent, finite or infinite, absolute or relative. An absolute being can be thought of or can exist without reference to another being. Things come into being and pass away. Is there a common ground from which they spring up and into which they return? Is this ground a thing, principle, anything or nothing? How far can we conceive a supreme being as the existing ground and substratum of everything? For any attempt to investigate this ground is bound to come up against not-being and the *nihil* and to experience the closeness of the negative in the very being of things, just as, seeking to demarcate the realm of beings, one must reckon with non-being, at the edge of the one whole of all that is.[38] Beings in the world, that is, outside the mind, exist not primarily as numbers, atoms, waves, or particles, but as entities or things. Heidegger, by giving thought to Being as the 'presencing of the present', succeeded in bringing together absencing and presencing, concealing and revealing, through the notion of *a-letheia* (un-concealment) or *Ereignis* (eventing).[39] "Instead of considering 'Being' (*Sein*), metaphysics has been dealing with the 'beingness' (*Seiendheit*) of entities (*Seinendes*) in its universality and ultimacy."[40] "Insofar as metaphysics considers the unity of entities in their abstracted universal trait, beingness, it is ontology; insofar as it inquires into the unity of entities as grounded in the highest entity, God, it is theology. As ontology and theology, metaphysics is onto-theo-logic."[41] According to Martin Heidegger the dominating or manipulating tendency of the subject – the epistemological approach – makes the whole of Western philosophy into a monolithic structure, characterized by its failure to consider Being.[42] In general it is assumed in the West that being is the primary category of understanding, and that 'nothingness' is simply a term which refers to the negating, denial or removal of being.[43] Non-being is not anything that has an existence of its own, but is a *dependent notion* referring to the *no-longer-being-ness* of a thing, situation or property of a being.[44]

> There does not exist a *non-being* as something having a value in itself, separately from being... *Non-being is only in being*, in the measure in which we discover its negativity... The forms of negativity are exactly correspondent to the correlative forms of positivity, because *non-being* is always the correlative of *being*. Therefore, there are as many forms of non-being as there are correlative forms of being. Non-being and nothingness are thus, not a priori creations of mind.[45]

There is an inadequacy of contemporary metaphysics. Quantum Mechanics with subatomic particles (and Big Bang) can help us to challenge the two-valued logic and go to a multi-valued logic and multi-valued understanding of being, non-being, not being, nothing (no being), relational being, absolute being etc. East has viewed language and reason as inadequate tools for the partial revelation of that which is neither verbal nor intellectual, but experiential. The entities exist primarily as substances. A substance exists *per se*, that is, in itself (independently). Substance is whatever is a natural kind of thing and exists in its own right. There are secondary modes of being that exist dependently called accidents, from the Latin, which means to inhere in. The substance is that in which the accidents inhere. Accidents actuate the substance in an accidental way, that is, in a way that does not change the substance itself. Accidents are the modifications that substance undergoes, but that do not change the kind of thing that each substance is. In a sense accidents reflect the structure of reality. The first accident quantifies a substance. A being is a thing that hasan *act of existing* (actuality) while non-being considers the potentiality of things. The knowing being (animate being) is not limited to its own being, but it is capable of being other than itself, while the non-knowing being (inanimate being) is limited to its own being. The knower has, in addition to his/her own form, the form of the thing known. Material things known must exist in the knower, not materially, but immaterially. So the material Universe has intelligibility which is composed of mass, energy and motion. It is not that material world is intelligent but it can be known, quantified and measured. Physics has discovered five layers (molecular, atomic, nuclear, hadronic and the layer of quarks) of the matter while *Advaita* has found five features – existence (*asti*), manifestation (*bhāti*), lovability (*priyam*), name (*nāma*), and form (*rūpa*).[46] Pictures, words, symbols, perceived objects, states of affairs, other minds, laws, and social conventions are all acknowledged as truly there, as sharing in being and as capable of appearing according to their own proper style.[47]

To cause an effect is to impart being. And it is existential judgment that apprehends being. Now, from nothing comes nothing.

For it is not possible to get being from non-being (nothing). And nothing is not a 'potency', for 'nothing' does not have 'ability', and 'ability' is a potentiality (an indeterminacy). Potentiality or ability is not nothing. It is intelligible – not in itself, but intelligible nonetheless. So it is not true that from nothing comes something. The Universe, or anything for that matter, cannot have been the effect of nothing or non-being, for nothing simply 'is not', and to effect is to impart being. But nothing has no being to impart, nor is it anything from which 'is' may emerge.

Now, if there is nothing, then there is no fluctuation, quantum or otherwise. As Parmenides knew long ago, non-being or nothing is unthinkable. It cannot be made an object of thought because 'nothing' has absolutely no referent. 'Nothing' is more referentless than 'zero' which refers to a place on a number line and mathematical operations. So if we refer to quantum fluctuation, we refer to something, not 'nothing.' Furthermore, if quantum fluctuation is going to have any intelligible value whatsoever, there will have to be a subject of that fluctuation. What is it that is fluctuating?

Change involves two terminals: the terminal from which (*terminus a quo*) a change commences, and a terminal towards which (*terminus ad quem*) the change moves and at which it terminates.[48] But nothing cannot be a terminus, because it is nothing. That is why creation (the bringing of something into being, by God, from nothing) is not change. The notion of creation from nothing, without God, of course, leaves us with nothing. So, we have the spontaneous appearance of the Universe from nothing, according to some scientists. It cannot be a change, since nothing is not a terminus. And there is no cause to this spontaneous appearance. So there is a potentiality that is actualized, but it is not 'somehow' actualized because there is no cause. We cannot ask 'how' or 'why.' To ask 'why' is to seek the cause, and there is no cause. But quantum fluctuation is put forth as an agent cause. This is inconsistent. So what then, is the existential status of this quantum fluctuation? What is it? If it is nothing, it cannot be the cause. If it is something, then the Universe did not proceed from nothing. Fluctuation is also a term whose meaning, like the meanings of all our words, is derived from our pre-scientific experience. Something fluctuates. The word itself means 'change.' Fluctuation implies a substrate and a *terminusa quo*. Something is changing, and the *terminus ad quem* of that change is the end of the change. Now, is there a cause of this quantum fluctuation? If not, then we posit a change that is not caused, that is, a fulfilment or a realization (actualization) of a potentiality without a prior act. But this too would mean getting something from nothing. There is no cause of the fluctuation, and so we cannot seek to know why there was a fluctuation. Now, if nothing precedes the fluctuation (which is to say that the fluctuation has no substrate), then the fluctuation has nothing for its *terminus a quo* (for it has no substrate). But nothing cannot be the *terminus a quo*, because nothing means non-being. It is absurd to posit nothing as being, a term 'from which' a change of the thing commences.

Finally, the notion of something coming from nothing is irrational and arbitrary. 'Everything is a matter of opinion', and that 'everyone has a right to one's own opinion', and 'that every opinion is just as valid as any other', or that 'what is right for me may not be right for others', and 'who am I to impose my morality on others', etc. deny the principle of identity. Then righteousness has no value even though language determines and describes reality in a limited way is equally absurd and irrational.

### 4.2.3 Existence and Non-existence

*Existence* is not what we *are*, but what we *have*. We have received the existence as human beings and rest of the things as they are. "'Is' refers to that by which something is actual. In the second existential sense, however, it expresses the truth of a proposition."[49] Existence is to have something in contrast to nothingness. We are aware that we came into existence in time and place and now we enjoy a received existence. Material thing is a composite of essence and existence. Something (or someone) must exist in its (his/her) own right, and not because of something else. That something which (or someone who) exists in its (his/her) own right and not as dependent on another is God. God simply IS, with the fullness of all that the word 'is' can contain. This is why God is called 'the Supreme Being.' God's existence is uncaused and independent. In God existence and essence are identical. God is the uncaused cause and source of all entities in the Universe. God's existence is ultimate, the default, and non-existence must be seen in relation to God's existence. *Non-existence* is the condition or something that does not exist nor have being. Before creation, there was only nothingness besides God - only He was in existence. As the existence is the essential property of a potential entity that has been actualized, non-existence can be defined as the general quality of un-actualized potential and nothingness can be defined as the sum of all non-actualized potentialities. Nothingness was infinite before the creation of the world, and it is still infinite, as God's creative potential is infinite. There must be someone who was not made by anyone else, someone who never had a beginning or end. That someone is God who is infinite good, eternal, all-knowing, all- present, almighty, life and love.

An existing being exists not by virtue of its substantial form, but by virtue of its *esse*, that is, its received act of existing. A substance is always a certain *kind of* thing. That is why we can ask the question: What is it? In other words, it has form, or *eidos* (idea). It has a certain intelligible *nature (physis)*. The substantial form is a *real principle of a substance*, the *principle of actuality*, the *formal principle*, or the *formal cause of the substance*. The substance has accidental qualities so we are able to perceive it. The substance does not exist separately from the accidents. It is matter's nature to *have*, to *receive*, to *be actualized by*, to *be determined by* an act, a form, a determination. A unifying principle is one, but the parts are many. The unifying principle of a living organism is the substantial form. Now the substantial form of an organism cannot be many, otherwise a thing would 'actually' be many things, which is a contradiction. Quantity is divided into continuous quantity (extension) and discrete quantity. Any sensible object is spread out in the three dimensions of length, breadth, and thickness. The substance has parts, but is not the sum of its parts. It is the whole substance that determines the parts to be what they are. *Artefacts* do not have a substantial nature that is whole and entire in every part. The essence of a material thing includes matter and form. All matter is a composite of essence and existence. *Abstract nouns* belong to the order of essences (what a thing is, expressed in concepts) and being belongs to the existential order, a radically different one from that of essences.[50]

Parmenides argued that change is impossible, because to change is to 'come into being' and to 'go out of being' (from 'is' to 'is not'). But outside of being is 'non-being' or nothing, and it is impossible to go into nothing, for there is nothing to go into. It is also impossible to come into being, because that implies that what came into being was outside of being, but outside of being is 'non-being' or nothing. A substance is a whole that is not determined by its parts. A substance can change in accidents (quantity...), and yet remain the same substance. Change is a 'transformation.' Note the word 'trans' and 'form'; change is a change in form, and not an absolute coming into being and going out of being, as Parmenides thought. So, if we were to define matter as that which has mass and extension, as our science books typically do, then it would follow that substance is more immaterial than material. 'I' is the substance that I am, which is not the same as the parts (quantity gives us 'parts outside of parts'), or atoms. Mathematical 'existence' meant only logical self-consistency and this neither required nor needed physical existence to complete it.[51] They are abstract entities. Science expresses the existence in five terms: *time, space, matter, power and motion.* We can find such truths in Genesis 1, 1-2: "In the beginning (time) God created (power) the heaven (space) and the earth (matter) ... And the Spirit of God moved (motion) upon the face of the 'waters'." Before God created anything, there was only nothingness or non-existence besides God - only He was in existence. Non-existence or nothingness was infinite before the creation of the world, and it is still infinite, as God's creative potential is infinite. Non-existence is the general quality of un-actualized potential or the sum of all non-actualized potentialities of the existence, the ultimate.

## 4.3 Suggestions for Complementarity

Nature itself entails complementarity in its manifold expression. The complementary nature in complementary pairs such as male~female, boy~girl, head~tail, heavy~light, 1~0, being~nothingness, space~time, energy~matter, particle~wave, faith~reason, active~passive, rational~intuitive, day~night, left~right, and so on. The reality lies somewhere in between opposites and polar aspects, in between something and everything, or in between life and death, or in between finite and infinite, or in between absolute and relative, etc. The complementary nature introduces a new meaning and application of the tilde or 'squiggle' character (~), as in yin~yang, body~mind, individual~collective... Unlike the hyphen, the squiggle does not represent a simple concatenation of words, but rather indicates the inextricable complementary relationship between them.[52] Every reality is a composite of *prime matter* and *form* which makes it as an integrated one. When the reality is perceived integrally it is perceived with being and non-being, as conscious and unconscious, as identified yet differentiated, in unity and diversity, as affirmed and negated, as observer and observed, as subject and object etc. The choice involves the reciprocal activity of intellect and will. Intelligence is the ability to grasp the existence and natures of things. We know that 'we' know something that is not us (the object of our knowledge). That is why we can say that we are subjects of knowledge. Hence, subjectivity and objectivity are, to intelligent persons, meaningful terms, for they describe a real intelligible relation. Freedom involves the choice between alternatives or means whereby the end is to be attained. The will is the intellectual appetite that follows upon the intellectual apprehension of beings and their relations, not a sensible appetite that follows upon sense knowledge. In everything that we will there is some good, and it is because of its goodness that we want it. The intellect moves the will, that is, presents the will with known goods, but the will in turn moves the intellect, causing it to continue presenting alternatives, that is, to continue deliberating. Decision occurs at the command of the will; for the very word 'decide' comes from the Latin:

*'de secare'* (dissect), which means literally 'to cut off.' At some point the will commands the intellect to 'cut off' its deliberation (decision). The will orders the intellect to impress upon the will (itself) a definite known good for the last time. Thus, the will, by terminating the intellectual process, is actually determining (de-terminating) the course of action to be followed, that is, which *means* is to be chosen.

### 4.3.1 Consciousness and Unconsciousness

All living beings have their life instincts yet only intelligent beings are aware of their consciousness and unconsciousness. "Our experience of consciousness may be subjective, but it is a biological feature of the brain, caused by the interactions between billions of individual cells."[53] "In terms of consciousness, matter and life have seen different stages. At the gross level, matter is unconscious. At the vital level, life is sub-conscious. At the emotional level, it is uni-conscious. At the intellectual level, it is conscious. At the spiritual level, it is super-conscious."[54] We are conscious or aware of ourselves and others or things. We have waking, dreaming, deep sleep and absolute consciousness. "We know that electrons make atoms. Atoms make molecules. Molecules make cells of body and blood. Blood circulates through heart, lungs, and brain to keep us alive and conscious and aware of self-identity."[55] Cognition is an act by which the knower actually becomes the object known. It is impossible to know an object unless we have in a cognitive way the form of the object we know. It means we are able to make an abstract concept of an object through our mental faculty. Consciousness consists of inner, qualitative, subjective, unified states of sentience, awareness, thoughts, and feelings.[56] The three features; qualitativeness, subjectivity, and unity, are not three distinct features, but different aspects of the very essence of consciousness. Consciousness is essentially consciousness 'of' something or other. "The consciousness of the individual is not static during life. Its ultimate destiny is to meet its source, or to express the Supreme Consciousness or the Universal Spirit completely."[57] Everything in the outside Universe can be represented in the inside of human consciousness as virtual or actual.[58] "The mind and the world are correlated with one another. Things do appear to us, things truly are disclosed, and we, on our part, do display, both to ourselves and to others, the way things are."[59]

The intellect can define things because it can apprehend what things are essentially. The senses do not grasp the 'what' of things, but only their sensible properties. *The first act* is that by which the intellect grasps the *essence* of a thing, that is, what a thing is, and this is called *simple apprehension.* It is through simple apprehension that the intellect conceives ideas or concepts, which are universal ideas within the mind (*eidos*). The *second act* of the intellect is not simple, but complex and thus, depends upon simple apprehension. This act is called *judgment*, which is either a *composition* or *division. The third act of the intellect* is called *reasoning*, which is the act of drawing a conclusion from two judgments.

Applying this to being and their relatedness to reality, we can bring in the Principle of Sufficient Reason: *Everything which is, to the extent to which it is, possesses a sufficient reason for its being so that it is capable of explaining itself to the intellect.*[60] Being conscious we find our identity and differentiate from others.

### 4.3.2 Identification and Differentiation

Every being or thing has its own identity. That is how things are different from each other. We can identify and differentiate due to our intellectual faculty and desire needed things due to our free will power. There is a relationship between 'doing' and 'being': we become (being) what we choose (doing). "What is the form that is not matter but that is the energizing principle that starts that organization?"[61] That form comes from the material itself for Aristotle, an instrumental efficient cause for Thomas Aquinas. We believe that every soul, whatever we mean by it, is uniquely customized, created for that being.[62] There are three structural forms a) the structure of parts and wholes, b) the structure of identity in a manifold, and c) the structure of presence and absence.[63] The wholes can be two different kinds of parts: pieces and moments. "Pieces are parts that can subsist and be presented even apart from the whole; they can be detached from their wholes. Pieces can be called independent parts."[64] "Moments are parts that cannot subsist or be presented apart from the whole to which they belong; they cannot be detached."[65] Mind and being are moments to each other; they are not pieces that can be segmented out of the whole to which they belong.[66] As the eye can see any object, but not itself, so the mind can know any object, but not itself, because it is not an object.[67] The structure of identity in a manifold is expressed in a manifold of ways, and the fact is other to any and all of its expressions. "Just as the cube belongs to a dimension different from that of the dies, aspects, and profiles, so the meaning or the fact belongs to a dimension different from that of the manifold of expressions and utterances through which it is given"[68] "Every act of consciousness we perform, every experience that we have, is intentional: it is essentially 'consciousness of' or an 'experience of' something or other. All our awareness is directed toward objects."[69] "Objectively, what is given to me when I see a cube is a blend made up of sides that are present and sides that are absent but cointended. The thing being seen involves a mixture of the present and the absent. Subjectively, my perception, my viewing, is a blend made up of filled and empty intentions."[70]

> Presence and absence are the objective correlates to *filled* and *empty intentions*. An empty intention is an intention that targets something that is not there, something absent, something not present to the one who intends. A filled intention is one that targets something that is there, in its bodily presence, before the one who intends.[71]

The intention begins with its appearance in three guises: intention for the future, the intention with which someone acts, and intentional action, as in the fact that I am typing these words intentionally.[72] "The presence and absence belong to the being of thing identified in them. Things are given in a mixture of presences and absences, just as they are given in a manifold of presentations.

We should also notice that it is this identity, this invariant in presence and absence, to which we refer when we use words to name a thing."[73] Intuition is not something mystical or magical; it is simply having a thing present to us as opposed to having it intended in its absence.[74] "The absent is given to us as absent; absence is a phenomenon, and it must be given its due. Hope and despair, for example, presuppose that we can intend some good that is not yet achieved and are either confident or diffident about attaining it."[75] The empty intention is correlated with the absence of the object, the filled intention is correlated with its presence.[76] In addition to empty and filled intentions, there is a third act, an act of recognition, or an act of identification that correlated with the identity of the object itself. The act of recognition or identification transcends the empty and filled intentions just as the object's identity transcends its presences and absences.

### 4.3.3 Unity and Diversity/Oneness and Otherness

Everywhere in the Universe, we are faced with one and many, unity and diversity or oneness and otherness. Unity or oneness is the process by which a being is not divided in itself, but divided from everything else. Oneness and otherness complement each other. "There is no unity without the plurality, and no plurality without unity, they found and sustain each other. One is in the other, and the other is in the one: unity is the foundation of plurality."[77] Space and time are vehicles of continuity by which the world's parts hang together. We know how an electron behaves but not what it is. Quantum theory insists that we cannot know the locality and velocity of particles at the same time, uncertainty relates to the measurement.[78] "All things cohere and adhere to each other somehow, and the Universe exists practically in reticulated or concatenated forms which make of it a continuous or 'integrated' affair due to causal unity, genetic unity, teleolical unity, aesthetic unity and moral unity."[79] Unity is not a creation of the human mind, but a discovering of what has already been there a discovery which is never complete.[80] From unity we derive the metaphysical principle of identity: 'A thing is what it **is**' and in its contradictory form 'A thing cannot **be** and **not be** the same thing at the same time and under the same respect.' It is the principle of uniformity of nature. If nature were not uniform there would be no scientific development. Even in the quantum or sub-atomic level matter has its probable measurement.

### 4.3.4 Affirmation and Negation/Purpose and Decision

Whatever exists is positive. Being positive is prior to being negative, for something must exist before it can be opposed or negated.[81] Each thing exists also as negative, for in whatever sense each thing is not any or all other things, it is both negated by them and negates them. The way in which it exists as not them is a part of the way in which it exists.[82] Being negative is prior to being positive, for when anything comes into existence. Actually, the positive and negative aspects of each thing occur together. Whatever exists is always in some sense positive and negative. "Negation exists always as an aspect of something which is both positive and negative. Negation never exists entirely alone. It exists in as many ways as each thing is not every other thing, and is as dynamic and variable as are the relations between changing things."[83]

Something acts with purpose means that it acts with an intention, that is, it acts for an end. What is the final cause of human existence? We all have the same formal cause, that is, the same nature. Therefore, we all have the same final cause or purpose. Change is always a movement from potentiality to actuality. Therefore, the terms 'purpose', 'direction', 'meaning', and 'end' have to do with a movement from potentiality to actuality. What is life's end? Act (an actuation, a realization). The perfection or completion of a movement is the complete actualization of the movement.

No experience is possible without negation. Our conception of the negative depends ultimately on the degree of legitimacy with which we can consider ourselves separate from the one world of which each of us forms a part. The relationship of apposite oppositeness is what it is in many different fundamental relationships in each of which apposite oppositeness occurs. Where complementary prevails, there is no escape from negativity because two polar positives constitute opposition and consequently become more negative as they become more positive.[84] "A negation or privation is never given a name of a 'cause.' A negation or privation is the absence of entity and as such is actually nothing. But what is actually nothing cannot exert a positive influence in the production of anything."[85]

### 4.3.5 The Observer and the Observed/Inside and Outside

The observer is the one who observes things from inside as well as from outside. By doing so the observer affects the observed things. Scientifically we may term it butterfly effect. The world is exclusive exteriority, thought is exclusive interiority: materialism and spiritualism – the primacy of matter (of exteriority) or the primacy of the spirit (of interiority).[86] "Does the distinction between matter and ideas disappear as we attempt to describe the limits of particle physics? Until today, the answer to this question is undecided and even unclear. The 'qwiff' is a 'quantum wave function' that at best can describe the probability of the observation and not the actual observation. Thus, qwiffs flow and qwiffs pop."[87] "Science is not viewed as totally objective and religions subjective. It used to be thought that the scientist was a detached observer but in relativity the basic measurements, such as the mass, velocity and length of an object depend on the frame of reference of the observer. There is the personal participation of the knower in all knowledge."[88] Does uncertainty principle refute realism? What we observe depends on how we observe it. The observed phenomenon depends on the observation, and therefore on the observer. Quantum theory raises doubts about one of the most deeply held articles of scientific faith-the belief in an objective world that is independent of our observations. Quantum theory and the uncertainty principle tell us that we cannot picture nature but can only predict the results of specific experiments- and these results will depend on how we choose to perform our experiments. Not only are we blind to the workings of nature, but even our brief glimpses are of no objective, independent reality but of a *subjective, observer-determined* world. "No one ever sees a radio wave, feels a radio wave through physiological tactile senses, or hears a radio wave directly."[89] We observe radio waves indirectly, by intercepting them with a receiving antenna, concerting them to electrical signals, processing these signals with electronic circuitry, then ultimately converting them to light on a screen or sound from a speaker.[90]

> "Only at the submolecular level does nature sometimes present us with sets of unambiguously discrete objects. Boundaries and definitions of entities are human constructs that nature is under no obligation to respects... But to believe that our definitions and groupings are the reality is to entertain a delusion, and can easily lead us to draw misleading or meaningless conclusions about the world around us."[91]

Machines and artefacts do not exist in themselves. They are made of different parts. The principle of unity and being comes to the machines or artefacts from the outside in regard to their production and in regard to the appreciation of the work. This is how the reductionist conceives of everything, and denies that things have a nature. The whole is one thing, that is, one unified entity that has a definite nature. It is the nature that determines it to be *what it is,* not the particles. The parts are parts of the substance, and so the parts have the same nature as the whole. If we come to something that does own something from within itself, it is either a nature or more parts. By appealing to smaller and smaller particles, we never really explain anything. The primary mode of being is not the particle or the atom. It is the substance, that is, the nature existing. A thing has a potential principle and a formal or actual principle. A thing is actually something because it has form, that is, an intelligible structure, or a nature. A material thing is not a pure form, but a composite of first matterand substantial form. The first accident of a material thing is *quantity,* which extends the substance. Quantity gives us parts outside of parts. The parts are not prior to the substance. The quantity of a substance can and does change while the substance itself remains the same (remains *what it is*). The laws of nature also as they are. The parts receive their order, their intelligible unity from the thing's form.

We hold ideas in common, implies the intellectual ability to grasp what is common and what is not common. In other words, it requires the ability to grasp universality, for I cannot deny what I cannot grasp. Not only does it require the ability to grasp universality, but it also implies the ability to 'step outside myself' so to speak. In other words, I am able to know something other than myself. I can see into other reality, enough to know that I do not hold any truth in common. I also presuppose that we can do the same, for I am telling that there is no common truth. Hence, I expect anybody to understand that.

If I communicate something to a person, I imply that I at least believe that the person has some abilities in common with us. For, we are able to communicate, enter into communion, enter into a common arena, so to speak. We have a lot in common, which is why we can communicate, and which is why I communicate to a person that 'there is no common truth.' Yet it is true that we have 'common ground' on which to communicate. We have this common ability to 'exit ourselves' and know something other than ourselves. There is a world outside of ourselves, something other than ourselves, otherwise the ability to exit ourselves would be entirely useless. If there is nothing outside of ourselves to know, why do we have the ability to exit ourselves? But there is something outside of ourselves, at least the person to whom I am communicating my idea that 'there is no common truth.' I can know something about him, namely that we have no truth in common. If I know that, then what I know about him is not mere opinion, but truth. Hence, there is a lot more that I can know than the inability to hold truth in common. No matter how we come at this problem, denying that we can hold the truth in common is *entirely self-refuting.*

In order to do any testing, any measuring, any evidence gathering, a scientist first needs to be able to know reality at a basic level, however imprecise. How does she/he test, gather evidence, measure, etc., in order to justify her/his knowing abilities so she/

he can trust her/his knowing abilities, ultimately so that she/he can proceed to test and gather evidence reliably, so that she/he may end up with solid, tested conclusions? One would have to be able to test and gather evidence before knowing anything at all, in order to verify that she/he can trust the knowing that takes place at the start of her/his evidence gathering. But this, of course, is absurd.

In other words, science cannot justify itself. Scientific knowledge can only be justified on the basis of a non-empirical mode of knowing, that is, a *philosophical mode of knowing*. That is why scientism, although it may not render science impossible (unless its logical implications are fully articulated and accepted), places science on a non-scientific foundation, namely *assumption (belief)*. If the only valid knowledge is empiriometric knowledge, then all science exists under the umbrella of an assumption.

A realist philosopher would argue that one's initial knowledge of the real, which is the pre-scientific foundation of the scientific process, is not an assumption, but genuine knowledge. It is the condition for the possibility of empirical science. But strict adherents of scientism could not agree with this without giving up scientism; for if one insists that the only genuine knowledge is tested knowledge, then science takes place on the basis of an assumption, and that means the entire scientific edifice is founded not on the hard cement of genuine knowledge, but on an assumption, that is, *a belief*.

Scientist lives in a world of beings (substances or things), that these 'things' are related to other things, that they can cause certain effects in other things, that they can be acted upon, that they reveal or disclose themselves through the way they act or react with other things, that they can undergo change, etc., and that is why the scientist begins to subject these things to experiment in order to investigate them more carefully, in order to understand them more precisely.

But scientist presupposes in order to begin his work. He does not attempt to justify the phenomenon of cause and effect. He does not ask whether it is really possible for one thing to bring about (cause) an effect in something else, i.e., Does this flame really cause this wood to change? Is cause and effect something that I can perceive with the senses? What am I doing when I declare something to be true? Is truth a relationship? Is it possible for me to actually say anything that is true?

In the mind of a scientist, the scientist knows that the flame causes the wood to burn, but she/he cannot justify these notions through her/his method of doing science, because she/he needs this 'initial knowledge' of cause and effect, the notion of substance or entity, an awareness that there is such a thing as truth, etc., as the starting points of her/his work.

That is why as scientist he is barred from pronouncing on cause and effect, the nature of truth, whether truth is a relationship or not, whether his initial general knowledge of things is certain or general, whether greater precision means absolute certainty or only a relative certainty, etc. Again, the scientist is barred from saying anything about the ultimate nature of things. To do so is to cross a line; it is to say something that exceeds the capacity of the empirical method of the scientist.

Physicist Erwin Schrödinger in 1935 tried to refute the principle of non-contradiction using Schrödinger's cat experiment. The principle of non-contradiction is that nothing can both be and not be at the same time and in the same respect. The logical formulation of this principle is that nothing can be both true and not true at the same time and in the same respect.

To deny the principle of non-contradiction is to pronounce on something that has a bearing upon what reality is ultimately, because the principle of non-contradiction is a first principle that bears upon being as being, that is, on whatever is, is. If it is refuted, this means that something can be *both true and not true* at the same time and in the same respect, or something can both be and not be at the same time and in the same respect.

Those who hold that the principle of non-contradiction is absolutely true, that it is a principle that bears upon whatever exists (numbers, particles, leptons, protons, light waves, possibilities, indeterminacies, etc.) are wrong because 'science has refuted the principle'.

But if they are wrong, then the principle of non-contradiction is true, and the realist philosophers are right. Why? Because it is said that they are wrong, not right. To declare that they are wrong, not right, is to declare that *they cannot be both right and not right* at the same time and in the same respect.

If the 'Schrödinger's cat' thought experiment refutes the principle of non-contradiction, then at the same time it proves it. In fact, it would mean that we could not ever again say that someone is wrong, for to do so would be to employ the principle. In fact, if the principle is not true, then to be wrong is to be right, and to be right is to be wrong.

Another example of exceeding the limits of the scientific method is the claim that a particular phenomenon occurs without a cause. This crosses the line because empirical science presupposes an initial, ordinary knowledge of cause and effect as a condition for the possibility of doing science. The relation of cause and effect and what that relation means ultimately, is not an object of scientific inquiry, for in itself that *relation is not measurable* and not empirical, but intelligible.

To claim that something happens without a cause is completely unwarranted; for how is it even logically possible for a person to know that a cause of a particular phenomenon does not exist, that there simply is no cause, especially in light of the fact that to understand a particular phenomenon is to understand its cause or reason? To know that the sufficient reason is not contained within that which we are seeking to understand, and to assert at the same time that there is no sufficient reason, reveals an Olympian audacity.

Perhaps we will never know the cause, or perhaps we cannot know the cause through empirical means, but to claim that the effect can be greater than the cause (for the cause does not exist, so it must be less than the effect) is to identify nothing with something: nothing is that out of which something comes to be. But to identify something with nothing and nothing with something is to eradicate the principle of non-contradiction, which in turn renders the entire scientific process impossible.

If the above view or scientism is upheld, then science inevitably rests on an assumption from which it cannot escape. The implication is that science cannot pronounce on anything about reality ultimately, but only on matters within the confines of that assumption. In short, science rests on a belief. Although adherents of scientism readily admit that science begins with assumption, they tend to want to forget that and will soon begin to behave like realists, forgetting that such privilege is not theirs; for the entire scientific edifice is founded upon *a belief.* All metaphysical conclusions stemming from scientific knowledge are per se impossible and must never be taken seriously, or they ought to be subjected to an entirely different kind of testing, the kind of testing that scientism denies is possible, namely a philosophical testing that does not depend upon an empirical approach to the real, but on reason.

A chemist might tell us that our bodies are 65% Oxygen, 18% Carbon, 10% Hydrogen, 3% Nitrogen, etc. But is a thing alive by virtue of its matter? Clearly not, for if a thing is alive by virtue of its matter, then all material things would be living. But this is clearly not the case. Matter is inert. So a thing is alive by virtue of a principle that is non-matter or immaterial. Water is a different *kind* of substance than hydrogen. And the human being, a living substance, is an entirely different kind of thing than the inanimate elements. A thing acts according to its nature (for we know the nature of a thing by its actions).

### 4.3.6 Inadequacy of Dualistic Metaphysics

Metaphysics is the science of being as being, of immaterial being, of the most abstract conceptions, of the most universal conceptions and of first principles. The formal object of metaphysics is being or beingness yet metaphysics is different from that of the other sciences. Immaterial beings like God and human soul exist without matter while for the understanding of abstract concepts like substance, cause, quality, number or knowledge of physical laws and metaphysical first principles do not require physical matter. The universal conceptions like unity, truth, goodness, beauty or duration are known as transcendentals which too do not need physical matter. In any system of metaphysics being, substance and cause are most important. The word 'Being' as a participle or noun is an 'act' of existence. The idea of 'Being' or more correctly, perhaps, the idea of 'something', is the first of all our ideas. Substance is a mode of being which is neither explicitly affirmed nor explicitly denied but only implicitly contained in the concept of Being. Everything is what it is, or everything is its opposite but the full truth is: Being is becoming. All reality is dynamic. Real being is dualistic in nature: finite and infinite, material (physical) and immaterial (spiritual), the world of senses and the world of forms or ideas, material body and immaterial mind, noumenon and phenomenon, theism and atheism, natural and supernatural, good and evil, light and darkness, etc. Finite being is composite of substance and accident. Accident is divided into nine categories: quantity, quality, relation, action, passion, place, time, posture, and habit/possession. There is an inadequacy of dualistic metaphysics for the ontological status of mathematical objects like sets and relations. Mathematical value cannot be limited to dualistic values of true and false as in the principle of excluded middle. It can be neutral, unknown, uncertain or probable too. "The application of the mathematics to the physical world has to assume a particular logic applies to its workings. At present there is no reason to believe that it has to be standard two-valued logic."[92] Three-valued logic prevails in the world of elementary particles: particle, wave and wavicle or positive, negative and neutral. Quantum Mechanics and Big Bang at the quantum and metaphysical level help us to go for a multi-valued logic from the two-valued logic for the better understanding of being, non-being, not being (negated being), nothing (*no* entity or being), analogical and relational being etc. 0 being quantitative number is neither positive nor negative, nor both positive and negative, nor neither positive nor negative but it is real and relational being in mathematical operations.

## Conclusion

The most ultimate remark we can make about a thing is that it is *something*, or, that it is not *nothing*. That something *is*. What is absolutely real is Being, the principle of all finite beings. The word 'Being', taken either as a participle or as a noun, has reference to the 'act' of existence (Be-ing) or the entity (being). Not-being is negation of being, non-being is unreal. Even if there is *no actual non-being* yet we represent empty set, empty placeholder, nothing, vacuum, empty space, non-being, non-existence, emptiness or *kenōsis* as numerical 0. Mathematical 0 is the *only one number* which has the implication of *nothing*. Relative zeros being abstractions have a hierarchy of zeros: natural 0, integral 0, rational 0 and real 0. Quantitative zeros imply 'nothing' of quantities like 0 litre, 0 gram, 0 rupees, etc. At absolute 0 K the object, atom or molecule, simply has no excess energy. The relativistic 0 is the black hole which is a *singularity*, an open wound in the fabric of the Universe. Things manifest in transcendental and analogous ways. Reality is everything we observe to be real. Non-reality simply means that there is no such thing as objective reality. Ultimately Reality or Existence is *Being Itself.* All particular beings participate in Infinite Being-Itself. But intelligent beings participate in the infinite being meaningfully. Being humans, we are called to be attentive, intelligent, critical and responsive for our decisive actions. We comprehend the ultimate nature, structure, and characteristics of reality through our simple apprehension, judgment and reasoning.Throughout history, it has been recognized that the human mind is capable of two kinds of knowledge, or two modes of consciousness, which have often been termed the *rational* and the *intuitive*, and have traditionally been associated with science and religion, respectively.[93]

Nothingness is something conceptual. It is representing absence. Mathematically it is 0 as a concept and number. It is an empty set as a set representing no elements.Mathematical 0 means *only one number* which has the implication of *nothing*. Relative zeros being abstractions have a hierarchy of zeros: natural 0, integral 0, rational 0 and real 0. Mathematical or quantitative zeros imply 'nothing' of quantities like 0 litre. Mathematical 0 has been operative in mathematics and physical sciences. We are created in such a way that we have body, mind and free will. We have sequence of cognitional acts; experience, understanding, judgment and decision. We have three domains of experience; internal, external and intellectual field of categorical objects. We use six questions *Why, How, When* and *Where* to delimit *What* and *Who.* Aristotle distinguished ten categories of being in two ways: 1) the primary as *substance (what or who)* and 2) the secondary way as nine accidents. Accidents are quantity, quality, position, place, time, state, action and passion. Immanuel Kant distinguishes twelve pure *concepts* of the understanding and divided them into four classes of three: 1) *Quantity*: Unity, Plurality, and Totality. 2) *Quality*: Reality, Negation, and Limitation. 3) *Relation*: Inherence and Subsistence (substance and accident), Causality and Dependence (cause and effect), and Community (reciprocity). 4) *Modality*: Possibility, Existence, and Necessity.

A living thing is characterized by *immanent activity*, that is, self-perfective activity. That is *essentially* different than the behaviour of non-living things: matter is inert; when it moves, it is moved by something outside of itself. Death is the full cessation of vital functions in the biological life. Death is Nature's answer to two properties of matter: its tendency to destroy; and its inability to respond, beyond a point, to the demands of spiritual growth. Immortality of the human soul, from a philosophical viewpoint, can be established from the immateriality or spirituality of certain fundamental operations like knowing, willing and remembering, which are immaterial or spiritual in themselves.

Nothingness is something conceptual. It represents absence, non-being, not being (negated being), nothing (*no* entity or being), empty set, empty placeholder, vacuum, empty space, non-existence, emptiness, nothingness as numerical 0, a concept and number. Nothingness and reality seem to be opposites but they are necessary correlatives and coevals yet reality is prior to nothingness and the nothingness represents the absence or shadow of reality. Two-valued logic is inadequate to express the reality of nothingness. This is the dynamic tensional or mutual relationship between nothingness and reality.

**Endnotes**

1. George Panthanmackel, "Being (Western)," in *ACPI Encyclopedia of Philosophy*, 2 Vols., Vol.1, ed. Johnson Puthenpurackal (Bangalore: Asian Trading Corporation, 2010), 157.
2. Robert Sokolowski, *Introduction to Phenomenology* (Cambridge: Cambridge University Press, 2000), 14.
3. Luigi Bogliolo, *Metaphysics,* trans., Myroslaw Alexander Cizdyn (Bangalore: Theological Publications in India, 1987), 57-58.
4. Johnson J. Puthenpurackal, "Essencing or Essence of God," *Indian Theological Studies* 29 (1-2) (March/June 1992), 105.
5. Isaac Parackal, "Person," in *ACPI Encyclopedia of Philosophy*, 2 Vols., Vol.2, ed. Johnson Puthenpurackal (Bangalore: Asian Trading Corporation, 2010), 1022.
6. Dilworth, "Nishida Kitaro", 472.
7. Dilworth, "Nishida Kitaro: Nothingness as the Negative Space of Experiential Immediacy," 477.
8. Puthenpurackal, "Essencing or Essence of God," 104.
9. Peter Kreeft & Ronald K. Tacelli, *Handbook of Christian Apologetics: Hundreds of Answers to Crucial Questions* (Downers Grove: InterVarsity Press, 1994), 15.
10. Puthenpurackal, "Essencing or Essence of God," 105-106.
11. John F. Haught, "Evolutionary Naturalism and the Future of Theology," in *Faith.Science.Culture: A 40 Year Retrospective Converging or Diverging Realities,* Proceedings of the ITEST 40th Anniversary Conference, September, 2008, eds. Marianne Postiglione and Thomas P. Sheahen {Missouri: ITEST (Institute for Theological Encounter with Science and Technology)}, 7.
12. Haught, "Evolutionary Naturalism and the Future of Theology," 10.
13. Peter Kreeft, *The Philosophy of Jesus* (South Bend, Indiana: St. Augustine's Press, 2007), 11.
14. Noel Q. King, "Metaphysical Analysis of God's Power and Personhood," in *Science and Spirituality*, ed. N. K. Singh (New Delhi: Global Vision Publishing House, 2005), 99.
15. Sokolowski, *Introduction to Phenomenology,* 5.
16. William Turner, "Metaphysics," in *The Catholic Encyclopedia*, Vol. 10 (New York: Robert Appleton Company, 1911) accessed March 14, 2011, http://www.newadvent.org/cathen/10226a.htm.

17. Cyril Desbruslais, *The Philosophy of Be-ing: Introduction to a Metaphysics for Today,* ed. Kuruvilla Pandikattu (Pune: Jnana-Deepa Vidyapeeth, 1997), 119.
18. The basic reality is existence. The existence is a pure entity without its circumstances. So it is in entitative order. Essence is the limitation of an existence. It receives its nature or essence from the existence. Quiddative order contains the essence of a thing as God is an essence fully constituted in its quiddative content as an act. In God alone essence and existence are identical, in creatures existence is participated, diversified, and multiplied, not by reason of itself but by reason of the essence which it actualizes.
19. Howard Robinson, "Substance," in *The Stanford Encyclopedia of Philosophy (Winter 2009 Edition)*, ed. Edward N. Zalta, accessed on March 2, 2011, http://plato.stanford.edu/entries/substance/
20. *Ibid.*
21. *Ibid.*
22. F. Leron Shults, *Christology and Science*, Ashgate Science and Religion Series, eds. Roger Trigg and J.Wentsel van Huyssteen (Burlington: Ashgate Publishing Co., 2008), 6.
23. Amie Thomasson, "Categories," in *The Stanford Encyclopedia of Philosophy*, accessed February 14, 2011, http://plato.stanford.edu/entries/categories/.
24. *Ibid.*
25. Sampooran Singh, "Modern Physics and Spirituality," in *Science and Spirituality*, ed. N. K. Singh (New Delhi: Global Vision Publishing House, 2005), 178.
26. *Ibid.*, 179.
27. M. K. Kaw, "Science and Spirituality in the 21st Century," in *Science and Spirituality*, ed. N. K. Singh (New Delhi: Global Vision Publishing House, 2005), 227.
28. Ernest Zebrowski, *A History of the Circle: Mathematical Reasoning and the Physical Universe* (London: Free Association Books, 1999), 187.
29. *Ibid.*, 188.
30. *Ibid.*, 189.
31. John D. Barrow, *The Book of Nothing* (London: Vintage, 2001), 238.
32. Nick Huggett, "Black Holes," in *Encyclopedia of Philosophy*, 2nd edition, Vol. 1, ed., Donald M. Borchert (Detroit: Thomson Gale, 2006), 606.

33. Heather R. Smith, "How Big Are Black Holes?" in *NASA Educational Technology Services*, accessed February 26, 2011, http://www.nasa.gov/audience/forstudents/k-4/stories/what-is-a-black-hole-k4.html.
34. Noel Sheth, "Budhism and Science," *Vidyajyoti: Journal of Theological Reflection* 68, 11 (November 2004): 844.
35. Sampooran Singh, "Modern Physics and Spirituality," in *Science and Spirituality*, ed. N. K. Singh (New Delhi: Global Vision Publishing House, 2005), 175.
36. Robert Sokolowski, *Introduction to Phenomenology* (Cambridge: Cambridge University Press, 2000), 226.
37. Luigi Bogliolo, *Metaphysics,* trans., Myroslaw Alexander Cizdyn (Bangalore: Theological Publications in India, 1987), 5.
38. J. L. Mehta, "Being and Non-Being," in *Studies in World Religions*, India and West: The Problem of Understanding Series, No. 4, ed. M. David Eckel (California: Scholars Press, 1985), 86.
39. Bosco Correya, "Absence," in *ACPI Encyclopedia of Philosophy*, 2 Vols., Vol. 1, ed. Johnson Puthenpurackal (Bangalore: Asian Trading Corporation, 2010), 10.
40. Johnson J. Puthenpurackal, "Essencing or Essence of God," in *Indian Theological Studies* 29, (1-2) (March/June 1992), 95.
41. *Ibid.,* 96.
42. *Ibid.,* 97.
43. Robert E. Carter, "The Nothingness beyond God," *Dialogue and Alliance* 1, 3 (Fall 1987): 70.
44. *Ibid.*
45. Luigi Bogliolo, *Metaphysics,* trans., Myroslaw Alexander Cizdyn (Bangalore: Theological Publications in India, 1987), 51.
46. R. Balasubramanian, "Spirituality of Matter and Materiality of Spirit," in *Science and Spirituality*, ed. N. K. Singh (Global Vision Publishing House, 2005), 162.
47. Sokolowski, *Introduction to Phenomenology,* 15.
48. Dough McManaman, "An Introduction to the Ten Categories," in*Lifeissues.net: Clear Thinking about Crucial Issues,* ed. Jerry Novotny, accessed March 13, 2011, http://www.lifeissues.net/writers/ mcm/ph/ph_01 philosophyyouth16.htm.
49. Barry Miller, "Existence," in *The Stanford Encyclopedia of Philosophy* (Fall 2009 Edition), ed. Edward N. Zalta, accessed February 26, 2011, http://plato.stanford.edu/archives/fall2009/entries/existence/.

50. Cyril Desbruslais, "Existence," in *ACPI Encyclopedia of Philosophy*, 2 Vols., Vol. 1, ed. Johnson Puthenpurackal (Bangalore: Asian Trading Corporation, 2010), 509.
51. John D. Barrow, *The Infinite Book: A Short Guide to the Boundless, Timeless and Endless* (London: Vintage, 2005), 30.
52. J. A. Scott Kelso and David A. Engstrøm, *The Complementary Nature* (London: The MIT Press, 2006), xiv-xv.
53. Daniel C. Matt, *God and the Big Bang: Discovering Harmony between Science and Spirituality* (Vermont: Jewish Lights Publishers, 1996), 62-63.
54. M. K. Kaw, "Science and Spirituality in the 21st Century," in *Science and Spirituality*, ed. N. K. Singh (New Delhi: Global Vision Publishing House, 2005), 229.
55. James N. Studer, "Consciousness and Reality: Our Entry into Creation," in *Cross Currents* (Spring 1998), 16.
56. John R. Searle, *Rationality in Action* (London: The MIT Press, 2001), 271.
57. Ramesh Bijlani, "Death: Biology and Beyond?" in *The Depth of Death: Scientific Insights, Religious Openness*, ed. Kuruvilla Pandikattu (New Delhi: Serials Publications, 2010), 24.
58. Sokolowski, *Introduction to Phenomenology,* 11.
59. *Ibid.,* 12.
60. "Faith and reason are like two wings on which the human spirit rises to the contemplation of truth; and God has placed in the human heart a desire to know the truth – in a word, to know himself – so that, by knowing and loving God, men and women may also come to the fullness of truth about themselves" (Ex 33, 18; Ps 27, 8-9; 63 2-3; Jn 14, 18; 1 Jn 3, 2). See John Paul II, *Encyclical Letter Fides et Ratio (Faith and Reason)* (Mumbai: Pauline Publications, 1998), 3.
61. Carla Mae Streeter, "Gaudium et Spes: Joy and Hope, The Church in the Modern World 43 years Later," in *Faith.Science.Culture: A 40 Year Retrospective Converging or Diverging Realities,* Proceedings of the ITEST 40th Anniversary Conference, September, 2008, eds. Marianne Postiglione and Thomas P. Sheahen {Missouri: ITEST (Institute for Theological Encounter with Science and Technology)}, 115.
62. *Ibid.*
63. Sokolowski, *Introduction to Phenomenology*, 22.
64. *Ibid.,* 22-23.

65. *Ibid.,* 23.
66. *Ibid.,* 25.
67. Peter Kreeft, *The Philosophy of Jesus* (South Bend, Indiana: St. Augustine's Press, 2007), 69-70.
68. Sokolowski, *Introduction to Phenomenology*, 28.
69. *Ibid.,* 8.
70. *Ibid.,* 17.
71. *Ibid.,* 33.
72. Kieran Setiya, "Intention," in *The Stanford Encyclopedia of Philosophy (Spring 2011 Edition)*, ed. Edward N. Zalta, accessed November 14, 2011, http://plato.stanford.edu/archives/spr2011/entries/intention/.
73. Sokolowski, *Introduction to Phenomenology,* 36.
74. *Ibid.,* 34.
75. *Ibid.,* 36.
76. *Ibid.,* 38.
77. George Panthanmackel, "Unity," in *ACPI Encyclopedia of Philosophy,* 2 Vols., Vol. 2, ed. Johnson Puthenpurackal (Bangalore: Asian Trading Corporation, 2010), 1447.
78. Robert Crawford, *Is God a Scientist? A Dialogue between Science and Religion* (New York: Palgrave Macmillan, 2004), 16.
79. Panthanmackel, "Unity," 1447.
80. George Panthanmackel, "Problem of One and Many," in *ACPI Encyclopedia of Philosophy,* 2 Vols., Vol. 2, ed. Johnson Puthenpurackal (Bangalore: Asian Trading Corporation, 2010), 990.
81. Archie J. Bahm, *Polarity, Dialectic and Organicity* (Albuquerque New Mexico: World Books, 1970), 265.
82. *Ibid.,* 265.
83. *Ibid.,* 266.
84. *Ibid.,* 262.
85. George Panthanmackel, "Causality (Western)," in *ACPI Encyclopedia of Philosophy*, 2 Vols., Vol. 1, ed. Johnson Puthenpurackal (Bangalore: Asian Trading Corporation, 2010), 240.
86. Luigi Bogliolo, *Metaphysics,* trans., Myroslaw Alexander Cizdyn (Bangalore: Theological Publications in India, 1987), 49-50.
87. Sampooran Singh, "Modern Physics and Spirituality," in *Science and Spirituality*, ed. N. K. Singh (New Delhi: Global Vision Publishing House, 2005), 170.

88. Robert Crawford, *Is God a Scientist? A Dialogue between Science and Religion* (New York: Palgrave Macmillan, 2004), 3.
89. Ernest Zebrowski, *A History of the Circle: Mathematical Reasoning and the Physical Universe* (London: Free Association Books, 1999), 189.
90. *Ibid.,* 190.
91. *Ibid.,* 43.
92. John D. Barrrow, *Pi in the Sky: Counting, Thinking, and Being* (Boston: Back Bay Books, 1992), 187.
93. Fritjof Capra, *The Tao of Physics: An Explanation of the Paralles between Modern Physics and Eastern Mysticism*, 3rd ed. (1982; reprint; London: Flamingo, 1991), 34.

# General Conclusion: Nothingness and Reality

In this concluding part we sum up our main insights and findings that we have arrived at in the earlier chapters. This is followed by restating the main findings of the book: the intimate contribution of nothingness towards the make-up of reality, as we understand it.

## The Reality of Triangular Mediation: Philosophy, Science and Religion

Philosophy, science and religion search for ways of making sense of the human *experience* of life in the cosmos. "Theology and science are both guided by a love of knowledge, and reflecting together on the way in which philosophical categories shape our inquiry can facilitate a deeper level of interaction. We are dealing here with a reciprocal *triangular mediation*"[1] The triangular mediation between *philosophy*, *science* and *religion* is reciprocal and relational. Philosophy, science and religion were *not separated* in the Greek culture in 6th century BCE.[2] Religion is associated with *faith*, in distinction from science, which is associated with *reason* while philosophy is associated with *reasonable faith*. While analysing the symbol of 'nothingness' from various perspectives, we have seen that it encompasses various disciplines such as Mathematics, Science and Religion. The symbols can be seen in the analogous fullness of the being and meaning of reality, through which all beings could be the symbol of the higher, intellectual realm of significance.[3] The symbols enable us to have a better understanding of reality. We ask why, how, when, and where to delimit what and who. Being efficient causes of effects we ask those six questions. The biggest questions in Philosophy, Science, and Religion are about nothingness and eternity, the void and the infinite, zeroand infinity.[4] It is Nicholas of Cusa's (1401-1464) premise that there can be only one infinite and this infinite also precedes all plurality and differentiation. Therefore, at true infinity there is one only and all are one.[5] In a holistic perspective we can understand 'nothingness' as the *starting point* for Science and Religion Dialogue. In sports, like tennis or shuttle, it begins with love (0 then 1). Further reflection would enable us to go to the extent of saying that the *end point* of Science and Religion Dialogue is oriented towards 'nothingness', where the 'fullness' lie hidden and opaque. Thus, we reach a paradoxical conclusion that the starting point and end point of Science and Religion Dialogue is 'nothingness', understood in the profoundly paradoxical and mystical sense. A paradox is the confluence or joining together of two or more seemingly incompatible ideas or events like beginning and end, nothing and everything, being and non-being, nothing and something, empty and full etc. Thus, the creative and enabling paradox of life is very well portrayed and articulated in the symbol of numerical nothingness, 0.

## Phenomenological Reality

Phenomenological reality includes the presence and absence of essences, events, facts and causes. We experience presence and absence, emptiness and fullness of things. It is we, human beings, who make statements about things, ourselves and others. "Making a rational judgment involves committing oneself to a belief, and faith involves making judgments about what is *trustworthy.* To believe something or to trust someone requires some knowledge of that thing or person. To know something or someone requires some level of commitment, a fiduciary connection to that which is known."[6] For we alone in the Universe are subjects, not objects. In us for the first time the Universe achieves self-consciousness. We are selves, subjects, whos, not things, objects, whats. "Under the influence of substance metaphysics, anthropology often began with a definition of a human person as an individual substance of a rational nature. The philosophical dichotomy between material substance and immaterial substance was the basis of the distinction between soul and body in the individual persons."[7] A 'substance' here means the kind of thing or person which can exercise active power whether in external activities such as pushing, carrying, fighting, speaking or teaching, or inner (immanent) activities such as enjoying, desiring, imagining or understanding. Only an intellectual substance can exercise external and internal activities. How one interprets divine *knowing*, *acting* and *being* will shape one's understanding of the *identity*, *agency* and *presence* of Jesus Christ in relation to God.[8] It is difficult to see the person as the author of one's own free actions without one being conceived as a causal agent: otherwise all one has is a collection of states of belief and desire engendering an action which is either determined or merely chance, and in neither case properly free. We can ask four basic questions about a thing: What is it? What is it made of? Where is it come from? Why is it good for? They are formal, material, efficient and final causes respectively. Rise of self-awareness and complex linguistic functions characterise our human knowing. We say 'I, myself; I am this particular, unique person.' What is other is everything else. In the same way as black implies white, self implies other. We have these polarities, this sort of differences, that what we call explicitly, or exoterically, they are different. But implicitly, esoterically, they are one. No element manifests itself without the agency of other materials already in existence or through direct intervention from a non material power like human or spiritual. We have a certain kind of *consciousness*, a reflexive consciousness – being aware of being aware. Being able to represent what goes on fundamentally in terms of a system of symbols, such as words and numbers. We put, as it were, two lives together at once, one representing the other. The symbols representing the reality, the money representing the wealth, and if we do not realize that the symbol is really secondary or the part is not equated with the whole then there is the danger of idolisation.[9] Reality is both presence and absence, paradoxical and relational. What is really out there? We, contingent beings, necessarily depend on one necessary being, God. God is immutable. He is eternally alive and perfect. What is not there? The existence of non-existence is *contradictory*. We have seen that mathematical zero is not mere nothingness. The concept 0 as a number represents what is 'not there.' It fills the empty position in the decimal numeration. It points to fullness and wholeness in interdisciplinary disciplines of physical or social sciences.

**Philosophical Zero**

We defined empty set {} or Ø as numerical 0. The category of substance lost its hold in mathematics and replaced by the concept of function. Zero is primarily a mathematical concept and a number. It is something, a finite amount which is defined. The concept of zero represents '*something*' that is '*not there*,' while zero as a number represents the lowest of all non-negative numbers. It has its mathematical operations. 'Nothing' differs in the way that it has *no* specific *basis* like zero (0) in numbers. Zero is the only digit which cannot stand alone. *By itself it is nothing*! 0 is having no substantial numeral value of its own but plays the key role in the system of decimal notation, to express all cardinal numbers with nine digits. It is a *catalyst*. Numbers 10 and greater are expressed by using a combination of the ten digits, with the *place* of the digit indicating the *value* of the digit. Zero is an independent value midway between + 1 and –1 of the number line. It indicates the division between BCE and CE. The 0 point is the startingpoint for both CE and BCE. A number is primarily *an abstraction* from things real. We invented them to *quantify* the external world around us. The limiting zero of an area is that of a closed figure, and is not a point or a straight line. A property of number is that it is either greater than some number or less than another number. Being the language of physical sciences, zero (0) means void, vacuum, or empty space. Most conceptuality is metaphysical; while reality is mostly physical.[10] Physical reality occupies space and time. Mental reality is in minds and their states which exists in time but not space. The abstract entities or universals are lying outside of time and space. Ontologically zero means *nothing*, complete *absence* or *negation*. We habitually think of the invisible as abstract and impersonal, as a set of ideas or ideals, words or principles as absence. We also think of only the visible as concretely alive and life-changing and dangerous animals as present. There are threekinds of complete ontological negations: absence of being, absence of difference, and absence of exclusion.[11] In the West, being is either isor is not, there is nothing in the middle. 'Is' or 'being' is affirmation and 'is not' (not being the state of matter) is negation. *Non-being* is different from *being* and negation of being (*not being*). The idea of non-being exists, but the *things* that would have non-being *do not*. So to have the idea of non-being is contradictory. The concept of absence is absence of *being*, not absence of distinction or absence of exclusion. Absences are things of a different type of any presence. Aristotle had 10 categories while Plato's five general kinds (*genōn*) are: 'that which is' or 'being' (*to on*), 'rest' (*stasis*), 'change' (*kinēsis*), 'the same' (*tauton*) and 'the different' (*heteron*).[12] The category of *difference* is applied to material quantities and relations but not to the mathematical and metaphysical realities. In Mahāyāna Buddhist tradition of India, being is *neither is*, *nor is not*, *nor both* is and is not, *nor neither* is nor is not. It is negation of negation which is ineffable. Here the concept of absence is absence of *difference*, including absence of *exclusion*, not absence of being. So ineffable is a being which we cannot conceptualise or imagine due to the limitation of human minds. But for some Chinese, being is both is and is not, *yang* (male) and *yin* (female), opposition is included. Here the concept of absence is absence of exclusion, not absence of being or absence of difference. Being (*tao)* has distinctions of *yang* and *yin,* balancing of the energy. The three ontological negations involve three logical negations: *exclusive negation*, *negation of all negation*, and *negation of exclusion*.[13] "All data are theory-laden. In other words, our experience of 'the world' is always and already interpreted through our linguistic categories and shaped by our participation within a world of shared meaning schemes."[14] Relationality, contextuality and interdisciplinarity are the three contemporary conceptual notions of the philosophy of science. Philosophers of science have described the *contexuality* of disciplinary activity in various ways, referring to the 'paradigms' of

Thomas Kuhn (1922-1996), 'research programs' of Imre Lakatos (1922-1974), or 'traditions' of Alasdair MacIntyre (b. 1929) that guide our inquiry.

## Mathematical Zero

Mathematical 0 is a neutral number, an empty placeholder, filler and at the same time becomes the power of 10 in the decimal positional system. 0 shows the paradox of empty placeholder and filler. Abstract entities – mathematical objects, universals and abstract concepts – exist only as ideas in the mind of God or human beings. The abstract objects are non-spatial (or non-spatiotemporal) or causally inefficacious (inert thing) or both. The mathematical theorems have no spatial location, and they exist nowhere in particular in time. The mathematical sets and functions are abstract entities too. An object is abstract if it fails to occupy anything like a determinate region of space (or spacetime). Concrete objects (whether mental or physical) have causal powers; numbers and functions and the rest make nothing happen. Vacuums are properties of things rather than things themselves. Vacuums are empty spaces. If there is no empty space there would be no motion, compression or absorption. Movement implies a mover and moved in the process of motion. Physical vacuums and the infinities are scientific paradoxes of 0 in science. Emptiness *(śūnyatā)* and fullness are other paradoxes of religious 0 or *kenōsis*. *Kenōsis* means self-emptying or dying for others. Life and sacrificial deaths are paradoxical. Mathematical 0 (number), physical 0 (vacuum) and religious 0 (self-emptying) are interconnected to each other in this dynamic world. Thus, the symbol of 'nothingness' can be a *catalyst* for fostering Science and Religion Dialogue for deepening human life. From a Christian perspective, "only in God's total *kenōsis* is everything, including the unjust and the sinner, natural and moral evil, forgiven, redeemed and satisfied, and the love of God completely fulfilled."[15]

## Quantum Zero

The hot Big Bang is the singularity, technically described by the cosmologist at a time equal to zero. This is known as T (time) = 0. Absolute zero tries to find out the unity or the equilibrium of the cosmos in triple temperatures. The micro world of Quantum Mechanics, the medium world of classical physics and the mega world of thermo dynamics are fashioned in the roots of quantum zero, relativistic zero and absolute zero respectively. General relativity theory holds sway in the realm of the mega world. Quantum Mechanics rules the domain of the micro world. Zero dwells at the juxtaposition of Quantum Mechanics and relativity; zero lives where the two theories meet and it causes the two theories to clash. A black hole is a zero in the equations of general relativity, the energy of a vacuum is a zero in the mathematics of quantum theory. The Big Bang leads to a zero in both the theories. The theory of everything is in fact a theory of 'nothing.' The empty space or 0 is not really empty. It is fluctuating with subatomic particles. This is zero-point energy, virtually infinity. A zero in Quantum Mechanics means that the entire Universe – including the vacuum – is filled with an infinite amount of energy. The vacuum is fluctuating constantly comes from Einstein's famous formula $E = mc^2$. Energy is getting converted to mass and mass is converting to energy. The Universe is continually active and dynamic. Where does the energy and matter come from? The Higgs boson is responsible for explaining the masses of the heavy fermions and bosons. After 40 years, scientists at CERN (European Organization for Nuclear Research), Geneva, announced the discovery of a particle consistent with long-sought Higgs boson on July 4, 2012. The state with least energy need not be empty; it can instead be filled with a physical quantity called the Higgs field.[16] Higgs field contains the particles which are responsible for masses. All the matter or mass that we can see, however, appears to be no more than about 4% of the total. The Higgs particle could be a bridge for understanding the 96% of the Universe that remains obscure like dark energy and dark matter.

Energy may be interpreted as a way to describe the grace of God. It is God who has created matter and energy in the world. By the very nature of creation, material being is endowed with its own stability, truth and excellence, its own order and laws.[17] The laws of nature tell us how the Universe behaves, but they do not answer the why questions: Why is there something rather than nothing? Why do we exist? Why the particular set of laws and not some other? Only the God who remains hidden continues to reveal Godself and is worthy of wonder and praise.[18]

> Philosophers and scientists do not create facts, they register them. Unless reality discloses itself, it remains unknown. Human's intellect is bound to accept the external data, the factual reality as well as the inner logic of human mind. Experience and reason are the two sources of natural knowledge.[19]

## Nothingness as Paradoxical Reality

*Mathematical nothingness* is numerical zero (0), a number and an empty placeholder in decimal numeration. Numerical zero is a mathematical symbol, an empty set, and an abstract quantity which is paradoxical in nature and existence. If a physical entity reaches 0 quantity of mass or volume then what would be its density? Mathematically it is indeterminate and paradoxical. Physically it is relativistic 0, Big Bang or black hole. At the quantum level it would be *quantum zero* which would be dynamic and seething with infinite quantum energy. Werner Heisenberg admitted that the position and movement of the particle is uncertain at the quantum level. So quantum zero in Quantum Mechanics is probable and uncertain. The *relativistic zero* in Big Bang Theory or in black hole would be again a paradoxical reality in its existence. The meaning of '*nothing*' is 'no thing', an entity 'no', 'no quantity', 'no quality', or 'no dignity' represented as numerical *0*.

Being, non-being, both and neither – all these four categories can be negated. It is negation of negation which is mystical. If being and non-being, both are negated, then something beyond both of them is presupposed. "God is the most real, therefore the most concrete of truth...Concrete does not mean physical. Concrete means absolute intelligibility, absolute real."[20]

**Conclusion**

Where does everything that exists come from? To understand or grasp the wholeness of reality we search for symbols like Zero, *Śūnyatā,* Trinity, Brahman, etc. Nothingness symbolised as numerical zero is the emptiness of the fullness of the dynamic aspect of the Reality of Existence. Mathematical zero, nothingness or an absence of quantity, is an empty set, {} or Ø represents numerically as 0. Zero numeral indicates *no* quantity, size, or magnitude. It is a number and placeholder in decimal numeration. 0 as a numeral is 'nothing' or 'no' entity yet represents the lowest value of non-negative numbers. When we calculate any value that is less than 1(it means 0 and lesser) and greater than nine (10 and greater) we need a symbol to represent the 'invisible', the *empty placeholder* in the decimal numeration. So, what better represents the 'invisible?' It is the *concept of nothing*, which is the *numerical zero*. A *concept* and *symbol* that connotes *nullity* represents a qualitative advancement of the human capacity of *abstraction. Being* is fundamental and *no-being* is *negation* of being. An absolute negation is *nothing*, it is non-being. It does not exist. Zero is a numerical being which is abstracted and quantified as *nothing* which exists. Mathematical 0 (a number), physical 0 (a vacuum) and religious 0 (self-emptying of a person) are interconnected to each other in this dynamic world. So 0 or *nothingness* is the mathematical expression of quantum 0, relativistic 0, absolute 0, *Nirguṇa* Brahman, *Śūnyatā* and *Kenōsis,* etc.

Mathematical 0 helps us to understand the physical nothingness (quantum 0 or vacuum) in Quantum Mechanics and relativistic 0 in Big Bang Theory. *Quantum 0* is not just a vacuous matter, quantity or mass, it is a fluctuating of energy. It is a zero-point energy. It is an *infinite energy*. This is a Universe of infinite energy like an atom bomb. The hot Big Bang is the singularity, the point technically described by the cosmologist at a time equal to zero. This is known as T (time) = 0. Absolute zero tries to find out the unity or the equilibrium of the cosmos in *triple temperatures*. Physical vacuums and the infinities are scientific paradoxes of 0 in science. Emptiness *(śūnyatā)* and fullness are other paradoxes of religious 0 or *kenōsis*. The Big Bang Theory reminds us that the Universe begun with singularity at the $0^{th}$ hour from a primordial atom.

Ontologically zero means *nothing*, complete *absence* or *negation*. There is a distinction between the three notions of *nothing, negation* and *non-being. Nothing* belongs to a quantity. It is a quantifier (*no*) combined with a variable (*thing*,...). There is an entity *no*in nothing. A real entity or an event of fact has two facets, *existence* and *nothingness*, fullness and emptiness, 1 and 0, quantity and quality, *form* and *matter*, and so on. The reality of quantities or qualities of 1 and 0 are coeval. Nothingness is the philosophy and science of empty space which is filled with fluctuations.

Phenomenological reality of nothingness and emptiness is expressed as nay or *nothing* in language, 0 in mathematics, vacuum in physical sciences, and emptiness or fullness in social sciences. In the psychological level existential nothingness gives rise to inner emptiness or nothingness of human beings. Languages and words are the function of marks. The different marks or notions like zero, nothing, *śūnya*, emptiness, *kenōsis* etc. are found in various fields like mathematics, science, philosophy, religion and mysticism. The reality and the nature of existence cannot be negated because the denial of something in question is identical with an existent which may be *absent or indeterminable or ineffable*. Reality is both presence and absence, paradoxical and relational. Zero has the most flexibility or elasticity and is the mark that has no 'original nature' at all. The concept of *zero* represents '*something*' that is '*not there*,' while zero as a number represents the lowest of all non-negative numbers. 'Nothing' differs in the way that it has *no* specific *basis* like zero (0) in numbers. As the mathematical empty set belongs to every other set so also nothingness belongs to every reality. The existence, presence or fullness is prior to non-existence, absence, vacuum, or emptiness. Affirmation is prior to negation. Negation is *not* of a being or thing. Absolute negation is nothing, it is *non-being*, which cannot exist. But relative negation, expressed through categories like nothing, none, absence, emptiness or nothingness is represented by numerical 0 and it exists.

# Bibliography


Abe, Masao., Patrick Henry and Wayne Teasdale, "Sunyata and Kenosis: The Rise of Universal Compassion in the Spiritual Journey." In *Monastic Interreligious Dialogue* 48 (October 1993). Accessed February 27, 2011. http://www.monasticdialog.com/a.php?id=704.

Adams, Fred., and Greg Laughlin, *The Five Stages of the Universe: Inside the Physics of Eternity*. New York: Touchstone, 1999.

Alles, David L., ed. "The Evolution of the Universe." Accessed January 11, 2011. http://fire.biol.wwu.edu/trent/alles/Cosmic_Evolution.pdf.

American Institute of Physics, "The Start of Scientific Cosmology." In *Cosmic Journey: A History of Scientific Cosmology*. Accessed January 4, 2011. http://www.aip.org/history/cosmology/ideas/start-of-scientific-cosmology.htm.

Aristotle. *Metaphysics* I. 5, translated by W. D. Ross in *The Internet Classic Archive* by Daniel Stevenson. Accessed February 27, 2011. http://classics.mit.edu/Aristotle/metaphysics.1.i.html.

Aristotle. *Physics* IV c.11, translated by Richard Hope. London: University of Nebraska Press, 1961.

Arsham, Hossein. "Zero in Four Dimensions: Cultural, Historical, Mathematical, and Psychological Perspectives." Accessed January 13, 2011. http://home.ubalt.edu/ntsbarsh/zero/ZERO.HTM.

Bahm, Archie J. "Three Zeros: A Comparative Philosophy of Voids." *International Philosophical Quarterly* 32, 4 (December 1992): 499-500.

__________. *Polarity, Dialectic and Organicity*. Albuquerque New Mexico: World Books, 1970.

Balasubramanian, R. "Spirituality of Matter and Materiality of Spirit." In *Science and Spirituality*, edited by N. K. Singh, 147-167. New Delhi: Global Vision Publishing House, 2005.

Barnes, Thomas G., David L. Bergman, Glen C. Collins and Charles W. (Bill) Lucas, "Our Consistent Approach to Life." In *Common Sense Science.* Accessed February 15, 2011. http://www. Common sense science.org/explaining_life.html.

Barrow, John D. *The Book of Nothing.* London: Vintage, 2001.

__________. *Pi in the Sky: Counting, Thinking, and Being.* Boston: Back Bay Books, 1992.

__________. *The Infinite Book: A Short Guide to the Boundless, Timeless and Endless.* London: Vintage, 2005.

Benacerraf, Paul., and Hilary Putnam, eds., *Philosophy of Mathematics: Selected Readings.* 2nd edition. 1964; Reprint. Cambridge: Cambridge University Press, 1998.

Bernays, Paul. "On Platonism in Mathematics." In *Philosophy of Mathematics: Selected Readings*, 2nd edition, edited by Paul Benacerraf and Hilary Putnam, 258-271. 1964; Reprint. Cambridge: Cambridge University Press, 1998.

Bhaskar, Roy. *Reflections on Meta-Reality: Transcendence, Emancipation and Everyday Life.* New Delhi: Sage Publications, 2002.

Bigelow, John., and Sam Butchart, "Number." In *Encyclopedia of Philosophy*, 2nd edition, 10 Vols., Vol. 6, edited by Donald M. Borchert, 670-697. Detroit: Thomas Gale, 2006.

Bijlani, Ramesh. "Death: Biology and Beyond?" In *The Depth of Death: Scientific Insights, Religious Openness*, edited by Kuruvilla Pandikattu, 17-30. New Delhi: Serials Publications, 2010.

Bingh, R. H. "Set Theory." In *McGraw-Hill Encyclopedia of Science and Technology*, 9th ed., 20 Vols., Vol. 16, edited by Mark D. Licker and others, 324-326. New York: McGraw Hill, 2002.

Blanc, Jill Le. "Infinity in Theology and Mathematics." *Religious Studies* 29 (1993): 51-62.

Bogliolo, Luigi. *Metaphysics*, translated by Myroslaw Alexander Cizdyn. Bangalore: Theological Publications in India, 1987.

Bond, H. Lawrence, trans. *Nicholas of Cusa: Selected Spiritual Writings*. The Classics of Western Spirituality Series, edited by Bernard McGinn. New York: Paulist Press, 1997.

Boyer, Carl B. "Mathematical Symbols." In *Microsoft Encarta Online Encyclopedia*. Accessed January 3, 2011. http://encarta.msn.com/encyclopedia_761577100/Mathematical_Symbols.html

Brown, James Robert. *Philosophy of Mathematics: A Contemporary Introduction to the World of Proofs and Pictures*, 2nd ed. New York: Routledge, 2008.

Bunson, Matthew E. "Fathers of Science." In *Catholic Answers Magazine*. Accessed October 10, 2011. http://www.catholic.com/magazine/articles/fathers-of-science.

Burde, Jayant. *Śūnya and Nothingness in Science, Philosophy and Religion*. Delhi: Motilal Banarsidass Publishers, 2009.

Burger, Edward B. "Zero to Infinity." In *Teaching Company*. Accessed January 6, 2011. http://www.teach12.com/ttcx/coursedesclong2.aspx?cid=1499&pc=Science%20and%20Mathematics.

Burgess, Cliff. "Higgs Boson Explains a Lot about Nothing." In *Thestar.com*. Accessed July 8, 2011. http://www.thestar.com/opinion/editorialopinion/article/1223002--higgs-boson-explains-a-lot-about-nothing.

Capra, Fritjof. *The Tao of Physics: An Explanation of the Paralles between Modern Physics and Eastern Mysticism*, 3rd edition. 1982; Reprint. London: Flamingo, 1991.

Carr, Bernard. "Mind and the Cosmos." In *Science, Consciousness and Ultimate Reality*, edited by David Lorimer, 33-64. Charlottesville: Imprint Academic, 2004.

Carter, Robert E. "God and Nothingness." *Philosophy East & West* 59, 1 (January 2009): 70-76.

*Catechism of the Catholic Church (CCC)*.1994; 8th Reprint. New Delhi: Theological Publications in India (TPI), 2006.

CERN. "Matter Particles." In *CERN (European Organization for Nuclear Research)*. Accessed July 10, 2012. http://user.web.cern.ch/public/en/Science/StandardModel-en.html.

__________. "Missing Higgs." In *(European Organization for Nuclear Research)*. Accessed July 10, 2012. http://user.web.cern.ch/public/en/Science/Higgs-en.html.

Chattopadhyaya, D. P. *Religion, Philosophy and Science: A Sketch of Global View.* Shimla: Indian Institute of Advanced Study, 2006.

Clarke, Chris. "Quantum Mechanics, Consciousness and the Self." In *Science, Consciousness and Ultimate Reality*, edited by David Lorimer. Charlottesville: Imprint Academic, 2004.

Coles, Peter, ed. *The Routledge Companion to The New Cosmology.* London: Routledge, 2001.

Colyvan, Mark. "Indispensability Arguments in the Philosophy of Mathematics." In *The Stanford Encyclopedia of Philosophy*. Accessed January 12, 2011. http://plato.stanford.edu/entries/mathphil-indis/.

Conze, Edward. *Buddhism: Its Essence and Development.* New York: Harper Colophon Books, 1975.

Coreth, Emerich. Forward to *Idols to Die, Symbols to Live: Dynamic Interaction between Language, Reality and the Divine* by Kuruvilla Pandikattu. New Delhi: Intercultural Publications, 2000.

Correya, Bosco. "Absence." In *ACPI Encyclopedia of Philosophy*, 2 Vols., Vol. 1, edited by Johnson Puthenpurackal, 7-11. Bangalore: Asian Trading Corporation, 2010.

__________. *Heidegger and Sankara: A Comparative Study of Thinking of Being and Advaita.* Kalamassery: Jyotir Dharma Publications, 2003.

Courant, R., and Herbert Robbins. *What Is Mathematics?: An Elementary Approach to Ideas and Methods*, 2nd ed. Oxford: Oxford University Press, 1996. Accessed January 9, 2011. http://mathworld.wolfram.com/InfiniteSet.html.

________. *What is Mathematics?* 5th Printing. London: Oxford University Press, 1951.

Crawford, Robert. *Is God a Scientist? A Dialogue between Science and Religion.* New York: Palgrave Macmillan, 2004.

Crosby, Donald A. "Nihilism." In *Routledge Encyclopedia of Philosophy*, edited by Edward Craig, 1-5. London: Routledge, 1998.

Crystal, Ellie. "Big Bang Theory." In *Crystalinks*, edited by Ellie Crystal. Accessed July 3, 2009. http://www.crystalinks.com/bigbang.html.

Cubbage, Norman Brian. "Nothingness and the Quarrel between Faith and Reason." *American Catholic Philosophical Quarterly* 78, 1 (2004): 1-24.

Curtis, David., and others. "Big Freeze Out." In *Science for the Millennium.*Illinois: The Board of Trustees of the University of Illinois, 1995. Accessed January 6, 2011. http://archive.ncsa.illinois.edu/Cyberia/Cosmos/BigFreezeOut.html.

________. "Quark Soup - The Elementary Particle Era." In *Science for the Millennium.* Illinois: The Board of Trustees of the University of Illinois, 1995. Accessed January 6, 2011. http://archive.ncsa.illinois.edu/Cyberia/Cosmos/QuarkSoup.html.

Darling, David. "Big Bang." In *The Internet Encyclopedia of Science*. Accessed January 6, 2011. http://www.daviddarling.info/encyclopedia/B/Big_Bang.html.

________. "Dark Energy." In *The Internet Encyclopedia of Science*. Accessed January 20, 2011. http://www.daviddarling.info/encyclopedia/D/dark_energy.html.

________. "Inflationary Model." In *The Internet Encyclopedia of Science*. Accessed January 5, 2011. http://www.daviddarling.info/encyclopedia/I/inflationary_model.html.

Davies, Paul. *God and the New Physics.* Middlesex, New York: Penguin Books, 1983.

________. Introduction to *Six Easy Pieces: Essentials of Physics Explained by Its Most Brilliant Teacher* by Richard P.

Feynman; originally prepared for publication by Robert B. Leighton and Matthew Sands. New York: Addison-Wesley Publishing Co., 1995.

Delsemme, Armand. *Our Cosmic Origins: From the Big Bang to the Emergence of Life and Intelligence.* Cambridge: Cambridge University Press, 1998.

Desbruslais, Cyril. *The Philosophy of Be-ing: Introduction to a Metaphysics for Today.* Edited by Kuruvilla Pandikattu. Pune: Jnana-Deepa Vidyapeeth, 1997.

__________. "Existence." In *ACPI Encyclopedia of Philosophy*, 2 Vols., Vol. 1, edited by Johnson Puthenpurackal, 508-511. Bangalore: Asian Trading Corporation, 2010.

__________. *The Philosophy of the Human Person: An Introduction to Philosophical Anthropology.* Edited by Kuruvilla Pandikattu. Pune: Jnana-Deepa Vidyapeeth, 1997.

__________. *The Philosophy of Religion.* Pune: Jnana-Deepa Vidyapeeth, 2000.

__________. *Western Philosophy.* Pune: Jnana-Deepa Vidyapeeth, 1976.

Drozdek, Adam. "Number and Infinity: Thomas and Cantor." *International Philosophical Quarterly* 39, 153 (March 1999): 35-46.

Easy Calculation, "Indian Numerals." In *Easycalculation.com.* Accessed January 11, 2011. http://www.easycalculation.com/funny/numerals/indian.php.

Educational Broadcasting Corporation, "Copernicus' Universe." In *Stephen Hawking's Universe*. Accessed January 4, 2011. http://www.pbs.org/wnet/hawking/universes/html/coper.htm.

*Essential Catholic Survival Guide: Answers to Tough Questions About the Faith, The.* San Diego: Catholic Answers, 2005.

Fact Monster. "The Age and Composition of the Universe." In Science Section of *Fact Monster*. Accessed January 18, 2011, http://www.factmonster.com/ipka/A0908644.html.

Fearn, Nicholas. *The Latest Answers to the Oldest Questions: A Philosophical Adventure with the World's Greatest Thinkers.* New York: Grove Press, 2005.

Ferrao, Victor. "Hermeneutical Proximity between Science and Religion." In *Omega: Indian Journal of Science and Religion* 2, 1 (June 2003): 88-96.

__________. "An Involving God in an Evolving World: An Emerging Paradigm in Science-Religion Dialogue." PhD diss., Jnana-Deepa Vidyapeeth of Pune, 2005.

Feynman, Richard P. *Six Easy Pieces: Essentials of Physics Explained by Its Most Brilliant Teacher*, originally prepared for publication by Robert B. Leighton and Matthew Sands. New York: Addison-Wesley Publishing Co., 1995.

Foregger, Thomas. "Set." In *PlanetMath.Org.* Accessed January 2, 2011. http://planetmath.org/encyclopedia/ProperSubset2.html.

Fox, Karen C. *The Big Bang Theory: What it is. Where it Came from, and Why it Works.* New York: John Wiley and Sons, 2002.

Francis, John. *Philosophy of Mathematics.* New Delhi: Global Vision Publishing House, 2008.

Freeman, J. B. *The Number Concept.* Bangalore: St Joseph's College, n. d.

Freudenrich, Craig. "Uniting the Fundamental Forces," of What are the Fundamental Forces of Nature. In *Howstuffworks?* Accessed March 1, 2011. http://science.howstuffworks.com/environmental/earth/geophysics/fundamental-forces-of-nature5.htm.

Fuerbacher, Björn., and Ryan Scranton, "Evidence for the Big Bang." In *The TalkOrigins Archive.* Accessed January 9, 2011. http://www.talkorigins.org/faqs/astronomy/bigbang.html.

Funes, José G. "Galaxy Evolution." In *Scientific Insight into the Evolution of the Universe and of Life: Plenary Session 31 October – 4 December 2008,* edited by Werner Arber, Nicola Cabibbo and Marcelo Sánchez Sorondo.Vatican: The

Pontifical Academy of Sciences, 2009. Accessed January 23, 2011. http://www.vatican.va/roman_curia/pontifical_academies/acdscien/documents/newpdf/acta20.pdf.

Gale, Richard M. "Nothingness." In *A Companion to Metaphysics*, edited by Jaegwon Kim and Ernest Sosa, 362. Oxford: Blackwell Publishers, 1995.

Gardner, Milo. "Egyptian Fraction." In *PlanetMath.org*. Accessed February 14, 2011. http://planetmath.org/EgyptianFraction2.html.

Gillon, Brendan S. "Negative Facts and Knowledge of Negative Facts." In *Indian Philosophy: A Collection of Readings*, edited by Roy W. Perrett, 82-103. New York: Garland Publishing, 2000.

Giorbran, Gevin. "When Zero Equals Infinity (God's Math)." In *Everything Forever: Learning to See the Timelessness*. Accessed January 1, 2011. http://everythingforever.com/st_math.html.

Gribbin, John. *Companion to the Cosmos*. New Delhi: Universities Press, 1999.

Grossmann, Reinhardt. *The Existence of the World: An Introduction to Ontology*. The Problems of Philosophy: Their Past and Present Series, edited by Ted Honderich. London: Routledge, 1992.

Gullberg, Jan. *Mathematics: From the Birth of Numbers*. New York: W. W. Norton & Company, 1997.

Gupta, R. C. "Spread and Triumph of Indian Numerals." *Indian Journal of History of Science* 18, 1 (1983): 23-38.

Halmos, P. R. "Mathematics as a Creative Art." *Science Today* 4, 1 (July 1969): 45-54.

Hanlon, Michael. "The Goddamn Particle and the Prophets of CERN: Some Thoughts on the Higgs Boson." In *Mail Online*. Accessed July 10, 2012. http://www.dailymail.co.uk/debate/article-2171448/The-Goddamn-particle-prophets-CERN-Some-thoughts-Higgs-Boson.html?ito=feeds-newsxml.

Haught, John F. "Evolutionary Naturalism and the Future of Theology." In *Faith. Science. Culture: A 40 Year Retrospective Converging or Diverging Realities,* Discussion Session 1, Proceedings of the ITEST 40th Anniversary Conference, September, 2008, edited by Marianne Postiglione and Thomas P. Sheahen, 1-18 and 63-88. Missouri: ITEST (Institute for Theological Encounter with Science and Technology), 2009.

Hawking, Stephen. *A Brief History of Time.* London: Bantam Books, 1988.

Heidegger, Martin. *What is called Thinking?* Cited by Johnson J. Puthenpurackal, *Heidegger Through Authentic Totality to Total Authenticity: A Unitary Approach to His Thought in Its Two Phases.* Louvain: Leuven University Press, 1987.

__________. *Being and Time*, trans. John Macquearie and Edward Robinson, 7th ed. Tübingen: Harper San Francisco, 1962.

*Holy Bible, New Revised Standard Version: Catholic Edition, The (NRSV).* Bangalore: Theological Publications in India (TPI), 2009.

Huzurbazar, V. S. "Proof in Mathematics." *Science Today* 2, 9 (March 1968): 34-37.

Ifrah, Georges. *The Universal History of Numbers II: The Modern Number System*, trans. David Bellos and others. New Delhi: Penguin Books, 2005.

Jayanth, Mathew. "Theology of Death: Experiencing the Fullness of Life through the Negation of Life in Death." In *The Depth of Death: Scientific Insights, Religious Openness*, edited by Kuruvilla Pandikattu, 150-125. New Delhi: Serials Publications, 2010.

Jetli, Priyedarshi. "Zero." In *ACPI Encyclopedia of Philosophy*, 2 Vols., Vol. 2, edited by Johnson Puthenpurackal, 1541-1543. Bangalore: Asian Trading Corporation, 2010.

Jusufi, Berat., Jon-Fredrik Stryker and Vegard Larsen, "The History of Indian Numerals." Accessed January 12, 2011. http://home.c2i.net/greaker/comenius/9899/indiannumerals/india.html.

Kaku, Michio. *Parallel Worlds: A Journey through Creation, Higher Dimensions, and the Future of the Cosmos.* New York: Anchor Books, 2005.

Kamal, Muhammad. "Consciousness and Nothingness." *Indian Philosophical Quarterly* 20, 4 (October1993): 373-380.

Kanamori, Akihiro. "Set Theory." In *Encyclopedia of Philosophy*, 2nd ed., 20 Vols., Vol. 8, edited by Donald M. Borchert, 831-847. Detroit: Thomas Gale, 2006.

Kaplan, Robert. *The Nothing that Is: The Natural History of Zero.* Oxford: Oxford University Press, 2000.

Kapur, J. N. "Fourth and Higher Dimensions." *Science Today* 4, 10 (April 1970): 17-25.

Kaup, Corey D. "General Nothingness Theory." Accessed January 15, 2011. http://www.nothingnesstheory.com/General%20 Nothingness%20Theory10%20VII.htm.

Kaw, M. K. "Science and Spirituality in the 21st Century." In *Science and Spirituality*, edited by N. K. Singh, 227-232. New Delhi: Global Vision Publishing House, 2005.

Kelso, J. A. Scott., and David A. Engstrøm, *The Complementary Nature*. London: The MIT Press, 2006.

King, Noel Q. "Metaphysical Analysis of God's Power and Personhood." In *Science and Spirituality*, ed. N. K. Singh. New Delhi: Global Vision Publishing House, 2005.

Kirshner, Robert P. *The Extravagant Universe: Exploding Stars, Dark Energy and the Accelerating Cosmos.* Princeton: Princeton University Press, 2002.

Kleppner, Daniel., and Roman Jackiw, "One Hundred Years of Quantum Physics." In *Science, Pathways of Discovery*, edited by Ivan Amato, 143-153. New York: John Wiley and Sons, 2002.

Kolb, Edward W. "The Big Bang Origin of the Universe." In *Cosmic Beginnings and Human Ends,* edited by Clifford N. Mattews and Roy Abraham Varghese. Chicago: Open Court, 1995.

Kozhamthadam, Job. "Creation Without a Creator: Reflections on Contemporary Scientific Cosmologies." In *Philosophy in Science*, Vol. 6, edited by Michael Heller, William R. Stoeger, and Jozef M. Zycinski, 4-46. Tucson: Pachart Publishing House, 1995.

Kreeft, Peter. *The Philosophy of Jesus*. South Bend, Indiana: St. Augustine's Press, 2007.

Kreeft, Peter., and Ronald K. Tacelli. *Handbook of Christian Apologetics: Hundreds of Answers to Crucial Questions*. Downers Grove: InterVarsity Press, 1994.

Lahav, Ofer., and Yasushi Suto, "Measuring our Universe from Galaxy Redshift Surveys." In *Living Reviews*. Accessed January 7, 2011. http://relativity.livingreviews.org/open?pubNo=lrr-2004-8&page=articlesu1.html.

Lineweaver, Charles H. "The Cosmic Microwave Background." In *The Routledge Companion to The New Cosmology*, edited by Peter Coles, 77-98. London: Routledge, 2001.

Malathi, K. N. "Number Down the Ages." *Science Today* 26, 4 (May 1992): 51-54.

Matt, Daniel C. *God and the Big Bang: Discovering Harmony between Science and Spirituality*. Vermont: Jewish Lights Publishers, 1996.

McInerny, Ralph., and John O'Callaghan, "Saint Thomas Aquinas." In *The Stanford Encyclopedia of Philosophy (Winter 2010 Edition)*, edited by Edward N. Zalta. Accessed February 24, 2011. http://plato.stanford.edu/entries/aquinas/.

McLeman, Cameron. "Zermelo-Fraenkel Axioms." Accessed January 4, 2011. http://planetmath.org/encyclopedia/ZermeloFraenkelAxioms.html.

McMahon, Arthur. "Meister Johann Eckhart." In *The Catholic Encyclopedia*, 15 Vols., Vol. 5. New York: Robert Appleton Company, 1909. Accessed December 3, 2011. http://www.newadvent.org/cathen/05274a.htm.

McManaman, Dough. "An Introduction to the Ten Categories." In *Lifeissues.net: Clear Thinking about Crucial Issues*, edited by Jerry Novotny. Accessed March 13, 2011. http://www.lifeissues.net/writers/mcm/ph/ph_01philosophyyouth16.html.

Mehta, J. L. "Being and Non-being." In *India and the West: The Problem of Understanding,* Studies in World Religions Series, No. 4, edited by M. David Eckel, 83-113. California: Scholars Press, 1985.

Mercier, Jean L. *Epistemology and the Problem of Truth.* Philosophy for All Series: No. 4. Bangalore: Asian Trading Corporation, 2000.

Midborn, Mark. "'A Day Without Yesterday': Georges Lemaitre & the Big Bang." In *Catholic Education Resource Centre.* Accessed January 4, 2011. http://www.catholiceducation.org/articles/science/sc0022.html.

Miller, Barry. "Existence." In *The Stanford Encyclopedia of Philosophy* (Fall 2009 Edition), edited by Edward N. Zalta. Accessed February 26, 2011. http://plato.stanford.edu/archives/fall2009/entries/existence/.

Narain, Harsh. *The Mādhyamika Mind.* Delhi: Motilal Banarsidass Publishers, 1997.

NASA Science. "Dark Energy, Dark Matter." In *NASA Sciencne.* Accessed February 22, 2011. http://science.nasa.gov/astrophysics/focus-areas/what-is-dark-energy/.

NASA Science Team. "Big Bang Cosmology." In *NASA*. Accessed January 9, 2011. http://map.gsfc.nasa.gov/universe/bb_theory.html.

__________. "Big Bang Theory." In *NASA*. Accessed January 8, 2011. http://map.gsfc.nasa.gov/universe/bb_theory.html.

__________. "Our Universe." In *NASA*. Accessed January 5, 2011. http://map.gsfc.nasa.gov/universe/bb_cosmo_infl.html.

__________. "Tests of Big Bang: Expansion." In *NASA*. Accessed January 10, 2011. http://map.gsfc.nasa.gov/universe/bb_tests_exp.html.

__________. "Universe." In *National Aeronautics Space Administration (NASA)*. Accessed January 5, 2011. http://map.gsfc.nasa.gov/universe/uni_age.html.

Nave, Carl Rod. "Unification of Gravity." In *HyperPhysics*. Georgia: Georgia State University, Department of Physics and Astronomy, 2005. Accessed February 24, 2011. http://hyperphysics.phy-astr.gsu.edu/hbase/forces/unigrav.html#c1.

Niles, Randall. "Theory of Evolution." In *All About the Journey*. Accessed January 15, 2011. http://www.allaboutthejourney.org/theory-of-evolution.htm.

O'Connor, J. J., and E F Robertson. "Mayan Mathematics." Accessed January 11, 2011. http://www-groups.dcs.stand.ac.uk/~history/HistTopics/Mayan_mathematics.html.

__________."Babylonian Numerals." In *The MacTutor History of Mathematics Archive*. Accessed January 10, 2011. http://www-history.mcs.st- andrews.ac.uk/HistTopics/Babylonian_numerals.html.

O'Grady, Patricia. "Thales of Miletus." In *The Internet Encyclopedia of Philosophy*, edited by James Fieser and Bradley Dowden.Accessed January 3, 2011. http://www.iep.utm.edu/t/thales.htm.

Pamplany, Augustine. *Cosmos, Bios and Theos: Introduction to Philosophy of Science, Scientific Cosmology and Science-Religion Dialogue*. Aluva: Institute of Science and Religion – Little Flower Seminary, 2004.

__________. "Quantum Mechanics." In *ACPI Encyclopedia of Philosophy*, edited by Johnson Puthenpurackal, 1116-1117, 2 Vols., Vol. 2. Bangalore: Asian Trading Corporation, 2010.

__________. *Theological Mysteries in Scientific Perspective*. Bangalore: Asian Trading Corporation, 2005.

Pamplany, Augustine., and Job Kozhamthadam. *East-West Interface of Reality: A Scientific and Intuitive Inquiry into the Nature of Reality*. Pune: ASSR (Association of Science, Society and Religion), 2003.

Pandikattu, Kuruvilla. "Ever Approachable, Never Attainable: Scientific and Philosophical Reflections on the Human Person." *Omega: Indian Journal of Science and Religion* 8, 1 (June 2009): 62-79.

__________. *Idols to Die, Symbols to Live: Dynamic Interaction between Language, Reality and the Divine.* New Delhi: Intercultural Publications, 2000.

__________.*Meaning through Science and Religion.* Pune: Jnana Deepa Vidyapeeth, 1999.

Panthanmackel, George. "Being (Western)." *In ACPI Encyclopedia of Philosophy*, 2 Vols., Vol.1, edited by Johnson Puthenpurackal, 153-159. Bangalore: Asian Trading Corporation, 2010.

__________. "Causality (Western)." In *ACPI Encyclopedia of Philosophy*, 2 Vols., Vol. 1, edited by Johnson Puthenpurackal, 235-240. Bangalore: Asian Trading Corporation, 2010.

__________. "Problem of One and Many." In *ACPI Encyclopedia of Philosophy,* 2 Vols., Vol. 2, edited by Johnson Puthenpurackal, 988-992. Bangalore: Asian Trading Corporation, 2010.

__________. "Unity." In *ACPI Encyclopedia of Philosophy,* 2 Vols., Vol.1, edited by Johnson Puthenpurackal, 1447-1451. Bangalore: Asian Trading Corporation, 2010.

Parackal, Isaac. "Person." In *ACPI Encyclopedia of Philosophy*, 2 Vols., Vol. 2, edited by Johnson Puthenpurackal, 1018-1023 Bangalore: Asian Trading Corporation, 2010.

Parappally, Jacob. "The Significance of Jesus' Resurrection for Humans and the World." In *The Depth of Death: Scientific Insights, Religious Openness*, edited by Kuruvilla Pandikattu, 126-138. New Delhi: Serials Publications, 2010.

Pasachoff, Jay M. "Big Bang Theory." In *McGraw-Hill Encyclopedia of Science and Technology,* 9th ed., 20 Vols., Vol. 2, edited by Elizabeth Geller and others, 719-723. New York: McGraw-Hill, 2002.

Paul II, John. Encyclical Letter *Fides et Ratio (Faith and Reason).* Mumbai: Pauline Publications, 1998.

__________. "Encyclical *Fides et Ratio*." *Origins*: CNS (Catholic News Service) Documentary Service 28, 19 (October 1998): 318-347.

Paulose, C.S., and Binoy Joseph. "Death: A Molecular Definition Death: A Molecular Definition." In *The Depth of Death: Scientific Insights, Religious Openness*, edited by Kuruvilla Pandikattu. New Delhi: Serials Publications, 2010.

Penrose, Roger. *The Road to Reality: A Complete Guide to the Law of the Universe*. London: Jonathan Cape, 2004.

Perumalil, Augustine. *Religious Cosmologies*. Delhi: ISPCK (Indian Society for Promoting Christian Knowledge), 2007.

Peterson, Doctor. "Difference between Math and Arithmetic." In *The Math Forum @ Drexel. The Math Forum. Ask Dr. Math*. Accessed January 20, 2011. http://mathforum.org/library/drmath/view/52282.html.

Pichalakkatt, Binoy. "Dialogue with Symbols: Exploring Zero, Śūnyatā and Trinity for a Holistic Reality." *Omega: Indian Journal of Science and Religion* 5, 2 (December 2006): 25-41.

Podimattam, Felix M. *Kenosis Spirituality: Paschal Path to Holiness*. Bangalore: Claretian Publications, 2002.

Polkinghorne, John. *Quantum Theory: A Very Short Introduction*. New Delhi: Oxford University Press, 2006.

Puthenpurackal, Johnson J. "Essencing or Essence of God." In *Indian Theological Studies* 29 (1-2) (March/June 1992): 93-106.

__________. *Heidegger Through Authentic Totality to Total Authenticity: A Unitary Approach to His Thought in Its Two Phases*. Louvain: Leuven University Press, 1987.

Ravindra, Ravi. "Yoga, Physics and Consciousness." In *Science, Consciousness and Ultimate Reality*, edited by David Lorimer, 93-108. Charlottesville: Imprint Academic, 2004.

Redondo, Joaquin. "Reality and Existence." In *Catholic Philosophy*. Accessed February 20, 2011. http://catholicphilosophy.com/sys-tmpl/door/index.html.

Rowlett, Russ. "CGS and MKS Units." In *How Many? A Dictionary of Units of Measurement.* Accessed October 12, 2011. http://www.unc.edu/~rowlett/units/cgsmks.html.

__________. "Coulomb (C)." In *How Many? A Dictionary of Units of Measurements*. Accessed November 12, 2011. http://www.unc.edu/~rowlett/units/dictC.html#coulomb.

__________. "Degree Celsius." In *How Many? A Dictionary of Units of Measurements*. Accessed November 12, 2011. http://www.unc.edu/~rowlett/units/dictD.html#celsius.

__________. "Digit." In *How Many? A Dictionary of Units of Measurements*. Accessed November 12, 2011. http://www.unc.edu/~rowlett/units/dictD.html.

__________. "Farad (F)." In *How Many? A Dictionary of Units of Measurements*. Accessed November 12, 2011. http://www.unc.edu/~rowlett/units/dictF.html#farad.

__________. "Gray (Gy)." In *How Many? A Dictionary of Units of Measurements*. Accessed November 12, 2011. http://www.unc.edu/~rowlett/units/dictG.html#gray.

__________. "Henry (H)." In *How Many? A Dictionary of Units of Measurements*. Accessed November 12, 2011. http://www.unc.edu/~rowlett/units/dictH.html#henry.

__________. "Lumen (lm)." In *How Many? A Dictionary of Units of Measurements*. Accessed November 12, 2011. http://www.unc.edu/~rowlett/units/dictL.html#lumen.

__________. "Names for Large Numbers." In *How Many? A Dictionary of Units of Measurement.* Accessed October 12, 2011. http://www.unc.edu/~rowlett/units/large.html.

__________. "Ohm (Ω)." In *How Many? A Dictionary of Units of Measurements*. Accessed November 12, 2011. http://www.unc.edu/~rowlett/units/dictO.html#ohm.

__________. "Tesla (T)." In *How Many? A Dictionary of Units of Measurements*. Accessed November 12, 2011. http://www.unc.edu/~rowlett/units/dictT.html#tesla.

__________. "The International System of Units (SI)." In *How Many? A Dictionary of Units of Measurement.*" Accessed

January 10, 2011. http://www.unc.edu/~rowlett/units/sipm.html.

__________. "The Metric System." In *How Many? A Dictionary of Units of Measurements*. Accessed November 12. 2011, http://www.unc.edu/~rowlett/units/metric.html.

__________. "Weber (Wb)." In *How Many? A Dictionary of Units of Measurements*. Accessed November 12, 2011. http://www.unc.edu/~rowlett/units/dictW.html#weber.

__________. "What Countries Besides the U.S. Have Not Adopted the Metric System." In *How Many? A Dictionary of Units of Measurements*. Accessed November 12, 2011. http://www.unc.edu/~rowlett/units/index.html.

Rudnicki, Konrad. "The Importance of Cosmological Principles for Research in Cosmology." In *Apeiron*, no. 4 (February 1989). Accessed January 7, 2011. http://redshift.vif.com/JournalFiles/Pre2001/V0N04PDF/V0N04RUD.pdf.

Russell, Bertrand. *Introduction to Mathematical Philosophy.* 1919; Reprint. London: George Allen and Unwin, 1930.

__________. *The Principles of Mathematics*. London: Bradford and Dickens, 1951.

Russell, Robert J. "Physics and Cosmology." In *Counterbalance*. Accessed January 8, 2011. http://www.counterbalance.net/physics/creat-frame.html.

Sanatani, Saurabh. "Physics, Mathematics and Philosophy – A Menage a Trois." In *The Journal of the Indian Academy of Philosophy* 31, 2 (1992): 23-37.

Sarcone, Gianni A. "Origins of the Numerals." In *Archimedes' Laboratory.* Accessed January 7, 2011. http://www.archimedes-lab.org/numeral.html.

Sartre, Jean-Paul. *Being and Nothingness: An Essay on Phenomenological Ontology*, translated by Hazel E. Barnes, 1st Indian Reprint. London: Routledge, 2004.

Schmidtz, David. "Nothing." In *Encyclopedia of Philosophy*, 2nd Edition, 16 Vols., Vol. 6, edited by Donald M. Borchert, 657-658. Detroit: Thomson Gale, 2006.

Schönborn, Christoph Card. "Pope Benedict XVI on 'Creation and Evolution'." In *Scientific Insight into the Evolution of the Universe and of Life: Plenary Session 31 October – 4 December 2008,* edited by Werner Arber, Nicola Cabibbo and Marcelo Sánchez Sorondo, 19-38.Vatican: The Pontifical Academy of Sciences, 2009. Accessed January 20, 2011. http://www.vatican.va/roman_curia/pontifical_academies/acdscien/documents/newpdf/acta20.pdf.

Schwarz, Patricia. "Cosmology: The Big Bang." In *The Official String Theory Web Site*. Accessed January 6, 2011. http://www.superstringtheory.com/cosmo/bang07.html.

Searle, John R. *Rationality in Action.* Cambridge: The MIT Press, 2001.

Seife, Charles. *Alpha and Omega: The Search for the Beginning and End of the Universe.* New York: Viking, 2003.

__________. *Zero: The Biography of a Dangerous Idea.* New York: Penguin Putnam, 2000.

Setiya, Kieran. "Intention." In *The Stanford Encyclopedia of Philosophy (Spring 2011 Edition)*, edited by Edward N. Zalta. Accessed November 14, 2011. http://plato.stanford.edu/archives/spr2011/entries/intention/.

Shapiro, Stewart. *Philosophy of Mathematics: Structure and Ontology.* Oxford: Oxford University Press, 1997.

Sharma, Chandradhar. *A Critical Survey of Indian Philosophy,* 8th ed. 1987; Reprint, Delhi: Motilal Banarsidass Publishers, 2000.

Sheth, Noel. "Buddhism and Science." *Vidyajyoti: Journal of Theological Reflection* 68, 11 (November 2004): 833-846.

Shults, F. Leron. *Christology and Science*. Ashgate Science and Religion Series, edited by Roger Trigg and J.Wentsel van Huyssteen. Burlington: Ashgate Publishing Co., 2008.

Silk, Joseph. *The Big Bang*, 3rd ed. New York: W. H. Freeman & Co., 2001.

Singh, Nagendra Kumar. "Aryabhatta." In *Encyclopedia of the Indian Biography,* 8 Vols., Vol. 1, 477-478. New Delhi: APH Publishing Corporation, 2000.

Singh, Sampooran. "Modern Physics and Spirituality." In *Science and Spirituality*, edited by N. K. Singh, 169-186. New Delhi: Global Vision Publishing House, 2005.

Singh, Simon. *Big Bang: The Origin of the Universe.* New York: Harper Perennial, 2005.

Smith, Frank Thomas. Review of *The Cosmological Principles* by Konrad Rudnicki. Cracow: Jagiellonian University, 1995. Accessed January 7, 2011. http://southerncrossreview.org/22/rudnicki.htm.

Smith, Gene. "The Big Bang: A Brief History of the Universe." In *Astronomy Education & Outreach*. Accessed January 7, 2011. http://cass.ucsd.edu/public/tutorial/BB.html.

Sokolowski, Robert. *Introduction to Phenomenology.* Cambridge: Cambridge University Press, 2000.

Sorensen, Roy. "Blanks: Signs of Omission." *American Philosophical Quarterly* 36, 4 (1999): 309-322.

Sorensen, Roy. "Nothingness." In *TheStanford Encyclopedia of Philosophy*. Accessed February 27, 2011. http://plato.stanford.edu/entries/nothingness/.

Steffney, John. "Existentialism's Legacy of Nothingness." In *Philosophy Today* 21 (Fall 1977): 216-226.

Stewart, Ian. *Nature's Numbers: Discovering Order and Pattern in the Universe.* London: Phoenix, 2001.

Stoll, Robert R. "Set Theory." In *The New Encyclopedia Britannica,* 15th ed. 32 Vols., Vol. 27, edited by Robert McHenry and others, 226-232. Chicago: Encyclopaedia Britannica, 1997.

Streeter, Carla Mae. "Gaudium et Spes: Joy and Hope, The Church in the Modern World 43 years Later." In *Faith.Science.Culture: A 40 Year Retrospective Converging or Diverging Realities,* Proceedings of the ITEST 40th Anniversary Conference, September, 2008, edited by Marianne Postiglione and Thomas

P. Sheahen, 39-54 and 99-122. Missouri: ITEST (Institute for Theological Encounter with Science and Technology), 2009.

Studer, James N. "Consciousness and Reality: Our Entry into Creation." In *Cross Currents* 48, 1 (Spring 1998): 15-33.

Suppe, Frederick. "Axiomatization." In *A Companion to the Philosophy of Science*. Edited by W. H. Newton-Smith, 9-1. Massachusetts: Blackwell Publishers, 2001.

Tabak, John. *Geometry: The Language of Space and Form*. 5 Vols., Vol. 2. New Delhi: Viva Books Private Ltd., 2006.

__________. *Numbers: Computers, Philosophers and the Search for Meaning*, The History of Mathematics Series, 5 Vols., Vol. 4. New Delhi: Viva Books Private Limited, 2006.

Taslaman, Caner. "Evidence of the Big Bang." Accessed January 4, 2011. http://www.bigbang.ws/.

Taylor, Barry N., and Peter J. Mohr, "Unit of Amount of Substance (Mole)." In *The NIST (National Institute of Standards and Technology) Reference on Constants, Units, and Uncertainty: Internatiional System of Units (SI)*. Accessed November 11, 2011, http://physics.nist.gov/cuu/Units/mole.html.

__________. "Unit of Electric Current (Ampere)." In *The NIST (National Institute of Standards and Technology) Reference on Constants, Units, and Uncertainty: Internatiional System of Units (SI)*. Accessed November 11, 2011. http://physics.nist.gov/cuu/Units/ampere.html.

__________. "Unit of Length (Metre)." In *The NIST (National Institute of Standards and Technology) Reference on Constants, Units, and Uncertainty: International System of Units (SI)*. Accessed November 11, 2011. http://physics.nist.gov/cuu/Units/meter.html.

__________. "Unit of Luminous Intensity (Candela)." In *The NIST (National Institute of Standards and Technology) Reference on Constants, Units, and Uncertainty: International System of Units (SI)*. Accessed November 11, 2011. http://physics.nist.gov/cuu/Units/candela.html.

__________. "Unit of Mass (Kilogram)." In *The NIST (National Institute of Standards and Technology) Reference on Constants, Units, and Uncertainty: International System of Units (SI)*. Accessed November 11, 2011. http://physics.nist.gov/cuu/Units/kilogram.html.

__________. "Unit of Thermodynamic Temperature (Kelvin)." In *The NIST (National Institute of Standards and Technology) Reference on Constants, Units, and Uncertainty: International System of Units (SI)*. Accessed November 11, 2011. http://physics.nist.gov/cuu/Units/kelvin.html.

__________. "Unit of Time (Second)." In *The NIST (National Institute of Standards and Technology) Reference on Constants, Units, and Uncertainty: International System of Units (SI)*. Accessed November 11, 2011. http://physics.nist.gov/cuu/Units/second.html.

Teilhard de Chardin, Pierre. *The Future of Man*, translated by Norman Denny. London: Collins, 1964.

__________.*The Heart of Matter*, trans. René Hague. London: Collins, 1978.

The NIST Reference on Constants, Units, and Uncertainty. "Prefixes for Binary Multiples." In *The NIST Reference on Constants, Units, and Uncertainty: International System of Units (SI)*, accessed January 21, 2011. http://physics.nist.gov/cuu/Units/binary.html.

Thomas, Alice. "Scientific and Religious Implications of Nothingness." In *Omega: Indian Journal of Science and Religion* 6, 1 (June 2007): 75-100.

Thomasson, Amie. "Categories." In *The Stanford Encyclopedia of Philosophy*. Accessed February 14, 2011. http://plato.stanford.edu/entries/categories/.

Tiles, Mary. "Philosophy of Mathematics." In *The Blackwell Companion to Philosophy,* edited by Nicholas Bunnin and E. P. Tsui-James, 325-357. Oxford: Blackwell Publishers, 1996.

Turner, William. "Metaphysics." In *The Catholic Encyclopedia*, Vol. 10. New York: Robert Appleton Company, 1911.

Accessed March 14, 2011. http://www.newadvent.org/cathen/10226a.htm.

Tyahla, Lori. "Edwin P. Hubble." In *National Aeronautics and Space Administration*. Accessed January 4, 2011. http://hubble.nasa.gov/overview/hubble_bio.php.

Vallabados, John Peter. "Abhāva." In *ACPI Encyclopedia of Philosophy*, 2 Vols., Vol. 1, edited by Johnson Puthenpurackal, 1-4. Bangalore: Asian Trading Corporation, 2010.

Valumkal, S. George. "Delaying or Defying Death through the Human Genome Project: Contribution of Science and Religion." In *The Depth of Death: Scientific Insights, Religious Openness*, edited by Kuruvilla Pandikattu, 31-48. New Delhi: Serials Publications, 2010.

Weinberg, Steven. *The First Three Minutes: A Modern View of the Origin of the Universe*, 2nd ed. New York: Basic Books, 1993.

Weinstein, Steven., and Dean Rickes, "Quantum Gravity." In *The Stanford Encyclopedia of Philosophy (Spring 2011 Edition)*. Edited by Edward N. Zalta. Accessed November 14, 2010. http://plato.stanford.edu/archives/spr2011/entries/quantum-gravity.

Weisstein, Eric W. "Axiom of Choice." In *Wolfram MathWorld*. Accessed February 12, 2011. http://mathworld.wolfram.com/AxiomofChoice.html.

__________. "Axiom of Foundation." In *Wolfram MathWorld*. Accessed February 12, 2011. http://mathworld.wolfram.com/AxiomofFoundation.html.

Wikipedia. "Blaise Pascal." In *Wikipedia: The Free Encyclopedia*. Accessed November 12, 2011. http://en.wikipedia.org/wiki/Blaise_Pascal.

__________."Empty Set: Notation." In *Wikipedia: The Free Encylopedia*. Accessed February 11, 2011. http://en.wikipedia.org/wiki/Empty_set.

__________. "Farad." In *Wikipdedia: The Free Encyclopedia*. Accessed November 12, 2011. http://en.wikipedia.org/wiki/Farad.

__________."Higgs Boson." In *Wikipedia: The Free Encyclopedia.* Accessed July 10, 2012. http://en.wikipedia.org/wiki/Higgs_boson.

__________. "Joule." In *Wikipedia: The Free Encyclopedia.* Accessed November 10, 2011. http://en.wikipedia.org/wiki/Joule.

__________. "Ohm." In *Wikipdedia: The Free Encyclopedia.* Accessed November 12, 2011.http://en.wikipedia.org/wiki/Ohm.

__________. "Omega Point." In *Wikipedia: The Free Encylopedia.* Accessed February 26, 2011. http://en.wikipedia.org/wiki/Omega_Point.

__________."Sidereal Time." In *Wikipedia: The Free Encyclopedia.* Accessed October 13, 2011. http://en.wikipedia.org/wiki/Sidereal_time.

__________. "Siemens (Unit)." In *Wikipdedia: The Free Encyclopedia*, accessed November 12, 2011.http://en.wikipedia.org/wiki/Siemens_(unit).

__________."The God Particle: If the Universe Is the Answer, What Is the Question?" In *Wikipedia:The Free Encyclopedia.* Accessed July 15, 2012. http://en.wikipedia.org/wiki/The_God_Particle:_If_the_Universe_Is_the_Answer,_What_Is_the_Question%3F.

__________. "Volt." In *Wikipdedia: The Free Encyclopedia.* Accessed November 12, 2011. http://en.wikipedia.org/wiki/Volt.

__________. "Watt." In *Wikipedia: The Free Encyclopedia.* Accessed November 12, 2011. http://en.wikipedia.org/wiki/Watt.

Woods, Mike. "Standard Model of Particle Physics." In *SLD*, accessed July 10, 2012. http://www-sldnt.slac.stanford.edu/alr/standard_model.htm.

Zebrowski, Ernest. *A History of the Circle: Mathematical Reasoning and the Physical Universe.* London: Free Association Books, 1999.

Zichichi, Antonino. “Rigorous Logic in the Theory of Evolution.” In *Scientific Insight into the Evolution of the Universe and of Life: Plenary Session 31 October – 4 December 2008,* edited by Werner Arber, Nicola Cabibbo and Marcelo Sánchez Sorondo. Vatican: The Pontifical Academy of Sciences, 2009. Accessed January 25, 2011. http://www.vatican.va/roman_curia/pontifical_academies/acdscien/documents/newpdf/acta20.pdf.

Zimmerman, Otto. “Infinity.” In *The Catholic Encyclopedia*, 15 Vols., Vol. 8. New York: Robert Appleton Company, 1910. Accessed March 3, 2011. http://www.newadvent.org/cathen/08004a.htm.

# Index

**Q**



**R**



**S**